WiMAX

A Wireless Technology Revolution

WiMAX

A Wireless Technology Revolution

G. S. V. Radha Krishna Rao
G. Radhamani

CRC Press
Taylor & Francis Group
Boca Raton London New York

CRC Press is an imprint of the
Taylor & Francis Group, an **informa** business

AN AUERBACH BOOK

First published 2008 by Aurbach Publications

Published 2019 by CRC Press
Taylor & Francis Group
6000 Broken Sound Parkway NW, Suite 300
Boca Raton, FL 33487-2742

First issued in paperback 2019

No claim to original U.S. Government works

ISBN-13: 978-0-367-45289-6 (pbk)
ISBN-13: 978-0-8493-7059-5 (hbk)

Library of Congress Cataloging-in-Publication Data

Radha Krishna Rao, G.S.V., 1973-
    WiMAX : a wireless technology revolution / G.S.V. Radha Krishna Rao and G. Radhamani.
        p. cm.
    ISBN-13: 978-0-8493-7059-5 (alk. paper)
    ISBN-10: 0-8493-7059-0 (alk. paper)
    1. Mobile communication systems. 2. Wireless communication systems. 3. Broadband communication systems. 4. IEEE 802.16 (Standard) I. Radhamani, G., 1968- II. Title.

TK6570.M6R36 2008
621.384--dc22   2007008287

Visit the Taylor & Francis Web site at
http://www.taylorandfrancis.com

and the Auerbach Web site at
http://www.auerbach-publications.com

Contents

Foreword

New telecommunications services and applications are the strong drivers of progress, and they pose new requirements to the network technologies. Indeed, in the last few years, we have witnessed an explosion of IP connectivity demand, yielding rapid development of the corresponding technologies in the wireless access network domain. IP services provision anytime and anywhere becomes very challenging and is seen by operators as a major opportunity for boosting the average revenue per unit (ARPU). The further success of IP services deployment requires true mobile broadband IP connectivity on a global scale. The third-generation mobile cellular systems are the main player, but insufficient throughput for support of broadband IP traffic stimulates 3GPP to account WiMAX and Wi-Fi (IEEE 802.11 family) as complementary broadband wireless access (BWA) technologies and speed up HSxPA standardization.

This book addresses the technologies implementing broadband wireless networks. The cornerstone of the book is the newborn technology WiMAX (IEEE 802.16 family) and the metropolitan scale BWA. Still in its infancy, the first piece of WiMAX-compatible equipment was just certified at the start of 2006. But the authors strongly believe that WiMAX is capable of occupying a very significant part of the wireless broadband market and will promote brand new telecommunications services.

The book brings to the field a comprehensive study on up-to-date BWA standardization, including 3G networks and WiMAX. It also provides an updated, detailed, and thorough analysis of WiMAX architectures, security, development scenarios, and business issues. A variety of case studies are also addressed. Very special attention is given to the technology contemporary to WiMAX, the WiBro. This technology is being developed by the Korean telecom industry, and it is expected that WiMAX and WiBro will be compatible.

The depth of treatment is intended to provide a general understanding of BWA concepts, along with deep and essential insights into specific technologies and standards that provide opportunities for the reader to get acquainted with advanced BWA developments. The book is useful for communication engineers and scientists. Students who need a general survey of these topics will also benefit. It may also serve as a reference and textbook in graduate level courses.

Overall, I find this book extremely useful and personally believe that the authors managed to successfully consolidate their mastery of BWA technologies. I hope the reader finds the book useful in enhancing and understanding broadband wireless networks.

Yevgeni Koucheryavy

Preface

Worldwide Interoperability for Microwave Access (WiMAX) is a standards-based wireless technology for providing high-speed, last-mile broadband connectivity to homes and businesses and for mobile wireless networks. WiMAX is similar to Wi-Fi but offers larger bandwidth, stronger encryption, and improved performance over longer distances by connecting between receiving stations that are not in the line of sight. WiMAX uses Orthogonal Frequency Division Modulation (OFDM) technology, which has a lower power consumption rate. WiMAX can be used for a number of applications, including last-mile broadband connections, hotspots and cellular backhaul, and high-speed enterprise connectivity for business. It supports broadband services such as VoIP or video. WiMAX is also a possibility for backhaul technology in municipal Wi-Fi networks. WiMAX or 802.16 is definitely a hot topic and has a fair list of industry supporters. Internationally, WiMAX has been finding a home among emerging markets that don't have a decent wired infrastructure. In the United States, several carriers, such as wireless, wireline, and cable operators, have voiced interest in WiMAX. Intel is shipping its highly integrated WiMAX chip, Rosedale. The Pro/Wireless 5116 chip has two ARM9 cores and an OFDM modem, and targets low-cost, low-chip-count access points and gateways supporting WiMAX. Intel is also working on putting Wi-Fi and WiMAX on the same chip. WiMAX equipment makers, such as Nortel Networks Ltd. and Motorola, say they have been garnering interest from cable providers.

WiMAX is essentially a next-generation wireless technology that enhances broadband wireless access. WiMAX comes in two varieties, fixed wireless and mobile. The fixed version, known as 802.16d-2004, was designed to be a replacement or supplement for broadband cable access or DSL. A recently ratified version, 802.16e-2005, also can support fixed wireless applications, but it allows for roaming among base stations as well. Thus, the two standards are generally known as *fixed* WiMAX and *mobile* WiMAX. WiMAX is designed to run in licensed bands of spectrum. It is a more innovative and commercially viable adaptation of a technology already used to deliver broadband wireless services in proprietary installations around the globe. Wireless broadband access systems are already deployed in more than 125 countries. WiMAX, like Wi-Fi, uses unregulated radio frequency spectrum, but unlike Wi-Fi, it does not require line of sight and is not limited to a dozen or so clients per access point. WiMAX can deliver ultra-fast Internet access over many miles. WiMAX is primarily built around broadband data, rather than voice, whereas 3G is primarily built around voice, with support for data services. WiMAX could prove disruptive to wireless carriers. Existing mobile operators who want to provide broadband data and voice services could also utilize the technology. WiMAX is also expected to solve the problems of rural connectivity, as it is suited for remote places that don't have an established infrastructure of power lines or telephone poles. WiMAX offers both increased range and download speeds.

The demand for broadband connectivity from urban homes and SMBs is growing rapidly, but this cannot be met effectively by existing wireline technologies. Today, we live in a world where communication has evolved into a landscape that a person in 1990 would scarcely recognize. WiMAX has the potential to provide widespread Internet access that can usher in economic growth, better education and health care, and improved entertainment services. WiMAX can be described as a framework for the evolution of wireless "broadband" rather than a static implementation of wireless technologies. Due to the trend toward mobile applications, WiMAX has a promising future. This sounds ambitious, but it may indeed be just what history has shown: when the highway is built the traffic will follow. Low network investment costs and non-line-of-sight operation over licensed or non-licensed radio spectrum make WiMAX an attractive technology. The ongoing development of the technology is expected to see WiMAX in digital cameras, phones, and iPod devices. Mobile WiMAX is based on OFDMA technology, which has inherent advantages in throughput, latency, spectral efficiency, and advanced antennae support, ultimately enabling it to provide higher performance than today's wide area wireless technologies. Many next-generation 4G wireless technologies may evolve toward OFDMA, and all IP-based networks are ideal for delivering cost-effective wireless data services. Although we all look forward to WiMAX Mobile and 4G, we can take a large step along the path to this vision of broadband ubiquity via portable services.

The WiMAX Forum is an industry nonprofit group that establishes standards for the emerging technology. The WiMAX Forum's goal is to accelerate the introduction of standard broadband devices into the market with fully interoperable WiMAX Forum Certified products supporting metropolitan area fixed, portable, and mobile broadband applications. Certification means that a WiMAX device complies with the IEEE 802.16 and ETSI HiperMAN standards based on 100 percent success in a series of authorized WiMAX Forum tests covering protocol conformance, radio conformance, and device interoperability. Product certification is a positive development for carriers seeking interoperable equipment choices.

The WiMAX Forum is already working toward a framework that will encourage the establishment of global roaming relationships among service providers.

The purpose of this book is to present WiMAX as a revolutionary wireless technology that, we believe, could change the wireless technology landscape considerably. This book presents the unique features of WiMAX technology and evaluates the revolutionary approach of WiMAX over contemporary technologies. This book also showcases the ongoing WiMAX development and deployment activities around the world. It analyzes future prospects of WiMAX and its contribution to the wireless and mobile communication technology field. It also explores the economic and opportunity costs of WiMAX implementation. This book covers the mission, product, and services of WiMAX as well as its specific features, such as security and mobile WiMAX. This book presents the best features of WiMAX technology for wireless and can be used as a guide for WiMAX for students, engineers, scientists, professionals, telecommunication business leaders, and technology lovers. This book is comprised of six chapters and the scope of the chapters is summarized in the following text.

The first chapter provides a complete introduction to WiMAX technology followed by an introduction to the WiMAX Forum and its activities. Chapter 2 presents contemporary technologies of WiMAX such as Wi-Fi, 3G, WiBro, etc. Chapter 3 showcases various features of WiMAX technology and provides a complete technical discussion. Chapters 4 and 5, respectively, present the development and deployment trends of WiMAX technology around globe. Finally, the last chapter presents an analysis of WiMAX's future prospects. This chapter also showcases a few applications of WiMAX technology, such as rural deployment, where we are personally involved. We also give some of our research concepts on WiMAX security, etc., in this same chapter.

We would like to thank Professor Datuk Dr. Ghauth Jasmon, president of Multimedia University (MMU), Malaysia, and Dr. Ewe Hong Tat, dean of the faculty of information technology at MMU for kind assistance and support. Our special thanks to Professor Alfredo Terzoli and Professor Hippolyte N'sung-nza Muyingi of Telkom Center of Excellence, South Africa, for their valuable comments and in-depth discussions. Much of this book's content was collected through continuous monitoring of the Internet for the last few years. Thanks to the Internet and special thanks to "Google Alerts." Acknowledgments are due to Rich O' Hanley and Catherine Giacari of Taylor & Francis for production of this book. Their efficiency and amiable manner made working together a pleasure. We are grateful to all others who have indirectly helped us in successfully bringing out this book.

G. Subrahmanya V. Radha Krishna Rao
G. Radhamani

Chapter 1

Introduction

The usable spectrum of electromagnetic radiation frequencies extends over a wide range. The lower frequencies are used primarily for terrestrial broadcasting and communications. The higher frequencies include visible and near-visible infrared and ultraviolet light, and x-rays. The standard frequency band designations are listed in Table 1.1 and Table 1.2. Alternate and more detailed subdivision of the VHF, UHF, SHF, and EHF bands is given in Table 1.3 and Table 1.4.

The primary bands of interest for radio communications are given in Table 1.5.

High-frequency radio (2 to 30 MHz) provides reliable medium-range coverage. The primary applications include broadcasting, fixed and mobile services, telemetering, and amateur transmissions. Very high (VHF) and ultrahigh (UHF) frequencies (30 MHz to 3 GHz), because of the greater channel bandwidth possible, can provide transmission of a large amount of information either as television detail or data communication. Furthermore, the shorter wavelengths permit the use of highly directional parabolic or multielement antennas. Reliable long-distance communication is provided using high-power tropospheric scatter techniques. The multitude of uses includes, in addition to television, fixed and mobile communication services, amateur radio, radio astronomy, satellite communication, telemetering, and radar.

At microwave (3 to 300 GHz) frequencies, many transmission characteristics are similar to those used for shorter optical waves, which limit the distances covered to line-of-sight (LoS). Typical uses include television relay, satellite, radar, and wide-band information services.

Infrared, visible, and ultraviolet light portions of the spectrum visible to the eye cover the gamut of transmitted colors ranging from red through yellow, green, and blue. It is bracketed by infrared on the low-frequency side and ultraviolet (UV)

1

Table 1.1 Standardized Frequency Bands

Extremely low-frequency (ELF) band	30 Hz–300 Hz
Voice-frequency (VF) band	300 Hz–3 kHz
Very low-frequency (VLF) band	3 kHz–30 kHz
Low-frequency (LF) band	30 kHz–300 kHz
Medium-frequency (MF) band	300 kHz–3 MHz
High-frequency (HF) band	3 MHz–30 MHz
Very high-frequency (VHF) band	30 MHz–300 MHz
Ultrahigh-frequency (UHF) band	300 MHz–3 GHz
Super high-frequency (SHF) band	3 GHz–30 GHz
Extremely high-frequency (EHF) band	30 GHz–300 GHz

on the high-frequency side. Infrared signals are used in a variety of consumer and industrial equipments for remote controls and sensor circuits in security systems.

In wireless technology, data is transmitted over the air, and it is an ideal platform for extending the concept of home networking into the area of mobile devices around the home. Consequently, wireless technology is portrayed as a new system that complements phone-line and power-line networking solutions. It is not clear whether wireless technology will be used as a home network backbone solution (as suggested by some proponents of the IEEE 802.11 standard); however, it will definitely be used to interconnect the class of devices that could constitute a subnetwork with mobile communications. These mobility subnetworks will interface with other subnetworks and with the Internet by connecting to the home network backbone whether it is wired or wireless. Wireless networks transmit and receive data over the air, minimizing the need for expensive wiring systems. With a wireless-based home network, users can access and share expensive entertainment devices without installing new cables through walls and ceilings. At the core of wireless communication are the transmitter and the receiver. The user may

Table 1.2 Standardized Frequency Bands at 1 GHz and above

L band	1 GHz–2 GHz
S band	2 GHz–4 GHz
C band	4 GHz–8 GHz
X band	8 GHz–12 GHz
Ku band	12 GHz–18 GHz
K band	18 GHz–26.5 GHz
Ka band	26.5 GHz–40 GHz
Q band	32 GHz–50 GHz
U band	40 GHz–60 GHz
V band	50 GHz–75 GHz
W band	75 GHz–100 GHz

Table 1.3   Detailed Subdivision of UHF, SHF, and EHF Bands

L band	1.12 GHz–1.7 GHz
LS band	1.7 GHz–2.6 GHz
S band	2.6 GHz–3.95 GHz
C(G) band	3.95 GHz–5.85 GHz
XN(J, XC) band	5.85 GHz–8.2 GHz
XB(H, BL) band	7.05 GHz–10 GHz
X band	8.2 GHz–12.4 GHz
Ku(P) band	12.4 GHz–18 GHz
K band	18 GHz–26.5 GHz
V(R, Ka) band	26.5 GHz–40 GHz
Q(V) band	33 GHz–50 GHz
M(W) band	50 GHz–75 GHz
E(Y) band	60 GHz–90 GHz
F(N) band	90 GHz–140 GHz
G(A) band	140 GHz–220 GHz
R band	220 GHz–325 GHz

interact with the transmitter — for example, if someone inputs a URL into his PC, this input is converted by the transmitter to electromagnetic waves and sent to the receiver. For two-way communication, each user requires a transmitter and a receiver. Therefore, many manufacturers build the transmitter and receiver into a single unit called a transceiver.

Rapid growth in demand for high-speed Internet/Web access and multiline voice for residential and small business customers has created a demand for last-mile

Table 1.4   Subdivision of VHF, UHF, and SHF Lower Part of the EHF Band

A band	100 MHz–250 MHz
B band	250 MHz–500 MHz
C band	500 MHz–1 GHz
D band	1 GHz–2 GHz
E band	2 GHz–3 GHz
F band	3 GHz–4 GHz
G band	4 GHz–6 GHz
H band	6 GHz–8 GHz
I band	8 GHz–10 GHz
J band	10 GHz–20 GHz
K band	20 GHz–40 GHz
L band	40 GHz–60 GHz
M band	60 GHz–100 GHz

Table 1.5   Radio Frequency Bands

Longwave broadcasting band	150–290 kHz
AM broadcasting band	550–1640 kHz (1.640 MHz) (107 channels, 10-kHz separation)
International broadcasting band	3–30 MHz
Shortwave broadcasting band	5.95–26.1 MHz (8 bands)
VHF television (channels 2–4)	54–72 MHz
VHF television (channels 5–6)	76–88 MHz
FM broadcasting band	88–108 MHz
VHF television (channels 7–13)	174–216 MHz
VHF television (channels 14–83)	470–890 MHz

broadband access. Typical peak data rates for a shared broadband pipe for residential customers and small office/home office (SOHO) are around 5 to 10 Mbps on the downlink (DL) (from the hub to the terminal), and 0.5 to 2 Mbps on the uplink (UL) (from the terminal to the hub). This asymmetry arises from the nature and dominance of Web traffic. Voice- and videoconferencing require symmetric data rates. Although long-term evolution of Internet services and the resulting traffic requirements are hard to predict, demand for data rates and quality of broadband last-mile services will certainly increase dramatically in the future. Many wireless systems in several bands compete for dominance of the last mile. Methods considered include point-to-point, point-to-multipoint (PMP), and multipoint-to-multipoint for bringing broadband communications information into the home and providing networking capabilities to end users. Broadband access is currently offered through digital subscriber line (xDSL) 47,48 and cable, and broadband wireless access (BWA), which can also be referred to as fixed broadband wireless access (FBWA) networks. Each of these techniques has its unique cost, performance, and deployment trade-offs. Although cable and DSL are already deployed on a large-scale basis, BWA is emerging as an access technology with several advantages. These include avoiding distance limitations of DSL and high costs of cable, rapid deployment, high scalability, lower maintenance and upgrade costs, and incremental investment to match market growth. Nevertheless, a number of important issues, including spectrum efficiency, network scalability, self-installable customer premise equipment (CPE) antennas, and reliable non-line-of-sight (NLoS) operation, need to be resolved before BWA can penetrate the market successfully. In recent years, broadband technology has rapidly become an established, global commodity required by a high percentage of the population. This healthy growth curve is expected to continue steadily over the next few years. DSL operators, who initially focused their deployments in densely populated urban and metropolitan areas, are now challenged to provide broadband services in suburban and rural areas where new markets are quickly taking root. Governments around the world are prioritizing broadband to overcome the "broadband gap," also known as the "digital divide."

WiMAX stands for Worldwide Interoperability for Microwave Access. WiMAX may be used in a wireless metropolitan area network (MAN) technology to connect IEEE 802.11(Wi-Fi) hot spots to the Internet and provide a wireless extension to cable and DSL for last-mile (last-kilometer) broadband access. IEEE 802.16 provides up to 50 km (31 mi) of linear service area range and allows users connectivity without a direct line of sight to a base station (BS). The technology also provides shared data rates up to 70 Mbps, which is enough bandwidth to simultaneously support more than 60 businesses with T1-type connectivity, and well over a thousand homes at 1-Mbps DSL-level connectivity. The original WiMAX standard, IEEE 802.16, specifies WiMAX in the 10- to 66-GHz range. 802.16a added support for the 2- to 11-GHz range, of which most parts are already unlicensed internationally, and only very few still require domestic licenses. Most business interest will probably be in the 802.16a standard, as opposed to licensed frequencies. The WiMAX specification improves upon many of the limitations of the Wi-Fi standard by providing increased bandwidth and stronger encryption. It also aims to provide connectivity between network endpoints without direct line of sight in some circumstances. It is commonly considered that spectrum under 5 to 6 GHz is needed to provide reasonable NLoS performance and cost effectiveness for point-to-multipoint deployments. WiMAX makes clever use of multipath signals but does not defy the laws of physics. With WiMAX, Wi-Fi-like data rates are easily supported, but the issue of interference is lessened. WiMAX operates on both licensed and nonlicensed frequencies, providing a regulated environment and viable economic model for wireless carriers. Much of the buzz about WiMAX has centered on customers receiving signal through walls, windows, etc., by eliminating the NLoS problem. This absolutely requires a licensed band solution. This is because the licensed band spectrum, being an exclusive (and thus, interference-protected) band, is allowed to use much more power radiation than the unlicensed band gear. Unlicensed band radios, WiMAX or otherwise, will all have power limitations.

In practical terms, WiMAX would operate similar to Wi-Fi but at higher speeds over greater distances and for a greater number of users. WiMAX could potentially erase the suburban and rural blackout areas that currently have no broadband Internet access because phone and cable companies have not yet run the necessary wires to those remote locations.

A WiMAX system consists of two parts:

A WiMAX tower (similar in concept to a cell phone tower) — a single WiMAX tower can provide coverage to a very large area, as big as 3000 sq mi (~8000 sq km).

A WiMAX receiver — the receiver and antenna could be a small box or Personal Computer Memory Card International Association (PCMCIA) card, or they could be built into a laptop the way Wi-Fi access is today.

A WiMAX tower station can connect directly to the Internet using a high-bandwidth, wired connection. It can also connect to another WiMAX tower using a LoS, microwave link. This connection to a second tower (often referred to as a backhaul), along with the ability of a single tower to cover up to 3000 sq mi, is what allows WiMAX to provide coverage to remote rural areas.

A typical WiMAX operation will comprise WiMAX BSs to provide ubiquitous coverage over a metropolitan area. WiMAX BSs can be connected to the edge network by means of a wireless point-to-point link or, where available, a fiber link. PMP wireless solutions based on WiMAX address the performance and economic challenges associated with providing cost-effective broadband access in the last mile. For fixed services, end-user locations are reached over the PMP–air interface by means of WiMAX subscriber end devices that are either rooftop mounted or customer-installable indoor units. Varied interface options will be available to enable connection for in-building distribution to end users. Interfaces for residential applications typically will include an RJ-45 Ethernet connection and an RJ-11 telephone connection, enabling the delivery of high-speed Internet data or voice services without the need for any additional equipment other than a PC and a telephone. Subscriber terminals for businesses typically would be equipped with a T1/E1 interface along with a 10/100BT Ethernet connection. Combining a wireless router with the WiMAX terminal will enable wireless distribution within the building premises by means of a Wi-Fi LAN. Because of the relatively limited spectrum assignments in the lower-frequency bands, WiMAX deployments usually will be capacity limited, requiring BS spacing on the order of 2 to 3 km. In lower-density rural areas, deployments will often be range limited, thus taking advantage of the full coverage capability of WiMAX, which can achieve NLoS coverage over an area of 75 sq km in the 3.5-GHz band.

The IEEE 802.16 Air Interface standard was developed from the outset with broadband and has resulted in a standard ideally suited to broadband data-centric services. Quality of service (QoS) is accomplished deterministically to enable the service provider to provision services on a customer-by-customer basis, with SLAs tailored to each customer's needs. Communications security is assured with the ability to select from multiple security modes, including 56-bit DES with data authentication. Adaptive modulation, spectral efficiency, and range capability help ensure a minimal number of BSs for a given spectrum allocation and coverage area. WiMAX equipment configured with smart-antenna systems further enhances the link budget and range. The WiMAX standard is beneficial to every link in the broadband wireless chain, such as consumers, operators, and component makers.

Consumers
■ Receive services in areas that were previously out of the broadband loop.
■ More players in the market translates into more choices for receiving broadband access services.

- Quick "trickle down" effect of cost savings to consumers, translating into lower monthly rates.

Operators
- Wireless systems significantly reduce operator investment risk.
- Common platform drives down costs, fosters healthy competition, and encourages innovation.
- Enables a relatively low initial CAPEX investment and incremental expenditures that reflect growth.
- No more commitments to a single vendor, a typical by-product of the proprietary technology model.

Equipment Vendors
- Concentrate on specialization (i.e., BSs or CPEs); there is no need to create an entire end-to-end solution as in a proprietary model.
- Standards-based, common platform fosters rapid innovation and the addition of new components and services.

Component Makers
- Standardization creates a volume opportunity for chip-set vendors/silicon suppliers.

During the development of 802.16e, which specifically addresses mobility, it became clear that the OFDM-256 PHY used in fixed WiMAX could not meet the requirements of mobile applications. Further, unlike the 802.11b/802.11a situation, there was no installed base of fixed WiMAX when this decision was made. Because the WiMAX fixed and mobile PHYs are fundamentally incompatible, the two versions will be deployed in different applications. BWA is one application touted for fixed WiMAX. WiMAX evangelists would have you believe that fixed WiMAX can deliver triple-play (voice/video/data) services, just like DSL or cable. But a WiMAX channel is a shared medium, and current profiles for licensed bands deliver a maximum DL speed of 26 Mbps at the PHY layer. After the MAC overhead, WiMAX can carry perhaps three standard TV streams or a single HDTV stream. This bandwidth is not enough for a single home, much less a large number of subscribers. Each application has specific requirements for latency, jitter, and bandwidth that WiMAX is able to meet to assure QoS. The WiMAX operator can also target a wide range of end-user types from stationary users to mobile users with varied service-level requirements.

WiMAX has been increasingly called the technology of the future. A question facing wireless designers and developers is to what extent WiMAX will gain adequate acceptance for them to base their designs on [1]. Belonging to the IEEE 802.16 series, WiMAX will support data transfer rates up to 70 Mbps over link distances up to 30 mi. Supporters of this standard tout it for a wide range of applications in fixed, portable, mobile, and nomadic environments, including wireless backhaul for Wi-Fi hot spots and cell sites, hot spots with wide area coverage, broadband data services at pedestrian and vehicular speeds, last-mile broadband access, etc. Aggressive support of many leading IT companies — Intel, Fujitsu, Samsung, Alcatel, Nortel, Huawei, ZTE, Motorola, Siemens, to name a few — is one of the most important reasons for the great interest in WiMAX. Membership of WiMAX Forum, an association of silicon suppliers, OEMs, and carriers committed to promoting WiMAX standards and certifying WiMAX-compliant products, has soared to over 250 in the last two years [1]. The designer will have to look beyond hype to know what expectations are realistic. Will WiMAX have the runaway success of Wi-Fi, or will it have to confine itself to niche applications? If confined to niche segments, which are the areas where it can make a mark over competitors? There is no dearth of competing technologies. At this moment, WiMAX seems to be emerging most strongly in access networks and MAN segments. In the access network segment comprising home offices, small and medium enterprises, and Internet connection for residences, WiMAX will mainly compete with xDSL, cable modem, fiber-to-premises, and T1 lines. In the MAN segment, where it will serve applications such as mobile communication, data services, and campus networks, it will compete with SONET/SDH and DWDM over optical fiber [2].

OFDMA is building up as the technology for mobile WiMAX as well as for 4G standards. Sprint Nextel has signed up with South Korea's Samsung to provide communications equipment and handsets for a WiBro test in the United States. WiBro is a TDD-based BWA technology developed by South Korean companies Samsung, Korea Telecom (KT), and the Electronics and Telecommunications Research Institute (ETRI). Operating at 9 MHz radio channel at 2.3 GHz with OFDMA as its access technology, WiBro is planned to support BWA at mobile speeds of up to 120 km per hr. Samsung is shipping WiBro equipment to Japan's KDDI and British Telecom. These developments show that WiMAX is an emerging technology.

What makes fixed WiMAX attractive for equipment designers is the availability of application-specific chips. A number of vendors offer system-on-chip (SoC) products that implement OFDM-256 baseband and 802.16 MAC functions. A separate set of vendors offers WiMAX radio transceivers for various bands. Intel is a high-profile supporter of WiMAX, and the company was first to market an SoC device. The PRO/Wireless 5116 integrates all of the digital functions for a fixed-WiMAX CPE design. The highly programmable chip includes a pair of ARM9 CPUs for MAC and upper-PHY processing as well as a DSP for the modem. A 10/100 Ethernet port provides the connection to a PC or router. Fujitsu is the second major chip vendor to offer a WiMAX SoC. The SoC includes a pair of CPUs for the MAC function, whereas the modem is implemented in hardware. Like Intel's chip, Fujitsu's MB87M3400 can be used as the heart of a CPE design. Unlike Intel's chip, the Fujitsu device can also be used in BS designs. French start-up Sequans Communications sampled its first chip in September 2005. The company's WiMAX SoC provides a number of features not found in the Intel and Fujitsu designs. Wavesat offers a WiMAX PHY chip plus MAC intellectual property. WiMAX-specific radios are now available from both large and small vendors. Texas Instruments offers chips for all three WiMAX bands: 2.5 GHz, 3.5 GHz, and 5.8 GHz. Radio specialists RF Magic and Sierra Monolithics (SMI) were the first vendors to offer merchant WiMAX radio chips. Better known for Wi-Fi power amplifiers, SiGe Semiconductor now offers WiMAX transceiver chips as well.

For enterprises, WiMAX can provide a cost-effective broadband access alternative. Its user-friendly installation process can break down the monopoly of local telecommunication companies (telcos). Because companies can set up their own private networks, telcos may be forced to add value or lower their prices in order to compete. Industries similar to oil and gas, mining, agriculture, transportation, and construction may find WiMAX useful when they need to operate in remote locations. WiMAX can provide Internet access to residential customers in suburban and "really" rural areas, the window to a whole new world that the now-obsolete cabled broadband could not offer. A wider coverage gives room for Internet telephony to expand. With wireless broadband, one can use the mobile phone to make cheaper international calls [3]. For countries that have skipped wired infrastructure as a result of inhibitive costs and unsympathetic geography, WiMAX can enhance wireless infrastructure in an inexpensive, decentralized, deployment-friendly, and effective manner. Another application under consideration is gaming. Sony and Microsoft are closely considering the addition of WiMAX as a feature in their next-generation game console. It will allow gamers to create ad hoc networks with other players. This may prove to be one of the "killer apps" driving WiMAX adoption: Wi-Fi-like functionality with vastly improved range and greatly reduced network latency and the capability to create ad hoc mesh networks. Global WiMAX trials have been running for several years, but none has been rolled out commercially so far.

Mobile broadband services might be attractive to a whole slew of businesses, such as real estate and insurance agents, who could carry laptops or PDAs to access documents or e-mail while out of the office. WiMAX is being seen in the United States as both a potential G3-killer and as a competitor to DSL. The success of WiMAX depends on its positioning with other technologies, most notably 2.5G/3G used for nomadic/mobile service. To capture initial success as a personal broadband solution, providers must position WiMAX as complementary to 3G. In addition, WiMAX must interoperate with the 3G ecosystem, including IMS and the proposed SDP framework, and, where appropriate, aim to leapfrog the legacy service infrastructure from which 3G is evolving. Longer-term success for WiMAX depends on whether it is successful in creating a more definitive value proposition. It could provide a means for mitigating the traditional telecom technology lock-in controlled by a small number of industry players and may enable nontraditional wireless telecom players such as Google to participate more actively in the mobile market. In addition, future positioning of WiMAX may see it being optimized for specific applications such as peer-to-peer multimedia and mobile video. WiMAX has significant potential to disrupt traditional business models by enabling new market entrants not encumbered by traditional mass-market wireless mobile business models. The network throughput performance for WiMAX will exceed that of 3G largely because of the efficiencies of WiMAX (OFDM) across broadband channels. This will enable WiMAX to offer a higher performance overlay network in localized areas such as urban centers. Compatibility and interoperability with 3G is critical for WiMAX. Radio spectrum availability and consistency is a major challenge for WiMAX, with a variety of frequency bands, including 2.3-, 2.5-, 3.3-, and 3.5-GHz bands. The market positioning of WiMAX goes beyond a technology discussion. Major equipment vendors such as Alcatel, Ericsson, Fujitsu, Lucent, Motorola, Nokia, Nortel, and Siemens are positioning themselves to support WiMAX, 3G, and evolved 3G solutions. WiMAX is a candidate for super-3G. However, it has many hurdles to overcome before it can fulfill this role. Furthermore, because the telecom industry has a complex value chain with significant interdependencies, accelerated success of WiMAX will depend on it being focused on the aspects of the value chain that are most vulnerable to disruption. Presenting WiMAX solely as a superior network technology is not enough. The industry must pay greater attention to the service ecosystem to leapfrog other installed telecom solutions.

WiMAX can compete successfully with DSL and cable performance and can cost-effectively reach outlying areas where DSL or cable is not now available. With indoor self-installable terminals, provisioning costs are minimal. With WiMAX, a service provider can meet the requirements of small and midsize businesses economically in low-density environments, and can provide alternatives to leased lines and DSL in highly competitive urban areas as well. WiMAX provides an economical way to expand deployment of Wi-Fi hot spots throughout campus environments, shopping centers, and other outdoor venues where other backhaul alternatives are not readily available. WiMAX also provides an economical option to wireline backhaul alternatives where DSL and leased lines are available.

Public Safety: Support for nomadic services and the ability to provide NLoS ubiquitous coverage over a metropolitan area can enable local law enforcement, fire protection, and other public safety organizations to maintain critical communications under a variety of adverse conditions. WiMAX can also be used to quickly restore communications in disaster recovery situations. Wireless private networks for industrial complexes, universities, and other campus-type environments represent an additional application for WiMAX. The range and security capabilities of WiMAX provide an advantage over Wi-Fi for these applications. With the availability of 802.16e, public transportation vehicles such as buses, trains, and trolleys can be connected to a broadband WiMAX network. This connection in conjunction with a Wi-Fi hot spot within the vehicles will enable passengers to take advantage of high-speed access during their commuting time. Personal broadband with WiMAX-enabled handheld devices and broadband services will be available to anyone anywhere within the WiMAX coverage area. The ability to provide a mixed suite of services to a wide range of end users reduces the investment risk for the WiMAX operator. It also gives the operator the opportunity to optimize spectral and backhaul efficiency by aggregating services and end-user types with varied traffic patterns on a common infrastructure.

Developed economies are highly competitive, with DSL and cable operators battling for market share. Sophisticated end users also have high expectations for services and responsiveness. WiMAX operators can win market share by offering differentiated services ranging from fixed to mobile applications to differentiate themselves from the incumbent competitors. Poor economic conditions and underdeveloped telecom infrastructure are potential obstacles in emerging markets, but access solutions based on WiMAX provide operators the ability to expand their network opportunistically as market conditions evolve. In both developed and emerging markets, equipment vendors will target both existing operators and emerging new operators. Although DSL has achieved wide acceptance as a broadband access alternative in both developed and emerging markets, distance and network constraints prevent operators from being able to provide broadband service to all of their dial-up customers. WiMAX can provide a cost-effective way for incumbent local exchange carriers (ILECs) to extend the network reach for their broadband services beyond DSL coverage and also provide a means for attracting new customers through new service offerings. Cable has also proven to be a viable broadband access alternative in countries and cities where it is available. Not all cable networks, however, are 100 percent upgraded for two-way services; and cable is generally not available in lower-density exurban and rural environments. Overcoming either of these obstacles requires significant capital investment and time. WiMAX can provide MSOs a lower-cost solution for extending the reach of their cable networks, and it also can be used to expand network capacity in selected high-traffic areas where their broadband cable network is not meeting customer expectations. The cable operator also can use WiMAX to address new market segments not typically served by cable, such as SME, hot spot backhaul, etc. WiMAX can be used to overlay existing cellular networks to add capacity for new data-centric services. This approach provides the operator the opportunity to add network capacity without jeopardizing the existing revenue-generating voice-centric network. Mobile operators can reuse most of the existing cell sites for WiMAX BSs, and in the core network they only need to add equipment specific to the new services to be offered. WiMAX provides competitive local exchange carriers (CLECs), ISPs, and other new competitive service providers a cost-effective, pay-as-you-grow way to become facilities-based operators, as opposed to leasing access facilities from incumbent operators with whom they are competing.

WiMAX is a standards-based wireless access solution that fills a critical gap in the end-to-end communications network. Lower equipment costs for a standards-based solution and assured interoperability greatly reduce the risks for operators wishing to roll out services. The ability to address multiple market segments with a common infrastructure further reduces risk and enhances revenue potential for the operator. With the 802.16e amendment, WiMAX offers the potential for the convergence of fixed, nomadic, portable, and mobile services. Multimode chips supporting both Wi-Fi and WiMAX will be available for notebook computers, PDAs, smart phones, and other handheld devices, thus enabling end users a seamless transition between 802.11-based LANs and 802.16-based MANs. What this points out is that WiMAX actually can provide two forms of wireless service: there is the NLoS, Wi-Fi sort of service, where a small antenna on your computer connects to the tower. In this mode, WiMAX uses a lower frequency range, i.e., 2 to 11 GHz (similar to Wi-Fi). Lower-wavelength transmissions are not as easily disrupted by physical obstructions; they are better able to diffract, or bend, around obstacles. There is LoS service, where a fixed dish antenna points straight at the WiMAX tower from a rooftop or pole. The LoS connection is stronger and more stable, so it is able to send a lot of data with fewer errors. LoS transmissions use higher frequencies, with ranges reaching a possible 66 GHz. At higher frequencies, there is less interference and lots more bandwidth. Wi-Fi-style access will be limited to a 4- to 6-mi radius (perhaps 25 sq mi or 65 sq km of coverage, which is similar in range to a cell-phone zone). Through the stronger LoS antennas, the WiMAX transmitting station would send data to WiMAX-enabled computers or routers set up within the transmitter's 30-mi radius (2800 sq mi or 9300 sq km of coverage). This is what allows WiMAX to achieve its maximum range.

WiMAX operates on the same general principles as Wi-Fi — it sends data from one computer to another via radio signals. A computer (either a desktop or a laptop) equipped with WiMAX would receive data from the WiMAX transmitting station, probably using encrypted data keys to prevent unauthorized users from stealing access. The fastest Wi-Fi connection can transmit up to 54 Mbps under optimal conditions. WiMAX should be able to handle up to 70 Mbps. Even once that 70 Mb is split up between several dozen businesses or a few hundred home users, it will provide at least the equivalent of cable-modem transfer rates to each user. The biggest difference is not speed; it is distance. WiMAX outdistances Wi-Fi by miles. Wi-Fi's range is about 100 ft (30 m). WiMAX will blanket a radius of 30 mi (50 km) with wireless access. The increased range is due to the frequencies used and the power of the transmitter. Of course, at that distance, terrain, weather, and large buildings will act to reduce the maximum range in some circumstances, but the potential is there to cover huge tracts of land.

802.16/HiperMAN Technology Specs

■ Based on IEEE 802.16 and ETSI HiperMAN, WiMAX selected the common mode of operation of these two standards — 256FFT OFDM.
■ Concentrated in 2- to 11-GHz WMAN, with the following set of features:
  • Service area range 50 km
  • NLoS
  • QoS designed in for voice/video, differentiated services

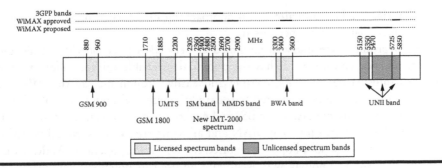

Figure 1.1   WiMAX spectrum. (Courtesy of www.wimaxforum.org.)

- Very high spectrum utilization: 3.8 bit/Hz
- Up to 280 Mbps per BS
- Speed — 70 Mbps
- Defines both the MAC and PHY layers and allows multiple PHY-layer specifications

WiMAX is a cost-effective technology as it can be deployed quickly and efficiently in regions that otherwise would not have broadband access. Although it has great potential, a key decision with regard to spectrum choice is whether to use the licensed or unlicensed spectrum (Figure 1.1). The use of the licensed spectrum has the obvious advantage of providing protection against interference from other wireless operators. The disadvantage is dealing with the licensing process. The use of the unlicensed spectrum gives the wireless operator the advantage of being able to deploy immediately but runs the risk of interference. With a large number of countries tightly controlling the wireless spectrum, WiMAX needs all the encouragement that the industry can provide it. Two primary bands are under consideration — the licensed 3.5-GHz band and the unlicensed 5.8-GHz UNII band frequencies (Table 1.6). Of these, the 3.5-GHz band seems to offer more promise, given the

Table 1.6   Key WiMAX Frequencies

Frequency (GHz)	Allocation	Countries	Target Group
2.5	Licensed	United States, Mexico, Brazil, Southeast Asia, and Korea (2.3 GHz)	Operators
3.5	Licensed	Most of the countries	Most of the countries
5.8	Unlicensed or light licensing	Most of the countries	ISPs (grass root)

Source: From www.wimaxforum.org.

fact that the 5-GHz spectrum is fast approaching its limits in most technologies and countries where it has been used.

Early products are likely to be aimed at network service providers (SPs) and businesses, not consumers. It has the potential to enable millions more to have wireless Internet connectivity, cheaply and easily. Proponents say that WiMAX wireless coverage will be measured in square kilometers, although that of Wi-Fi is measured in square meters. These BSs will eventually cover an entire metropolitan area, making that area into a WMAN and allowing true wireless mobility within it, as opposed to hot-spot hopping required by Wi-Fi. Proponents of WiMAX are hoping that the technology will eventually be used in notebook computers and PDAs. True roaming cell-like wireless broadband, however, will require 802.16e. True broadband for portable users, based on IEEE 802.16e, enables the creation of a "CPE-less" broadband market, providing broadband connectivity for laptops and PDAs with integrated WiMAX technology.

Governments globally are starting to prioritize broadband as a key political objective for all citizens to overcome the "broadband gap," also known as the "digital divide." In last-mile markets where traditional cable or copper/fiber infrastructures are saturated, outdated, or simply out of reach, BWA technology fills the void admirably, providing highly efficient and cost-effective access services for a large number of subscribers who would otherwise be left out of the loop in developed markets. The growing demand for broadband services on a global scale is clear and uncontestable. Businesses, public institutions, and private users regard it as an enabling technology, and it has become a given requirement for delivering communications services in the information age. The introduction of WMAN standards (802.16 and HiperMAN), and the guidelines set forth by the WiMAX Forum to ensure its success, will do much to encourage the growth of broadband wireless markets everywhere, benefiting everyone in the delivery chain — from equipment vendors to carriers to end users. As the wireless industry's most experienced solutions provider, Alvarion has a long and impressive record of commitment to developing and introducing standardized protocols. The buzz on WiMAX these days is electric. Internationally, it seems that WiMAX is already poised to take off as it is a hungrily awaited product.

Numerous countries have aggressive service providers fielding broadband services largely in the 3.5-GHz spectrum. The results of various investigations show that there is a positive business case for operators who want to add services and applications comparable to other existing broadband technologies (e.g., cable or DSL) for both high-volume residential and high-revenue business customers in greenfield and overlay scenarios, and also want to address the problems associated with the digital divide (e.g., limited range and, hence, limited penetration in underserved areas). The emerging markets can also benefit from the WiMAX technology, particularly those operators who are interested in using WiMAX for low-cost voice transport and delivery, which has been very difficult with proprietary solutions. Overall, markets without any fixed infrastructure pose the greatest opportunities.

They benefit from the absence of steep installation or rental costs because no outside-plant costs are necessary for copper/fiber and scalable equipment, matching the rollout to the acquired subscribers.

WiMAX seems new but, in many ways, it is nothing new at all. Much of the technology has been around for several years. Several vendors had offered variations of the current WiMAX flavor earlier — indeed they donated the seed technology to the WiMAX Forum. However, these firms all built 802.11 proprietary systems. Each fielded a Media Access Control (MAC) that offered specific improvements over the Wi-Fi standard. What was missing among these numerous vendors was interoperability. At its core, WiMAX is just such a standards initiative. Virtually everyone agrees that broadband wireless is here to stay and that standardization is essential. How quickly WiMAX gear is adopted will fuel expected price reductions. Having defined WiMAX in terms of its economic impact, there do remain important technical and business considerations to examine. With the advent of WiMAX, BWA is undergoing a dramatic change. What differentiates WiMAX from earlier BWA developments is standardization. Current broadband wireless deployments are based on proprietary solutions in which each BWA vendor custom-builds its solution, which adds time and cost to the process. Similar to what has happened recently in the WLAN arena with Wi-Fi, WiMAX plans to enforce standards compliance among vendor members. This compliance will result in interoperability and ultimately plug-and-play products, the cost of which will benefit from economies of scale and hence bring dramatic improvement to the business case for the operator. WiMAX products are set to become the mainstream broadband wireless platform. Although the overall number of subscriber lines is quite small relative to DSL or cable, the dollar value is growing to the point where even major carriers are beginning to pay close attention. It is not only the developed markets that can benefit from WiMAX. For emerging markets, operators are interested in using WiMAX for low-cost voice transport and delivery, which has been very difficult with proprietary solutions. As noted previously, the markets without any fixed infrastructure pose the greatest opportunities. Developments such as WiMAX chipsets embedded in laptops and other mobile devices will lead to broadband portability and to a CPE-less business model, which makes the case even more compelling for an operator because the user is subsidizing the model.

The main problems with broadband access are that it is expensive and it does not reach all areas. The main problem with Wi-Fi access is that hot spots are very small, so coverage is sparse. WiMAX has the potential to do to broadband Internet access what cell phones have done to phone access. In the same way that many people have given up their "landlines" in favor of cell phones, WiMAX could replace cable and DSL services, providing universal Internet access just about anywhere you go. WiMAX will also be as painless as Wi-Fi — turning your computer on will automatically connect you to the closest available WiMAX antenna. An important aspect of the IEEE 802.16 is that it defines a MAC layer that supports multiple physical layer (PHY) specifications. This is crucial to allow equipment makers to differentiate their offerings. Enhancements to current and new technologies and potentially new basic technologies incorporated into the PHY can be used. A converging trend is the use of multimode and multiradio SoCs and system designs that are harmonized through the use of common MAC, system management, roaming, IMS, and other levels of the system. WiMAX may be described as a bold attempt at forging many technologies to serve many needs across many spectrums. The MAC is significantly different from that of Wi-Fi. In Wi-Fi, the MAC uses contention access — all subscriber stations wishing to pass data through an access point are competing for the AP's attention on a random basis. This can cause distant nodes from the AP to be repeatedly interrupted by less sensitive, closer nodes, greatly reducing their throughput. By contrast, the 802.16 MAC is a scheduling MAC where the subscriber station only has to compete once (for initial entry into the network). After that, it is allocated a time slot by the BS. The time slot can enlarge and constrict, but it remains assigned to the subscriber station, meaning that other subscribers are not supposed to use it but take their turn. This scheduling algorithm is stable under overload and oversubscription (unlike 802.11). It is also much more bandwidth efficient. The scheduling algorithm also allows the BS to control QoS by balancing the assignments among the needs of the subscriber stations.

BWA is being revolutionized by standardization. Operators can benefit from interoperability and economies of scale of WiMAX equipment, which will dominate the wireless technologies available on the market, with the first products becoming available soon. Although operators have deployed broadband services to many subscribers who are within reach of central office locations, there is still an untapped market of subscribers who do not benefit from them. With WiMAX, operators are being given the chance to extend their customer base to include these subscribers using a highly efficient and cost-effective complementary access technology. In emerging markets, operators will be able to capitalize on the benefits that are associated with standardized equipment, such as economies of scale. WiMAX deployment will follow a two-stage development. Once mobility and broadband have been combined in step two in the form of in integrated CPEs in 2006, WiMAX will coexist alongside Universal Mobile Telecommunications System (UMTS).

Although wireless connectivity options have expanded rapidly in recent years, wireless network access is available now only in limited physical areas. Internet and intranet users need broadband access that extends over longer distances to more locations. The WiMAX standard, developed to create certified standards-based products from a wide range of vendors, enables system vendors to create many different types of products, including various configurations of BSs and customer premise equipment. WiMAX supports a variety of wireless broadband connections: In addition to supporting the 2- to 11-GHz frequency range, the 802.16d standard supports three PHYs. The mandatory PHY mode is 256-point FFT orthogonal frequency modulation (OFDM). The other two PHY modes are single carrier (SC) and 2048 orthogonal frequency division multiple access (OFDMA) modes. The corresponding

European standard — the ETSI HiperMAN standard — defines a single PHY mode identical to the 256-point OFDM mode in the 802.16d standard.

For security, the 802.16d standard specifies the Data Encryption Standard (DES) as the mandatory encryption mechanism for data, and triple DES for key encryption. The allowed cryptographic suites are

- CBC-mode 56-bit DES, no data authentication and 3-DES, 128
- CBC-mode 56-bit DES, no data authentication and RSA, 1024
- CCM-mode AES, no data authentication and AES, 128

Several features of the WiMAX protocol ensure robust QoS protection for services such as streaming audio and video. As with any other type of network, users have to share the data capacity of a WiMAX network, but WiMAX's QoS features allow service providers to manage the traffic based on each subscriber's service agreement on a link-by-link basis. Service providers can therefore charge a premium for guaranteed audio/video QoS, beyond the average data rate of a subscriber's link. One aspect of WiMAX QoS provisioning is a grant-request mechanism for letting users into the network. This mechanism's operation and value become apparent from a comparison of WiMAX with the CSMA/CD or CSMA/CA mechanisms used in LAN technologies such as 802.11. When a CSMA/CA-based wireless LAN has fewer than ten users per access point, the network experiences little contention for use of airtime. Occasional packet collisions occur, and they require back off and retransmissions, but the resulting overhead does not waste a significant amount of bandwidth. If the number of CSMA/CA access-point users goes up to dozens or hundreds of users, many more users tend to collide, back off, and retransmit data. In such an environment, average network loading factors can easily rise past 20 to 30 percent, and users notice delays — especially in streaming-media services. WiMAX avoids such issues by using a grant-request mechanism that allocates a small portion of each transmitted frame as a contention slot. With this contention slot, a subscriber station can enter the network by asking the BS to allocate a UL slot. The BS evaluates the subscriber station's request in the context of the subscriber's service level agreement (SLA) and allocates a slot in which the subscriber station can transmit (send UL packets). The WiMAX grant-request mechanism establishes a fixed overhead for airtime contentions and prevents large numbers of subscribers from interfering with one another. Overall, the mechanism allows for much higher utilization of available channel resources. Even when a BS has thousands of users and a high load factor, the network does not bog down with packet collisions and retransmissions. As more users join a WiMAX network, the BS schedules the subscribers using dynamic scheduling algorithms that the service provider can define and modify to achieve the promised level of service to each subscriber.

Another aspect of WiMAX QoS provisioning is link-by-link data-rate manageability. The signal strength between base and subscriber stations affects a wireless link's data rate and ability to use various modulation schemes within the 256 OFDM framework. Signal strength depends mainly on the distance between the two stations. If the network were restricted to a single modulation scheme per carrier, subscribers that are farther away from the BS would limit the network's ability to use the most efficient scheme. WiMAX enables optimization of each subscriber's data rate by allowing the BS to set modulation schemes on a link-by-link basis. A subscriber station close to the BS could use 64QAM modulation, although the weaker signal from a more remote subscriber might only permit the use of 16QAM or QPSK. The 802.16 MAC can even use a different modulation method for each subscriber's DL and UL bursts. The minimum granularity of a DL or UL burst is one OFDM symbol. Optimizing overall bandwidth usage and maximizing each subscriber's data rate establishes a solid foundation for high QoS. In addition to these general-purpose QoS features, WiMAX provides specific QoS support for voice and video. To enable toll-quality voice traffic, for example, voice packets can be tagged as such. The base station's scheduler then manages the passage of these packets through the air interface to provide deterministic latency.

All WiMAX products will be interoperable using the 802.16-2004 standard. The industry group WiMAX Forum will test and certify products for interoperability much the same way Wi-Fi Alliance does for Wi-Fi products. This will produce an equipment market of standardized components. Products based on prestandard versions of the 802.16-2004 specification are already in the market. Analysts estimate that subscriber stations for home access will initially cost up to $300. BSs will cost as little as $5,000 but will reach $100,000, depending on their range. In some cases, consumers would lease subscriber stations from carriers the way they do with cable set-top boxes, as part of their service plans. Even Wi-Fi, embedded in nearly every new computing gadget to provide short-range networking, has not yet established a service market with significant revenues. However, the opportunities are much higher in the wireless broadband market than they are in wireless networking, making WiMAX something service providers and carriers cannot dismiss as just another fad.

When fully realized, WiMAX will be used in nationwide networks that deliver wireless broadband service, offering a blend of speed, range, and price beyond what is offered by current wireless services. Subscribers will receive a WiMAX signal on their laptop computer, handset, or other electronic device from antennas that provide coverage from 1 to 5 mi in urban settings, and up to 30 mi in rural areas. Intel hopes to sell WiMAX chips in a variety of electronic equipment such as cameras, camcorders, and MP3 players [7]. Alvarion is already betting on the WiMAX technology. Among their first results, a technical platform, BreezeMax, that delivers primary voice services using existing TDM infrastructure, in addition to its broadband service capabilities, means ILECs and CLECs [9]. When it goes fully mobile, WiMAX can boast of an intriguing set of advantages. It will offer a greater range than Wi-Fi and the ability to provide access to people on the move or in a moving vehicle, something that Wi-Fi is still trying to work out. Because it works on a licensed spectrum, it does not face some of the interference and security problems that plague Wi-Fi. WiMAX can also reach rural or remote customers who are not wired for DSL or cable modem service. In the end, Wi-Fi will probably continue to exist alongside WiMAX, providing a choice of wireless options. WiMAX is expected to fare well against cellular broadband, which was introduced in the Bay Area last year by Sprint, Verizon Wireless, and Cingular Wireless. WiMAX should provide better speeds, about 2 to 4 Mbps, compared to 400 to 700 kbps for cellular broadband providers. Sprint has not announced a price, but industry observers say the service will be about the same price as DSL, $30 to $40 a month. Although cellular broadband has some of the same characteristics of WiMAX, it has had a tough time attracting customers because of its price: about $80 a month for laptop users, or $60 a month with a cell-phone plan. Concerns about capacity have also dogged the emerging 3G service, which uses existing voice networks. WiMAX's architecture is capable of handling more users per antenna site than cellular, making it more cost effective. There are a number of other wireless data and broadband technologies being tested by companies looking for alternatives to wires. Power line broadband and next-generation cellular technologies such as EvDO are also being kicked around. There are examples for hsdpa and WiMAX being complementary. For instance, WiMAX could be used for backhaul, reducing expensive leased line or fiber connections. The fact is that if a customer sends a megabyte of data on WiMAX, that megabyte will not be sent on hsdpa, and if a WiMAX service offers cheap flat-rate Voice-over-IP (VoIP) services as well, there will be a huge impact on both revenues and margins for the 3G operators [9]. Another standard that is considered very similar to 802.16 specifications is 802.20. Supporters of the 802.20 envision megabit-per-second data transfers with ranges of several miles. Initial enthusiasm was behind 802.20, which was designed as a standard for mobile devices, but the shift of industry support to WiMAX's 802.16 specifications has put the brakes on 802.20. In fact, some of its major proponents have joined the WiMAX Forum.

The major trend that is already emerging is the migration of mobile networks to fully IP-based networks. The next generation of wireless systems, i.e., 4G systems, will use new spectrum and emerging wireless air interfaces that will provide a very high bandwidth of 10+ Mbps. It will be entirely IP-based and will use packet-switching technology. It is expected that 4G systems will increase usage of the wireless spectrum. According to Cooper's law, on average, the number of channels has doubled every 30 months since 1985. Figure 1.2 shows the user mobility and data rates for different generations of wireless systems, and for wireless PANs and LANs. The 3G, and later 4G, systems will provide multimedia services to users everywhere, although WLANs provide broadband services in hot spots and WPANs connect personal devices together at very short distances. Spread-spectrum technology is presently used in 3G systems.

There is a substantial unmet need for very high-speed wireless wide area Internet access to both fixed and mobile devices. WiMAX is an advanced technology

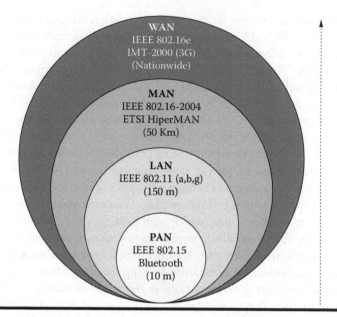

Figure 1.2   Network range expansion to meet current needs. (Courtesy of http://www. qoscom.de/documentation/51 _WiMAX%20Summit%20paris%20-%20may04.pdf; The Implications of WiMax for Competition and Regulation, OECD document [dated March 2, 2006].)

solution, based on an open standard designed to meet this need and to do so in a low-cost, flexible way. WiMAX networks are optimized for high-speed data and should help spur innovation in services, content, and new mobile devices. Both fixed and mobile applications of WiMAX are engineered to help deliver ubiquitous, high-throughput, broadband wireless services at a low cost. It is believed [2] that WiMAX, with its technical and economic advantages, should help enable mainstream adoption of personal broadband. WiMAX is the leading contender for mobile services among wireless solutions, according to the market research analyst firm Semico Research Corp., which said WiMAX revenue could grow from $21.6 million in 2005 to $3.3 billion in 2010, pending necessary factors. A recent report from the analyst firm Infonetics suggests that 22 percent of carriers and service providers worldwide have already deployed fixed WiMAX networks based on the 802.16d standard, with that figure set to rise to 50 percent by 2007. It concludes that use of both WiMAX and 3G wireless links as backhaul solutions in telecommunications networks will grow dramatically by 2007, possibly indicating a general trend away from fixed-line solutions. WiMAX represents a global connectivity opportunity in highly developed mobile market segments and developing countries, where this technology may help provide affordable broadband services. WiMAX is expected to enable true broadband speeds over wireless networks at a cost point to enable mass market adoption. Soon, WiMAX will be a very well-recognized term to describe wireless Internet access throughout the world. It is the only wireless standard today that has the ability to deliver true broadband speeds and help make the vision of pervasive connectivity a reality.

WiMax Forum

The WiMAX Forum is an industry-led, nonprofit corporation formed to help promote and certify the interoperability of broadband wireless products compliant with the IEEE 802.16 and ETSI HiperMAN standards. The Forum's goal is to accelerate global deployments of, and grow the market for, standards-based, interoperable, BWA solutions. The WiMAX Forum is working with member companies to develop standardized profiles and interoperable WiMAX products around specific spectrum bands, mainly 2.3 GHz, 2.5 GHz, 3.5 GHz, and 5.8 GHz. Until the equipment passes standards compliance and interoperability testing, it is essentially proprietary, and does not offer the scale or plug-and-play benefits of standard kit. But don't trot down to Circuit City to buy your WiMAX PCMCIA card just yet; the new testing tools are part of a phased rollout of compliance tests, and are not final or complete. They will merely help equipment vendors make sure their equipment is being designed on the path to compliance [10]. Because WiMAX's goal is to promote the interoperability of equipment based on either the 802.16d or the HiperMAN standard, the forum has chosen to support the 256 OFDM mode exclusively. To ensure worldwide interoperability, the WiMAX Forum will only certify equipment supporting that particular PHY mode. The WiMAX Forum's certification laboratory works with each WiMAX equipment supplier to conduct series of stringent and extensive test procedures consisting of protocol conformance, radio conformance, and interoperability testing. The issuing of a "WiMAX-Certified" label will serve as a seal of approval that a particular vendor's system or component fully corresponds to the technological specifications set forth by the new WMAN protocol.

To ensure the success of wireless technology as a stable, viable, and cost-effective alternative for delivering broadband access services in the last mile, the introduction of industry standards is essential. The companies that have already joined the WiMAX Forum represent over 75 percent of revenues in the global BWA market. Membership of the WiMAX Forum is not only limited to leading industry BWA providers; numerous multinational enterprises such as Intel and Fujitsu have also joined the WiMAX Forum. The Forum represents a cross-industry group of valued partners, including chip set manufacturers, component makers, and service providers. All of these organizations recognize the long-term benefits of working with standardized, interoperable equipment and are committed to the design, development, and implementation of WiMAX-compliant solutions. To date, there are more than 368 member companies in the WiMAX Forum, including 136

**Table 1.7   WiMAX Forum Board
Member List (as of November 2006)**

Airspan Networks
Alvarion
Aperto Networks
AT&T
British Telecom
Fujitsu
Intel Corporation
KDDI
KT Corp.
Motorola
Samsung
Sprint Nextel
ZTE Corporation

Source: From www.wimaxforum.org.

service providers (Table 1.7, Table 1.8, and Table 1.9). The WiMAX Forum is also evaluating these long-standing choices in light of recent advances in encryption technology. ABI Research projects the certified product line to grow, with larger numbers of products reaching the market. Aside from market expansion, wireless ISPs' deployment of certified fixed WiMAX solutions will also be available for some time. Early on, several initial deployments of pre-WiMAX networks are under way across the globe, including a growing number from South America.

Table 1.8   WiMAX Forum Principal Member List (as of November 2006)

Adaptix	BelAir Networks
Airvana	Bell Canada
Alcatel	BellSouth Corporation
Alpha Networks	Bridgewater Systems
Altair Semiconductor Ltd.	BRN Phoenix Inc.
Amicus Wireless Technology Inc.	Broadcom
ApaceWave Technologies	Cibernet Corporation
ArrayComm	Cisco Systems
ASUSTek Computer Inc.	Clearwire
AT4 Wireless	Delta Networks Inc.
Atmel	DesignArt Networks
Axxcelera Broadband Wireless	eAccess Ltd.
BB Mobile Corp.	EADS Secure Networks
Beceem	EION Wireless

Table 1.8   WiMAX Forum Principal Member List (as of November 2006) (Continued)

Ericcson	Pipex
ETRI	PMC-Sierra
FRC	PointRed Telecom Pvt. Ltd.
GCT Semiconductor Inc.	POSDATA
Gemtek Technologies Co. Ltd.	Protel
Globetel Wireless	Proxim Wireless Corporation
Hitachi Kokusai Electric Inc.	Quanta Computer Inc.
Hitachi Ltd.	RedDot Wireless Inc.
Huawel Technologies	Redline Communications
Hughes Systique Corporation	Runcom Technologies Ltd.
Hulu Sweden AB	Sagem Communication
Iberbanda	Sanyo Electric Co. Ltd.
Industrial Technology Research Institute	Selex Communications
Innowireless	SEQUANS Communications
Institute for Information Industry	SIAE Microelettronica
Intracom	Siemens SPA
Ixia	SK Telecom
Japan Radio	SK Telesys
Kyocera	SkyPilot Networks
LG Electronics	Solectek Corporation
LOGUS Broadband Wireless Solutions	SOMA Networks
Lucent Technologies	SR Telecom
M/A-COM Inc.	Starent Networks
Marvell International Ltd.	STMicroelectronics
MediaTek Inc.	Stratex Networks
MITAC Technology Corporation	Telecis Wireless
Mitsubishi Electric	Telemar
Modacom Inc.	Telsima
Navini	Toshiba America Research Inc. (TARI)
NEC	Tranzeo Wireless Technologies Inc.
Netgear	UTStarcom
NextWave Wireless LLC	VCom Inc.
Nippon Telegraph and Telephone	Walt Disney Company
Nokia	Wateen Telecom (Pvt.) Limited
Nortel	Wavesat Wireless Inc.
Oki Electric Industry Co. Ltd.	WiNetworks
ORZA NETWORKS	XRONet Corporation
PCTEL	Yozan
PicoChip	Z-Com

Source: From www.wimaxforum.org.

Table 1.9 WiMAX Forum Regular Member List (as of November 2006)

7 layers Inc.	BII Group
ACCA	Booz Allen and Hamilton
Accenture	Borusan Telekom
Accton Technology Corporation	bracNet
Adesta	Broadspectrum Ltd.
Advance Data Technology Corporation	butlerNetworks
ADVANTFST CORPORATION	CableMatrix Technologies Inc.
Aeroflex	Cameo Communications
Aeronix Inc	Casema N.V.
Agilent	CATR
Air Broadband Communications	Cedar Point Communications
Air Network Solutions	Celestica
airBand	CelPlan Technologies
AirMagnet Inc.	Ceragon
AirNet Communications	CETECOM Inc.
Alan Dick & Co Ltd.	China Motion Telecom
Albentia Systems	China Network Communications
Aloha Partners	Group
Alpha Technologies	Corporation
Alps Electric	Chung-Shan Institute of Science &
Analog Devices	Technology
Anite Telecoms Ltd.	Chunghwa Telecom Co. Ltd.
Anritsu Limited	CMP Media
AOL	Comcast
Aptilo Networks	Communication Technologies Inc.
Arab Telecommunication	Compliance Certification Servises
Arasor Corporation	CompUSA
Artiza Networks Inc.	Comsys Communication & Signal
Asia Pacific Broadband Telecom	Processing
AsicAhead	Couei Corporation
Astra Microelectronic	Covad Communications
Technologies Ltd.	CoWare Inc.
ATDI	Cushcraft Corporation
Austar Entertainment	CyberTAN Technology Inc.
Award Solutions	DBD Deutsche Breitband Dienste
Axtel	GmbH
Azaire Networks	Deutsche Telekom
Azimuth Systems	Digiweb
Azonic System Inc	Direct On PC Limited
Azotel Technologies Ltd.	Dishnet Wireless Limited
Aztech Systems Ltd.	Doceo Tech Incorporated
BAE Systems	EDX Wireless
Barik	Eircom
Bechtel Telecommunications	Elcoteq

Table 1.9 WiMAX Forum Regular Member List (as of November 2006) (Continued)

Elektrobit	IDEA Cellular Limited
Elitecore Technologies Ltd.	IDT Telecom
EMPRESA DE TELECOMM-	InfiNet Wireless Ltd.
UNICACIONES DE	Intertek Testing Services Taiwan
BOGOTA ETB. E.S.P.	Ltd. ETL
Enforta	SEMKO Devision
Entel Chile SA	IntroMobile
Ertach	Invenova
ETS-Lindgren	IRI Ubiteq. Inc.
European Antennas	Irish Broadband Internet Services
Euskaltel S.A.	IT&S. HOLDING LTD
EUTELSAT S.A.	Jacket Micro Devices
Far Esatone Telecommunications	JDSU
Co. Ltd.	JSC "OptiTelecom"
Filtronic	JSC CEDICOM
Finnet	Juniper Networks
Firetide	Kapsch CarrierCom
First International Telecom CORP	KenCast
Flextronics	Koenet Telecommunication
Fortress Technologies	Technologies and Communication
FPT Telecom	Services Corporation
France Telecom	WFI
FREEBOX SA	KTL
Freescale Semiconductor Inc.	Larsen & Toubro Infotech Limited
Fundacao CPqD	Lattice Semiconductor
Fusion Communications Corporation	LCC
GEMALTO	LitePoint
General Dynamics Canada	M2Z Networks Inc.
Geodesic Information Systems Ltd.	M3 Wireless Ltd.
Globalcom	Maravedis Inc
GlobalWave Telecom	Max Telecom Ltd.
GO Networks	Maxim Integrated Products
Golden Telecom	Maxim Communications Berhad
HCL Infinet	MAXTEL
HCL Technologies	McKinsey and Co.
Hong Kong Applied Science and	MetroBridge Networks
Technology	Microelectronics Technology Inc
Research Institute Limited	Microsoft Corporation
Hopling Technologies	MindTree Consulting Private Limited
Huber+Suhner	MLL Telecom Ltd.
Hughes Network Systems	Mobile Mark
Hypres	Mobile Metrics

(continued)

**Table 1.9   WiMAX Forum Regular Member List (as of November 2006)
(Continued)**

MobilePro	Quiconnect
MoblTV Inc.	Qwest
Mocana	Redpine Signals
Morpho Technologies	ReignCom
Mpower Communications	Reliance Communications, A D Ambani
MSkylink Telecom Inc.	Group
MSV	RF Magic Inc.
MTI Wireless Edge	RFI
MTN Group	Roamware Inc.
Murandi Communications Ltd.	Rogers
NasionCom Sdn. Bhd.	Rohde&Schwarz
Neotec	SAI Technology Inc.
NeoviaTelecomanicacacoes S/A	Sanjole
Nera Networks AS	SC Lithuanian Radio & TV Center
NetHawk Oyj	Seasolve Software Inc.
Nexcom Telecom	Secgo Software Oy
Nextel de Mexico	SES Americom
NextGenTel	SGS Taiwan Ltd.
NextPhase Wireless	Sierra Monolithics
North Rock Communications	Sierra Wireless
Omnivision C.A.	Sify Limited
OPNET Technologies Inc	SiGe Semiconductor Inc.
Orascom Telecom Holding (OTH)	SingTel
Orbitel S.A. E.S.P	SkyTel/MCI
OxfordSVl	Skyworks Solutions
PA Consulting Group	SmartBridges
Pacific Internet Corporation	Sony Electronics Inc.
Panasonic Electronic Devices Europe	Spanco TeleSystems & Solutions Limited
PCCW	Spirent Communications
PCTEST Engineering Laboratory Inc.	Sporton International Inc.
(PCTEST WIRELESS)	Sri Lanka Telecom
Pegasus Communications	Start Telecom
Philips Semiconductors.b.v.	Stealth Microwave
Portugal Telecom Inovao	Sumitomo Electric Industries Ltd.
Powerwave Technologies	Summa Telecom Ltd.
PricewaterhouseCoopers	SUPERONLINE
Prisma Engineering	Swift Networks Limited
Pronto Networks	Symbol Technologies Inc.
PT Indosat Mega Media	Synterra
PT Telekomunikasi Indonesia, Tbk	Syntronic AB
Q-Ware Systems & Services Corp.	Tata Elxsi Limited
Qdelo Inc.	TATUNG CO.

Table 1.9 WiMAX Forum Regular Member List (as of November 2006) (Continued)

TDC Solutions	Trillion
Techxact	TriQuint Semiconductor
Tecom Co. Ltd.	TruePosition Inc.
Tektronix Inc.	TTA
Telabria	Turbonet A.S
TelASIC Communications	TUV Rheinland Group
Telcordia Technologies	UNI-COM S.A
Telecom Italia	UNISTARS Holding
Telecom Technology Center	UNITLINE
Telediffusion de France	Universal Scientific Industrial Co. Ltd.
Telefonica I+D	Unwired Australia
Telenor	Urmet Telecomunicazioni Spa
TeleSonera	Venturi Wireless
Telkom SA	VeriSign
TELMEX	VIA Telecom
Telsa srl	Videsh Sanchar Nigam Limited
Telus	Vietnam Multimedia Corporation (VTC)
TenXc Wireless Inc.	VimpelCom
Texas Instruments	Warner Music Group
The Cloud Networks	Wi-LAN
The MITRE Corporation	Wi-MAN
Theta Microelectronics SA	Wichorus
TietoEnator	Wimax Telecom AG
Time Warner Telecom	Wind River
TM Research & Development	Wintegra
TNO Information and Communication	Wipro Technologies
Technology	WirelessLogix
Towerstream	WiTech
TRDA	XTS TELECOM
Trendsmedia Inc.	Yokogawa Electric Corporation
Tridea Works, LLC	ZyXEL Communications Corp.

Source: From www.wimaxforum.org.

As an organization comprising nearly 400 member companies and overseeing a range of activities that span the globe, the WiMAX Forum now has added operations and marketing directors — along with a staff of project managers — to ensure that it meets the needs of membership and achieves stated goals. To handle the expected deluge of WiMAX gear, the WiMAX Forum chose Spain's Cetecom Laboratories as the first laboratory and recently added Seoul, South Korea's TTA (Telecommunications Technology Association, www.tta.or.kr) as the second. TTA will likely specialize in certification of products that conform to the coming mobile flavor of WiMAX, IEEE 802.16e. It expects to certify the first commercial mobile WiMAX product in the first quarter of 2007. Cetecom Laboratories is also preparing to offer mobile WiMAX certification. The lab is jointly developing a protocol-conformance tester with Aeroflex. Cetecom and U.K.-based picoChip have announced that the tester would rely on the PC102 DSP-array chips and the PC8530 software stack from picoChip. To date, few fixed WiMAX products have received the "WiMAX Forum Certified" seal; a few of them are introduced in the following text.

The RedMAX AN-100U BS uses OFDM optical LoS and NLoS technology to overcome typical urban obstacles, although the long-range capabilities and high-capacity of the AN-100 allows wireless connectivity to remote locations with a minimum number of repeater stations.

SEQUANS Communications, a fabless semiconductor company and leading supplier of WiMAX silicon and software for BWA, announced recently that the company's subscriber station and BS reference designs, based respectively on its SQN1010 and SQN2010 SoCs, and S-Cube software solution, have achieved certification by the WiMAX Forum. The SQN2010 SoC BS solution delivers unique RF capabilities through a fully digital front end, integrating A/D and D/A converters and operating with channel width ranging from 1.25 to 28 MHz. Sequans is the first silicon provider to offer a complete end-to-end certified chipset solution. Sequans' SQN2010-RD BS reference design was certified by the WiMAX Forum earlier, and Sequans' subscriber station reference design, the SQN1010-RD, has also received the Forum's seal of approval. Sequans' products passed stringent and extensive testing, consisting of protocol conformance, radio conformance, and interoperability testing, to obtain the WiMAX Forum Certification seal. SEQUANS' reference designs allow equipment manufacturers to quickly develop a wide range of products from high-end BSs to pico-BSs and from outdoor to feature-rich, indoor, self-install terminals and home gateways. Equipment manufacturers benefit from Sequans' unique implementation of mandatory and optional IEEE 802.16/ETSI HiperMAN features that together drastically improve cell coverage and throughput and enable low-latency support for real-time voice, video, and data applications.

The miniMAX CPE solution features a full-range of standard-based integrated circuits, software, and reference system designs for BWA 802.16 compliant applications that require flexible product and network configurations.

Montreal-based Wavesat is the first supplier worldwide to receive this certification for a customer premise equipment solution. Wavesat's Minimax CPE passed extensive tests related to protocol conformance, radio conformance, and interoperability testing to attain the WiMAX Forum Certification seal. The Minimax CPE solution, part of the Evolutive WiMAX Series, is available to manufacturers and operators worldwide to accelerate the design of 3.5-GHz WiMAX-certifiable CPE compliant with the IEEE 802.16-2004 standard and its corrigendum.

Minimax is the subscriber platform included in Wavesat's Evolutive Reference Kit to guide and support the design of 3.5-GHz WiMAX-certifiable wireless systems using Wavesat's DM256 integrated circuit. Wavesat's Evolutive Series consists of a range of standard-based integrated circuits, software, and reference designs compliant with IEEE 802.16-2004 and intended for forward compatibility with the IEEE 802.16e mobility amendment. Wavesat products fit design requirements for CPE as well as BS infrastructures, providing wireless connectivity for a range of network sizes and coverage.

WiMAX Forum has certified Siemens' products for having passed the interoperability tests in the Forum's international standardization laboratory. The WayMAX@vantage solution from Siemens, which is certified for the WiMAX FDD 3.5-GHz system, consists of a BS, modems, and routers. The product is now ready for the future IEEE 802.16e-2005 OFDM profile and the ETSI HiperMAN standard. The IEEE 802.16 standard used today allows data transmission at rates as high as 10.5 Mbps in 3.5 MHz bandwidth.

WiMAX Spectrum Owners Alliance

WiMAX Spectrum Owners Alliance (WiSOA) is the first global organization composed exclusively of owners of WiMAX spectrum [8]. WiSOA is focused on the regulation, commercialization, and deployment of WiMAX spectrum in the 2.3- to 2.5-GHz and the 3.4- to 3.5-GHz ranges. WiSOA is dedicated to educating and informing its members, industry representatives, and government regulators of the importance of WiMAX spectrum, its use, and the potential for WiMAX to revolutionize broadband.

References

1. http://www.wirelessdesignasia.com/article.asp?id=2049.
2. http://www.intel.com/netcomms/events/wimax.htm.
3. http://www.btimes.com.my/Current_News/BT/Monday/Column/BT583229.txt/ Article/ [dated August 24, 2006].
4. www.wimaxforum.org.
5. http://www.qoscom.de/documentation/51_WiMAX%20Summit%20paris% 20-%20may04.pdf.
6. The Implications of WiMax for Competition and Regulation, OECD document [dated March 2, 2006].
7. http://www.sfgate.com/cgi-bin/article.cgi?f=/c/a/2006/12/18/BUG8NN0HIT1.DTL [dated December 18, 2006].
8. http://electronicxtreme.blogspot.com/2006/12/wi-max.html [dated December 11, 2006].
9. http://21talks.net/voip/voice-over-wimax.
10. http://news.techdirt.com/news/wireless/article/6929 [dated October 26, 2006].
11. www.intel.com.

Chapter 2

Contemporary Wireless Technologies

Wireless Technologies

Today, there are many wireless technologies that are used for a variety of applications. Wireless radio communications are based on transmission of radio waves through the air. Radio waves between 30 MHz and 20 GHz are used for data communications. The range lower than 30 MHz could support data communication; however, it is typically used for frequency modulation (FM) and amplitude modulation (AM) radio broadcasting because these waves reflect on the Earth's ionosphere to extend the communication. Radio waves over 20 GHz may be absorbed by water vapor and, therefore, they are not suitable for long-distance communication.

Microwave transmission is based on the same principles as radio transmission. The microwave networks require a direct transmission path, high transmission towers, and antennas. Satellite communications are used for a variety of broadcasting applications. The two most popular frequency bands for satellite communications are C-band (frequency range 5.9 to 6.4 GHz for uplink and 3.7 to 4.2 GHz for downlink) and Ku-band (frequency range 14 to 14.5 GHz for uplink and 11.7 to 12.2 GHz for downlink). The radio transmission system consists of a transmitter and a receiver. The main components of a radio transmitter are a transducer, an oscillator, a modulator, and an antenna. A transducer converts the information to be transmitted to an electrical signal. An oscillator generates a reliable frequency that is used to carry the signal. A modulator embeds the voice or data signal into the carrier frequency. An antenna is used to radiate an electrical signal into space in the form of electromagnetic waves. A radio receiver consists of an antenna, an oscillator, a demodulator, and an amplifier. An antenna captures radio waves and converts them into electrical signals. An oscillator generates electrical waves at the carrier frequency that is used as a reference wave to extract the signal. A demodulator detects and restores modulated signals. An amplifier amplifies the received signal that is typically very weak.

Modulation Techniques

Modulation techniques embed a signal into the carrier frequency. They can be classified into analog and digital modulations. Traditional analog modulations include AM and FM. In digital modulations, binary 1s and 0s are embedded in the carrier frequency by changing its amplitude, frequency, or phase. Subsequently, digital modulations are called keying techniques, such as amplitude shift keying (ASK), frequency shift keying (FSK), and phase shift keying (PSK). Other popular keying techniques include Gaussian minimum shift keying (GMSK) and differential quadrature phase shift keying (DQPSK). GMSK is a type of FSK modulation that uses continuous phase modulation so that it can avoid abrupt changes. It is used in Groupe Speciale Mobile systems, and digital enhanced cordless telecommunications (DECT). DPSK is a type of phase modulation that defines four, rather than two, phases. A significant drawback of traditional radio frequency (RF) systems is that they are quite vulnerable to sources of interference. Spread-spectrum modulation techniques resolve the problem by spreading the information over a broad frequency range. These techniques are very resistant to interference. Spread-spectrum techniques are used in code division multiple access (CDMA) systems.

OFDM

Orthogonal frequency-division multiplexing (OFDM) is a transmission scheme that enables data to be encoded concurrently on multiple high-speed RFs. This allows for increased amounts of data throughput and robustness and currently achieves the most efficient use of bandwidth. OFDM is the basis of the PHY of the IEEE 802.11a and IEEE 802.11g standard (Wi-Fi). In addition, the IEEE 802.16 standard (WiMAX) has two PHYs that utilize OFDM techniques.

IEEE 802.11a/g OFDM

IEEE 802.11a (and g) use OFDM modulation. This particular OFDM implementation divides 16.25 MHz of bandwidth into 52 subcarriers that are 312.5 kHz wide. An OFDM data packet consists of a preamble, a header, and a data block. In the data block, 48 subcarriers are used to transmit data. The pilot signals allow the receiver to compensate for the OFDM signal's phase and amplitude distortion caused by the environment. Pilot subcarriers help maintain synchronization because each burst can act as a new reference point for each burst, whereas standard single carrier (SC) implementations only feature this on a per-packet basis within the preamble. These characteristics give OFDM implementation a distinct advantage within fast-fading multipath and reflective non/NLoS conditions.

Proprietary OFDM (pre-WiMAX)

Conceptually, OFDM techniques can be applied in many different ways above and beyond the "Wi-Fi-based" form. Certain wireless vendors (including the WiMAX Forum) have invested additional time and money into creating OFDM schemes specifically to address the needs of outdoor wide area broadband wireless network operations. Examples of these modifications include varying the guard interval, changing the number of subcarriers in use, adapting the type and style of coding, and lengthening or shortening the symbol burst-length of the carrier. Each specific modification has ramifications on the operation and performance of the radio system.

Frequency Division Duplexing

Frequency division duplexing (FDD) refers to the simultaneous transmission and reception of data over separate frequencies, allowing for bidirectional full-duplex communications. Thus, there is no substantial time delay and no technology limit to distance, so full throughput is achievable at any distance. Depending on the situation, this design also can provide for higher colocation possibilities through the synchronization of transmit-frequency channels.

Time Division Duplexing

Time division duplexing (TDD) refers to the interleaving of transmission and reception of data on the same frequency. A common frequency is shared between the upstream and downstream, the direction in transmission being switched in time. Under these circumstances, because of its ability to put both uplink and downlink in the same channel, TDD can be more spectrally efficient.

Wireless System Topologies

Two basic wireless system topologies are point-to-point (or ad hoc) and networked topology. In the point-to-point topology, two or more mobile devices are connected using the same Air Interface protocol. In a full mesh point-to-point configuration, all devices are interconnected. Limitations of this topology are that the wireless devices cannot access the Web, send e-mail, or run remote applications. In the networked topology, there is a link between the wireless devices connected in the wireless network and the fixed public or private network. A typical configuration includes wireless devices (or terminals), at least one bridge between the wireless and the physical networks, and the numbers of servers hosting applications used by wireless devices. The bridge between the wireless and the physical networks is called the base station (BS) or access point.

Performance Elements of Wireless Communications

Wireless communication is characterized by several critical performance elements:

■ Range
■ Power used to generate the signal
■ Mobility
■ Bandwidth
■ Actual data rate

The range is a critical factor that refers to the coverage area between the wireless transmitter and the receiver. It is strongly correlated with the power of the signal. A simplified approximation is that for 1 mW of power, the range is 1 m in radius. For example, 1 W of power will allow the range of 1 km in radius. As the distance from the BS increases, the signal will degrade, and data may incur a high error rate. Using part of the spectrum for error correction can extend the range; also, the use of multiple BSs can extend the range. The mobility of the user depends on the size of the wireless device. Miniaturization of the wireless device provides better mobility. This can be achieved by reducing the battery size and, consequently, by minimizing power consumption; however, this will cause the generated signal to weaken, giving reduced range. There should be a trade-off between range and mobility: the extended range will reduce the mobility, and better mobility will reduce the range of wireless devices. Bandwidth refers to the amount of frequency spectrum available per user. Using wider channels gives more bandwidth. Transmission errors could reduce the available bandwidth because part of the spectrum will be used for error correction.

The actual data rate mostly depends on the bandwidth available to the user; however, there are some other factors that influence it, such as the movement of the transceiver, position of the cell, and density of users. The actual data rate is typically higher for stationary users than for users who are walking. Users traveling at high speed (such as in cars or trains) have the lowest actual data rate. The reason for this is that part of the available bandwidth must be used for error correction due to greater interference that traveling users may experience. Similarly, interference depends on the position of the cell; with higher interference, the actual data rate will be reduced. Optimal location is where there is direct LOS between the user and the BS, and the user is not far from the BS. In that case, there is no interference, and the transmission requires minimum bandwidth for error correction. If the density of users is high, there will be more users transmitting within a given cell and, consequently, there will be less aggregate bandwidth per user. This reduces the actual data rate.

Generations of Wireless Systems Based on Wireless Access Technologies

From the late 1970s until today, there have been three generations of wireless systems based on different access technologies:

1. 1G wireless systems, based on FDMA (frequency division multiple access)
2. 2G wireless systems, based on TDMA (time division multiple access) and CDMA (code division multiple access)
3. 3G wireless systems, mostly based on W-CDMA (wideband code division multiple access)

The 1G Wireless Systems

The first generation of wireless systems was introduced in the late 1970s and early 1980s, and was built for voice transmission only. It was an analog, circuit-switched network that was based on FDMA air interface technology. In FDMA, each caller has a dedicated frequency channel and related circuits. For example, three callers use three frequency channels. An example of a wireless system that employs FDMA is AMPS (Advanced Mobile Phone Service).

The 2G Wireless Systems

The second generation of wireless systems was introduced in the late 1980s and early 1990s with the objective of improving transmission quality, system capacity, and range. Major multiple-access technologies used in 2G systems are TDMA and CDMA. These systems are digital, and they use circuit-switched networks.

TDMA Technology

In TDMA systems, several callers time-share a frequency channel. A call is sliced into a series of time slots, and each caller gets one time slot at regular intervals. Typically, a 39-kHz channel is divided into three time slots, which allows three callers to use the same channel. In this case, nine callers use three channels. The main advantage of the TDMA system is increased efficiency of transmission; TDMA systems can be used for transmission of both voice and data. They offer data rates from

64 kbps to 120 Mbps, which enables operators to offer personal communication services such as fax, voice-band data, and short messaging services (SMS). TDMA technology separates users in time, thus ensuring that they will not have interference from other simultaneous transmissions. It provides extended battery life because transmission occurs only part of the time. One of the disadvantages of TDMA is caused by the fact that each caller has a predefined time slot. The result is that when callers are roaming from one cell to another, all time slots in the next cell are already occupied, and the call might be disconnected. GSM is the best-known European implementation of services that use TDMA air interface technology. The other systems that deploy TDMA are DECT, the IS-136 standard, and Integrated Digital Enhanced Network (iDEN).

Global System for Mobile Communications (GSM) — The GSM protocol was created in 1980 in France. It uses the 890- to 915-MHz radio band for the upload traffic and the 935- to 960-MHz radio band for the download traffic. GSM is a 2G system based on FD-TDMA (frequency division–time division multiple access) radio access, which offers a 9.6-kbps rate. Millions of subscribers in the world use the GSM system for their wireless cellular communications (Figure 2.1). The problem is that GSM will not be able to satisfy news services such as data networks. GSM has applied the frequency-hopping technique, which involves switching the call frequency many times per second for security. A revision of the GSM specifications defines an extended GSM (EGSM) that extends the original GSM-900 operation band and stipulates lower-power terminals and smaller serving areas.

CDMA Access Technology

CDMA is a radically different air interface technology that uses the frequency-hopping (FH) spread-spectrum technique. The signal is randomly spread across the entire allocated 1.35-MHz bandwidth. The randomly spread sequences are transmitted all at once, which gives a higher data rate and improved capacity of the channels. CDMA provides better signal quality and secure communications. The transmitted signal is dynamic, bursty, and ideal for data communication. Many mobile phone standards currently being developed are based on CDMA.

CDMA is a form of multiplexing (not a modulation scheme) and a method of multiple access that does not divide up the channel by time (as in TDMA), or frequency (as in FDMA), but instead encodes data with a special code associated with each channel and uses the constructive interference properties of the special codes to perform the multiplexing. It also refers to digital cellular telephony systems that make use of this multiple-access scheme, such as those pioneered by Qualcomm, and W-CDMA by the International Telecommunication Union (ITU). CDMA has since been used in many communications systems, including the global positioning system (GPS) and the OmniTRACS satellite system for transportation logistics. A number

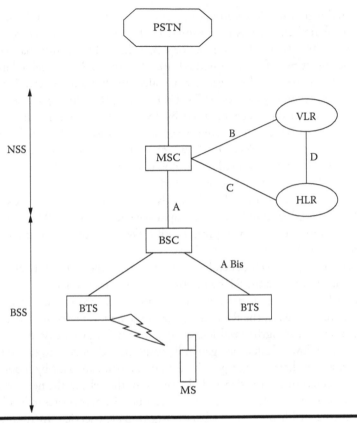

Figure 2.1   Architecture of a GSM network.

of different terms are used to refer to CDMA implementations. The original U.S. standard defined by Qualcomm was known as IS-95, the IS referring to an Interim Standard of the Telecommunications Industry Association (TIA). IS-95 is often referred to as 2G or second-generation cellular. The Qualcomm brand name cdma-One may also be used to refer to the 2G CDMA standard. CDMA has been submitted for approval as a mobile air interface standard to the ITU [5]. Whereas the GSM standard is a specification of an entire network infrastructure, the CDMA interface relates only to the air interface — the radio part of the technology. For example, GSM specifies an infrastructure based on an internationally approved standard, whereas CDMA allows each operator to provide the network features as it finds suitable. On the air interface, the signaling suite (GSM: ISDN SS7) work has been progressing to harmonize these. After a couple of revisions, IS-95 was superseded by the IS-2000 standard. This standard was introduced to meet some of the criteria laid out in the International Mobile Telecommunication System (IMT-2000) specification for 3G (or third-generation) cellular. It is also referred to as 1xRTT, which simply means

"1 times radio transmission technology" and indicates that IS-2000 uses the same 1.25-MHz shared channel as the original IS-95 standard. A related scheme called 3xRTT uses three 1.25-MHz carriers for a 3.75-MHz bandwidth that would allow higher data burst rates for an individual user, but the 3xRTT scheme has not been commercially deployed. More recently, Qualcomm has led the creation of a new CDMA-based technology called 1xEV-DO, or IS-856, which provides the higher packet data transmission rates required by IMT-2000 and desired by wireless network operators. This CDMA system is frequently confused with a similar but incompatible technology called W-CDMA, which forms the basis of the W-CDMA air interface. This air interface is used in the global 3G standard UMTS and the Japanese 3G standard Freedom of Mobile Multimedia Access (FOMA), by NTT DoCoMo and Vodafone; however, the CDMA family of U.S. national standards (including cdmaOne and CDMA2000) are not compatible with the W-CDMA family of ITU standards. Another important application of CDMA — predating and entirely distinct from CDMA cellular — is the GPS.

The size of a given cell depends on the power of the signal transmitted by the handset, the terrain, and the RF being used. Various algorithms can reduce the noise introduced by variations in terrain but require extra information be sent to validate the transfer. Hence, the RF and power of the handset effectively determine the cell size. Long wavelengths need less energy to travel a given distance versus short wavelengths, so lower frequencies generally result in greater coverage, and higher frequencies result in shorter coverage. These characteristics are used by mobile network planners in determining the size and placement of the cells in the network. In cities, many small cells are needed; the use of high frequencies allows sites to be placed more closely together, with more subscribers being provided service. In rural areas with a lower density of subscribers, use of lower frequencies allows each site to provide broader coverage. Various companies use different variants of CDMA to provide fixed-line networks using wireless local loops (WLL) technology. Because they can plan with a specific number of subscribers per cell in mind, and these are all stationary, this application of CDMA can be found in most parts of the world. CDMA is suited for data transfer with bursty behavior and where delays can be accepted. It is therefore used in WLAN applications; the cell size here is 500 ft because of the high frequency (2.4 GHz) and low power. The suitability for data transfer is the reason why W-CDMA seems to be the "winning technology" for the data portion of 3G mobile cellular networks. All forms of CDMA use spread-spectrum process gain to allow receivers to partially discriminate against unwanted signals. Signals with the desired chip code and timing are received, whereas signals with different chip codes (or the same spreading code but a different timing offset) appear as wideband noise reduced by the process gain [5].

Asynchronous CDMA's main advantage over CDM (synchronous CDMA), TDMA, and FDMA is that it can use the spectrum more efficiently in mobile telephony applications. TDMA systems must carefully synchronize the W times of all the users to ensure that they are received in the correct time slot and do not cause interference. Because this cannot be perfectly controlled in a mobile environment, each time slot must have a guard time, which reduces the probability that users will interfere but decreases the spectral efficiency. Similarly, FDMA systems must use a guard band between adjacent channels because of the random doppler shift of the signal spectrum that occurs due to the user's mobility. The guard bands will reduce the probability that adjacent channels will interfere, but decrease the utilization of the spectrum. Most importantly, asynchronous CDMA offers a key advantage in the flexible allocation of resources. There is a fixed number of orthogonal codes, time slots, or frequency bands that can be allocated for CDM, TDMA, and FDMA systems, which remain underutilized due to the bursty nature of telephony and packetized data transmissions. There is no strict limit to the number of users that can be supported in an asynchronous CDMA system; only a practical limit governed by the desired bit-error probability because the SIR (signal-to-interference ratio) varies inversely with the number of users. In a bursty traffic environment such as mobile telephony, the advantage afforded by asynchronous CDMA is that the performance (bit-error rate) is allowed to fluctuate randomly, with an average value determined by the number of users multiplied by the percentage of utilization. Suppose there are 2N users that only talk half of the time; then, 2N users can be accommodated with the same average bit-error probability as N users that talk all of the time. The key difference here is that the bit-error probability for N users talking all of the time is constant, whereas it is a random quantity (with the same mean) for 2N users talking half of the time [5].

Asynchronous CDMA is ideally suited to a mobile network where large numbers of transmitters each generate a relatively small amount of traffic at irregular intervals. CDM, TDMA, and FDMA systems cannot recover the underutilized resources inherent to bursty traffic due to the fixed number of orthogonal codes, time slots, or frequency channels that can be assigned to individual transmitters. For instance, if there are N time slots in a TDMA system and 2N users that talk half of the time, then, half of the time there will be more than N users needing to use more than N time slots. Furthermore, it would require significant overhead to continually allocate and deallocate the orthogonal code, time slot, or frequency-channel resources. By comparison, asynchronous CDMA transmitters simply send signals when they have something to say, and go off the air when they don't, keeping the same PN signature sequence as long as they are connected to the system [5].

CDMA One

The need for increased capacity was the great motivation for the advent of this American digital cellular technology. As demand for wireless services increased, mainly in dense urban areas, the old analog standard, known as AMPS, proved inadequate to satisfy the demand. TDMA technology, based on the EIA/TIA/IS-54 specifications (later on enhanced and renamed EIA/TIA/IS-136), was the first solution to the capacity problem of the old analog system. By offering roughly a threefold increase in capacity by dividing each 30-kHz AMPS channel into three time slots, this system was the first American response to the European cellular 2G, the GSM. This digital novelty, however, was not enough to soothe a number of service providers, who argued that such a technology would not be adequate for future growth in service. A mobile station may initiate a call in the CDMA system and, while the call is still in progress, it may migrate to the analog system if required. A number of innovations have been introduced in the CDMA system as compared to earlier cellular systems. Soft handoff is certainly a great novelty. In soft handoff, handoff from one BS to another occurs in a smooth manner. In soft handoff, the mobile station keeps its radio link with the original BS and establishes a connection with one or more BSs. The excess connections are given up only when and if the new link has sufficient quality. Another innovation introduced in the CDMA system is the use of GPS receivers at the BSs. GPSs are utilized so that BSs can be synchronized, a feature vital to the soft handoff operation. The first CDMA systems were employed under the TIA/EIA/IS-95A specifications. The A version of the specifications evolved to TIA/EIA/IS-95B, in which new features related to higher data rate transmission, soft handoff algorithms, and power-control techniques have been introduced. The name "cdmaOne" is then used to identify the CDMA technology operating with either specification.

2.5G Wireless Systems

An intermediate step in employing full packet-switching 3G systems is the 2.5G wireless systems. They use separate air interfaces — circuit switching for voice and packet switching for data — designed to operate in 2G network spectrum. The 2.5G provides an increased bandwidth to about 100 kbps, much larger than 2G systems but much lower than the expected bandwidth of 3G systems. General packet radio service (GPRS) is the 2.5G implementation of Internet protocol packet switching on European GSM networks. Enhanced data for global enhancement (EDGE) is another packet-switched technology that is a GPRS upgrade based on TDMA. The switch from the circuit-switched networks to packet-switched networks provoked the carriers to heavily invest in another new-generation technology — 2.5G. Based on the digital transmission protocols, the 2.5G is not a single wireless standard but a collection of several standards. Bolting on to existing 2G infrastructure built on the operational GSM, CDMA, and TDMA standards among others, 2.5G CPRS and CDMA2000 standards are to provide faster data speeds up to 171 kbps. Among the most important attributes that 2.5G wireless Internet technologies can offer is wide area coverage. Technologies of 2.5G standards are looked upon as an intermediary step on the way to the true fast-speed wireless Internet access promised by 3G technologies. Rollout of 2.5G is timed well with other supporting technologies such as location services through GPS and network-based location; biometrics offering personalization; miniaturization allowing integration of more memory, energy, and processing power in portable devices; voice recognition offering easy access and interface; Bluetooth; Wi-Fi; and others. Many see 2.5G as a great market experiment powerful enough to open new business models, new entrants, and a whole slew of new business and consumer products and services.

GPRS and EDGE

These are 2.5G networks enabling the offering of a 170-kbps data transfer rate. They will use the IP protocol for data transport. For these networks, the billing for data communication is based on the data exchanged, and not on the duration of the communication. GPRS networks can work in parallel with GSM networks: GSM is used for voice communications and GPRS for data communications. Therefore, a mobile station can be connected at the same time to the GSM and GPRS networks.

GPRS is based on two routers:

■ Serving GPRS support node (SGSN) for the packet transfer between the wireless radio subsystem and the fixed network. SGSN routers are connected to the basic service set (BSS) and to the GGSN routers.
■ Gateway GPRS support node (GGSN) for the management of the public data, for example, for the quality-of-service (QoS) negotiation.

GTP (GPRS Tunneling Protocol) is used for the encapsulation of data between SGSN and GGSN, by using TCP (Transmission Control Protocol) and UDP (User Datagram Protocol). Between the SGSN and the MS, it is the SNDCP (SubNetwork Dependent Convergence Protocol) that is used to manage the packets.

The GPRS architecture can be represented as shown in Figure 2.2.

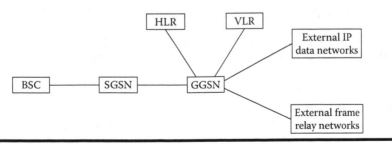

Figure 2.2 GPRS architecture.

3G Systems

The 3G wireless systems are digital systems based on packet-switched network technology intended for wireless transmission of voice, data, images, audio, and video. The 3G system IMT-2000 is based on the 2000-MHz radio band and is composed of

- UTRA (universal mobile telecommunication system terrestrial radio access), proposed by the ETSI (European Telecommunication Standard Institute)
- CDMA2000 (code division multiple access 2000), proposed by TIA (Telecommunications Industry Association), which is an evolution of the IS95 standard
- UWC136 (Universal Wireless Communications 136), proposed by TIA, which is an evolution of the IS136 standard
- W-CDMA, proposed by ARIB (Association of Radio Industries and Business), which is an evolution of the PDC standard.

W-CDMA is based on the FDD (frequency division duplex) mode. In the FDD mode, the uplink (reverse direction) and the downlink (forward direction) traffic use different frequencies. In the TDD (time division duplex) mode, the uplink and the downlink traffic are separated in time.

UMTS

The 3GPP (Third Generation Partnership Project) is composed of national standardization committees (ETSI, ARIB, TTC, TTA, T1P1, CWTS). It works on the development of UMTS standards through five technical committees (Radio Access Network, Core Network, Service and System Aspects, Terminals, and GSM Enhanced Radio Access Network).

The UTRA standard proposes five different accesses to the radio resources:

- W-CDMA (wideband CDMA), used by the FDD mode
- OFDMA (orthogonal frequency division multiplexing)
- TD-CDMA (time division CDMA), used by the TDD mode
- W-TDMA (wideband TDMA)
- ODMA (opportunity-driven multiple access), based on the ad hoc networks

UMTS integrates the TD-CDMA and the W-CDMA systems.

The RNS (radio network subsystem) (called BSS in GSM) is composed of

- UE (user equipment) (called MS in GSM)
- Node B (called BTS in GSM)
- RNC (radio network controller) (called BSC in GSM)

The RNC is the Iub interface (called Abis interface in GSM), which is used to connect the RNC to the node B.

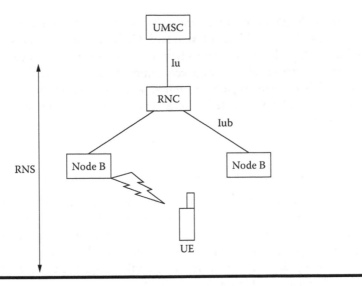

Figure 2.3   Architecture of a UMTS network.

The UMSC (UMTS MSC) is connected to the RNC through the Iub interface (called A interface in GSM).

The UMTS architecture can be represented as shown in Figure 2.3.

UMTS will offer a 2 Mbps: 384 kbps in urban areas and 144 kbps in rural areas. In summary, the target features of 3G wireless systems include

- High data rates, which are expected to be 2 to 4 Mbps for indoor use, 384 kbps for pedestrians, and 144 kbps for vehicles.
- Packet-switched networks, which provide that the users will always be connected.
- Voice and data network will be dynamically allocated.
- The system will offer enhanced roaming.
- The system will include common billing and will have user profiles.
- The system will be able to determine the geographic position of the users via mobile terminals and networks.
- The system will be well suited for transmission of multimedia and will offer various services such as bandwidth on demand, variable data rates, quality sound, etc.

CDMA2000

CDMA2000 is an evolution of the IS95 standard in which the packet mode is more efficient. The two protocols, CDMA2000 and IS95, use the same frequency band.

The PPP (Point-to-Point Protocol) does the interconnection between the IP protocol and the CDMA2000 standard. CDMA2000 is the most widely deployed 3G technology. It offers several advantages over other technologies, including open standards, interoperability, large economies of scale, removable user identity modules (R-UIM), seamless global roaming, post- and prepaid solutions, Java, Windows Mobile and BREW-enabled phones, and a large selection of rich and versatile value-added services [1].

W-CDMA Access Technology

W-CDMA uses a direct sequence (DS) spread-spectrum technique. DS spread spectrum uses a binary sequence to spread the original data over a larger frequency range. The original data is multiplied by a second signal, called *spreading sequence* or *spreading code*, which is a pseudorandom code (PRC) of much wider frequency. The resulting signal is as wide as the spreading sequence but carries the data of the original signal. (See Figures 2.4 and 2.5.)

Although the switch from the 1G cellular to the 2G digital networks was far more noticeable from the technology point of view, with the industry focusing on adjusting to a major technological paradigm shift, the move from the 2G to the 3G networks is still a little blurred, with the industry focusing more on the qualitative service provision characteristics and thus making it harder to agree on specific quantitative standards. In reality, the promise of 3G does not lie in the technical sophistication of the system but rather in the benefits that consumers and providers are hoping to derive from it. The benefits of 3G to consumers focus primarily on two dimensions: convenience and cost. 3G systems are being designed to get the most

Features	1G	2G	2.5G	3G
Air interfaces	FDMA	TDMA CDMA	TDMA	W-CDMA TD-CDMA CDMA2000
Bandwidth		~10 kbps	~100 kbps	~2 to 4 Mbps
Data traffic	No data	Circuit switched	Packet switched	Packet switched
Examples of services	AMPS	GSM IS-136 PDC IS-95	GPRS EDGE	UMTS CDMA2000
Modulation	Analog	Digital	Digital	Digital
Voice traffic	Circuit switched	Circuit switched	Circuit switched	Packet switched (VoIP)

Figure 2.4   Basic characteristics of generations of wireless systems.

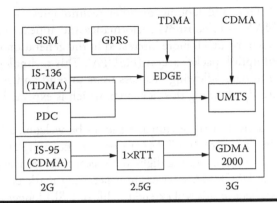

Figure 2.5   Migration path from 2G to 3G wireless systems.

efficient use of the spectrum, and the tight competition created in the 3G services providers' field will most likely result in lower costs and prices. (See Figure 2.6.)

1x evolution-data optimized, abbreviated as EV-DO or 1xEV-DO and often EVDO, is a wireless radio broadband data standard adopted by many CDMA mobile phone service providers [2]. It is standardized by 3GPP2, as part of the CDMA family of standards, and has few limitations [3].

HSDPA (high-speed downlink packet access) technology promises to deliver the 3G experience that subscribers have been waiting for and highlights the limitations of the existing implementations of the W-CDMA technology. Although it is being widely tested by businesses, HSDPA is best suited to download applications such as video streaming. Some far-sighted operators are even seeing the

	Generation	Channel BW (Hz)	Channel Rate (bps)	Principal Information Format
		GSM		
GSM	2	200 K	271 k	Voice and circuit data
EDGE	2.5	200 K	813 k	Voice and circuit data
GPRS	2.5	200 K	271 k	Packet data
E-GPRS	2.5	200 K	813 k	Packet data
W-CDMA/FDD	3	5 M	3.84 M	Multimedia
W-CDMA/TDD	3	5 M	3.84 M	Multimedia
		CDMA		
CDMA1	2	1.25 M	1.2288 M	Voice and circuit data
1XRTT	2.5	1.25 M	1.2288 M	Voice and circuit data
HDR	2.5	1.25 M	Uplink 2.4 M Downlink 153 k	Packet data
CDMA2000	3	3.75 M	3.6864 M	Multimedia

Figure 2.6   Advanced 2.5G and 3G cellular systems.

limitations of HSDPA and looking to other technologies — namely, HSUPA and Mobile WiMAX — to boost 3G performance and appeal to a wider range of users. Businesses will be much more interested in the generation beyond HSDPA called high-speed uplink packet access (HSUPA). This technology will enhance the uplink speed of data, allowing business users to send and receive large files. Operators are already planning this next step, which is expected to arrive in late 2006 to 2007.

Although the arrival of these launches should be welcomed by the end user, they highlight the failure of W-CDMA to deliver the complete 3G experience. W-CDMA's limitations are also highlighted by recent figures from ABI Research, which indicate that W-CDMA services are penetrating markets more slowly than expected. Analysts believe this will extend the life of GSM longer than it projected as few users are prepared to upgrade to 3G.

Analysts at Informa say that W-CDMA's failure to support compelling services has forced operators to bring forward their HSDPA plans. The knock-on effect of this move is that it will create a void between 3.5G (HSDPA/HSUPA) and what will become 4G. Informa says there is concern among operators that significant uptake of mobile triple-play services will overload the HSDPA infrastructure, creating the need for 3.99G, also known as Evolved UMTS or Super 3G. Interestingly, this timeframe for HSUPA puts it in the same window of opportunity as the mobile version of WiMAX based on IEEE 802.16e.

Broadband networks facilitate a large variety of applications. Some of these applications, such as browsing the Internet or checking e-mail, are also possible with networks that support relatively low bit rates. On the other hand, applications that involve media are generally not possible, or quite unpleasant to use, over networks that only support low bit rates. A large number of applications over broadband involve various forms of media (including speech, audio, image, video, and computer graphics), and these applications may be used for work, entertainment, or education. At the end of the broadband wireless era, billions of people worldwide will be communicating wirelessly using devices and services not yet designed. Many of these people will have access to multiple technologies that will allow them choices for an always best-connected advantage.

The Last Mile defines the access link that connects the end user to the Internet (the backbone or core network). This access link has been called the *last mile*. It has sometimes been referred to in a user-centric style as the "first mile." Regardless of nomenclature, the simple way of characterizing the challenge is to say that this mile should not be the weakest link in the chain.

In recent years, there has been increasing interest shown in wireless technologies for subscriber access as an alternative to traditional wired (e.g., twisted-pair, cable, fiber optics, etc.) local loop. These approaches are generally referred to as WLL, or fixed wireless access, or even last-mile broadband wireless access. These technologies are used by telecommunication companies to carry IP data from central locations on their networks to small low-cost antennas mounted on subscribers' roofs. Wireless cable Internet access is enabled through the use of a number of distribution technologies.

Standardization Activities in IEEE [8–11]

Active Working Groups and Study Groups

- 802.1 Higher Layer LAN Protocols Working Group
  - Link Security Executive Committee Study Group is now part of 802.1
- 802.3 Ethernet Working Group
- 802.11 Wireless LAN Working Group
- 802.15 Wireless Personal Area Network (WPAN) Working Group
- 802.16 Broadband Wireless Access Working Group
- 802.17 Resilient Packet Ring Working Group
- 802.18 Radio Regulatory TAG
- 802.19 Coexistence TAG
- 802.20 Mobile Broadband Wireless Access (MBWA) Working Group
- 802.21 Media Independent Handoff Working Group
- 802.22 Wireless Regional Area Networks

Inactive Working Groups and Study Groups

- 802.2 Logical Link Control Working Group
- 802.5 Token Ring Working Group
- 802.12 Demand Priority Working Group

Disbanded Working Groups and Study Groups

- 802.4 Token Bus Working Group (material no longer available on this Web site)
- 802.6 Metropolitan Area Network Working Group (material no longer available on this Web site)
- 802.7 Broadband TAG (material no longer available on this Web site)
- 802.8 Fiber Optic TAG (material no longer available on this Web site)
- 802.9 Integrated Services LAN Working Group (material no longer available on this Web site)
- 802.10 Security Working Group (material no longer available on this Web site)
- 802.14 Cable Modem Working Group (material no longer available on this Web site)
- QOS/FC Executive Committee Study Group (material no longer available on this Web site)

In the context of the IEEE 802 project, there are mainly three working groups (WGs) delivering standards for WLANs, WPANs, and fixed broadband wireless access (BWA) networks. These working groups, namely, 802.11, 802.15, and 802.16, are briefly discussed in the following text.

IEEE WG 802.11 (WLANs)

The IEEE 802.11 WG (www.ieee802.org/11/) develops WLAN consensus standards for short-range wireless networks.

- IEEE 802.11-1999, "Wireless LAN Medium Access Control (MAC) and Physical Layer (PHY) Specifications." This standard specifies the 802.11 MAC protocol as well as three physical layers (frequency hopping spread spectrum, direct sequence spread spectrum, and infrared) operating at speeds of 1 and 2 Mbps in the 2.4-GHz frequency range.
- IEEE 802.11a-1999, "High-Speed Physical Layer in the 5-GHz Band." This standard provides changes and additions to IEEE 802.11-1999 to support a physical layer (based on OFDM) operating at speeds up to 54 Mbps in the 5-GHz frequency band.
- IEEE 802.11b-1999, "Higher-Speed Physical Layer Extension in the 2.4-GHz Band." This standard provides changes and additions to IEEE 802.11-1999 to support a physical layer (based on complementary code keying) operating at speeds up to 11 Mbps in the 2.4-GHz frequency band.
- IEEE 802.11d-2001, "Operation in Additional Regulatory Domains." This amendment specifies the extensions to IEEE 802.11 for WLANs providing specifications for conformant operation beyond the original six regulatory domains of that standard. These extensions provide a mechanism for an IEEE 802.11 access point to deliver the required radio-transmitter parameters to an IEEE 802.11 mobile station, which allows that station to configure its radio to operate within the applicable regulations of a geographic or political subdivision. This mechanism is applicable to all IEEE 802.11 PHY types. A secondary benefit of the mechanism described in this amendment is the ability for an IEEE 802.11 mobile station to roam between regulatory domains.

The IEEE 802.11 WG continues its work for enhancing the published 802.11 specifications. The work is carried out in several task groups (TGs), which are tasked to deliver additional 802.11 standards.

IEEE 802.11 TGe (MAC enhancements for QoS): The purpose of TGe is to enhance the current 802.11 MAC to support applications with QoS requirements and to expand the capabilities and efficiency of the protocol. TGe is responsible for the IEEE 802.11e standard.

IEEE 802.11 TGf (Inter-Access Point Protocol): The purpose of TGf is to describe recommended practices for implementation of an Inter-Access Point Protocol (IAPP) on a distribution system (DS) supporting IEEE 802.11, WLANs. The recommended DS utilizes an IAPP that provides the necessary capabilities to achieve multivendor access point (AP) interoperability within the DS. This IAPP is described for a DS consisting of IEEE 802 LAN components utilizing an IETF IP environment. TGf is responsible for the IEEE 802.11f standard.

IEEE 802.11 TGg (further higher-speed physical layer extension in the 2.4-GHz band): The purpose of TGf is to specify a new physical layer (based on OFDM) operating at up to 54 Mbps in the 2.4-GHz frequency band. TGg is responsible for the IEEE 802.11g standard.

IEEE 802.11 TGi (enhanced security): The purpose of TGi is to enhance the IEEE 802.11 standard to enable advanced security features. TGi has defined the concept of the robust security network (RSN), which provides a number of additional security features not present in the basic IEEE 802.11 architecture. TGi is responsible for the IEEE 802.11i standard.

IEEE 802.11 (next-generation WLANs): In the May 2002 meeting of the IEEE 802.11 WG in Sydney, Australia, the Wireless Next Generation (WNG) Standing Committee moved to form two new study groups: the Radio Resources Measurements Study Group (RMSG) and the High Throughput Study Group (HTSG). The WNG and its study groups are investigating the technology for next-generation WLANs (with bit rates greater than 100 Mbps), including interworking schemes with other access technologies such as HiperLAN/2. In this context, WNG collaborates with European Telecommunications Standards Institute (ETSI) Broadband Radio Access Network (BRAN).

IEEE WG 802.15 (Wireless PANs)

The IEEE 802.15 WG develops WPAN consensus standards for short-distance wireless networks. These WPANs address wireless networking of portable and mobile computing devices such as PCs, PDAs, peripherals, cell phones, pagers, and consumer electronics, and allow these devices to communicate and interoperate with one another. The goal is to publish standards, recommended practices, or guides that have broad market applicability and that deal effectively with the issues of coexistence and interoperability with other wired and wireless networking solutions.

The IEEE 802.15 WG is divided into the following four TGs:

IEEE 802.15 TG1 (Bluetooth): The IEEE 802.15 TG1 (TG1) has delivered a WPAN standard (802.15.1) based on the Bluetooth v1.1 specifications. In particular, IEEE has licensed wireless technology from the Bluetooth Special Interest Group (SIG) to adapt and copy a portion of the Bluetooth specification as base material for IEEE Standard 802.15.1. This standard, which is fully compatible with the Bluetooth v1.1 specification, was conditionally approved on March 21, 2002.

IEEE 802.15 TG2 (coexistence): The IEEE 802.15 TG2 (TG2) is developing recommended practices to facilitate coexistence of 802.15 WPANs and 802.11 WLANs. The TG is developing a coexistence model to quantify the mutual interference of a WLAN and a WPAN. TG2 is also developing a set of coexistence mechanisms to facilitate coexistence of WLAN and WPAN devices.

IEEE 802.15 TG3 (high-rate WPAN): The IEEE 802.15 TG3 (TG3) is tasked to provide a new standard for high-rate (20 Mbps or greater) WPANs. Besides a high data rate, the new standard will provide for low-power, low-cost solutions that address the needs of portable consumer digital imaging and multimedia applications. TG3 has adopted a PHY proposal based on a 2.4-GHz orthogonal quadrature phase shift keying (OQPSK) radio design. The IEEE 802.15.3 specification features high data rates (11, 22, 33, 44, and 55 Mbps), a QoS isochronous protocol, security mechanisms, low power consumption, and low cost.

IEEE 802.15 TG4 (low-rate WPAN): The IEEE 802.15 TG4 (TG4) is tasked to provide a standard for a low data rate (from 20 to 250 kbps) WPAN solution with multimonth to multiyear battery life and very low complexity. It is intended to operate in an unlicensed, international frequency band (mainly in the 2.4-GHz band). Potential applications are sensors, interactive toys, smart badges, remote controls, and home automation.

IEEE WG 802.16 (Fixed BWA)

Since July 1999, the IEEE 802.16 WG [8–11] on BWA has been developing standards for wireless metropolitan area networks (WMANs) with global applicability. IEEE 802.16 provides standardized solutions for reliable, high-speed network access in the so-called last mile by homes and enterprises, which could be more economical than wireline alternatives.

The IEEE 802.16 WG has completed two IEEE standards:

1. The IEEE 802.16 WMAN Standard (air interface for fixed broadband wireless access systems), which addresses WMANs. The initial standard, covering systems between 10 and 66 GHz, was approved in December 2001. After that, the work has been expanded to cover licensed and license-exempt bands as well as in the range from 2 to 11 GHz. Note that a fixed BWA system in this frequency range is also being developed by the ETSI BRAN.

2. The IEEE Standard 802.16.2 is a recommended practice (coexistence of fixed broadband wireless access systems) covering between 10 and 66 GHz. The IEEE Standard 802.16.2 was published on September 10, 2001 [12]. The WMAN Medium Access Control (MAC) provides mechanisms for differentiated QoS support to address the needs of various applications. For instance, voice and video require low latency but tolerate some error rate. In contrast, generic data applications cannot tolerate error, but latency is not critical. The

standard accommodates voice, video, and other data transmissions by using appropriate features in the MAC layer. The WMAN standard supports both FDD and TDD. FDD requires two channel pairs, one for transmission and one for reception, with some frequency separation between them to mitigate self-interference. On the contrary, TDD provides a highly flexible duplexing scheme where a single channel is used for both upstream and downstream transmissions. A TDD system can dynamically allocate upstream and downstream bandwidth depending on traffic requirements.

To provide a standardized approach to WLL, the IEEE 802 committee set up the 802.16 WG 43 in 1999 to develop broadband wireless standards. IEEE 802.1617 standardizes the WMAN air interface and related functions for WMANs. This standard serves as a major driving force in linking businesses and homes to local telecommunication networks. A WMAN provides network access to buildings through exterior antennas, communicating with central radio BSs. It offers an alternative to cabled-access networks, such as fiber-optic links, coaxial systems using cable modems, and DSL links. This technology may prove less expensive to deploy and lead to more ubiquitous broadband access because wireless systems have the capacity to address broad geographic areas without the costly infrastructure development required in deploying cable links to individual sites. Such systems have been in use for several years, but the development of the new standard marks the maturation of the industry and forms the basis of new industry success using 2G equipment. In this scenario, with WMAN technology bringing the network to a building, users inside the building can be connected to it with conventional in-building networks such as Ethernet or WLANs. However, the fundamental design of the standard may eventually allow for an efficient extension of the WMAN networking protocols directly to the individual user. For instance, a central BS may someday exchange MAC protocol data with an individual laptop computer in a home. The links from the BS to the home receiver and from the home receiver to the laptop would likely use quite different PHY, but design of the Wireless MAN-MAC could accommodate such a connection with full QoS.

With the technology expanding in this direction, it is likely that the standard will evolve to support nomadic and, increasingly, mobile users such as a stationary or slow-moving vehicle. IEEE Standard 802.16 was designed to evolve as a set of air interfaces based on a common MAC protocol but with PHY specifications dependent on the spectrum of use and associated regulations. The standard, as approved in 2001, addresses frequencies from 10 to 66 GHz, where a large spectrum is currently available worldwide, but at which the short wavelengths introduce significant deployment challenges. A project has completed an amendment denoted IEEE 802.16a.18. This document extends the air interface support to lower frequencies in the 2- to 11-GHz band, including licensed and license-exempt spectra. Compared to the higher frequencies, such spectra offer a less expensive opportunity to reach many more customers, although at generally lower data rates. This suggests that such services will be oriented toward individual homes or small- to medium-sized enterprises.

In spite of the lack of deployment of fixed wireless IEEE 802.16 as of now, extensive specifications have been developed on standards for implementation. The operation is at the 11- to 66-GHz band with a data rate of 2 to 155 Mbps, with flexible asymmetry. The downstream transmission is TDMA in broadcast mode and the upstream is TDMA with demand-assigned multiple access (DAMA). The components to be managed are subscriber station, BS, wireless link, and RF spectrum. The IEEE 802.16 WG has recommended the adoption of 802 standards framework for LAN/MAN management ISO/IEC 15802-2(E). The security specifications address two levels of authentication — between subscriber station and BS at the MAC level, and between subscriber and the broadband wireless access system for authorization of services and privacy. IEEE 802.16.1 specifications support classes of service with various QoS for bearer services, bandwidth negotiation for connectionless service, state information for connection-oriented service, and various ATM traffic categories: constant bit rate, variable bit rate real-time, variable bit rate non-real time, and adjustable bit rate. IETF traffic categories of integrated services and differentiated services are also supported by the specifications.

IEEE 802.16d, a modified version of 802.16a and 802.16c, also known as WiMAX, is an extension of 802.16. The operation is in the 2- to 11-GHz band and is primarily intended as a MAN. The network management considerations specified in 802.16 may be applied to it. QoS and high performance are maintained by implementing TDMA downstream and TDMA/DAMA upstream.

The IEEE 802.16 specification on broadband wireless access systems facilitates implementation of interoperable fixed point-to-multipoint broadband wireless access networking solutions. These systems transport voice, video, and data in the spectrum between the 2- and 11-GHz frequencies and in the 10- and 66-GHz spectral bands. The IEEE 802.16 Working Group on Broadband Wireless Access Systems defines the radio–air interface for broadband wireless access configurations that operate in the licensed spectrum between the 2- and 11-GHz frequencies. This working group also delineates the radio–air interface for broadband wireless systems that operate in the spectrum between the 10- and 66-GHz frequencies. These frequencies also support Unlicensed-National Information Infrastructure (U-NNI) operations. Approaches for enabling the coexistence of broadband wireless access metropolitan networks and Local Multipoint Distribution System (LMDS) configurations that operate in the 23.5- and 43.5-GHz frequencies are also explored. IEEE 802.16 specifications conform to IEEE 802 standards governing LAN and MAN operations endorsed by the IEEE in 1990. As opposed to IEEE 802.11, which focuses on WLAN implementations and applications, the IEEE 802.16 Working Group develops affordable point-to-multipoint broadband wireless access configurations that enable multimedia services in MAN and WAN environments. The IEEE 802.16 Working Group works with the BRAN Committee sponsored by the ETSI in developing compatible broadband wireless access system specifications.

The IEEE 802.16a Extension clarifies operations, services, and the radio–air interface for broadband wireless access networks that operate in the spectrum between the 2- and 11-GHz frequencies. Sponsored by the IEEE 802.11 Working Group on Broadband Wireless Access Systems, the WirelessHUMAN (high-data-rate unlicensed metropolitan area network) initiative fosters implementation of broadband wireless access metropolitan network specifications. These specifications provide the foundation and framework for the IEEE 802.16b Extension.

Approved in 2001, the IEEE 802.16b Extension clarifies broadband wireless access metropolitan network functions and capabilities of the radio–air interface. License-exempt BWA metropolitan networks support multimedia services in the license-exempt spectrum between the 5.15- and 5.25-GHz frequencies, between the 5.25- and 5.35-GHz frequencies, and between the 5.725- and 5.825-GHz frequencies. To facilitate the standardization process, the WirelessHUMAN initiative supports utilization of the PHY OFDM Protocol defined in the IEEE 802.11a Extension and MAC layer operations defined in the IEEE 802.16 standard.

The IEEE 802.20 Standard

The IEEE 802.20 standard is a broadband wireless networking technology that is being standardized for deployment by mobile communications service providers, in portions of their licensed spectrum. The capacity of 802.20 is projected to be 2 Mbps per user, and its range is comparable to 3G cellular technologies, namely, up to 5 km. More typical deployments will be in the neighborhood of 1 to 3 km. Finalization of the 802.20 standard is not expected soon. To understand how wireless home networking is going to evolve, one must look at the short term and the long term. The short term is guided mostly by the performance capabilities of the various technologies today. With the notable exception of television-quality video, most of the typical applications found in homes today can be accommodated within the current performance capabilities of the various wireless networking technologies. Given the variety of performance capabilities among wireless networking technologies and the range of application requirements, the technology or technologies deployed in any particular wireless home network will be driven by the bandwidth requirements of the applications that will run on the network. This argues for hybrid solutions incorporating multiple networking technologies (wired and wireless) to achieve the desired results.

The 802.20 standard has been under development since late 2002, but the going has been slow, to say the least. 802.20 and 802.16e, the mobile WiMAX specification, appear similar at first glance but differ in the frequencies they will use and the technologies they are based on. Standard 802.20 will operate below 3.5 GHz, whereas mobile WiMAX will work within the 2-GHz to 6-GHz bands. Further, as the name suggests, 802.16e is based on WiMAX, with the goal of having WiMAX transmitters being able to support both fixed and mobile connections [4]. Although the 802.20 group will be back at work later, the 802.20 technology is alluring, with promises of low-latency 1-Mbps connections being sustained even at speeds of up to 150 mph, but we are going to have to wait a couple of years for it.

Wi-Fi

Wi-Fi, which stands for "wireless fidelity," is a radio technology that networks computers so they connect to each other and to the Internet without wires. Users can share documents and projects, as well as an Internet connection, among various computer stations and easily connect to a broadband Internet connection while traveling. By using a Wi-Fi network, individuals can network desktop computers, laptops, and PDAs and share networked peripherals such as servers and printers. A Wi-Fi network operates just like a wired network, but without the restrictions imposed by wires. It uses radio technologies called IEEE 802.11a, 802.11b, or 802.11g to provide secure, reliable, fast wireless connectivity. A Wi-Fi network can be used to connect computers to each other, to the Internet, and to wired networks (which use IEEE 802.3 or Ethernet). Wi-Fi networks operate in the unlicensed 2.4- and 5-GHz radio bands with an 11-Mbps (802.11b) or 54-Mbps (802.11a) data rate, or with products that contain both bands (dual band). They can provide real-world performance similar to the basic 10BaseT wired Ethernet networks. A Wi-Fi network can connect computers together to share such hardware and software resources as printers and the Internet.

The Wi-Fi Alliance is the global Wi-Fi organization that created the Wi-Fi brand. The Wi-Fi Alliance was originally established as the Wireless Ethernet Compatibility Alliance (WECA) in August 1999 by several of the leading WLAN manufacturers. A nonprofit organization, the Alliance was formed to certify interoperability of IEEE 802.11 products and to promote them as the global, wireless LAN standard across all market segments. The Wi-Fi Alliance has instituted a test suite that defines how member products are tested to certify that they are interoperable with other Wi-Fi-Certified products. These tests are conducted at an independent laboratory.

Wi-Fi networks also work well for small businesses, providing connectivity between mobile salespeople, floor staff, and behind-the-scenes finance and accounting departments. Large corporations and campuses use enterprise-level technology and Wi-Fi-Certified wireless products to extend standard wired Ethernet networks to public areas such as meeting rooms, training classrooms, and large auditoriums. Many corporations also provide wireless networks to their off-site and telecommuting workers to use at home or in remote offices. Large companies and campuses often use Wi-Fi to connect buildings. Service providers and wireless ISPs are using Wi-Fi technology to distribute Internet connectivity within individual homes and businesses, as well as apartments and commercial complexes.

Table 2.1 Versions of Wi-Fi

802.11	Throughput (Mbps)	Range (ft)	Frequency Band (GHz)
g	1–54	100–300	2.4
a/g	1–54	100–300	2.4–5.0
n	320	100–300	2.4–5.0

Wi-Fi, in its several different versions (IEEE 802.11b, 802.11a, 802.11a/g, and 802.11n) (Table 2.1), is the most mature of any wireless home networking technology. As a result, it has achieved the most widespread deployment in homes, public areas such as airports, and so-called hot spots such as hotels, coffee shops, and restaurants. Wi-Fi also operates in the unlicensed 2.4-GHz range of the wireless spectrum, as well as the 5-GHz frequency band. It has been developed as a WLAN technology; as such, the reach of its wireless signals extends outward to a range of 40 to 100 m. To a certain extent, its signals can also penetrate the walls in a typical home construction. Depending on the version of Wi-Fi deployed and the size of the house, a Wi-Fi WLAN often can cover an entire house, though reducing the data rate to below 1 Mbps at far distances of coverage. Where greater coverage is required, additional Wi-Fi access points (APs) can be installed. Some Wi-Fi WLANs have achieved much larger coverage areas by increasing the power output considerably. Data rate is a function of distance for all wireless and wireline technologies: the shorter the distance, the higher the data rate; the longer, the lower.

The 802.11 Standard

The IEEE ratified the original 802.11 specification in 1997 as the standard for WLANs. That version of 802.11 provides for 1- and 2-Mbps data rates and a set of fundamental signaling methods and other services. One of the disadvantages with the original 802.11 standard is that the data rates are too slow to support most general business requirements. Recognizing the critical need to support higher data transmission rates, the IEEE ratified the 802.11b standard for transmissions of up to 11 Mbps. With 802.11b, WLANs are able to achieve wireless performance and throughput comparable to wired 10-Mbps Ethernet. The 802.11a standard offers speeds of up to 54 Mbps but runs in the 5-GHz band.

Several task groups are working on further developments for the 802.11 standard. Like all 802.x standards, 802.11 focuses on the bottom two layers of the OSI Reference Model: the physical and the data-link layers. In fact, the standard covers three PHY implementations: direct sequence (DS) spread spectrum, frequency hopping (FH) spread spectrum, and infrared (IR). A single MAC layer supports all three PHY implementations.

The 802.11 Architecture

Each computer (mobile, portable, or fixed) is referred to as a station in 802.11. Mobile stations access the LAN during movement. The 802.11 standard defines two modes: infrastructure mode and ad hoc mode. In the infrastructure mode, the wireless network consists of at least one AP connected to the wired network infrastructure, and a set of wireless end stations. This configuration is called a basic service set (BSS). An extended service set (ESS) is a set of two or more BSSs forming a single subnetwork. Two or more ESSs are interconnected using a distribution system (DS). In an ESS, the entire network looks like an independent BSS to the logical link control (LLC) layer; this means that stations within the extended service set can communicate or even move between BSSs transparently to the LLC. The distribution system can be thought of as a backbone network that is responsible for MAC-level transport of MAC service data units (MSDUs). The distribution system, as specified by 802.11, is implementation independent; therefore, the distribution system could be a wired 802.3 Ethernet LAN, an 802.4 token bus LAN, an 802.5 token ring LAN, a Fiber Distributed Data Interface (FDDI) MAN, or another 802.11 wireless medium. Although the distribution system could physically be the same transmission medium as the BSS, they are logically different because the distribution system is solely used as a transport backbone to transfer packets between different BSSs in the ESS. An ESS can provide gateway access for wireless users into a wired network such as the Internet. This is accomplished via a device known as a *portal*. The portal is a logical entity that specifies the integration point on the distribution system where the 802.11 network integrates with a non-802.11 network. If the network is an 802.x, the portal incorporates functions that are analogous to a bridge, i.e., it provides range extension and the translation between different frame formats. The ad hoc mode (also called peer-to-peer mode or an independent basic service set, or IBSS) is simply a set of 802.11 stations that communicate directly with one another without using an access point or any connection to a wired network. In ad hoc networks, there is no base, and no one gives permission to talk; these networks are spontaneous and can be set up rapidly, but are limited both temporally and spatially.

The Physical Layer (PHY)

The three PHY originally defined in the 802.11 standard included two spread-spectrum radio techniques and a diffuse infrared specification. The radio-based standards operate within the 2.4-GHz ISM (industrial, scientific, and medical) band. These frequency bands are recognized by international regulatory agencies such as the FCC (United States), ETSI (Europe), and the MKK (Japan) for unlicensed radio operations. As such, 802.11-based products do not require user licensing or special training. Spread-spectrum techniques, in addition to satisfying regulatory requirements, boost throughput and allow many unrelated products to share the spectrum without explicit cooperation and with minimal interference. The original 802.11 wireless standard defines data rates of 1 and 2 Mbps via radio waves using FH spread spectrum or DS spread spectrum. It is important to note that these are fundamentally different transmission mechanisms and will not interoperate with each other. DS has a more robust modulation and a larger coverage range than FH even when FH uses twice the transmitter power output level. FH gives a large number of hop frequencies, but the adjacent channel interference behavior limits the number of independently operating collocated systems. Hop time and a smaller packet size introduce more transmission time overhead into FH, which affects the maximum throughput. Although FH is less robust, it gives a more graceful degradation in throughput and connectivity. Under poor channel and interference conditions, FH will continue to work over a few hop channels a little longer than over the other hop channels.

DS, however, still gives reliable links for a distance at which very few FH hop channels still work. For collocated networks (access points), DS gives a higher potential throughput with fewer access points than FH, which has more access points. The smaller number of access points used by DS lowers the infrastructure cost.

The Data-Link Layer (DLL)

The DLL within 802.11 consists of two sublayers: LLC and MAC. The 802.11 standard uses the same 802.2 LLC and 48-bit addressing as other 802.x LANs, allowing for very simple bridging from wireless to wired networks, but the MAC is unique to WLANs. Of particular interest in the specification is the support for two fundamentally different MAC schemes to transport asynchronous and time-bounded services. The first scheme, distributed coordination function (DCF), is similar to traditional legacy packet networks. The DCF is designed for asynchronous data transport, where all users with data to transmit have an equally fair chance of accessing the network. The point coordination function (PCF) is the second MAC scheme. The PCF is based on polling that is controlled by an access point.

The basic access method, DCF, is drawn from the family of Carrier Sense Multiple Access with Collision Avoidance (CSMA/CA) protocols. The collision detection (CD) mechanism, as used in the CSMA/CD protocol of Ethernet, cannot be used under 802.11 due to the near/far problem: to detect a collision, a station must be able to transmit and listen at the same time, but in radio systems the transmission drowns out the ability of the station to hear a collision. So, 802.11 uses CSMA/CA, under which collisions are avoided by using explicit packet acknowledgment (ACK) to confirm that the data packet arrived intact. The 802.11 standard supports three different types of frames: management, control, and data. The management frames are used for station association and disassociation with the access point, timing and synchronization, and authentication and deauthentication. Control frames are used for handshaking during a contention period (CP), for positive acknowledgment during the CP, and to end the contention-free period (CFP). Data frames are used for the transmission

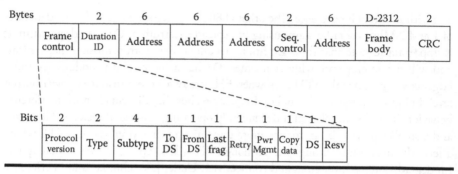

Figure 2.7   Standard 802.11 frame format.

of data during the CP and CFP, and can be combined with polling and acknowledgments during the CFP. Figure 2.7 shows the standard 802.11 frame format, and Figure 2.8 shows the 802.11 standard and the ISO model. (See also Table 2.2.)

Security Technologies

WPA, WPA2, and other wireless security methods operate strictly between the Wi-Fi-enabled device and Wi-Fi-Certified access point. When data reaches the access point or gateway, it is unencrypted and unprotected while it is being transmitted out on the public Internet to its destination — unless it is also encrypted at the source with SSL when purchasing on the Internet or when using a virtual private network (VPN). So, although using WPA/WPA2 affords the user protection from external intruders, additional techniques need to be implemented to protect transmissions when using public networks and the Internet.

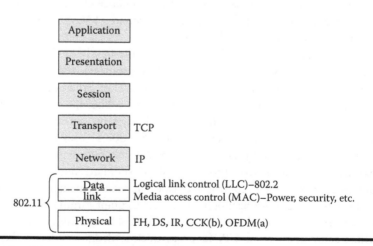

Figure 2.8   802.11 standard and the ISO model.

Table 2.2   Wi-Fi Task Group Activities

Task Group	Activities
802.11	Initial Standard, 2.4-GHz band, 2 Mbps
802.11a	High-speed PHY layer in the 5-GHz band, up to 24 or 54 Mbps
802.11b	High-speed PHY layer in the 2.4-GHz band, up to 11 Mbps
802.11d	New regulatory domains (countries)
802.11e	Medium access control (MAC) enhancements: multimedia, QoS, enhanced security
802.11f	Interaccess point protocol for AP interoperability
802.11g	Higher data rate extension in the 2.4-GHz band, up to 22 Mbps
802.11h	Extensions for the 5-GHz band support in Europe

WPA2 (Wi-Fi Protected Access 2)

WPA2 (Wi-Fi Protected Access 2) provides network administrators with a high level of assurance that only authorized users can access the network. Based on the ratified IEEE 802.11i standard, WPA2 provides government-grade security by implementing the National Institute of Standards and Technology (NIST) FIPS 140-2-compliant AES encryption algorithm. WPA2 can be enabled in two versions — WPA2-Personal and WPA2-Enterprise. WPA2-Personal protects unauthorized network access by utilizing a setup password. WPA2-Enterprise verifies network users through a server. WPA2 is backward compatible with WPA.

Extended EAP (Extensible Authentication Protocol)

Extended EAP is an addition to the Wi-Fi Protected Access (WPA) and WPA2-Enterprise certification programs, which further ensures the interoperability of secure Wi-Fi networking products for enterprise and government users. EAP types include

- EAP-TLS
- EAP-TTLS/MSCHAv2
- PEAPv0/EAP-MSCHAPv2
- PEAPv1/EAP-GTC
- EAP-SIM

Though the previously mentioned existing technologies are indeed useful for helping secure Wi-Fi, the Wi-Fi Alliance and IEEE have both realized the importance of security enhancements to Wi-Fi itself. Two important initiatives are the proposed 802.11i standard and Wi-Fi Protected Access.

The 802.11i Standard

Task Group i within IEEE 802.11 is a standard for WLAN security. The 802.11i standard is designed to embrace the authentication scheme of 802.1X and EAP while adding enhanced security features, including a new encryption scheme and dynamic key distribution. Not only does it fix WEP, it takes WLAN security to a higher level. The proposed specification uses the Temporal Key Integrity Protocol (TKIP) to produce a 128-bit "temporal key" that allows different stations to use different keys to encrypt data. TKIP introduces a sophisticated key generation function, which encrypts every data packet sent over the air with its own unique encryption key. Consequently, TKIP greatly increases the complexity and difficulty of decoding the keys. Intruders simply are not allowed enough time to collect sufficient data to decipher the key. The 802.11i standard also endorses the Advanced Encryption Standard (AES) as a replacement for WEP encryption. AES has already been adopted as an official government standard by the U.S. Department of Commerce. It uses a mathematical ciphering algorithm that employs variable key sizes of 128, 192, or 256 bits, making it far more difficult to decipher than WEP. AES, however, is not readily compatible with Wi-Fi-Certified WLAN devices. It requires chipsets, which, for WLAN customers, means investments in wireless devices. Those looking to build new WLANs will find it attractive. Those with previously installed wireless networks must justify whether AES security is worth the cost of replacing equipment.

Wi-Fi Protected Access (WPA)

The Wi-Fi Alliance addresses the need for an immediate, software-upgradeable security solution. Realizing the importance of enhanced Wi-Fi security, the Alliance has led an effort to bring strongly improved, interoperable Wi-Fi security to market. The result of that effort is WPA. WPA is a specification of standards-based, interoperable security enhancements that strongly increase the level of encryption and authentication for existing and future WLAN systems. WPA is derived from the upcoming IEEE 802.11i standard and will be forward compatible with it. It addresses the vulnerabilities of WEP encryption and adds user authentication. Thus, WPA will provide WLAN users with a high level of assurance that their data will remain protected and that only authorized network users can access the network. Significantly, it is designed as a software upgrade to Wi-Fi-Certified devices, requiring no additional hardware. WPA includes 802.1X and TKIP technology. Cryptographers working with the Wi-Fi Alliance have reviewed WPA and endorsed the fact that it solves all of WEP's (Wired Equivalent Privacy) known vulnerabilities. The Wi-Fi does interoperability certification testing on WPA. As Wi-Fi interoperable solutions improve, users might find that the expense and complexity of add-on solutions such as VPNs is no longer necessary — at least not for the express purpose of securing the wireless link in a Wi-Fi network. The future holds that promise in the form of 802.11i and WPA.

WMM QoS

WMM QoS is a set of features for Wi-Fi networks that improve the user experience for audio, video, and voice applications by prioritizing data traffic. Since the WMM certification program was launched in September 2004, more than 200 Wi-Fi devices have been Wi-Fi-Certified for WMM. WMM QoS is based on a subset of the IEEE 802.11e standard.

WMM Power Save

WMM Power Save is a set of features for Wi-Fi networks that help conserve battery power in small devices such as phones, PDAs, and audio players. The certification for both access points and client devices uses mechanisms from the IEEE 802.11e standard and is an enhancement of 802.11 Power Save. WMM Power Save helps pave the way for rapid proliferation of Wi-Fi technology into devices dependent on battery power.

Wi-Fi Pros and Cons

Wi-Fi networks and customer premise equipment (CPE) are low-cost alternatives.

- Pre-WiMAX base stations cost around 200 times more.
- Pre-WiMAX CPE averages $500.

Wi-Fi uses unlicensed spectrum.

- Zero entry cost.
- Interference likely to be minimal in rural areas.

Wi-Fi is not a carrier grade solution for network access.

- Contention access.
- No QoS management yet.

Wi-Fi is not intended for long range (Wi-Fi Alliance).

- Typically 20 to 50 m.
- Can be extended up to a couple of kilometers but speed is less.

WiBro

WiBro (wireless broadband) is an Internet technology being developed by the Korean telecom industry (Figure 2.9). In February 2002, the Korean government allocated 100 MHz of electromagnetic spectrum in the 2.3-GHz band, and in late 2004, WiBro Phase 1 was standardized by the TTA (Telecommunications Technology Association) of Korea. WiBro is the newest variety of mobile wireless broadband access. It is based on the same IEEE 802.16 standard as WiMAX but is designed to maintain connectivity on the go, tracking a receiver at speeds of up to 37 mi per hr (60 km/hr). WiMAX is the current standard in the United States, offering wireless Internet connectivity to mobile users at fixed ranges of up to 31 mi (50 km) from the transmitting base. However, it is not designed to be used while the receiver is in motion. WiBro can be thought of as mobile WiMAX, though the technology and its exact specifications will change as it undergoes refinements throughout its preliminary stages. Korean-based fixed-line operators KT, SK Telecom, and Hanaro Telecom were awarded licenses by the South Korean government to provide WiBro commercially. According to *Asia Media News Daily*, the *Korean Times* reported a glitch in the initial excitement of WiBro, as published in 2005. Hanaro Telecom gave up its license for WiBro after concerns that the considerable investment required would not see a return, and SK Telecom was also said to be hanging back. Only KT Corp remained enthusiastically committed in the push to make WiBro a reality. Meanwhile, Samsung has shown great interest in providing devices with WiBro capability (Figure 2.9, Figure 2.10, Figure 2.11, and Figure 2.12).

WiBro BSs will offer an aggregate data throughput of 30 to 50 Mbps and cover a radius of 1 to 5 km, allowing for the use of portable Internet usage within the range of a BS. The technology will also offer QoS. The inclusion of QoS allows for WiBro to stream video content and other loss-sensitive data in a reliable manner. In contrast to WiMAX, an American wireless technology, WiBro uses licensed radio spectrum. From one point of view, this is a stronger advantage for the technology; the spectrum it uses is licensed and correspondingly protected from unlicensed use, negating any potential interference from other sources using the same spectrum. These all appear to be (and may be) the stronger advantages over the WiMAX standard, but the proprietary nature of WiBro and its use of licensed spectrum that may not be available across the globe may keep it from becoming an international standard. Although WiBro is quite exacting in its requirements from spectrum use to

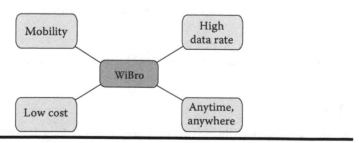

Figure 2.9   WiBro, as defined. (Courtesy of Hong, D., 2.3GHz Portable Internet (WiBro) for Wireless Broadband Access, ITU-APT Regional Seminar 2004.)

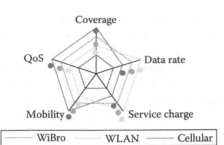

Figure 2.10   WiBro explained. (Courtesy of Samsung.)

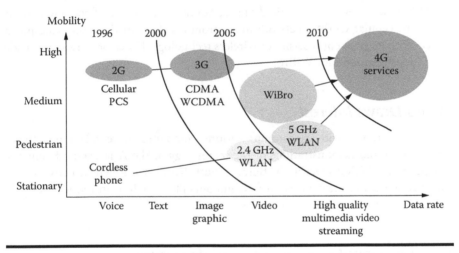

Figure 2.11   WiBro, as compared to other competitor technologies. (Courtesy of Samsung.)

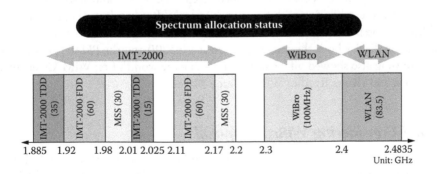

Figure 2.12   WiBro spectrum allocation. (Courtesy of Samsung.)

equipment design, WiMAX leaves much of this up to the equipment provider while providing enough detail to ensure interoperability between designs. SK Telecom and Hanaro Telecom have announced a partnership to roll out WiBro nationwide in Korea, excluding Seoul and six provincial cities, where independent networks will be rolled out. In November 2004, Intel and LG Electronics executives agreed to ensure compatibility between WiBro and WiMAX technology. In September 2005, Samsung Electronics signed a deal with Sprint Nextel Corporation to provide equipment for a WiBro trial. As it may become the 4G (fourth-generation) wireless standard, the global market will be watching. WiBro will operate in the 2.3-GHz band and is interoperable with WiMAX. In South Korea, broadband Internet access is widespread via DSL, cable, and Wi-Fi. South Korea is also quickly commercializing 3G cellular services such as CDMA2000, a faster version of the CDMA network. As in the United States, South Korea is one of the few nations to use the cellular CDMA network more prominently than the more widespread GSM. With its great enthusiasm for wireless technology, Korea promises to provide a solid testing ground for WiBro.

WiBro Draws Interest

Korean electronics and telecommunications companies have taken on WiBro development and demonstrations of the technology at the Asia Pacific Economic Cooperation (APEC) meeting in Busan, South Korea. Commercial networks are expected to start in the country, and Reigncom's player will be introduced roughly in line with the launch of the networks.

Samsung Unveils First WiBro Mobile Handsets

Samsung has demonstrated the WiBro mobile phones and systems at the 2005 APEC IT Exhibition during the APEC meeting in Busan. Various applications such as broadcasting, home networking, video telephony, VOD, and navigations were presented at the exhibition with Samsung's latest WiBro handsets (Figure 2.13). As WiBro gets prepared to be fully implemented and utilized in the market, Samsung also put on display both the mobile phone-type H1000 and the PDA-type M8000.

Samsung also showed off what it claims to be the world's first WiMAX-enabled notebook and IRiver Readies WiBro Game Player.

VNPT Considering WiBro Proposal

Vietnam's dominant fixed-line telco VNPT is considering a proposal from South Korea's KT Corp that would see the two companies collaborating over a rollout of WiBro technology. WiBro could be the key to Vietnam increasing its relatively

Figure 2.13   WiBro handset. (Courtesy of Samsung.)

low Internet penetration of just 12.9 percent. It was also hinted that the Vietnamese government was mindful of the country's large landmass, and consequently preferred wireless solutions to Internet connectivity over fixed-line technologies such as DSL.

WiBro, WiMAX Get Closer: Intel, LG Agree on Mobile Internet Compatibility

WiBro is increasing its level of cooperation with WiMAX, the next-generation wireless Internet protocol. Analysts say these two standards will be compatible with each other and will grow into a gigantic wireless Internet technology protocol. The agreement is intended to preempt the world's mobile Internet market through the standardization of WiBro and WiMAX protocols. LG, for its part, plans to build itself on WiBro and expand into WiMAX in its ultimate bid to enter the mobile Internet equipment and handset markets. Intel is also seeking to enlarge the scope of WiMAX by inducing LG and then preempting South Korea's WiBro market (Figure 2.14). Both WiBro and WiMAX make it possible to log on to the Internet broadband while moving, cheaply and without a hitch, opening a new horizon in the Internet use by such mobile handsets as cell phones, smart phones, and PDAs. These two standards will help replace the existing high-speed Internet access such as DSL and cable modems because of their ubiquitous features.

South Korea's wireless data service market reaches nearly $4 billion, thanks in part to the introduction of HSDPA service as well as the country's own spin on mobile WiMAX service, according to a report from the Federation of Korean Information Industries. The country's wireless data service market is expected to

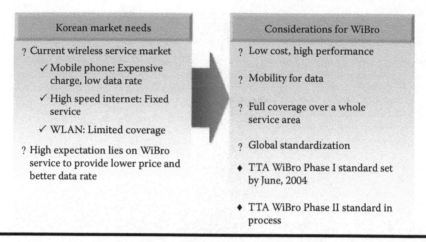

Figure 2.14   Considerations for WiBro. (Courtesy of Hong, D., 2.3GHz Portable Internet (WiBro) for Wireless Broadband Access, ITU-APT Regional Seminar 2004.)

grow 11.8 percent to 3.8 trillion won ($3.96 billion) from an estimated 3.4 trillion won (roughly $3.52 billion) in 2005. Of that total, according to the report, the HSDPA market is expected to account for roughly $2.6 billion, while the market for services based on Korea's WiBro wireless standard is expected to claim about $1.25 billion. Conventional wireless data services will account for the remainder.

South Korea became the first country to launch commercial 3.5G HSDPA service, an advanced version of the 3G wireless CDMA technology. WiBro service is slated to debut.

Mobile WiMAX Gets Hearing at CES

Samsung Telecom demonstrated WiBro infrastructure and handheld devices that promise to deliver wireless video calling and wireless data at average downlink speeds of 2 Mbps per user at vehicular speeds up to 75 mph. WiBro is a Korean-spectrum 2.3-GHz band technology based on the mobile WiMAX standard, but Samsung will be rebanding the technology for use by Sprint Nextel for trials in the U.S. 2.5-GHz spectrum owned by that carrier. At International CES, Samsung demonstrated a WiBro-equipped PDA phone, cellular phone, and wireless PC Card. Service demos will include Voice-over-IP (VoIP) telephony, simultaneous voice and data, video calling, video-on-demand, and push-to-all, or simultaneous push voice, data, and video. Mobile WiMAX's average data speeds exceed those of other finalized wireless standards, including the W-CDMA HSDPA technology that Cingular is rolling out. That technology promises average download speeds of 550 kbps to 1.1 Mbps, according to 3G Americas, the trade group that represents GSM manufacturers and carriers in the Americas.

WiBro for the U.S. Military

The *Korea Times* reports that the U.S. military is interested in Samsung's WiBro technology and is negotiating a $3-billion deal with the company [14]. The mobile WiMAX technology is already being implemented by the South Korean military as part of its "ubiquitous defense" project.

WiBro Bus

Speaking of WiBro, Korea Telecom gave the industry a WiBro Experience bus ride around Seoul [15]. Passengers could use PDAs and laptops equipped with PCMCIA WiBro cards to experience WiBro service, no external antenna required.

WiBro Going to India

South Korean companies have a pretty interesting plan to turn their version of (mobile) WiMAX aka WiBro into a global standard: go after some of the fastest growing emerging markets and get the necessary scale to compete with rivals, mostly from the United States. A few months after making a WiBro play in Brazil, South Korean companies are now targeting India. Samsung, encouraged by some of the recent spectrum allocations in the 2.3-GHz to 2.5-GHz and 3.5-GHz bands in India, is now attempting to sell its gear that would allow 2 Mbps download speed and upload of 1 Mbps. The company sees huge potential in the rural areas and regions that are off the main grids. Samsung Vice President (Global Marketing Group) Dr. Hung Song says the company is in talks with some Indian operators for the possible rollout of WiBro in India in the near future.

The United States Adopts Samsung's WiBro Technology

Samsung Electronics forged an alliance with three firms — Sprint Nextel, Intel, and Motorola — for the launch of WiBro in the United States [16]. Sprint aims to have 100 million people covered by the go-anywhere Internet application in 2008. Together with Intel and Motorola, Samsung will provide Sprint with BS equipment, terminals, and chipsets for WiBro.

WiMAX

The new wireless platform, WiMAX holds promise of high-speed Internet delivered to handheld devices. It delivers higher speeds than Wi-Fi over a much longer distance. The technology does not require a line of sight, and it is more efficient in transporting bandwidth-intensive applications, particularly time-sensitive services such as real-time video [17]. WiMAX also can be used as a complementary system to

Wi-Fi. One could use Wi-Fi in a coffee shop or home with WiMAX infrastructure quickly connecting the Internet traffic to the outside world. Nortel Networks says that WiMAX is ideally positioned for the "time/place shift" in modern society. That shift is illustrated by such popular consumer electronic devices as the TiVo, iPod, and Slingbox, which enable consumers to listen to music and watch video whenever and wherever they want. But whether WiMAX evolves into a major industry ultimately will depend on how many vendors and carriers participate, experts say. That will determine whether prices are low enough to attract consumers and whether information can be sent across multiple networks [17]. WiMAX can be used for the mobile market or as a "fixed wireless" technology going into homes and offices. There's a lot of interest in developing countries that do not have infrastructure at all, such as Pakistan and India. Australia, Japan, and South Korea also have been aggressive in adopting different flavors of WiMAX. South Korea calls its platform WiBro [17]. It is possible to stay connected to the world — if you want to — wherever you go [17].

Analysis

Within the marketplace, WiMAX's main competition comes from widely deployed wireless systems with overlapping functionality such as UMTS and CDMA2000, as well as a number of Internet-oriented systems such as HIPERMAN and WiBro [18].

Both of the two major 3G systems, CDMA2000 and UMTS, compete with WiMAX. Both offer DSL-class Internet access, in addition to phone service. UMTS has also been enhanced to compete directly with WiMAX in the form of UMTS-TDD, which can use WiMAX-oriented spectrum, and it provides a more consistent (lower bandwidth at peak) user experience than WiMAX (Figure 2.15). Moving forward, similar air interface technologies to those used by WiMAX are being considered for the 4G evolution of UMTS [18].

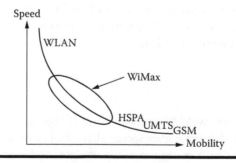

Figure 2.15 Competing technologies. (Courtesy of http://technology.indoblogs. com/?p=40 [dated November 28, 2006].)

The IEEE has approved the 802.16e BWA protocol, better known by some as mobile WiMAX. In a move that should help the development of BWA systems across the globe, the IEEE has approved the 802.16e WiMAX standard. RF chipmakers will welcome the move, which extends the existing 802.16 standard to include combined fixed and mobile BWA subscriber stations moving at speeds typical of car travel. Mobile WiMAX will operate in licensed bands below 6 GHz. A number of compound semi-conductor chip companies, such as Nitronex, Cree, Eudyna Devices, and TriQuint Semiconductor are targeting WiMAX already, with components based on either GaAs, SiC, or GaN transistors. WiMAX technology has enormous potential, as it promises to satisfy a strong demand for ubiquitous mobile broadband, but competing technolo-gies are significant threats, reports In-Stat (Figure 2.16). Although much uncertainty remains in this market, the high-tech market research firm foresees the WiMAX chipset market reaching as high as $950 million in 2009. Another plausible, more conservative

Standard	Family	Primary Use	Radio Tech	Downlink (Mbps)	Uplink (Mbps)	Notes
802.16e	WiMAX	Mobile Internet	SOFDMA	70	70	Quoted speeds only achievable at short range.
HIPERMAN	HIPERMAN	Mobile Internet	OFDM	56.9	56.9	
WiBro	WiBro	Mobile Internet	OFDM	50	50	Short range (<5km) HSDPA downlink widely deployed.
UMTS W-CDMA HSDPA+ HSUPA	UMTS/3GSM	Mobile phone	CDMA/FDD	.384 3.6	.384 5.76	Roadmap shows HSDPA up to 28.8Mbps.
UMTS-TDD	UMTS/3GSM	Mobile Internet	CDMA/TDD	16	16	Reported speeds according to IPWireless.
LTE UTMS	UMTS/4GSM	General 4G	OFDM/ MIMO (HSOPA)	>100	>50	Still in development.
1XRTT	CDMA2000	Mobile phone	CDMA	0.144	0.144	Obsoleted by EV-DO.
EV-DO 1x Rev. 0	CDMA2000	Mobile phone	CDMA/FDD	2.45	0.15	Proposed Rev. B improves downlink to nearly 5Mbps.
Rev. A				3.1	1.8	

Figure 2.16   Comparison of various technologies. (Courtesy of http://technology. indoblogs.com/?p=40 [dated November 28, 2006].)

scenario pegs this market at $450 million in 2009. Competing technologies include 3G technologies on the cellular side (EV-DO Release 0, A, and B; HSDPA) and Wi-Fi (coupled with wireless mesh networking and multiple-input multiple-output (MIMO) enhancements within 802.11n) on the networking side. According to In-Stat, persuading the large service providers to build infrastructures to support WiMAX will be the key for WiMAX boosters, especially convincing cellular operators, who already have built out expensive 3G infrastructures.

The first version of the IEEE 802.16 standard released addressed LoS environments using comparatively HF bands in the 10- to 66-GHz range. The most recently published standard, 802.16-2004, describes 2 GHz to 11 GHz, allowing support for NLoS environments. Three completely new PHYs were added, together with a number of modifications to the MAC, with knock-on effects in terms of the required digital processing. Further changes have been proposed to allow more efficient use of the radio spectrum at lower frequencies such as 450 MHz. With 802.16-2004 published, attention has shifted to developing the 802.16e standard, adding mobility and opening up competition with 3G cellular networks. This standard will add further complex PHY-layer processing along with handoff signals to allow users in vehicles to switch from BS to BS seamlessly. WiMAX was created to promote 802.16, but the two are not identical; WiMAX has deliberately defined a small subset of options and predefined pro-

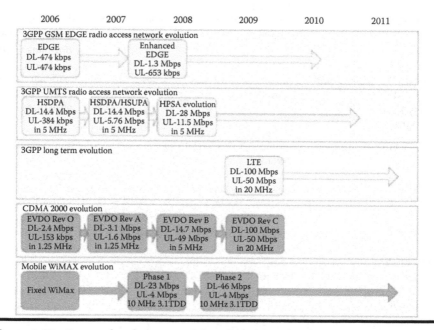

Figure 2.17   Future development of data transfer technologies. (Courtesy of http://www.digit-life.com/articles2/mobile/wimax.html.)

files. This simplifies implementation, although there are still many configurations and optional features to which designers have to cater.

Having split in the 2G, cellular communication technologies were reduced to a common denominator — WCDMA. It is a 3G standard that underlies UMTS networks. It is not surprising because sooner or later high data-transfer rates require the same technologies. That's why the GSM–GPRS–EDGE–UMTS tree has grown branches for encoding and multiplexing channels, and the AMPS–CDMA–CDMA2000–W-CDMA tree for division into subbands and OFDM (Figure 2.17) [6].

At the same time, wireless technologies that had been initially created solely for data exchange use code division of bands and OFDM. It is inevitable. Data transfer technologies in cellular communication networks and wireless networks could not compete with each other but supplemented each other at the previous stage (when the market was dominated by 2G and 2.5G standards). However, now, with the increased Internet access rates in cellular communication networks on one hand, and enlarged coverage of wireless networks on the other, different "worlds" started to compete with each other. We have a unique opportunity to see which approach will survive: cellular communication networks designed for voice transmission and offering broadband access to digital networks (Internet in particular), or wireless networks designed for data transfers, which successfully mastered VoIP technologies. To all appearances, that's the reason why engineers are not in a hurry to deliver 4G specifications, though some information still leaks to the press. There is a well-grounded opinion that when 4G standards are ready, they will include technical solutions that are currently used in wireless as well as cellular communication networks [6].

The HSPDA technology belongs to the family of solutions that use packet data transmissions. This family also includes GPRS and EDGE. Physically, HSDPA is a superstructure over the WCDMA/UMTS networks, so it's often called 3.5G. The "half" in this informal name is also justified by the fact that the startup HSDPA bandwidth is 1.8 Mbps, whereas the theoretical maximum is 14.4 Mbps. But it's far from the theoretical maximum so far — this technology has just exceeded 3.6 Mbps for two years. However, the strategy adopted by many suppliers (Option in particular) consists in delivering ready devices that support higher throughputs than provided by the operator. They can only wait for the bright day when an operator will upgrade its BSs (operators have to change their equipment) and voila! — you can download files at 7.2 Mbps. An obvious advantage of this technology is that the communication range practically equals the distance range of a BS (with some reservations to be mentioned at the end of this chapter). The drawback here is that high speed is available only for downlink; uplink will be at the baseline W-CDMA speed of 384 kbps. We can expect this drawback to be fixed with the appearance of HSUPA. The HSDPA + HSUPA combo will be called high-speed packet access (HSPA) [6].

Research and Markets has added "2006 Australia — Mobile Data & Content — The Battle between HSDPA & WIMAX" to their offering. Cellular mobile networks have been built for voice services and, even more importantly, have been fine-tuned over the years for efficient and effective voice transmission. Although both 2G and 3G allow, in principle, for a large range of mobile data services, these networks can never be optimized for that. Voice will remain the killer application for mobile with some data services included as support services and niche market services. WiMAX and 4G are the real solutions for mobile data, but by then it will be called wireless personal broadband [7].

This report analyses the industry: HSDPA, GPRS, WAP, EDGE, CDMA2000 1X, EV-DO, i-mode, and BlackBerry. The industry is awash with a multitude of acronyms and fancy names for somewhat inexplicable technologies and services. The range of services promoted as midway between conventional 2G mobile services offering plain voice and SMS, and the 3G multimedia + voice applications, is known as the 2.5G range of wireless data services. The report looks at some of these 2.5G services, including GPRS, PTT (post office, telegraph, and telecommunications), USSD, and EDGE. The latest addition is HSDPA to the 3G networks. Like the GSM technology, CDMA has also delivered a range of mobile data technologies, namely, 1X and EV-DO. However, with the withdrawal of CDMA from the Australian market, these services are no longer relevant to the market. They will be replaced by HSDPA. The report also covers the failure of i-mode. BlackBerry, one of the most successful business mobile data applications, is also discussed. The SMS technology, based on GSM, is examined in the report, from its faltering beginnings to its present relevance to mobile data. Key issues in relation to market trends, marketing, technology developments, and regulatory and policy matters are all discussed. Premium SMS is also covered. SMS remains a major growth area for mobile operators. However, revenue growth is only a fraction of the growth in messages. Australians did send well over 8 billion SMS messages in FY 2005/2006, an average of at least 300 messages for each subscriber. By the end of the decade, over 10 billion messages will be sent. The importance of SMS to mobile phone service operators is also increasing, with SMS now accounting for an average of between 10 and 15 percent of revenue for mobile operators. As an extension of the immensely popular SMS service, MMS was aimed at providing longer text messages, in addition to music and pictures. It also allows for the sending of messages to multiple recipients. Launched in 2001, MMS has failed to take off. Elements of MMS have been introduced in other technologies similar to where WAP ended up. The current technology and, more importantly, its business models, don't yet stack up. The same applies to the mobile TV technology, perhaps a great engineering feat, but with no proper business model [7]! Up till now, the mobile market has mainly revolved around mobile calls and SMS. However, this market is reaching the end of its life. On the other side, we see the emergence of wireless broadband, and the mobile aspects of this market are going show us the way forward where mobile data failed. This is the new market of "mobility." This will further develop into an artificial intelligence (AI) network infrastructure linked to personal devices with high storage capacity and parallel processing. Data will move freely around this wireless grid, which, of course, will also be linked into the fixed network. Both WiMAX and 4G are vying for this market [7].

References

1. www.cdg.org.
2. http://en.wikipedia.org/wiki/EVDO.
3. Anderson, N., The Limits of 'Unlimited' EVDO, http://arstechnica.com/news.ars/ post/20060727-7365.html [dated July 27, 2006].
4. http://arstechnica.com/news.ars/post/20060921-7798.html [dated September 21, 2006].
5. http://sachin-electronovel.blogspot.com/2006/11/something-about-cdma.html [dated November 25, 2006].
6. http://www.digit-life.com/articles2/mobile/wimax.html.
7. http://www.sda-india.com/sda_india/psecom,id,102,site_layout,sdaindia,news,1414 1,p,0.html.
8. http://grouper.ieee.org/groups/802/dots.html.
9. http://ieee802.org/16/docs/01/80216-01_58r1.pdf.
10. http://grouper.ieee.org/groups/802/16/index.html.
11. http://grouper.ieee.org/groups/802/11/index.html.
12. http://standards.ieee.org/getieee802/download/802.16.2-2001.pdf.
13. Hong, D., 2.3GHz Portable Internet (WiBro) for Wireless Broadband Access, ITU-APT Regional Seminar 2004.
14. http://www.dailywireless.org/2006/10/27/wibro-for-the-us-military/.
15. http://www.union-network.org/unitelecom. nsf/0/6FF154A370318ED1C12571FD002688AA?OpenDocument.
16. http://times.hankooki.com/lpage/200608/kt2006080917403310440.htm.
17. http://www.rockymountainnews.com/drmn/tech/article/0,2777,DRMN_23910_5087124,00.html [dated October 23, 2006].
18. http://technology.indoblogs.com/?p=40 [dated November 28, 2006].

Chapter 3

WiMAX — A Technology

802.16

IEEE 802.16 Working Group on Broadband Wireless Access Systems

The IEEE 802.16 Working Group on Broadband Wireless Access Systems defines the radio–air interface for BWA configurations that operate in the licensed spectrum between the 2- and 11-GHz frequencies. This Working Group also delineates the radio–air interface for broadband wireless systems that operate in the spectrum between the 10- and 66-GHz frequencies (Figure 3.1). IEEE 802.16 specifications conform to IEEE 802 standards governing LAN and metropolitan area network (MAN) operations endorsed by the IEEE in 1990. As opposed to IEEE 802.11, which focuses on WLAN implementations and applications, the IEEE 802.16 Working Group (WG) develops affordable point-to-multipoint BWA configurations that enable multimedia services in MAN and WAN wide area network (WAN) environments. The IEEE 802.16 Working Group works with the Broadband Radio Access Network (BRAN) Committee sponsored by the European Telecommunications Standards Institute (ETSI) in developing compatible BWA system specifications.

IEEE 802.16a Extension

The IEEE 802.16a Extension clarifies operations, services, and the radio–air interface for BWA networks that operate in the spectrum between the 2- and 11-GHz frequencies.

> 163 members
> 67 "potential members"
> 62 official observers
> 700 different individuals have attended a session
> 2.8 million file downloads in year 2000
> Members and potential members from
>   ❖ 10 countries
>   ❖ >110 companies

Figure 3.1   802.16 by the numbers. (Courtesy of http://ieee802.org/16/docs/ 01/80216-01_58r1.pdf.)

IEEE 802.16b Extension: The WirelessHUMAN Initiative

Sponsored by the IEEE 802.11 WG on BWA systems, the WirelessHUMAN (high-data-rate unlicensed metropolitan area network) initiative fosters implementation of BWA metropolitan network specifications. These specifications provide the foundation and framework for the IEEE 802.16b Extension. Approved in 2001, the IEEE 802.16b Extension clarifies broadband wireless access metropolitan network functions and capabilities of the radio–air interface. License-exempt BWA metropolitan networks support multimedia services in license-exempt spectrum between the 5.15- and 5.25-GHz frequencies, between the 5.25- and 5.35-GHz frequencies, and between the 5.725- and 5.825-GHz frequencies. To facilitate the standardization process, the WirelessHUMAN initiative supports utilization of the Physical Layer Orthogonal Frequency Division Multiplexing (PHYOFDM) Protocol defined in the IEEE 802.11a Extension and MAC (media access control) layer operations defined in the IEEE 802.16 standard (Figure 3.2).

The MAC Layer

The IEEE 802.16 MAC protocol was designed to support point-to-multipoint BWA applications. It addresses the need for very high bit rates, both uplink (UL) and downlink (DL). Access and bandwidth allocation algorithms must accommodate hundreds of terminals per channel, with terminals that may be shared by multiple end users. The services required by these end users are varied, and include legacy TDM voice and data, Internet Protocol (IP) connectivity, and packetized Voice-over-IP (VoIP).

> Mesh mode
>   ❖ Optional topology
>   ❖ Subscriber to subscriber communication
> OFDM support
> ARQ

Figure 3.2   Enhancements to 802.16. (Courtesy of http://ieee802.org/16/ docs/01/80216-01_58r1.pdf.)

➢ Support both TDD and FDD in the PHY
➢ Provide network access
➢ Address the wireless environment
  ❖ Eg. very efficient use of spectrum
➢ Broadband services
  ❖ Very high bit rates, downlink and uplink
  ❖ A range of QoS requirements
  ❖ Ethernet, IPv4, IPv6, ATM etc.
➢ Likelihood of terminal being shared
  ❖ Base station may be heavily loaded
➢ Security
➢ Protocol-independent engine
  ❖ Convergence layers to ATM, IP, Ethernet etc.

Figure 3.3   802.16 MAC overview. (Courtesy of IEEE.)

To support this variety of services, the 802.16 MAC must accommodate continuous and bursty traffic. Additionally, these services are expected to be assigned quality of service (QoS) in keeping with the traffic types. The 802.16 MAC provides a wide range of service types analogous to the classic asynchronous transfer mode (ATM) service categories, as well as newer categories such as guaranteed frame rate (GFR) (Figure 3.3). The 802.16 MAC protocol must also support a variety of backhaul requirements, including ATM and packet-based protocols. Convergence sublayers are used to map the transport-layer-specific traffic to a MAC that is flexible enough to carry any traffic type efficiently. Through such features as payload header suppression, packing, and fragmentation, the convergence sublayers and MAC work together to carry traffic in a form that is often more efficient than the original transport mechanism. Issues of transport efficiency are also addressed at the interface between the MAC and the PHY layer. For example, modulation and coding schemes are specified in a burst profile that may be adjusted to each subscriber station (SS) adaptively for each burst. The MAC can make use of the bandwidth-efficient burst profiles under favorable link conditions but shift to more reliable, though less efficient, alternatives as required to support the planned 99.999 percent link availability. The request-grant mechanism is designed to be scalable, efficient, and self correcting. The 802.16 access system does not lose efficiency when presented with multiple connections per terminal, multiple QoS levels per terminal, and a large number of statistically multiplexed users. It takes advantage of a wide variety of request mechanisms, balancing the stability of connectionless access with the efficiency of contention-oriented access. Along with the fundamental task of allocating bandwidth and transporting data, the MAC includes a privacy sublayer that provides authentication of network access and connection establishment to avoid theft of service, and key exchange and encryption for data privacy. To accommodate a more demanding physical environment and different service requirements of the frequencies between 2 and 11 GHz, the 802.16a project upgraded the MAC

> Point-to-multipoint
> Metropolitan area network
> Connection-oriented
> Supports multiple 802.16 PHYs
> Supports difficult user environments
   ❖ High bandwidth, hundreds of users per channel
   ❖ Continuous and burst traffic
   ❖ Very efficient use of spectrum
> Protocol-independent core (ATM, IP, Ethernet, ...)
> Balances between stability of contentionless and efficiency of contention-based operation
> Flexible QoS offerings
   ❖ CBR, rt-VBR, nrt-VBR, BE, with granularity within classes

Figure 3.4   MAC requirements. (Courtesy of IEEE.)

to provide automatic retransmission request (ARQ) and support for mesh, rather than only point-to-multipoint, network architectures (Figure 3.4).

MAC Layer Details

The MAC includes service-specific convergence sublayers that interface to higher layers above the core MAC common part sublayer that carries out the key MAC functions. Below the common part sublayer, the privacy sublayer is located.

Service-Specific Convergence Sublayers

IEEE Standard 802.16 defines two general service-specific convergence sublayers for mapping services to and from 802.16 MAC connections. The ATM convergence sublayer is defined for ATM services, and the packet convergence sublayer is defined for mapping packet services such as IPv4, IPv6, Ethernet, and virtual local area network (VLAN). The primary task of the sublayer is to classify service data units (SDUs) to the proper MAC connection, preserve or enable QoS, and enable bandwidth allocation. The mapping takes various forms depending on the type of service. In addition to these basic functions, the convergence sublayers can also perform more sophisticated functions such as payload header suppression and reconstruction to enhance airlink efficiency.

Common Part Sublayer

In general, the 802.16 MAC is designed to support a point-to-multipoint architecture with a central base station (BS) handling multiple independent sectors simultaneously. On the downlink, data to the SSs are multiplexed in TDM fashion. The uplink is shared between SSs in TDMA fashion. The 802.16 MAC is connection oriented. All services, including inherently connectionless services, are mapped to a connection. This provides a mechanism for requesting bandwidth, associating QoS and traffic parameters, transporting and routing data to the appropriate convergence sublayer, and all other actions associated with the contractual terms of the service. Connections are referenced with 16-b connection identifiers and may require continuous availability of bandwidth or bandwidth on demand. Each SS has a standard 48-b MAC address that serves mainly as an equipment identifier because the primary addresses used during operation are the connection identifiers. Upon entering the network, the SS is assigned three management connections in each direction, which reflect the three different QoS requirements used by different management levels. The first of these is the basic connection, which is used for the transfer of short, time-critical MAC and radio link control (RLC) messages. The primary management connection is used to transfer longer, more delay-tolerant messages such as those used for authentication and connection setup. The secondary management connection is used for the transfer of standard-based management messages such as Dynamic Host Configuration Protocol (DHCP), Trivial File Transfer Protocol (TFTP), and Simple Network Management Protocol (SNMP). The MAC reserves additional connections for other purposes. One connection is reserved for contention-based initial access. Another is reserved for broadcast transmissions in the downlink as well as for signaling broadcast contention-based polling of SS bandwidth needs. Additional connections are reserved for multicast, rather than broadcast, contention-based polling. SSs may be instructed to join multicast polling groups associated with these multicast polling connections.

MAC PDU Formats

The MAC PDU is the data unit exchanged between the MAC layers of the BS and its SSs. A MAC PDU consists of a fixed-length MAC header, a variable-length payload, and an optional cyclic redundancy check (CRC). Two header formats, distinguished by the HT field, are defined: the generic header (Figure 3.5) and the

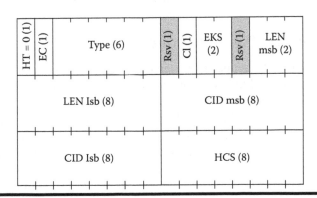

Figure 3.5   Generic header for MAC PDU.

bandwidth request header. Except for bandwidth containing no payload, MAC PDUs have MAC management messages or convergence sublayer data.

Three types of MAC subheader may be present:

1. A grant management subheader, used by SS to convey bandwidth management needs to its BS
2. A fragmentation subheader, indicating the presence and orientation within the payload of any fragments of the SDUs
3. The packing subheader, used to indicate packing of multiple SDUs into a single PDU

Immediately following the generic header, grant management and fragmentation subheaders may be inserted into MAC PDUs if so indicated by the Type field. The packing subheader may be inserted before each MAC SDU if shown by the Type field.

Transmission of MAC PDUs

The IEEE 802.16 MAC supports various higher-layer protocols such as ATM or IP (Internet Protocol). Incoming MAC SDUs from corresponding convergence sublayers are formatted according to the MAC PDU format, possibly with fragmentation and/or packing, before they are conveyed over one or more connections in accordance with the MAC protocol. After traversing the air link, MAC PDUs are reconstructed back into the original MAC SDUs so that the format modifications performed by the MAC layer protocol are transparent to the receiving entity. IEEE 802.16 takes advantage of packing and fragmentation processes, whose effectiveness, flexibility, and efficiency are maximized by the bandwidth allocation process. *Fragmentation* is the process in which a MAC SDU is divided into one or more MAC SDU fragments. *Packing* is the process in which multiple MAC SDUs are packed into a single MAC PDU payload. Both processes may be initiated by a BS for a DL connection or by an SS for an uplink connection. IEEE 802.16 allows simultaneous fragmentation and packing for efficient use of the bandwidth.

PHY Support and Frame Structure

The IEEE 802.16 MAC supports time division duplex (TDD) and frequency division duplex (FDD). In FDD, continuous as well as burst downlinks are possible. Continuous downlinks allow for certain robustness enhancement techniques, such as interleaving. Burst downlinks (FDD or TDD) allow the use of more advanced robustness and capacity enhancement techniques, such as subscriber-level adaptive burst profiling and advanced antenna systems. The MAC builds the DL subframe starting with a frame control section containing the DL-MAP (downlink MAP) and UL-MAP (uplink MAP) messages. These indicate PHY transitions on the downlink, as well as bandwidth allocations and burst profiles on the uplink. The DL-MAP is always applicable to the current frame and is always at least two FEC blocks long. To allow adequate processing time, the first PHY transition is expressed in the first FEC block. In TDD and FDD systems, the UL-MAP provides allocations starting no later than the next DL frame. The UL-MAP can, however, start allocating in the current frame as long as processing times and round-trip delays are observed.

Radio Link Control

The advanced technology of the 802.16 PHY requires equally advanced RLC, particularly the capability of the PHY to change from one burst profile to another. The RLC must control this capability as well as the traditional RLC functions of power control and ranging. RLC begins with periodic BS broadcast of the burst profiles that have been chosen for the uplink and downlink. Among the several burst profiles used on a channel, one in particular is chosen based on a number of factors such as rain region and equipment capabilities. Burst profiles for the downlink are each tagged with a downlink interval usage code (DIUC), and those for the uplink are tagged with an uplink interval usage code (UIUC). During initial access, the SS performs initial power leveling and ranging using ranging request (RNG-REQ) messages transmitted in initial maintenance windows. The adjustments to the SS's transmit time advance, as well as power adjustments, are returned to the SS in ranging response (RNG-RSP) messages.

For ongoing ranging and power adjustments, the BS may transmit unsolicited RNG-RSP messages instructing the SS to adjust its power or timing. During initial ranging, the SS can also request service in the downlink via a particular burst profile by transmitting its choice of DIUC to the BS. The selection is based on received DL signal quality measurements performed by the SS before and during initial ranging. The BS may confirm or reject the choice in the ranging response. Similarly, the BS monitors the quality of the UL signal it receives from the SS. The BS commands the SS to use a particular UL burst profile simply by including the appropriate burst profile UIUC with the SS's grants in UL-MAP messages. After initial determination of uplink and DL burst profiles between the BS and a particular SS, RLC continues to monitor and control the burst profiles. Harsher environmental conditions, such as rain fades, can force the SS to request a more robust burst profile. Alternatively, exceptionally good weather may allow an SS to operate temporarily with a more efficient burst profile. The RLC continues to adapt the SS's current UL and DL burst profiles, always striving to achieve a balance between robustness and efficiency. Because the BS is in control and directly monitors the UL signal quality, the protocol for changing the UL burst profile for an SS is simply by BS merely specifying the profile's associated UIUC whenever granting the SS bandwidth in a frame. This eliminates the need for an acknowledgment because the SS will always receive both the UIUC and the grant or neither. Thus, no chance of UL burst profile mismatch between the BS and the SS exists.

In the downlink, the SS is the entity that monitors the quality of the receive signal, and therefore knows when its DL burst profile should change. The BS, however, is the entity in control of the change. Two methods are available to the SS to request a change in the DL burst profile, depending on whether the SS operates in the grant per connection (GPC) or grant per SS (GPSS) mode. The first method would typically apply (based on the discretion of the BS scheduling algorithm) only to GPC SSs. In this case, the BS may periodically allocate a station maintenance interval to the SS. The SS can use the RNG-REQ message to request a change in the DL burst profile. The preferred method is for the SS to transmit a DL burst profile change request (DBPC-REQ). In this case, which is always an option for GPSS SSs and can be an option for GPC SSs, the BS responds with a downlink burst profile change response (DBPC-RSP) message confirming or denying the change. Because messages may be lost due to irrecoverable bit errors, the protocols for changing an SS's DL burst profile must be carefully structured. The order of the burst profile change actions is different when transitioning to a more robust burst profile than when transitioning to a less robust one. The standard takes advantage of the fact that any SS is always required to listen to more robust portions of the downlink as well as the profile that has been negotiated.

Channel Acquisition

The MAC Protocol includes an initialization procedure designed to eliminate the need for manual configuration. Upon installation, SS begins scanning its frequency list to find an operating channel. It may be programmed to register with one specific BS, referring to a programmable BS ID broadcasted by each. This feature is useful in dense deployments in which the SS might hear a secondary BS due to selective fading or when the SS picks up a sidelobe of a nearby BS antenna. After deciding on which channel or channel pair to start communicating, the SS tries to synchronize to the DL transmission by detecting the periodic frame preambles. Once the PHY is synchronized, the SS looks for periodic DCD and UCD broadcast messages that enable the SS to learn the modulation and FEC schemes used on the carrier.

After registration, the SS attains an IP address via DHCP and establishes the time of day via the Internet Time Protocol. The DHCP server also provides the address of the TFTP server from which the SS can request a configuration file. This file provides a standard interface for providing vendor-specific configuration information.

Physical Layer

10–66 GHz

In the design of the PHY specification for 10 to 66 GHz, line-of-sight (LOS) propagation has been deemed a practical necessity. With this condition assumed, single-carrier modulation could be easily selected to be employed in designated air interface WMAN-SC. However, many fundamental design challenges remain. Because of a point-to-multipoint architecture, BS basically transmits a TDM signal, with individual subscriber stations allocated time slots sequentially. Access in the UL direction is by TDMA. Following extensive discussions on duplexing, a burst design has been selected that allows TDD (in which the uplink and downlink share a channel but do not transmit simultaneously) and FDD (the uplink and downlink operate on separate channels, sometimes simultaneously) to be handled in a similar fashion. Support for half-duplex FDD subscriber stations, which may be less expensive because they do not simultaneously transmit and receive, has been added at the expense of some slight complexity. TDD and FDD alternatives support adaptive burst profiles in which modulation and coding options may be dynamically assigned on a burst-by-burst basis.

2–11 GHz

Licensed and license-exempt 2- to 11-GHz bands are addressed in the IEEE Project 802.16a. This currently specifies that compliant systems implement one of three air interface specifications, each of which can provide interoperability. Design of the 2- to 11-GHz physical layer is driven by the need for NLoS operation. Because residential applications are expected, rooftops may be too low for a clear sight line to the antenna of a BS, possibly due to obstruction by trees. Therefore, significant multipath propagation must be expected. Furthermore, outdoor-mounted antennas are expensive because of hardware and installation costs. The three 2- to 11-GHz air interfaces included in 802.16a, draft 3, and the specifications are

- *WirelessMAN-SC2* uses a single-carrier modulation format.
- *WirelessMAN-OFDM* uses OFDM with a 256-point transform. Access is by TDMA. This air interface is mandatory for license-exempt bands.
- *WirelessMAN-OFDMA* uses OFDMA with a 2048-point transform. In this system, multiple access is provided by addressing a subset of the multiple carriers to individual receivers. Because of the propagation requirements, the use of advanced antenna systems is supported. It is premature to speculate on further details of the 802.16a amendment prior to its completion. The draft seems to have reached a level of maturity, but the contents could significantly change by ballots. Modes could even be deleted or added.

Physical Layer Details

The PHY specification defined for 10 to 66 GHz uses burst single-carrier modulation with adaptive burst profiling in which transmission parameters, including the modulation and coding schemes, may be adjusted individually to each SS on a frame-by-frame basis. TDD and burst FDD variants are defined. Channel bandwidths of 20 or 25 MHz (typical U.S. allocation) or 28 MHz (typical European allocation) are specified, along with Nyquist square-root raised-cosine pulse shaping with a roll-off factor of 0.25. Randomization is performed for spectral shaping and ensuring bit transitions for clock recovery. The FEC uses Reed–Solomon GF (256) with variable block size and appropriate error-correction capabilities. This is paired with an inner block convolutional code to transmit critical data robustly, such as frame control and initial accesses. The FEC options are paired with quadrature phase shift keying (QPSK), 16-state QAM (16-QAM) and 64-state QAM (64-QAM) to form burst profiles of varying robustness and efficiency. If the last FEC block is not filled, that block may be shortened. Shortening in the uplink and downlink is controlled by the BS and is implicitly communicated in the uplink map (UL-MAP) and downlink map (DL-MAP). The system uses a frame of 0.5, 1, or 2 ms divided into physical slots for the purpose of bandwidth allocation and identification of PHY transitions. A *physical slot* is defined to be four QAM symbols. In the TDD variant of the PHY, the UL subframe follows the DL subframe on the same carrier frequency. In the FDD variant, the UL and DL subframes are coincident in time but carried on separate frequencies. The DL subframe starts with a frame control section that contains the DL-MAP for the current DL frame, as well as the UL-MAP for a specified time in the future. The DL map specifies when PHY transitions (modulation and FEC changes) occur within the DL subframe. The DL subframe typically contains a TDM portion immediately following the frame control section. DL data is transmitted to each SS using a negotiated burst profile. The data is transmitted in order of decreasing robustness to allow SSs to receive their data before being presented with a burst profile that could cause them to lose synchronization with the downlink. In FDD systems, the TDM portion may be followed by a TDMA segment that includes an extra preamble at the start of each new burst profile. This feature allows better support of half-duplex SSs. In an efficiently scheduled FDD system with many half-duplex SSs, some may need to transmit earlier in the frame than they are received. Due to their half-duplex nature, these SSs may lose synchronization with the downlink. The TDMA preamble allows them to regain synchronization.

Due to the dynamics of bandwidth demand for a variety of services that may be active, the mixture and duration of burst profiles and the presence or absence of a TDMA portion vary dynamically from frame to frame. Because the recipient SS is implicitly indicated in the MAC headers rather than in the DL-MAP, SSs listen to all portions of the DL subframes that they are capable of receiving. For full-duplex SSs, this means receiving all burst profiles of equal or greater robustness than they have negotiated with the BS. Unlike the downlink, the UL-MAP grants bandwidth to specific SSs. The SSs transmit in their assigned allocation using the burst profile specified by the UIUC in the UL-MAP entry granting them bandwidth. The UL subframe may also contain contention-based allocations for initial system access and broadcast or multicast bandwidth requests. The access opportunities for initial system access are sized to allow extra guard time for SSs that have not resolved the transmit time advances necessary to offset the round-trip delay to the BS. Between the PHY and MAC is a transmission convergence (TC) sublayer. This layer performs

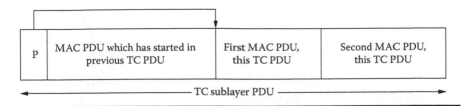

Figure 3.6 TC PDU format.

the transformation of variable length MAC PDUs into the fixed-length FEC blocks (plus possibly a shortened block at the end) of each burst. The TC layer has a PDU sized to fit in the FEC block currently being filled (Figure 3.6). It starts with a pointer indicating where the next MAC PDU header starts within the FEC block. The TC PDU format allows resynchronization to the next MAC PDU in the event that the previous FEC block had irrecoverable errors. Without the TC layer, a receiving SS or BS could potentially lose the entire remainder of a burst when an irrecoverable bit error occurs.

Base and Subscriber Stations

WiMAX BS can range from units that support only a few subscriber stations to elaborate equipment that supports thousands of subscriber stations and provides many carrier-class features. Whatever number of subscriber stations a BS supports, the latter must manage a variety of functions that are not required in subscriber equipment. Some BSs must support sophisticated antenna capabilities, for example, and implement efficient frequency reuse. As a result, WiMAX BSs will have many different configurations. They will likely range from simple stand-alone units that support a few users to redundant, rack-mounted systems and server blades that operate alongside wireline networking equipment. On the hardware side, this equipment will typically use off-the-shelf microprocessors and discrete RF components. Required software includes an 802.16 MAC, scheduler and many other software applications such as network management services and protocol stacks. A typical presentation of WiMAX system components is given in Figure 3.7 with emphasis on different levels of interface [2].

The typical configurations of this topology are illustrated in Figure 3.7, Figure 3.8, and Figure 3.9. The key difference in these topologies is that daisy-chaining reduces overall path availability performance and increased delay and delay variability. The daisy chain, however, allows the effective reach of the metro fiber PoP to be considerably extended [2].

In this topology, an Ethernet mesh is used to aggregate and backhaul WiMax hub sites, delivering the traffic to the metro fibered PoP location (Figure 3.9). In this case, the network delivers superior path availability due to the inherent angle diversity and location diversity within the meshed backhaul layer (Figure 3.9). These gains

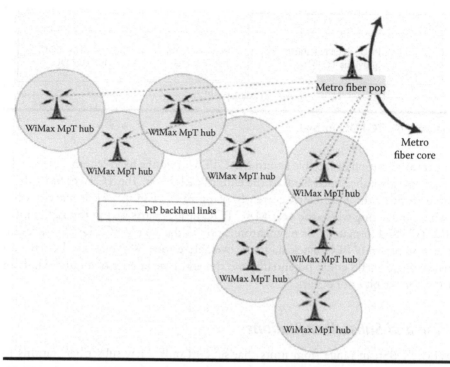

Figure 3.7 WiMax MpT Access + PtP backhaul. (Illustrative subset of a metro network portion shown.) (Courtesy of http://www.convergedigest.com/bp-bbw/ bp1.asp?ID=391&ctgy=Mesh [dated August 30, 2006].)

can provide 5–10 X improvements in availability. Additionally, compared to the single-layer PtP topology, the meshed solution often results in reduced (average) path lengths, further enhancing availability performance.

As a general goal, a key design objective of the network design is the minimization of delay and delay variability. Delay performance directly impacts the operation of time-sensitive applications, which include items such as VoIP and VIDoIP, and TDM over IP (TDMoIP) services. Delay variability affects the operation of handoff processing applicable to mobile applications.

IEEE 802.16 MAC and Service Provisioning

Implementation Challenges of the WiMAX MAC and QoS Models

The tasks performed by the 802.16 MAC Protocol can be roughly partitioned into two different categories: periodic (per-frame) "fast path" activities and aperiodic "slow path" activities. Fast path activities (such as scheduling, packing, fragmentation,

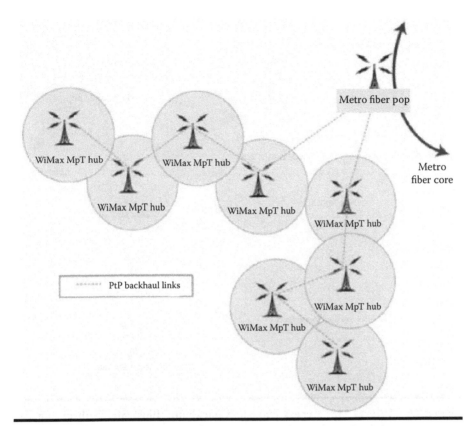

Figure 3.8 WiMax MpT Access + Daisy-chained PtP backhaul. (Illustrative subset of a metro network portion shown.) (Courtesy of http://www.convergedigest.com/bp-bbw/bp1.asp?ID=391&ctgy=Mesh [dated August 30, 2006].)

and ARQ) must be performed at the granularity of single frames, and they are subject to hard real-time deadlines. They must complete in time for transmission of the frame they are associated with (Figures 3.10 and 3.11). In contrast, slow path activities typically execute according to timers that are not associated with a specific frame or the frame period, and as such do not have stringent deadlines [3].

The 802.16 MAC microcode has been modeled using the Intel Architecture Development Tool for IXP 2850 and IXP 2350 network processors. The performance estimations done on the model indicate a large processing headroom, guaranteeing scalability and making IXP network processors a perfect choice for multichannel and multisector WiMAX BS implementations. The analysis shows that both types of IXP processors can easily handle four RF channel or four sector configurations on a single chip [3]. The 802.16 specification defines a complex, powerful MAC Protocol for achieving high bandwidth and robust service offerings. In addition to the MAC features and functionality, the following design

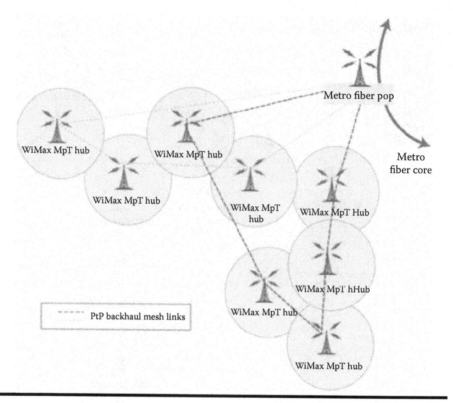

Figure 3.9 WiMax MpT Access + meshed backhaul. (Illustrative subset of a metro network portion shown.) (Courtesy of http://www.convergedigest.com/bp-bbw/bp1.asp?ID=391&ctgy=Mesh [dated August 30, 2006].)

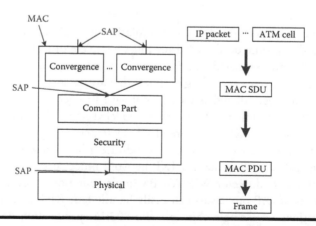

Figure 3.10 WiMax layered architecture. (Courtesy of Barbeau, M., WiMax/802.16 Threat Analysis, Q2SWinet'05, October 13, 2005, Montreal, Quebec, Canada.)

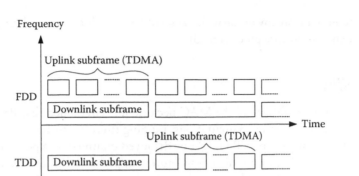

Figure 3.11 Framing. (Courtesy of Barbeau, M., WiMax/802.16 Threat Analysis, Q2SWinet'05, October 13, 2005, Montreal, Quebec, Canada.)

considerations were used in architecting the Intel Architecture BS MAC implementation of 802.16 with the OFDMA PHY. Extensibility, as described previously, was a primary requirement in the Intel Architecture BS MAC implementation. Scalability, both in the design of the software MAC as well as in the BS design itself, was another key requirement (Figure 3.12).

Portability of the MAC implementation was also a key design consideration, which goes hand in hand with scalability. A portable MAC implementation should

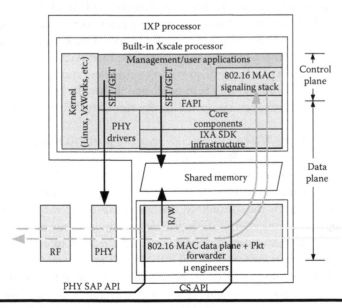

Figure 3.12 Sample WiMAX BS software partitioning. (Courtesy of Nair, G., Chou, J., Madejski, T., Perycz, K., Putzolu, D., and Sydir, J., IEEE 802.16 medium access control and service provisioning, *Intel Technology Journal*, 8(3), 2004.)

be able to execute on any of the wide range of Intel Architecture and XScale Architecture general-purpose processors [3].

Scalability

Scalability is a key feature of the MAC because it is envisioned that BSs will have a wide variety of physical configurations, ranging from "pico" BSs to "macro" systems. In this context, a pico BS might be deployed mounted on a pole with a small, single sector and single omnidirectional antenna, perhaps with limited bandwidth and tight power and heat limitations, and subject to outdoor environment-level temperatures. At the other extreme, a heavy iron BS might be rack mounted, support multiple sectors, have many antennae, and be in an environmentally controlled cabinet or small building, with a large antenna tower connected to it. As such, it must be possible for the MAC software implementation to be usable with the wide range of processor performance levels available with general-purpose processors such as Intel Architecture processors. The system must be implemented such that performance scales in a predictable fashion with processor performance, allowing appropriate processors to be chosen for executing the MAC software.

Portability

Portability is a key feature of the Intel Architecture MAC implementation for similar reasons. The wide range of performance and price points likely to be associated with WiMAX BSs creates the need to easily choose different processors based on power, price, heat, and performance metrics. The Intel Architecture MAC design takes this feature as a primary goal, providing a complete and robust MAC offering, while at the same time allowing it to be ported across the range of Intel general-purpose processor architectures, including Pentium M, Pentium 4, Xeon, XScale, and Celeron.

A handful of "pre-WiMAX" solutions using the Intel PRO/Wireless 5116 chipset exist, each showing promise. But the success of each is contingent on how well it fares in terms of reliability, features, and protection. As with other disruptive technologies, expediency to market is key if OEMs wish to survive, let alone thrive, in the WiMAX space. However, given the streamlined and standards-based nature of 802.16, networking and communications OEMs benefit greatly in terms of developing common platform WiMAX-enabled devices — at least relative to accommodating the almost innumerable standards of Wi-Fi. OEMs will find themselves competing for first-to-market position not so much on the strength and impenetrability of their devices' security infrastructure but on how well they integrate with innovative converged platforms providing support for enterprise applications such as VoIP, video, and management. The battle for first-to-market will be met with anticipation from service providers, end-users, and, perhaps most important, enterprises that stand to gain the most of what WiMAX has to offer. The recent spate of converged WLAN security appliances has created many innovative all-in-one solutions for collaboration and productivity, but they operate at the bottlecapped speed of the 802.11 standard. To realize the full potential of these products and what they promise for VoIP, VoD, and other low-latency applications, WiMAX-enabled equipment must be fully tested and certified by OEMs and standards bodies alike. Yet, with the rush to deploy converged systems for the WiMAX ecosystem, OEMs stand to risk releasing products with beta, or premature, security components derived from Wi-Fi specifications, leaving uncertainty as to the protection of the network — especially given the absence of learned lessons from trial deployments. What many consider to be the future-proof standard for wireless enterprise communication could be fatally flawed if OEMs do not exercise due diligence in developing robust software security infrastructure. As the release of certified WiMAX hardware approaches, it is important to understand the security challenges presented by current standards as well as those to come in the future. Designing a network with a wireless segment is not an easy task, and should be approached only after carefully weighing all the facts.

Mobile WiMax

Mobile WiMAX is a major opportunity for systems designers who understand the value of multi-antenna signal processing (MAS) technologies such as multiple input/multiple output (MIMO) and adaptive antenna systems. MAS technology addresses those service provider requirements by extending cell radii, ensuring QoS and high throughput, and improving network capacity, all of which reduce the need for additional BSs or repeaters. These savings make the operator better able to price its mobile WiMAX services competitively yet profitably. By selecting the right DSP for their MAS-enabled mobile WiMAX products, systems designers can differentiate their products (Figure 3.13). That ability is a major asset in a market as crowded and competitive as WiMAX, where features and performance are must-haves for standing out from the pack and justifying a price premium (Figure 3.14) [4].

Conformance Testing for Mobile WiMAX

Centro de Tecnologia de las Comunicaciones (Cetecom), in Spain, has been selected by the WiMAX Forum to develop the Radio Conformance Test Tester (RCTT) for mobile WiMAX. Cetecom has participated, together with other test equipment manufacturers, in an RCTT RFP activity conducted by the Forum. This test system is based on MINT T2110, the first RF conformance test system for IEEE 802.16-2004 devices. MINT T2110 will be supporting both fixed WiMAX and mobile RF testing. The MINT family of test solutions for WiMAX comprises a radio conformance tester (MINT T2110), a protocol conformance tester (MINT

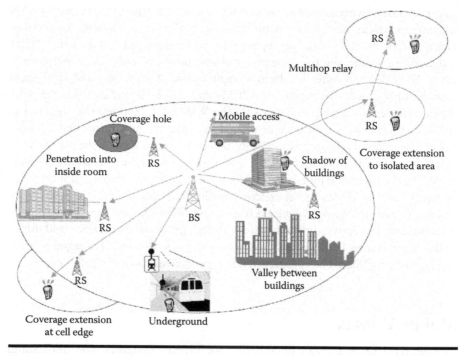

Figure 3.13 Concept of 802.16 mobile multihop relay (CMMR). (Courtesy of http://www.ieee802.org/16/sg/mmr/.)

- 802.16 mmr
  - interworks with the others following 802.16, and
  - different from those of 802.1D, 802.1Q, 802.1ad, and 802.11s,
  - happy to work together with those, if necessary.

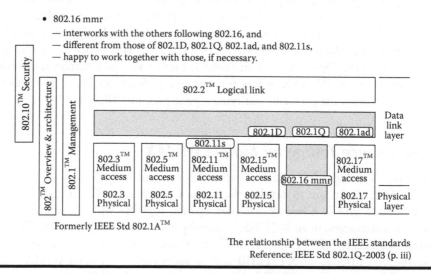

The relationship between the IEEE standards
Reference: IEEE Std 802.1Q-2003 (p. iii)

Figure 3.14 Distinction of MMR with other technologies. (Courtesy of http://www.ieee802.org/16/sg/mmr/.)

T2230), and a protocol analyzer tool (MINT T2240). MINT T2110 is based on Cetecom's technology and a set of standard test equipments, and it covers the transmitter and receiver test cases for BS and SS, supports several profiles, and provides a powerful Test Manager to automate the testing processes. MINT T2230 protocol conformance tester for mobile WiMAX testing, according to the IEEE 802.16e-2005 standard, is under development. The architecture is based on Cetecom's Dynamically Reconfigurable Wireless Signalling Unit built with picoChip's hardware PC102 that allows scalability and software reconfigurability. The MINT T2230 will include the official TTCN code delivered by ETSI for certification. Using the same architecture, the MINT T2240 is a protocol analyzer tool (sniffer) suitable to debug, test, and verify the development of the 802.16e-2005 protocol, which provides capturing, decoding, filtering, and displaying features.

Next-Generation OFDM: OFDMA

OFDMA is a multiple-access/multiplexing scheme closely related to OFDM. Like OFDM, OFDMA works by subdividing bandwidth into multiple frequency subcarriers. In OFDM, the input data stream is divided into several parallel substreams of reduced data rate, and each substream is modulated (by an Inverse Fast Fourier Transform, or IFFT) and transmitted on a separate orthogonal subcarrier. OFDMA takes things one step further, multiplexing data streams from multiple users onto DL subchannels and providing UL multiple access by means of UL subchannels. The OFDMA used in 802.16e is based on the scalable OFDM model. As a result, mobile WiMAX can use variable bandwidths; all you need to do is adjust the FFT size while fixing the subcarrier frequency spacing at 10.94 kHz. For now, mobile WiMAX supports both 5 MHz- and 10 MHz-wide systems. The next revision of the specification allows bandwidths of 7 MHz and 8.75 MHz using 7.81 KHz and 9.77 KHz for the spacing [6]. OFDMA uses data subcarriers for data transmission, pilot subcarriers for estimation and synchronization purposes, and null subcarriers for guard bands. OFDMA groups active (data and pilot) subcarriers into subsets called *subchannels*. The minimum frequency-time resource unit of subchannelization is one slot, which is equal to 48 data tones (subcarriers). There are two types of subcarrier permutations for subchannelization: diversity and contiguous. The diversity permutation draws subcarriers pseudorandomly to form a subchannel. This provides frequency diversity and intercell interference averaging. The contiguous permutation groups a block of contiguous subcarriers to form a subchannel. However, when formed, the subchannel is home to adaptive modulation and coding (AMC) for uploads and downloads. AMC enables multi-user diversity by allowing users to choose the subchannel with an optimal frequency response. Diversity is best suited for mobile applications, whereas contiguous works best for fixed, portable (moving from one fixed site to another fixed site), and low-mobility situations [6].

OFDMA is the solid center of the 802.16e specification, but it is not the whole show. For instance, Time Division Duplex (TDD) will be the supported mode of operation in the specifications first release. With TDD, the DL/UL ratios are adjustable, and it supports channel reciprocity, which is important when using MIMO and other antenna technologies. Also, TDD only uses a single channel for uplink and downlink. Another feature, hybrid auto repeat request (HARQ), enables fast response to packet errors, which are reported by a dedicated ACK channel in the uplink. HARQ also enables asynchronous operation, with a variable delay between retransmissions. Of course, retransmission overhead will slow throughput down somewhat, but the need for data integrity is just as important as blazing speed [6]. Mobile WiMAX's QoS support looks pretty spiffy. The QoS parameters associated with the specific kind of data to be transmitted define the transmission ordering and the scheduling for the on-the-air interface. The parameters can be dynamically managed through MAC messages for whatever service is in use. For example, VoIP wants a maximum sustained rate and has a high latency and "jitter" tolerance. Streaming audio or video also wants the maximum sustained rate but with a traffic priority. The MAC allows these kinds of adjustments using a scheduler located at each base station. You can use the scheduler to allocate available resources to satisfy bursty data traffic and any variations in the channel's condition. The scheduler works on both the uplink and DL parts of transmissions. The specification calls for two types of power consumption (besides "on") in the mobile unit: sleep mode and idle mode. In sleep mode, the mobile unit prenegotiates a period of unavailability between itself and the BS. The idle mode differs in that the mobile unit makes itself periodically available for downloaded broadcast traffic. In idle mode, a mobile unit is not linked with any specific BS. This means the mobile may traverse multiple BSs without going through a hand-off operation (which would require that power be expended in functionally unneeded radio transmissions). A mobile unit in idle mode can be paged to alert it to pending download traffic. For security, 802.16e relies on a key-management protocol, device and user authentication, and traffic encryption (using the AES algorithm for block encryption). The traffic encryption uses a periodic key refresh to avoid brute force and dictionary attacks. Handovers between cells utilize a three-way handshake designed to block monkey-in-the-middle attacks. The security is end-to-end and seems reasonably designed [6]. Mobile WiMAX really means the practical, real-world extensions to IEEE 802.16e, which are being developed under the WiMAX Forum industry group to allow solutions to real-world problems like interoperability. Although mobile WiMAX is envisioned as a global standard, the frequencies at which the Air Interface Standard operates will vary from country to country. It is too high-powered for unlicensed use, so it needs licensed frequencies around the 2-GHz transmission sweet spot, though 5 GHz is a possibility [6].

Today's operators require a smooth path to mobility, one that provides a future-proof solution, protects their investment, and provides a sound business case. OFDM with subchannelization may be just the cost-effective solution they are after for their fixed-to-basic mobility business model [7] — a solution that drives strong value differences in today's broadband mobility market. In contrast to OFDMA, OFDM has already gone through the definition stage and is now heading to full implementation. Today, a growing number of chip manufacturers, as well as original design manufacturers (ODMs) and equipment makers, are developing their solutions based on OFDM256 WiMAX technology. This technology is field proven, making it a safe choice for current and future deployments. By the end of 2005, many manufacturers will benefit from low-cost CPE packaging such as miniPCI and other high-volume manufacturing formats, providing broadband service providers access to cost-effective solutions. OFDM 802.16e highlights the operator's need for a smooth path to mobility, one that provides a future-proof solution, protects their investment, and provides a sound business case. For the operator who is deploying fixed wireless access solutions today, and who wants to offer nomadic or mobile services in the future, OFDM256 is the only choice [7].

WiMAX Architecture

WiMAX offers a rich feature set and flexibility, which also increases the complexity of service deployment and provisioning for fixed and mobile networks.

Figure 3.15 shows the management reference model for BWA networks. This consists of a network management system (NMS), some nodes, and a database. BS- and SS-managed nodes collect and store the managed objects in an 802.16 MIB format. Managed objects are made available to NMS using the Simple Network Management Protocol (SNMP). When a customer subscribes to the WiMAX service, the service provider asks the customer for the service flow information.

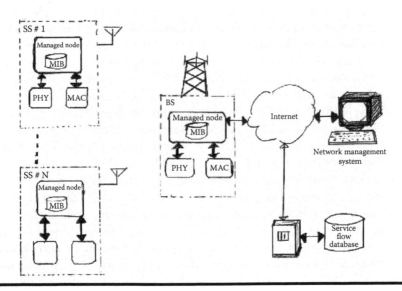

Figure 3.15 WiMAX management information base. (From Nair, G., Chou, J., Madejski, T., Perycz, K., Putzolu, D., and Sydir, J., IEEE 802.16 medium access control and service provisioning, *Intel Technology Journal*, 8(3), 2004.)

This would include number of UL/DL connections with the data rates and QoS parameters. The customer also needs to tell the kind of applications that he or she proposes to run. The service provider then proceeds to preprovision the services and enters the information in the service flow database.

The IEEE has specified how QoS is scheduled at the MAC layer, and this is currently being expanded by the WiMAX Forum to specify the architecture for delivering new services. Included in the emerging WiMAX standards is the ability to dynamically request premium delivery from the BS on behalf of applications and subscribers authorized by the wireless service Internet provider (WISP). Although the standards are not yet complete, the WiMAX Forum already has incorporated many of the concepts associated with the IP Multimedia Subsystem (IMS), a service delivery framework standardized by 3G PP. This framework specifies a common functional platform for next-generation converged multimedia services. The policy decision function (PDF) is responsible for dynamically allocating network resources on behalf of premium delivery walled garden services, whether voice, video, or gaming. The PDF combined with the intelligent edge SIP proxy, otherwise called the P-CSCF (call session control function), reserves and commits resources when a call is initiated (or received) by the WISP subscriber.

Offering Premium Services Over WiMAX

Like the evolution of voice services, broadband data services are rapidly migrating from a single-provider, fixed-connection environment to a multiple-provider, wireless offering. The promise of wireless broadband is that, regardless of where a subscriber is located or the current capabilities of the incumbent wireline service provider, broadband data services are readily available over the air. One wireless delivery technology that makes this both possible and practical is WiMAX [8]. Whether due to its sheer bandwidth capabilities or emerging extensions that will add mobility, WiMAX's ability to enable premium mobile broadband services is unparalleled. Its underlying MAC Protocol, borrowed substantively from the cable industry's Data Over Cable Service Interface Specifications (DOCSIS) standard, offers Wireless Internet Service Providers (WISPs) the ability to precisely manage the QoS to the individual subscriber and application in real time [8]. What this means for the subscriber is nearly flawless delivery of IP data. For WISPs, it means the ability to offer high-quality, revenue-generating applications such as VoIP, streaming video, gaming, and commercial services [8]. WiMAX's MAC layer includes a traffic scheduler that is primarily responsible for queuing both upstream and downstream data flows by shaping the IP flows at the MAC layer with firmware located in the BS. Previous broadband wireless technologies offered only coarse prioritization capabilities. WiMAX, however, based on the core IEEE 802.16 standard, offers a menu of QoS management techniques that are available for applications to request parameterized QoS, defined by precise allocation of bandwidth, latency, and jitter to each specific service flow. Within this framework, external network elements, acting on behalf of applications and service provider policies, can direct the traffic scheduler in the BS regarding how to shape the traffic. For VoIP data, this means that the CODEC-specific bandwidth can be scheduled with a latency that minimizes dropped packets. For real-time, high-resolution streaming video, the bandwidth can be temporarily and dynamically increased — beyond WISP's statically provisioned values. Each service flow is specified by a flow specification interpreted by the BS that incorporates the application-specific QoS characteristics. Included in this flow specification is the type of service that defines how upstream flows are scheduled. WiMAX service providers can statically provision their access networks and provide best-effort treatment to most IP data, and QoS policy management technology offers them the unique ability to intelligently manage their network and become a "Smart RAN."

By managing the data flow specific to each application or content, WISPs can differentiate their own walled garden services from those of third-party content providers such as Vonage or Google. Leveraging this capability, a WISP not only gains the ability to further monetize the value of its underlying capital investment but it also becomes a mission-critical partner, particularly to its business customers. QoS policy management is an essential ingredient in order for WISPs to offer service level agreements (SLAs) to its most demanding, and often highest margin, customers. When the call goes off hook, the SIP message is processed by the P-CSCF, which authorizes the call by verifying the subscriber in the subscriber database (known as the HSS). It then requests the network resources required for the specific CODEC from the PDF. The PDF can admit or deny a request for QoS, depending on whether the network resources are available over the subscriber-specific RAN and on the WISP usage policies [8]. If the VoIP service is charged incrementally versus flat fee, the PDF generates a Remote Dial-In User Service (RADIUS) event message to a billing system. It further maps the IMS core to a multitude of BSs, thereby allowing the service provider to centrally locate its policy management — and, in particular, coordinate its network policies with other network elements and even access network types. In addition to Session Initiation Protocol (SIP)-based communications, this architecture can support premium-delivery legacy desktop applications such as peer-to-peer PC gaming, file transfers, and VoIP. Whereas centrally hosted application servers can dynamically request bandwidth for the duration of an authorized user's session, peer-to-peer or third-party applications can use a client smart agent, similar to an IMS SIP client, to monitor application network usage and signal for QoS on behalf of authorized applications. The agent is authenticated and authorized by either the P-CSCF or a discreet application function that performs similar functionality in concert with a specific application's resource requirements [8]. By adopting a best-in-breed IMS architecture for WiMAX, service providers can confidently start deploying new, premium-delivery services today with an eye on the future. For example, toll-quality SIP-based VoIP can be deployed with a PDF, SIP proxy or session border controller (SBC), feature server, and media gateway, in addition to a WiMAX-compatible BS. Once the service provider has comfortably deployed its voice service, additional services can be supported, such as video, PC games, and commercial services. This requires gracefully adding additional application and feature services to the aforementioned core network elements [8]. Because the PDF plays the crucial role of applying service-provider policies to the performance of applications over the RAN, it must incorporate a rich rule set that accounts for application types, BS capability, and business logic. In addition, it should be capable of maintaining ongoing sessions (called statefulness) in case of system failures and emergency preemption [8].

The Deployment Outlook

The first form of the WiMAX standard primarily supports fixed wireless access, so the initial deployment will most likely be in non-cellular data-networking applications. Companies that have been marketing proprietary OFDM systems have a market foothold from which to deploy WiMAX-certified BS in small towns or cities. Service providers in metropolitan areas may use WiMAX as their technology of choice over DSL and cable modems. Rural service providers in both developed and developing countries may need to deploy the WiMAX BS, introduce an attractive sign-up package, and then provide the CPEs to subscribers via the mail or in-store pickup. Other WiMAX players will include Wi-Fi product vendors, pure-play CPE companies, and traditional networking equipment manufacturers. The Wi-Fi product vendors can leverage their existing sales channels by incorporating WiMAX into their products as a way to backhaul hot spot traffic to the public WAN. Because WiMAX deployment requires the push of service providers, the Wi-Fi product vendors must work with these providers for product launch. The pure-play CPE companies will most likely either partner with BS companies that have service provider ties or solicit the service providers to evaluate their products.

Understanding the enormous potentials of the fixed wireless networking market, networking equipment makers have shown great interest in WiMAX. Like the Wi-Fi product vendors, networking equipment makers will have to work with the service providers for deployment. As the 802.16d standard evolves, a variety of wireless products such as WiMAX-enabled Internet access cards will appear. Similarly, as 802.16e becomes the mobile standard for the WMAN, products such as laptops, PDAs, and cell phones will be the revenue drivers. In the early days of deployment, trial networks will be scattered around the globe. Once users understand WiMAX's benefits, the adoption rate could spread like wildfire — a possible scenario for 2006 and beyond. Toward that goal, the companies participating in WiMAX product development are establishing a foundation of high-performance, affordable silicon and systems that customers will find irresistible. To address the unique demands posed by broadband mobility and to bring about further increases in range and throughput, as well as meet user demands for flexibility, new air interfaces, modulation techniques, smart antenna systems, and digital signal processing devices had to be designed. A number of local operators have approached the challenge of providing connectivity to the mobile Internet user, whose appetites are for much higher data rates, in unique and varied ways. Analysts said the first WiMAX-certified products will likely be BSs for carriers looking to expand coverage in remote areas and take on traffic burdens in congested areas. BSs are similar to cell towers in that they send and receive transmissions. WiMAX BSs can blanket an area by connecting to a wired connection or linking with other BSs. Figures 3.16 through Figure 3.21 illustrate various deployment scenarios of WiMAX 802.16.

The high-speed WBA based on WiMAX promises an economically viable solution for accelerating Internet adoption, and through that, bettering the education system, healthcare, E-governance, and citizen and entertainment services. WiMAX will coexist with the existing DSL, just as Wi-Fi is being used as an overlay to the existing wired network. WiMAX 802.16d will speed up broadband deployment and will be useful in inaccessible regions [10]. Then there is a citizen multiple video conferencing setup, wherein the city administration and officials can interact with citizens at the telecenter, and all this is being enabled through WiMAX (operating in 3.3- to 3.4-GHz frequencies with 2 Mbps of broadband bandwidth available for video conferencing). This setup is helping in faster resolution of citizen queries, issues, and complaints by saving on travel time [10].

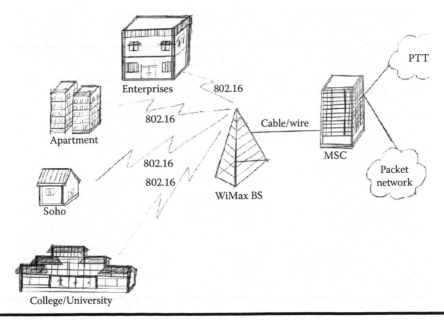

Figure 3.16 A general configuration of 802.16. (Courtesy of Smith, C. & Meyer, J., *3G Wireless with WiMax and Wi-Fi*, McGraw Hill Publishing, 2005, pp. 1–234.)

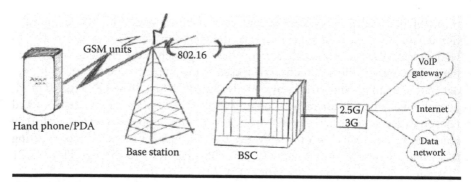

Figure 3.17   A backhaul configuration of 802.16 with GSM/UMTS networks.
(Courtesy of Smith, C. & Meyer, J., *3G Wireless with WiMax and Wi-Fi,*
McGraw Hill Publishing, 2005, pp. 1–234.)

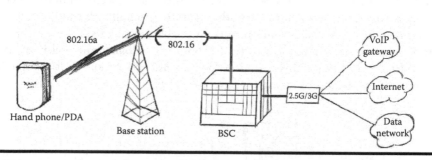

Figure 3.18   A last-mile configuration of 802.16 with GSM/UMTS networks.
(Courtesy of Smith, C. & Meyer, J., *3G Wireless with WiMax and Wi-Fi,*
McGraw Hill Publishing, 2005, pp. 1–234.)

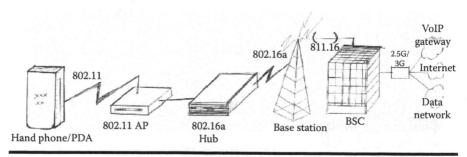

Figure 3.19   A backhaul configuration of 802.16 with Wi-Fi and 3G networks.
(Courtesy of Smith, C. & Meyer, J., *3G Wireless with WiMax and Wi-Fi,*
McGraw Hill Publishing, 2005, pp. 1–234.)

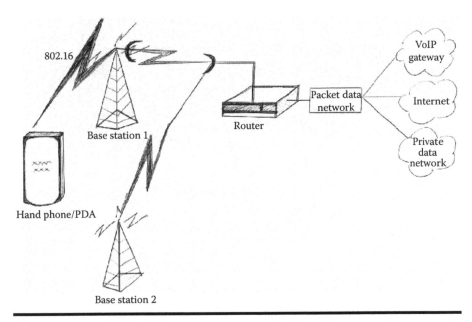

Figure 3.20 A general campus mobility configuration of 802.16e. (Courtesy of Smith, C. & Meyer, J., *3G Wireless with WiMax and Wi-Fi,* McGraw Hill Publishing, 2005, pp. 1–234.)

Although many competing access network technologies claim QoS capability, none are nearly as robust as the 802.16-2000 specification in combination with the WiMAX architecture (Figure 3.22). By intelligently managing the RAN, WISPs can not only maximize the value of their capital investments but reduce their operational expenses with carefully coordinated network management policies. True WiMAX service providers are uniquely positioned to not only maximize subscriber satisfaction in the face of enormous competition but also to gain incremental revenues associated with differentiated services. To do this, they must implement a centralized approach to policy management that coordinates the performance and functionality of applications including VoIP, video, and beyond. WiMAX is a standardized wireless technology designed to offer connectivity in a MAN. Prior to the emergence of WiMAX, proprietary technologies such as LMDS and MMDS occupied this segment, with varying degrees of success due to lack of client device installations, high BS costs, and the general barrier to market entry encumbering all proprietary solutions in a new market [11].

WiMAX will enter the communications market eventually in spite of potential architectural issues that arise when integrating multiple radio types into a small package, such as a mobile phone. Motorola's mobile device plans include integrating WiMAX into their complete phone portfolio. Nextel is among the lucky recipients. Motorola appears to be halfway through the process, but in the time frame of the

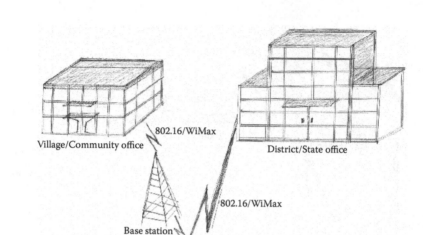

Figure 3.21 An E-Governance configuration with 802.16. (Courtesy of Smith, C. & Meyer, J., *3G Wireless with WiMax and Wi-Fi,* McGraw Hill Publishing, 2005, pp. 1–234; http://www.expresscomputeronline.com/20060814/market01. shtml [dated August14, 2006].)

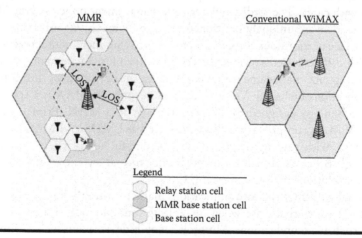

Figure 3.22 Network architecture — MMR versus conventional WiMAX. (Courtesy of http://www.ieee802.org/16/sg/mmr/.)

next 18 months, the 802.16 profile is not likely to be mature enough to support existing end products. In addition, the significant geographic areas that have true, unimpeded, drivers for mobile WiMAX are those with populations that, coincidentally, use public transportation on a broad scale. The United States, which represents roughly ⅓ of the world market for cell phones, is not a predominant public transportation consumer [11]. Although promising opportunities exist in areas and countries where wiring is exorbitant or impossible to provide, the necessary WiMAX infrastructure is by no means cost-effective in all such areas and communities. Finding its best opportunity, with regard to cost-effectiveness, in outlying but semi-urban suburbia at home, or abroad in countries where power grids are nonexistent, the market for WiMAX is limited in this sense, and, despite its promise, is still a long way from home base. Unlike ZigBee (IEEE 802.15.4) or Wi-Fi (IEEE 802.11x), both of which are upgrades and replacements of existing network infrastructures, the predominant market for WiMAX (IEEE 802.16d-2004) is in new infrastructure installations (Figure 3.23). This has likely been a barrier to an earlier success, but it seems that now WiMAX has finally found its way into the mainstream of market acceptance.

At the same time, the struggle is not yet quite over; mobile WiMAX (IEEE 802.16e) is rapidly gaining ground, threatening to leapfrog the recently defunct 802.20. The real eye-opening realization is that the tremendous interest in IEEE 802.16e is threatening the growth of WiMAX fixed applications. The IEEE 802.16e specification can address mobile applications and stationary applications, but WiMAX is today largely limited to stationary segments. If investing infrastructure capital in high-speed wireless for MAN applications, why would it make sense to invest in two technologies when it is possible to invest in only one?

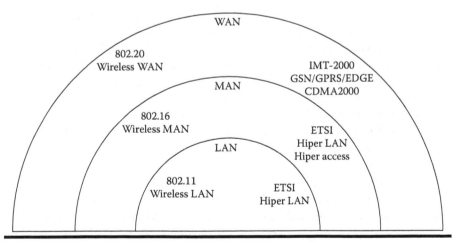

Figure 3.23   802.16 with respect to network deployment. (Courtesy of Smith, C. & Meyer, J., *3G Wireless with WiMax and Wi-Fi*, McGraw Hill Publishing, 2005, pp. 1–234.)

This last factor is the locus of major expenditure in creating the ubiquitous WiMAX grid. Most of the companies developing components for this market are hedging their bets, however, and bringing to market dual-band products that enable deployment of both mobile and fixed WiMAX environments. In Asia, WiMAX is emerging as the wireless technology of choice; Tokyo, Japan, has several WiMAX MAN installation projects in varying degrees of completion, involving a number of companies. Airspan and Yozan began with a budget of $12 million in November 2005 and has since expanded its range to Osaka and Nagoya with an additional $26 million. Okayama trials are under way now. Clearly, the aim is to make the endeavor a successful one and in no time introduce versatility by way of the upgrading option to mobile WiMAX (IEEE 802.16e). Airspan already offers a WiMAX USB adapter for mobile users. The Airspan and Yozan teams are not alone in their effort to successfully introduce WiMAX to mainstream communication. NTT-DoCoMo, working in collaboration with other NTT group companies, will conduct wireless WiMAX tests in the Yoyogi area of Tokyo for about one year from March 2006, assessing wireless throughput, optimal parameters, and characteristics of handset speed to name the most obvious, using the 2.5-GHz frequency band. In the United States, there are obstacles of a different sort, whereas other countries are hamstrung by regulatory hurdles, corruption, or lack of economic maturity. Given that the market structure is demand driven, the delay or sluggish interest is caused by the absence of a market driver. One need only look at the example of Wi-Fi as an indicator, to be repeated again and again in whatever next big thing that is coming along. The first move that elevated the visibility of Wi-Fi into market cognizance came with its name change from IEEE 802.11 to WECA-compatible to Wi-Fi. The second was that Apple included Wi-Fi as "airport" option in its 1999 laptops, but it was not until Intel launched its Centrino chip in conjunction with Wi-Fi in its laptops did Wi-Fi catch on. It was, of course, dependent on a growing availability of hot spots, which was, in turn, driven by Intel's $200,000 Wi-Fi marketing campaign. However, there is an ancillary caution to this: the hot spot explosion was anything but a financial boom, as service providers realized that little profit was to be had from hot spot offerings, for both Wi-Fi and Bluetooth. Given this, and the fact that at this point in time there is little visible interest in WiMAX on the part of the general population, it is most likely that in the United States WiMAX will play a minor market role, and mobile WiMAX (IEEE 802.16e) will quickly come from behind and take the lion's share of the WiMAX market within a very short time.

Some of this may not be as far-fetched as it seems. Intel is certainly talking to companies and governments in Third World countries, South America, Europe, and the Eastern countries of the European periphery. Motorola, too, has expanded its horizons. Primary target markets today include those geographical areas with high GDP growth potential: South Africa, Vietnam, Pakistan, and India. This makes sense given the broad market reach of Motorola today and its requirement to reach into the nebulous underdeveloped Third World regions to increase overall market share. Why not China? First, China does not have the spectrum allocated for fixed WiMAX use at this point. Second, China is single-handedly undermining the entire semiconductor industry by building subsidized fabs and offering manufacturing services at or below cost. Intel is today moving to Third World countries with WiMAX technology. In Nigeria, with a population of roughly 130 million, fixed WiMAX is beginning to take off, with six licensees introducing services and 13 more in the works, all in the 3.5-GHz band. The topology of Nigeria is largely flat, and hence WiMAX will fare well in the environment and, all things being equal, could become a significant factor in the economic revitalization and modernization of the country.

Standardization and interoperability are keys to a successful integration of WiMAX into products, as evidenced by the existence of the hitherto customary collaboration between the IEEE and technology industry alliances, in this case the WiMAX Forum. Keeping in mind that WiMAX is capable of proprietary applications on top of the IEEE 802.16e standard, there is not likely to be an end to the search for the easiest, fastest, user-friendliest, always on status in the wireless high-speed arena. Rather than being a disruptive technology, WiMAX is evolutionary, which means that it is likely to graduate rapidly from fixed to mobile, i.e., its IEEE 802.16e version. Already WiMAX mobile is not the only contender in the high-speed wireless arena; it has a rival in WiBro, the Korean version of mobile WiMAX, licensed by South Korea's KT Corp. (KTC). WiBro allows Internet access at any traveling speed, making download links possible even if moving at 60 mi/hr. Yet, already a new wireless mobile communication service on the horizon in Korea, the 3.5G technology HSDPA (High-Speed Downlink Packet Access), is capable of being more than six times faster in data transfer. This means that whereas downloading an MP3 music file takes 10 s today, it would take 2 s with HSDPA; and to download data from a station could theoretically be as fast as 14 Mbps, though more likely 2 to 7 Mbps. Further, although most advanced countries are still, often slowly, rolling out broadband, South Korea is ready to move to the next level, which is nationwide 50–100 Mbps fiber-to-the-home (FTTH) and mobile access to a single IP-based network capable of handling and offering every thinkable service, especially multimedia services. Broadband with 8 to 10 Mbps now reaches 70 to 80 percent of the homes and businesses in South Korea, which means there is a burgeoning demand for better and faster data communications. More than 30 million of the nation's 48 million population carry wireless Internet-capable cell phones, and hence it is simply the next step for the government to maintain the momentum and to deploy WiBro today, and most likely HSDPA tomorrow. Therefore, it is understandable that South Korea's Samsung Electronics and LG Electronics have invested heavily in WiMAX development, and all of the country's telecom firms are members of the WiMAX Forum, including now Samsung. South Korea has also reached an agreement with the IEEE 802.16 Working Group on the specifications of WiBro. Other members of the WiMAX Forum are mindful of the fact that South Korea is moving into a leading position, ready to export its know-how. In the United States, Texas Instruments recently completed three chip sets for both WiMAX fixed and mobile applications. The fabless semiconductor company, Athena, also chimed in with an RF transceiver that supports both WiMAX and WiBro. GigaBeam and Adaptix showcased their WiMAX and WiBro technology at a recent Broadband Wireless World Forum. However, Samsung is likely to be the link that will bridge the technological divide between South Korea and the ROW, of which the United States, by all appearances, seems to be one.

Quality of Service (QoS)

WiMAX QoS depends crucially on the 802.16 Layers 1 and 2, as these govern the all-important BS/user-terminal radio access — an inherently difficult environment compared to, say, a wireline broadband network. Because the d/e forms of 802.16 are aimed at different applications — fixed terminals and mobile terminals, respectively — there are significant differences in technology between them. In particular, 802.16d used OFDM, or ODM for those in a hurry, and 802.16e uses OFDMA or ODMA. The capabilities of these technologies have a direct impact on end-user services and QoS [12]. Table 3.1 summarizes some of the key technical features of the fixed and mobile forms of 802.16. Two basic characteristics are a radio interface that uses adaptive modulation to adapt performance to the prevailing channel conditions of the user, and OFDM techniques to reduce the impact of multipath interference. This makes WiMAX suitable for near- and NLoS environments such as urban areas [12].

Table 3.1   Features of Fixed and Mobile WiMAX

WiMAX Fixed (IEEE 802.16-2004/ETSI HiperMAN)	WiMAX Mobile (802.16e)
Frequencies specified as sub-11 GHz	Frequencies specified as sub-6 GHz
Scaleable channel widths specified (1.75 MHz to 20 MHz)	Scaleable OFDMA 128, 512, 1024, 2048 (not 256)
256-Carrier OFDM	Subchannelization
FDD and TDD multiplexing	Questions over backward compatibility (256-carrier OFDMA not specified)
Deterministic QoS	
Adaptive modulation(BPSK/QPSK/16QAM/QAM)	
Uplink subchannelization	

Source: Light Reading, 2006; http://www.unstrung.com/document.asp?site=unstrung&doc_id=103315&page_number=1.

Table 3.2   Wireless Technologies and Their MAC Characteristics

	3G HSPDA	3G EV-DO	WiMAX 802.16.2004	WiMAX 802.16e	Wi-Fi
Bandwidth, MHz	5	1.25	<20	<20	20
Data rates, Mbit/s	14.4	2.4	75	75	11, 54
Bit/Hz	2.9	1.92	3.75	3.75	2.7
Multiple access	TDMA, CDMA	CDMA	OFDMA	OFDMA	CSMA/CA
Duplexing	FDD	FDD	TDD/FDD/HD-FDD	TDD	
Mobility	Full	Full	Portable	Nomadic/full	Portable
Coverage	Large	Large	Mid	Mid	Small

Source: Freescale Semiconductor, 2006; http://www.unstrung.com/document.asp?site=unstrung&doc_id=103315&page_number=1.

Another important feature is the 802.16 MAC, which, if required, can offer deterministic QoS. This is crucial because it makes it practical to offer services such as voice and T1/E1-type services. The 802.16e revision was important primarily because it introduced the new physical layer based on OFDMA but with variable subcarrier permutations from 128 to 2048 carriers. This is sometimes called scalable OFDMA (SOFDMA) because the number of subcarriers would typically scale with the channel bandwidth. Bandwidth scalability is one of the most important advantages of OFDMA. Table 3.2 summarizes some of the MAC/silicon characteristics of these technologies [12].

It is fairly clear from this perspective that the two 3G technologies and Wi-Fi are very different and occupy opposite poles as far as mobility and (current geographical) coverage are concerned. WiMAX is more in the middle. However, because of the efficiency of its air interface and the channel sizes used, 802.16 supports higher data rates than both 3G and Wi-Fi. Also, says Rouwet, 802.16 has been very well designed as an IP-based network, which allows a very high level of QoS [12].

WiMAX QoS Architecture

The WiMAX Forum Applications Working Group (AWG) has determined five initial application classes, as listed in Figure 3.24. Initial WiMAX Forum-certified systems are capable of supporting these five classes simultaneously.

One metric missing from Figure 3.24 is mobility, specifically the handover between sectors and cells. This is likely to be added in the forthcoming wave of mobile WiMAX profiles due to start later in 2006. As luck would have it, the

Class	Application	Bandwidth Guideline		Latency Guideline		Jitter Guideline	
1	Interactive gaming	Low bandwidth	50 kbit/s	Low latency	80 ms	N/A	
2	Voice Telephone (VOIP) video conference	Low bandwidth	32–64 kbit/s	Low latency	160 ms	Low jittering	<50 ms
3	Streaming media	Moderate to high bandwidth	<2 Mbit/s	N/A		Low jittering	<100 ms
4	Instant messaging Web browsing	Moderate bandwidth	2 Mbit/s	N/A		N/A	
5	Media content download	High bandwidth	10 Mbit/s	N/A		N/A	

Figure 3.24 WiMAX application classes. (Courtesy of www.wimaxforum.org.)

application classes map to the five QoS classes specified in the 802.16 standards, as shown in Table 3.3.

The really big question is: how do you map radio resources to a user's service classes? This is the task of the scheduling algorithm, which is likely to be a key area of differentiation among BS equipment vendors. To a degree, this is seen in the 3G HSDPA systems being rolled out currently — the performance of the scheduler is a potential differentiator among equipment providers in what is otherwise a quite standardized environment, as it helps operators use spectrum more efficiently and deliver better services [12]. In simplistic terms, for, say, DL operation, packets arrive from the network at the BS, and are placed in DL user traffic queues. The scheduler decides which user traffic to map into a frame from the queues, and the appropriate burst is generated, together with the appropriate MAP information element. Users are scheduled according to their service classes (UGS, rtPS, ertPS, nrtPS, and BE). MAPs contain information on transmission to or from all users for each frame, including modulation and coding type, and size and position of allocation [12]. Scheduling in this way on a frame-by-frame basis gives a lot of flexibility, but it does create issues, particularly in the frame allocation overhead needed (as shown in red in Figure 3.25 for OFDMA).

A further issue is the amount of padding bytes needed to ensure that each burst forms a rectangle that can be packed correctly into an OFDMA frame. Ideally, to maximize transmission efficiency, the number of padding bytes should be zero, but

Table 3.3   802.16 QoS Classes

Class	Description	Minimum Rate	Maximum Rate	Latency	Jitter	Priority
Unsolicited grant service	VoIP, E1; fixed-size packets on periodic basis	—	x	x	x	—
Real-time polling service	Streaming audio/video	x	x	x	—	x
Enhanced real-time polling service	VoIP with activity detection	x	x	x	x	x
Non-real-time polling service	FTP	x	x	—	—	x
Best-effort	Data transfer, Web browsing, etc.	—	x	—	—	x

Note: x = QoS specified. *Source:* Light Reading, 2006.

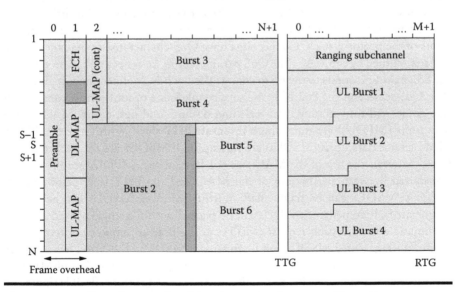

Figure 3.25   Allocation overhead for OFDMA. (Courtesy of http://www. freescale.com/.)

this may not be possible, and will depend on the number of users, their QoS, the applications they are running, and, of course, on the decisions the scheduler is taking. So, WiMAX operators may face trade-offs between transmission efficiency and service offerings, depending on the scenarios they plan to support [12]. Generally speaking, OFDM allows a simple, relatively straightforward scheduler design, giving good performance for larger packet sizes, as the overhead/padding problem is not so important. This makes it suitable for the needs of certain data services, such as legacy TDM. However, a larger packet size increases the latency of the connection, which can be an issue [12]. OFDMA, on the other hand, gives a smaller granularity of bandwidth grants than OFDM, so there is less overhead wasted for small packet sizes. Similarly, the smaller granularity of MAPs means that less overhead is wasted in MAP allocation. Also, OFDMA has the potential for using AMC in "fixed" environments with known channel responses. It can, for example, pre-allocate specific subchannels that have a known good performance over the physical layer to a certain user. However, this use of AMC has the drawback that, by reserving certain subchannels for one user, it reduces the pool of subchannels available to other users and, therefore, limits the scheduler's flexibility and dynamic range [12].

WiMAX supports both TDD and FDD modes of operation on air, along with a range of channel bandwidths. The OFDM PHY mode, which is also known as WMAN-OFDM, is specified for use between 2 and 11 GHz. The 802.16 MAC controls access of the BSs and SSs to the air through a rich set of features. The on-air timing is based on consecutive frames that are divided into slots. The size of frames and the size of individual slots within the frames can be varied on a frame-by-frame basis under the control of a scheduler in the BS. This allows effective allocation of on-air resources to meet the demands of the active connections with their granted QoS properties. The 802.16 MAC provides a connection-oriented service to upper layers of the protocol stack. Connections have QoS characteristics that are granted and maintained by the MAC. The QoS parameters for a connection can be varied by the SS, making requests to the BS to change them while a connection is maintained [15]. QoS service in the 802.16 MAC service takes one of four forms: constant bit rate grant, real-time polling, non-real-time polling, and best effort. MAC packet data units (MPDUs) are transmitted in on-air PHY slots. Within these MPDUs, MAC service data units (MSDUs) are transmitted. MSDUs are the packets transferred between the top of the MAC and the layer above. MPDUs are the packets transferred between the bottom of the MAC and the PHY layer below. Across MPDUs, MSDUs can be fragmented. Within MPDUs, MSDUs can be packed (aggregated). Fragments of MSDUs can be packed within a single packed MPDU. Automatic retransmission request (ARQ) can be used to request the retransmission of unfragmented MSDUs and fragments of MSDUs. The MAC has a privacy sublayer that performs authentication, key exchange, and encryption of MPDUs. Through the use of flexible PHY modulation and coding options, flexible frame and slot allocations, flexible QoS mechanisms, packing, fragmentation, and ARQ, the 802.16 standard can be used to deliver broadband voice and data into cells that may have a wide range of properties. This includes a wide range of population densities, a wide range of cell radii, and a wide range of propagation environments. Convergence sublayers at the top of the MAC enable Ethernet, ATM, TDM voice, and IP services to be offered over 802.16. WiMAX defines interoperable system profiles targeted for common licensed and unlicensed bands used around the world. This enables 802.16-based equipment to be used in diverse spectrum allocations around the world [15]. IEEE 802.16 also considers optional subchannelization in uplink. This feature is particularly useful when a power-limited platform such as a laptop is considered in the subscriber station in an indoor portable or mobile environment. With a subchannelization factor of $\frac{1}{16}$, a 12-dB link budget enhancement can be achieved. Sixteen sets of twelve subcarriers each are defined, where one, two, four, eight, or all sets can be assigned to an SS in uplink. The eight pilot carriers are used when more than one set of subchannels is allocated. To support and handle time variation in the channel, the 802.16 standard provisions optional, more frequent repetition of preambles. In the UL path, short preambles, called mid-ambles for this purpose, can be repeated with a programmable repetition period. In the DL direction, a short preamble can be optionally inserted at the beginning of all DL bursts in addition to the long preamble that is presented by default at the beginning of the frame. A proper implementation of the BS scheduler guarantees the minimum required repetition interval for channel estimation [15].

Security

The 802.16 security methods are derived from those defined in DOCSIS. DES in cipher block chaining (CBC) mode is used to encrypt the payload of MPDUs on transport and secondary management connections. The PKM Protocol is used for certificate-based authorization of the SS and to perform transfer of keys between the BS and the SS. Although the encipherment process takes place over the payload of the MPDU, all the details of fragmentation, packing, grant requests, and ARQ are hidden from view. The PKM Protocol uses certificates and RSA public key methods to authenticate an SS to a BS. The SS provides its X.509 certificate to the BS, thus revealing its identity and public key to the BS. The BS returns an authorization key to the SS, protected by the SS's public key using the RSA algorithm. The SS can decrypt the authorization key using its private key. The authorization key is then used to derive key encryption keys (KEKs), the SS and BS, because they both know the authorization key can derive the same KEKs. To transfer a TEK (temporal encryption key) from the BS to the SS, the TEK is encrypted using the Data Encryption Standard (DES) in EDE mode, keys with a KEK. The TEKs are those used by the CBC-DES algorithm to encrypt the MPDU data [16]. In light of the increased security threats and concerns in a mobile environment, the 802.16e specification includes security enhancements to use the AES-CCM cipher mode and EAP-based authentication. There are also proposals to address new features in future standardization work. These proposed new features include directed mesh extensions and point-to-point enhancements [16].

Michel Barbeau [17] examined threats to the security of the WiMAX/802.16 BWA technology. Threats associated with the PHY and MAC layer were reviewed, and the likelihood, impact, and risk were evaluated according to a threat assessment methodology proposed by the ETSI. Threats are listed and ranked according to the level of risk they represent. This work can be used to prioritize future research directions in WiMAX/802.16 security. An analysis of the threats to the security of the WiMAX/802.16 BWA networks has been conducted [17]. Critical threats are eavesdropping of management messages, BS or MS masquerading, management message modification, and DoS attack. Major threats are jamming and data traffic modification (when AES is not applied). Countermeasures need to be devised for networks using the security options with critical or major risks. An intrusion detection system approach can be used to address some of the threats. More research is needed in this direction [17]. With WiMAX promising to solve the bandwidth bottleneck, many carriers are looking to networking OEMs to provide robust security solutions—particularly VPNs and firewalls — in their edge devices, allowing them to securely deliver feature-rich services to subscribers while protecting their own networks. Software original design manufacturers are now entering the fray to ensure that device vendors can provide carriers with these next-generation converged platforms while adhering to the strict certification processes and rigid standards of quality in shorter development cycles [16]. Building on the exploits and flaws found in the 802.11 protocol, the WiMAX standard was drafted with security in mind, offering more robust protection in the form of certificate-based encryption. However, regardless of the inherently stronger and more robust authentication measures in the 802.16a Protocol, there remains a battery of implications that OEMs face in developing their networking devices with this new access technology, each as multifaceted as the next, but none too unfamiliar to the seasoned developer [16]. In a WiMAX installation, a fixed wireless BS, similar in concept to a cell phone tower, serves an "always-on" radio signal directly accessible by WiMAX-enabled clients, with no need for leased lines or an intermediate AP. Similar to 802.11, the 802.16 MAC Protocol, a sublayer of the data-link layer, governs the client's access to the physical layer. However, the scheduling algorithm within the 802.16 MAC Protocol offers optimal prioritization of this traffic based on first-in first-out (FIFO) scheduling, in which clients seeking access to the BS are assigned bandwidth upon time of initial access instead of random queue assignment based on the order of the MAC address (as in 802.11). Furthermore, the 802.16 MAC Protocol ensures optimal QoS over its Wi-Fi predecessor, allocating bandwidth effectively by balancing clients' needs instead of "best-effort service," i.e., equal distribution of what remains after allocation to other clients. Additionally, rather than encrypt the radio signal using WEP, WPA/PSK, or any other existing Layer 2 WLAN security protocol, 802.16a's baseline authentication architecture, by default, employs X.509-based PKI (public key infrastructure) certificate authorization, in which the BS validates the client's digital certificate before permitting access to the PHY. A wireless network should be treated as having a higher security risk than an internal

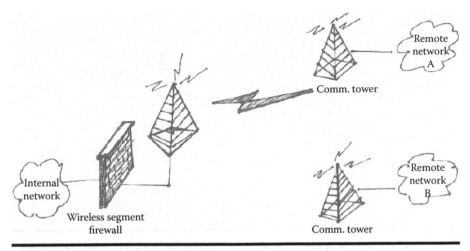

Figure 3.26   Wireless segment separated by a firewall. (Courtesy of http://rfdesign.com/mag/508RFDF1.pdf.)

physical network. It is always a good idea to separate the wireless network from sensitive resources. System administrators should police all traffic passing between a wireless segment and the rest of the network [16]. Figure 3.26 illustrates a wireless segment separated from the rest of the network by a firewall. In this case, the firewall is a logical concept and can mean just another Ethernet port on your existing firewall [16]. Figure 3.27 illustrates a wireless environment with a firewall at every location participating in a hub-and-spoke VPN [16].

However, in some scenarios, it might be desirable to implement a full intrusion detection system (IDS) in a wireless segment. This allows administrators to monitor the links for traffic anomalies, attack signatures and other malicious traffic. In the Figure 3.26 and Figure 3.27 scenarios, IDS can be deployed just after the wireless segment firewall. If malicious traffic manages to evade the security measures of the firewall, it will be caught by the IDS system [16]. Some IDS systems will allow you to implement advanced technologies such as Honeypot or Darknet, allowing proactive monitoring of hacker activity on both wireless and wired networks [16]. In an emergency, communication is crucial for government officials as they try to determine the cause of the problem, find out who may be injured, and coordinate rescue efforts or cleanup operations. A gas-line explosion or terrorist attack could sever the cables that connect leaders and officials with their vital information networks. WiMAX could be used to set up a backup (or even primary) communications system that would be difficult to destroy with a single, pinpoint attack. A cluster of WiMAX transmitters would be set up in the range of a key command center but as far from each other as possible. Each transmitter would be in a bunker hardened against bombs and other attacks. No single attack could destroy all of the transmitters, so the officials in the command center would remain in communication at all times

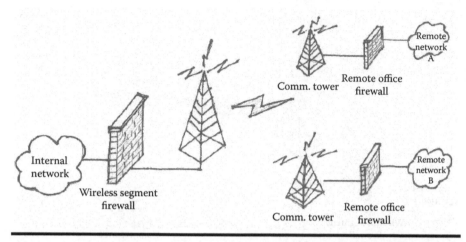

Figure 3.27   Firewall at every location. (Courtesy of http://rfdesign.com/mag/508RFDF1.pdf.)

[18]. Despite good intentions for WiMAX security, there are several potential attacks open to adversaries, including rogue BSs, DoS attacks, man-in-the-middle attacks, and network manipulation with spoofed management frames. The real test of WiMAX security will come when providers begin wide-scale network deployments, and researchers and attackers have access to commodity customer premises equipment (CPE). Other attacks, including WiMAX Protocol fuzzing, may enable attackers to further manipulate BSs or SSs. Until then, the security of WiMAX is limited to speculation. Recognizing the importance of security, the 802.16 working groups designed several mechanisms for authentication and encryption to protect the service provider from theft of service and to protect the customer from unauthorized information disclosure [19].

References

1. http://ieee802.org/16/docs/01/80216-01_58r1.pdf.
2. http://www.convergedigest.com/bp-bbw/bp1.asp?ID=391&ctgy=Mesh [dated August 30, 2006].
3. Nair, G., Chou, J., Madejski, T., Perycz, K., Putzolu, D., and Sydir, J., IEEE 802.16 medium access control and service provisioning, *Intel Technology Journal*, 8(3), 2004.
4. http://www.ddj.com/dept/embedded/193004406?pgno=3.
5. http://www.ieee802.org/16/sg/mmr/.
6. http://www-128.ibm.com/developerworks/library/wi-roam49.html?ca=dgr-lnxw-09Mobile-WiMAX [dated August 17, 2006].
7. Dube, V., Mobile WiMax by enhanced OFDM, not OFDMA? WaveSat certainly thinks so..., WaveSat's White Paper, 2006.

8. http://www.telephonyworld.com/cgi-bin/news/viewnews.cgi?category=all&id=11527 54660 [dated July 12, 2006].
9. Smith, C. & Meyer, J., *3G Wireless with WiMax and Wi-Fi,* McGraw Hill Publishing, 2005, pp. 1–234.
10. http://www.expresscomputeronline.com/20060814/market01.shtml [dated August 14, 2006].
11. http://www.researchandmarkets.com/reportinfo.asp?report_id=342995&t=o&cat_id=.
12. http://www.unstrung.com/document.asp?site=unstrung&doc_id=103315&page_number=1.
13. www.wimaxforum.org.
14. http://www.freescale.com/.
15. http://www.commsdesign.com/design_corner/showArticle.jhtml?articleID=17500156 [dated January 20, 2004].
16. http://rfdesign.com/mag/508RFDF1.pdf.
17. Barbeau, M., WiMax/802.16 Threat Analysis, Q2SWinet'05, October 13, 2005, Montreal, Quebec, Canada.
18. http://computer.howstuffworks.com/wimax2.htm.
19. http://www.networkworld.com/columnists/2006/121106-wireless-security.html?page=2.

Chapter 4

WiMAX Product Development Trends

New products and key deployments are accelerating WiMAX growth. By 2010, the worldwide WiMAX market is forecasted to reach $3.5 billion and account for 4 percent of all broadband usage. This growth will be driven by new equipment from a growing list of hardware suppliers and an increasing number of WiMAX trials and deployments. WiMAX has attracted many leading equipment manufacturers and component suppliers. Many are also forming strategic partnerships. Alcatel and Intel have implemented a dedicated WiMAX program. Nokia, which views WiMAX as a complement to third generation (3G), partnered with Intel to incorporate WiMAX into future handsets. Other key suppliers include Airspan Networks, Alvarion, Aperto Networks, Fujitsu, Motorola, Navini, Nortel, Proxim, Redline Communications, Sequans, SR Telecom, Wavesat Wireless, and Wi-LAN. WiMAX systems and services are being evaluated/deployed in suburban business districts that lack high quality DSL access, in urban markets to compete against DSL and broadband cable, by wireline carriers and ISPs to compete with integrated operators' converged fixed–mobile offers, and by mobile carriers to overcome 3G network saturation and transition to 4G. These service providers include: Altitude Telecom, AT&T, BT, Clearwire, France Telecom, Iberbanda, Korea Telecom, Monaco Telecom, Telekom Austria, TelstraClear, Towerstream, Verizon, and Yozan. On a worldwide basis, WiMAX systems can be deployed in a large number of licensed and unlicensed frequency bands.

Range of WiMAX Hardware Is Expanding

The third WiMAX PlugFest at the European Telecommunications Standards Institute (ETSI) was held in the French town of Sophia Antipolis. At the meeting of developers and operators, featuring broadband radio data transmission issues and organized by the manufacturers association WiMAX Forum, a total of ten companies tested the interoperability of their products, whereupon Airspan, Axxcelera, Sequans, Siemens, and Wavesat were happy to see their products certified for stationary use. The certificates for frequency division duplexing (FDD) operation in the 3.5-GHz band were issued by the Spanish laboratory Cetecom after checking the conformity of the products in question with the WiMAX standard 802.16. The number of successfully tested products is thereby growing. Stationary WiMAX promises to boost the expansion of high-speed broadband networks in regions where high-speed access has to date been nonexistent.

WiMAX Chip Has an Eye for Mobile Services

A WiMAX device enables both fixed services and a "portable" services market with vast potential and room for growth years before the advent of standardized "mobile" services. Telecis Wireless claimed a WiMAX industry breakthrough with the introduction of its TCW 1620 chip, which enables both low-cost, indoor "self-installed" customer premises equipment (CPE) for fixed WiMAX services and a portable services market. The TCW 1620 is based on the standard (IEEE 802.16-2004) for "fixed" WiMAX services that are being rolled out now. The chip offers numerous design and performance advantages that would enable consumers to buy and install their own fixed indoor equipment — which makes the residential market more viable for carriers — and also enjoy portable connectivity via PC cards and small USB devices while traveling away from their home or office. The portable capability, in particular, is attractive to network operators because a WiMAX system or network-supporting classic last-mile access applications can also support portable operation, and hence addresses a much larger market need than does a strictly fixed WiMAX implementation that must be plugged in or bolted to walls. Consumers, particularly the millions around the world accustomed to Wi-Fi-like roaming and portability, also stand to benefit sooner from the higher connection speeds, quality of service (QoS)-enabled applications, and larger coverage area afforded by WiMAX service.

InfiNet Wireless Announces 802.16d/802.16e WiMAX Design Win With picoChip

InfiNet Wireless selected the picoChip software upgradeable WiMAX solution for 802.16d and 802.16e WiMAX system designs. InfiNet, a leading vendor of Broadband Wireless Access (BWA) equipment in Russia, Eastern Europe, and other key countries of the emerging markets, supplied pre-WiMAX gear for more than 300 carrier-class wireless networks throughout the world. InfiNet Wireless was spun out from the integration business of CompTek International in 2003. The company was responsible for rolling out the first WMAN in Russia in 1995, and boasts world-class Russian laboratories for hardware and software development.

Xilinx Announces Industry's Most Comprehensive Suite of Programmable WiMAX Solutions

Central to the new suite of solutions is the bundled suite of application-specific IP for Forward Error Correction (FEC). Offering a 60 percent cost savings, the FEC IP bundle enables quick implementation of WiMAX designs optimized for use with Xilinx high- performance Virtex-4 and Spartan-3 FPGA families. Xilinx and Wavesat, a fabless semiconductor developer of broadband wireless chips, unveiled a jointly developed WiMAX Mini-PCI Reference Design. The design provides a plug-and-play development platform designed to accelerate time-to-market for WiMAX equipment manufacturers.

Green Hills Software Adds WiMAX to Platform for Wireless Devices

Green Hills Software, Inc., added WiMAX support to the Green Hills Platform for Wireless Devices, accelerating the development of both WiMAX mobile and BS devices. The Green Hills Platform solves this paradox by providing a pre-integrated platform with the latest WiMAX security protocols built on the INTEGRITY real-time operating system. This platform allows companies to get their WiMAX-based products to market faster with higher quality and lower production costs. The WiMAX BS configuration includes support for both the Mobile IP Home Agent and Foreign Agent protocols, including the necessary extensions to support fast handoffs. This is a key enabler for Voice-over-IP (VoIP) in the next generation mobile WiMAX (802.16e) network. The WiMAX Mobile Station configuration includes support for the Mobile IP node protocol.

Vendors Preview FPGA-Based WiMAX Modem

Altera and Wi-LAN partnered to deliver a programmable, low-cost, WiMAX-compliant BTS (base transceiver station) modem. The IEEE 802.16-2004-compliant modem will allow BS developers to deliver WiMAX products that can be upgraded in the field to meet changing customer requirements and market conditions. The partnership will combine Wi-LAN's 802.16-2004 MAC (media access control) and PHY (physical layer) intellectual property with Altera's FPGAs and building blocks such as FEC (forward-error correction).

Wavesat Brings Mini-PCI to WiMAX

WiMAX Mini-PCI reference design opens the way to low-cost and small form-factor WiMAX CPE, driving fast deployment of WiMAX solutions. Wavesat has released the world's first WiMAX Mini-PCI reference design, a 3.5-GHz development platform to guide and support efforts in designing WiMAX-compliant wireless systems, based on its Evolutive WiMAX DM256 chip. Wavesat's Mini-PCI design enables OEMs and ODMs to rapidly design and manufacture cost-effective WiMAX CPE solutions by providing a plug-and-play complete solution for the lower-layer air interface and time-critical low-level MAC functionality. The industry-standard-compliant Mini-PCI format simplifies the overall WiMAX CPE design, enabling customers to bring WiMAX solutions to market faster and more cost efficiently, while allowing for flexibility to address further changes driven by the WiMAX emerging market dynamics, application diversity, and customer profiles. Wavesat's reference design fully supports the WiMAX profiles included in the first round of certification, with 3.5-GHz radio frequency (RF) interface, 3.5-MHz bandwidth, and time division duplexing (TDD), as well as hybrid FDD (HFDD) operation. The reference design includes the physical layer (PHY) and low-level MAC functionality with standard interface to customer motherboard, as well as the RF circuitry. In addition, because the Mini-PCI design is fully tested and WiMAX compliant, the solution accelerates customers' CPE WiMAX certification. The Evolutive WiMAX DM256 family of products is a complete and cost-effective solution supporting all the necessary features to design BSs and subscriber units for both licensed and license-exempt RFs. It consists of a full-range of standard-based integrated circuits, software, and reference designs supporting WiMAX 802.16-2004 certification and intended for forward compatibility with 802.16e for basic mobility. Wavesat products fit design requirements for CPE as well as BS infrastructure, providing effective wireless connectivity for a wide range of network sizes and coverage from urban to rural applications.

Fetish Electric Car Goes WiMAX

Venturi and Intel Corporation have combined their technological forces to give the all-electric car Fetish a completely new data communication capability by incorporating an Alvarion pre-WiMAX wireless connection box into the car. The Monaco car maker presents its vehicle of the future: good-looking, clean, and built with the future goal of sharing its energy. Intel and Venturi Automobiles announced a pooling of their talents and resources that led to the WiMAX wireless data communication technology being incorporated into the Fetish. A technology-edged car, Fetish has changed the perception of electrical motorization. It takes into account current ecological challenges while combining a positive vision of tomorrow's car. Fetish is just the first step on the road toward optimized energy management. Thanks to WiMAX technology, the future Venturi vehicle — a solar powered electric vehicle — will usher in a new era of electric power-sharing networks in an urban environment. Using WiMAX technology, the fleet of vehicles will be remotely managed. Better yet, each vehicle will be able to communicate with the others.

WiMAX Parabolic Dish Antennas

Parabolic dish antenna systems offered by Pacific Wireless are constructed of an aluminum alloy dish with powder-coat paint finish for excellent mechanical, electrical, and environmental performance.

The Pacific Wireless parabolic reflector is made with a special one-step molding technology that achieves excellent consistency and long-term stability. The Pacific Wireless parabolic dish antennas come complete with universal galvanized steel, powder-coat paint, and a mounting system for pole mount applications. Because of its superb electrical performance and mechanical stability, the parabolic dish antenna can be used in a wide variety of high-performance 3.5-GHz wireless applications.

Features of parabolic reflectors:

- High gain — choice of 25 dBI or 28 dBI antenna
- Adjustable tilt pole mount
- Vertical or horizontal polarization
- Type n female connector
- DC grounded for lightning protection
- Rugged, lightweight, and waterproof

Applications of parabolic reflectors:

- 3.5-GHz wireless local loop (WLL)
- Long-distance backhaul data links
- Point-to-point (P2P) data links
- Building-to-building high-speed links

picoChip and Wintegra Announce Partnership: New 802.16e Reference Design Provides Increased Flexibility and Performance for WiMAX BS

The solutions combine picoChip's picoArray family of massively parallel digital signal processors (DSP) and software for the WiMAX PHY with Wintegra's WinMax processor and software for a complete MAC solution. Coupled with Wintegra's existing WinPath family of access packet processors and software for transport and backhaul functionality, the joint reference designs offer flexibility for both radio (air) interface access cards and network interface transport cards, with scalability to cover pico, micro, and macro BS architectures. A unique aspect of the joint design is that it is software defined: both companies offer fully tested software and vendor-independent APIs that permit rapid integration of MAC, PHY, and RF components, as well as additional system software. Usually, most WiMAX reference designs have focused solely on "closed" board-level solutions, providing benefits for those seeking to directly manufacture the design but little flexibility for those seeking to add their own features. The picoChip/Wintegra design offers the same benefits of complete integration and interoperability testing while retaining a programmable, scalable, open approach enabling OEMs to customize and differentiate their offerings.

picoChip and ETRI Sign Software Defined Radio Development Partnership for 3G and WiMAX

picoChip announced that it has signed a development partnership agreement with the Electronics and Telecommunications Research Institute (ETRI) of Korea in the area of Software Defined Radio for W-CDMA (Code Division Multiple Access)/ HSDPA (High-Speed Downlink Packet Access) and WiMAX. The arrangement takes the form of an engineering cooperation, including joint development and research into future wireless technologies. As part of this, a team from ETRI will be based at picoChip's Bath, U.K., headquarters for a year.

picoChip First to Demo Advanced Features of WiMAX

picoChip showed both BS and subscriber station (SS) reference designs with multi-user subchannelization and multiple antennas for both input and output (STC and MRC, 2*TX, 2*RX). According to the WiMAX Forum, these features can increase the area covered twenty times compared to a standard WiMAX chipset and are critical for indoor (self-install) CPE. Both systems are programmable and software-upgradable from 802.16d to 802.16e. Multi-user subchannelization is a technique in 802.16d that shares the uplink (UL) tones and allows many SSs to transmit simultaneously. The advantage is that UL power can be "concentrated," increasing effective power and hence range. This is essential if CPE are to be self-installed indoors, as opposed to the traditional outdoor fixed-wireless systems that needed expensive installation, dramatically impacting the economics of a network. Several OEMs have announced SS products that support subchannelization: picoChip's is the first solution to offer this capability for full end-to-end operation — for both BSs and SSs.

Nokia Makes First WiMAX Data Call

Nokia has announced that its networks business group has completed a data call as part of its WiMAX (802.16e) development program. The error-free call was made between computing and baseband modules at Nokia's research and development facility in Germany according to Nokia's WiMAX development timetable, and was conducted on a high-speed preproduct test platform. Nokia will be expanding to WiMAX trials.

Lucent's Multimedia Access Platform Supports Integrated FTTX, WiMAX, and DSL Services

Lucent Technologies introduced its Multimedia Access Platform — an Internet Protocol (IP)-based platform that enables service provider delivery of high-bandwidth video/IPTV, VoIP, and multimedia services on a mass-market scale. The company says the platform, based on the Advanced Telecommunications Computing Architecture (AdvancedTCA) standard, is designed to support DSL, FTTX, and WiMAX wireless broadband services in a single frame, helping service providers deliver interactive IP multimedia applications over a wide variety of networks.

JISP Announces OSS/BSS to Build Profitable WiMAX

JISP's portfolio includes pre-WiMAX deployments in Africa where the technology finds ready acceptance due to lack of infrastructure. In addition, it supports current WiMAX deployments in India. With industry analysts forecasting a $3 to 5 billion WiMAX market by 2009, the technology is set to penetrate the service provider market. JISP's comprehensive platform lowers operating costs and ensures easy management, making WiMAX deployment a highly attractive proposition from day zero. To enable the deployment of profit-ready WiMAX, JISP is partnering with leading WiMAX equipment vendors such as Redline, WiLAN, and BelAir Networks, among others, reducing the time lag between deployment of WiMAX-certified equipment and the launch of profitable WiMAX services.

New PXI Modules from Aeroflex Address WLAN, WiMAX Applications

Airspan's AS.MAX 802.16-2004 and 802.16e WiMAX product line supports indoor, self-install WiMAX modems and end user devices. The AS.MAX product line comprises four BSs (Macro-Cell: HiperMAX and MacroMAX;

Micro-Cell: MicroMAX-SDR and MicroMAX-SOC) and three CPE types (Indoor Self-Install: EasyST; Outdoor Professional Install: ProST; Wi-Fi/WiMAX Hot-Zones: ProST-Wi-Fi). All of the AS.MAX products include support for VeriSign's Custom Device Certificate Service.

Alvarion Launches Indoor WiMAX CPE Gear

Alvarion Ltd. unveiled inexpensive, self-installable indoor CPE for the wide-area wireless solution. The CPE, called the BreezeMAX Si, features simple plug-and-play installation and will lead to nomadic and portable services. O'Neal said the CPE is the size of "a one-slice bagel toaster" and will be priced below $500 when pricing is firmed. He expects that the Si CPE will be sold in retail outlets. The BreezeMAX Si is a product within Alvarion's BreezeMAX 3500 family and has been designed to integrate easily with Alvarion's existing WiMAX deployments. Although WiMAX deployments across the world have generally been established in rural and suburban regions, O'Neal said the Si CPE is best suited for urban and in-building situations. The Si CPE, which uses Intel's PRO/Wireless 5116 broadband interface chip, has been successfully tested with ten different operators, Alvarion said. Using dual-mode FDD/TDD software-defined radio (SDR), the Si CPE operates in either the FDD or TDD mode to enable users to keep their options open for future network designs. Using Web interfaces, the device connects via integrated 9 dBi antennas or external 12 dBi window mount antennas. A single 10/100 Base-T interface provides easy connectivity with Wi-Fi and voice solutions.

Foursome Converges to Deliver VoIP Over WiMAX

AudioCodes (www.audiocodes.com), CableMatrix (www.cablematrix.com), Emergent Networks (www.emergentnetworks.net), and VCom (www.v-com.com) have joined forces to deliver a WiMAX-based VoIP platform for service providers. The companies had demonstrated at the joint solution week at GLOBALCOMM 2006.

Redline Introduces RedMAX Management Suite for WiMAX Networks

Network and element management enables true carrier-class WiMAX deployments and seamless integration with the core network. Redline Communications introduced the RedMAX Management Suite (RMS), enabling seamless integration and management of WiMAX technologies within operators' core networks. By integrating the RMS with their RedMAX network, operators can establish and manage a true carrier-class WiMAX network. RMS is an element management system that enables broadband network operators to easily deploy, control, monitor, and upgrade Redline products in their network, acting as a gateway to the operators' NMS and OSS and enabling full automation of operations. RMS is standards based and platform independent to easily integrate with any IT infrastructure. It monitors equipment, collects traffic statistics and enables provisioning of services, and reports inventories and alarm propagation via a Northbound Interface. To help ensure uninterrupted service and to maximize the network capacity, RMS includes programmable TCAs for varying levels of alarms. In addition, it enables operators to perform scheduled automated software upgrades to all Redline equipment on the network from a central location.

Redline's RedPATH Architecture Roadmap

RMS is an important component of Redline's RedPATH™ architecture roadmap, which provides carriers with a clear business and network deployment strategy that leverages their WiMAX investment. RedPATH is a three-stage approach that guides Redline's RedMAX product development from supporting fixed and portable services to products that will enable carriers to expand and enhance their services, and delivering on the promise of full mobility. With the first phase now complete, operators can establish a WiMAX network that delivers on the performance and interoperability requirements of WiMAX Forum-certified products, with an open architecture and management system that is a key component for carrier-class networks.

Redline is now delivering on phase two of RedPATH, which will enable operators to expand their services to enhanced fixed services and portable applications. The RedMAX Indoor Subscriber Unit will accelerate the expansion of WiMAX networks to include residential and small business users. Also in this phase, operators can benefit from a new RedMAX BS architecture that will support either or both of today's WiMAX standards. The third phase of RedPATH will enable RedMAX network operators to evolve to mobile service offerings with advanced PHY technologies, including multiple-input multiple-output (MIMO) and AAS antennas that ensure the ubiquitous coverage required for a profitable mobile business model.

Redline's RedMAX products have been chosen by carriers in international markets for nationwide deployments and network trials. Among the first to install RedMAX for a nationwide network is Hrvatske Telekomunikacije d.d (T-HT), a Croatian telecommunications company owned by Deutsche Telecom. The T-HT deployment is being managed by MICROLINK, a distributor and system integrator of wireless communication systems for digital data transmission. RedMAX is also being deployed by Integrated Telecom Company Ltd. (ITC), a licensed data service provider in Saudi Arabia, as part of the $22.2 million first phase of its region wide broadband network.

Samsung Planning GSM-WiMAX Phone

Samsung is planning a jump into the mobile WiMAX business as early as possible. Their plans are to release a dual-mode handset, with WiMAX and GSM protocols. The phone will be available all over the world to take advantage of its full functionality. The phone will be another in Samsung's line of products aimed at taking advantage of WiMAX, the newest wireless network technology on the block. They are also working on WiMAX-based PDAs and notebooks.

RF Transceivers Support 802.16e WiMAX

Philips has unveiled its next-generation laterally diffused metal oxide semiconductor (LDMOS) WiMAX lineup for BS solutions, which delivers up to 3.8 GHz of performance over an 802.16e mobile WiMAX platform. Available immediately, the Philips Gen6 LDMOS solution enables the highest efficiency WiMAX in an LDMOS platform, offering users access to broadband communication any time, anywhere. Philips' Gen6 LDMOS technology features enhanced RF performance as well as unparalleled linearity and power gain. The new LDMOS WiMAX BS also offers high levels of system efficiency, requiring less energy to power the network infrastructure so that network operators can deliver next-generation WiMAX services and connectivity to consumers for less operational expenditure.

For system architects, Philips provides a full suite of intuitive development tools, including software models and S-parameters, making it easy to design and integrate their solutions in the shortest time possible, so that integrators can save valuable time in bringing high-value services to market. Philips delivers a comprehensive solution for the emerging WiMAX standard by also offering RF transceivers for 802.16e WiMAX. The Philips UXF234xx series is a set of fully integrated, low-power, dual conversion transceivers that enable easy, robust, and reliable broadband communication for mobile devices such as phones, Personal Computer Memory Card International Association (PCMCIA) cards, laptops, and PDAs. Featuring ultra low noise, high dynamic range, and high linearity, the UXF234xx transceivers allow seamless handover between BSs.

WiMAX Transceiver Cuts Equipment Down to Size

A WiMAX Mini-PCI reference design provides the industry's lowest cost WiMAX-compliant CPE. Atmel Corporation is working with Wavesat to create such a WiMAX mini-PCI reference design. Developed to provide OEMs with a quickly deployable WiMAX end product, the reference design will include Atmel's MAX-Link AT86RF535A 3.5-GHz WiMAX-specific transceiver, Wavesat's DM256 baseband, interfaces, all external filters and components, and software in a mini-PCI module. With an expected bill of materials (BOM) of under $100, this design is projected to save OEMs 25 percent in cost compared with competing WiMAX CPE solutions. The low BOM cost of the reference design is largely attributable to Atmel's AT86RF535A MAX-Link low IF transceiver. The MAX-Link transceiver achieves −34 dBm of TX-EVM, including balun, exceeding the requirement for WiMAX certification, and has fewer external components than conventional, off-the-shelf 802.16 radios. It includes a bandwidth-programmable integrated channel filter for receive and transmit, complete integrated synthesizer, digital gain setting for the receive path with a 96 dB gain range, digital transmit power control with a more than 50 dB control range, integrated image rejection, and LO leakage digital control settings and detectors. It does not require any external SAW filters. Unlike dual conversion radios, the AT86RF535A does not require offset cancellation circuitry, a high-resolution controlled TCVCXCO, or a high-resolution synthesizer. It requires only 10 μs to switch between TX and RX modes — a significant savings over the 100 μs typically required by dual conversion radios. An integrated on-chip programmable synthesizer provides frequency resolution up to the required −30 dB subcarrier certification limit. The AT86RF535A's supply current is 200 mA in receive mode and 320 mA in transmit mode at −5 dBm, including balun. This comparatively low power consumption reduces the average power requirement of the mini-PCI by more than 30 percent to just 3.2 W. The high level of integration of the AT86RF535A, combined with its low IF architecture, results in a mini-PCI WiMAX end product that has 20 percent fewer components and $30 less cost in the BOM than any currently available reference design. The mini-PCI board with Atmel RF will be included in Wavesat WiMAX reference kits. Kits will include a complete WiMAX system, software license with full maintenance contract, and reference design including BOM and Gerber files. Atmel's AT86RF535A MAX-Link radio is available now in an 8 × 8 mm 56-lead QFN package and is priced at $18 in quantities of 10,000. Atmel is developing additional MAX-Link radios to be introduced in 2006 and 2007 that will cover the full range of WiMAX frequency profiles.

WiMAX Is the Focus for Cree's GaN HEMTs

Cree, the Durham, North Carolina, chip manufacturer, has begun sampling a GaN HEMT for use in broadband wireless BSs. Cree has launched a new GaN HEMT product that it hopes will find uptake in the emerging market for the WiMAX BWA technology. It says that its 15-W power transistor, which has been optimized for the 3.3- to 3.9-GHz frequency band, is aimed primarily at applications in base stations. Unlike the SiC-based MESFET launched for similar applications a year ago, this latest device is designed for 28 V operations.

Although GaN-based transistors have long been regarded as technologically superior to their GaAs or silicon LDMOS equivalents at these frequencies, particularly in terms of power output and efficiency, their relatively high price has always been a stumbling block. However, Cree says the GaN devices it is now starting to roll out will be priced competitively with alternative technologies for WiMAX applications. The GaN HEMTs are manufactured on semi-insulating SiC substrates at Cree's new fabrication facility, located just a few miles from its Durham, NC, headquarters. Although there have been difficulties in standardizing the various protocols associated with WiMAX technology, some of the semiconductor industry's biggest players have targeted it as a key growth area.

Flextronics Unveils WiMAX Signaling Solution

Flextronics Software Systems (FSS), an end-to-end communication solutions provider based in India, has launched Sig ASN, a signaling framework for developing the WiMAX Forum-defined ASN gateway. FSS's Sig ASN, a platform-independent software-signaling framework, enables telecom equipment manufacturers (TEMs) to quickly develop ASN gateway, a key component for enabling mobility in WiMAX networks. Based on 802.16e specifications, Sig ASN reportedly provides a modular control plane implementation and open interfaces for user plane (fast path) integration. The solution is expected to help TEMs develop a complete ASN gateway of the required network configuration over a platform of their choice by integrating the WiMAX standard-based software control plane solution from FSS. It also offers customization and integration services that enable the development and creation of a complete ASN gateway solution, including the fast-path engine.

New WiMAX Reference Library for CoWare Platform-driven ESL Design

CoWare(R), Inc., the leading supplier of platform-driven electronic system-level (ESL) design software and services, announced a new WiMAX Reference Library integrated into CoWare Signal Processing Designer (formerly known as SPW). Covering IEEE 802.16/16e standards, this library will allow system-on-chip (SoC) design teams using the CoWare platform-driven ESL design solution to reduce time-to-market introduction by six months for every product generation. The CoWare solution allows optimization of WiMAX SoC implementation performance for the noise performance relevant in rural areas and interference performance in densely populated areas, both of which impact the operator's network capacity. Platform-driven ESL design starts with the creation of new hardware and software components at the algorithm level. These components are often complex signal processing functions bound to a particular standard, just as in this case for WiMAX. The algorithmic design includes modeling and performance simulation, as well as fixed-point optimization, specifically for hardware components. The new WiMAX Library for CoWare Signal Processing Designer provides ready-to-use reference systems, all delivered with source code, from which design teams can start to add their particular implementations and optimize them in the overall system context by executing Signal Processing Designer simulations on a server farm. Furthermore, algorithms designed with CoWare Signal Processing Designer are often implemented as programmable accelerators using CoWare Processor Designer. This integration into the CoWare design solution makes the new WiMAX Library a very powerful enabler for design teams, which cuts six months off the overall schedule from specification to working products.

Motorola Continues MOTOwi4 Momentum, Advances WiMAX Adoption

Motorola continues to be the leading provider in WiMAX technology with plans to develop a comprehensive ecosystem for personal broadband "on the go." The commitment furthers the company's MOTOwi4 strategy and extends its recent product introductions — including a carrier-class WiMAX access point — by incorporating plans to work with multiple chipset suppliers to help ensure that a proliferation of WiMAX-enabled devices are available at attractive prices to meet the anticipated global demand for WiMAX technology. Motorola is building on its previously announced relationship with Intel to promote 802.16e WiMAX by working with other technology leaders to ensure that there will be a complete ecosystem for delivering the benefits of WiMAX and for demonstrating its value proposition at every point — from WiMAX-enabled handsets and CPE to BSs, PC cards, and chipsets.

Motorola Showcases First Public Demo of 802.16e-based MOTOwi4 WiMAX Solution

Motorola has unveiled its MOTOwi4 WiMAX solutions. Using a suite of infrastructure and subscriber products, it demonstrated IP telephony over its MOTOwi4 WiMAX platform. Motorola's first MOTOwi4 WiMAX system focuses on delivering low-cost fixed and nomadic services in underserved markets and developing countries using the 3.5-GHz spectrum available across most of the world. In addition, by using a common core network, Motorola will enable operators to use a complementary combination of licensed and unlicensed spectra to cover new territories with broadband service and IP telephony. The MOTOwi4 WiMAX system is an "ultralight access point" and can be mounted virtually anywhere to provide high-speed wireless broadband coverage. Retaining the benefits of Motorola's highly successful MOTOwi4 Canopy solution, this 3.5-GHz system is compact, lightweight, and easy to deploy, making it an ideal solution for new and existing carriers with 3.5-GHz fixed-wireless access licenses in developing countries, as well as rural areas in developed countries, especially in Europe, the Middle East, and Latin America. Motorola's MOTOwi4 WiMAX products are designed to address the full scope of fixed, nomadic, portable, and mobile applications. It is expected to be interoperable with subscriber modem devices manufactured by third parties. Many early shipments are also in conjunction with a carrier class IP core based around Motorola's leading IP Multimedia Subsystem platform. MOTOwi4 delivers a comprehensive platform of wireless broadband solutions and services, and its solutions create, complement, and complete IP networks — extending coverage, connecting the unconnected, and helping to deliver "personal broadband on-the-go" throughout both developed and undeveloped markets. The MOTOwi4 platform includes WiMAX, canopy solutions, mesh, broadband over powerline, and backhaul solutions for private and public networks.

ZyXel Announces WiMAX Products

ZyXel Communications announced a new line of WiMAX products. The new products include a WiMAX CPE product and a WiMAX PCMCIA notebook card. Both of the products were designed to be compliant with the 802.16e standard, but although they have the broadband capabilities found in DSL networking products, they also have QoS features. The MAX-200 Series WiMAX CPE is meant to be used like a DSL modem, except that it connects to a WiMAX broadband Internet connection, said ZyXel. ZyXel designed the CPE product to be a simple plug-and-play router for home users. The flip side to the announcement is the MAX-100 Series WiMAX PCMCIA card for mobile laptop users. According to ZyXel, both products enable service providers to deliver last-mile wireless broadband access to customers as an alternative to cable and DSL. The products will provide a completely new and enhanced broadband wireless experience. ZyXel's comprehensive WiMAX product line comes in several models to operate at different frequency bands including 2.5 GHz, 3.5 GHz, and 2.3 GHz. With the products, ZyXel is offering the option to service providers to provide broadband IP telephony and IPTV services to their customers without the necessity of additional hardware on the customer's site, said ZyXel. According to the ZyXel, the MAX-200 is ideal for wireless ISPs because it enables them to offer services such as VoIP and IP TV, which rely on a high level of QoS. An advanced firewall with DoS protection built into it blocks attacks from hackers, and the addition of Advanced Encryption Standard (AES) for wireless connection allows the MAX-200 series to offer an all-in-one solution for the end-user. There's also an SMA removable high-gain antenna for outdoor antenna installation and SNMP support, enabling service providers to remotely manage the CPE. The MAX-100 series PCMCIA card is designed for mobile users who have Windows XP/2000 laptops. It is also compliant with the IEEE 802.16e-2005 WiMAX standard and has a 23-dBm powerful RF design for a long-range and high-speed connection. This allows the user to access the Internet on the go with much wider coverage.

WiMAX Card for Windows

Polonix Corporation, a global distributor of the ENTE e!MAX series of WiMAX products, has made available the WiMAX PCI card for personal computers (PCs) that run a Microsoft Windows operating system. The cards deliver direct access to WiMAX broadband Internet/Network services [1]. The e!MAX PCI card features a powerful WiMAX chipset from Wavesat, the WiMAX industry leader, and it works for both line-of-sight (LoS) and non-line-of-sight (NLoS) communications. The card simply plugs into an open PCI slot, an antenna plugs into the card, and broadband connectivity to an e!MAX BS is achieved. The BS could be located at a service provider's facility or in/on any building within a radius of several kilometers.

Orthogon Systems Introduces Its Latest Fully WiMAX Solution, OS-Spectra Lite

Orthogon Systems, provider of fixed wireless solutions for reliable connectivity in difficult environments, has launched OS-Spectra Lite, a secure point-to-point (P2P) wireless Ethernet bridge that delivers reliable, carrier-grade connectivity at a lower entry level price without compromising high performance. OS-Spectra Lite connects separate networks for up to 125 mi with performance of up to 150 Mbps aggregate user throughput. Fully WiMAX compatible, it addresses the high-bandwidth networking requirements for both telecommunications backhaul as well as applications for large enterprises, including those used in healthcare, education, and government industries. Orthogon Systems also announced the availability of its OS-Spectra 58200 software release for download. With this new software release, OS-Spectra Lite customers will be able to activate a single T1/E1 port, bridging both switched-circuit and Ethernet traffic over a single wireless connection. Furthermore, the addition of the T1/E1 port activation enables enterprises to eliminate recurring monthly costs from leased lines. The 58200 software release also provides customers with bandwidth allocation on demand. With this capability, the OS-Spectra system intelligently detects when more bandwidth is needed in order to transport large files, such as those affiliated with video. Instead of the usual 50/50 split for upstream and downstream traffic, the system allocates a greater amount of bandwidth on the fly to move large amounts of data, making the wireless network more efficient around the clock. Further, this process is done automatically, eliminating the need for any manual input. The OS-Spectra Lite is the newest edition to Orthogon's OS-Spectra family of products. It has been expressly designed for customers who only require 150 Mbps and who, at the same time, have specific budget constraints. For companies that need higher bandwidth, Orthogon offers 300 Mbps through its OS-Spectra 300 product. The OS-Spectra Lite operates in the unlicensed 5.8-GHz band and is Federal Communications Commission (FCC) and ETSI certified. It maintains exceptional link availability, up to 99.9999 percent in long-range LoS and NLoS environments, as well as over large bodies of water. A truly software-defined radio, the OS-Spectra Lite provides feature and performance upgrades via simple software downloads, and is easy to install and manage. Built upon Orthogon's proven radio technology, it offers customers the following features:

- Multibeam Space–Time-Coding — The OS-Spectra Lite minimizes signal fading due to path obstructions or atmospheric disturbances.
- Advanced Spectrum Management with intelligent Dynamic Frequency Selection (iDFS) — Interference-free operation is ensured by constantly monitoring the link for congestion and automatically switching to the most interference-free channel.
- WiMAX Compatibility — OS-Spectra Lite features a narrow 30-MHz channel, making it an ideal system to backhaul up to 150 Mbps of traffic from a WiMAX BS to the wide area network (WLAN) and allowing organizations to preserve spectrum for last-mile access. In addition, OS-Spectra Lite supports the WiMAX MIB (management information base), enabling users to seamlessly integrate the solution into a complete end-to-end broadband wireless network.
- Security — For the highest levels of security, customers are provided with an advanced Air Interface that incorporates a proprietary data scrambling technique as well as AES encryption. It acts as a transparent Ethernet bridge enabling customers to superimpose complete end-to-end network security solutions such as virtual private networks (VPN).
- Multiple Interfaces — The OS-Spectra Lite has multiple interfaces that support both small and large IP networks, including 10/100/1000 Base-T and optional Fiber Optic 1000 Base-SX.

Intel's WiMAX Chip

Intel is shipping its highly integrated WiMAX chip, formerly codenamed Rosedale. The Pro/Wireless 5116 chip has two ARM9 cores and an OFDM (orthogonal frequency division multiplexing) modem, and targets low-cost, low-chip-count access points and gateways supporting WiMAX, an IEEE standard for long-distance wireless broadband. The Pro/Wireless 5116 is a highly integrated SoC meant to combine with third-party RFIC (radio chips) and power amplifiers in low-chip-count wireless broadband equipment. It features two ARM946E-S cores for MAC, PHY, and application processing. The SoC also includes a DSP (digital signal processor) and an in-line security processor. Additionally, the Pro/Wireless 5116 integrates a 256-channel OFDM modem supporting channel bandwidths of up to 10 MHz, says Intel. The OFDM modem can support licensed and unlicensed frequencies, and should simplify the design of WiMAX CPE, such as the design blocked out below. The Pro/Wireless 5116 can also be used at the other end of the virtual wire in WiMAX access points, thanks to a TDM (time division multiplexing) interface that enables it to connect to T1/E1 lines, Intel says, through an off-chip SLIC/SLAC (subscriber line interface/access controller). The TDM interface also supports legacy analog phones in gateway applications, Intel says.

Other I/O interfaces include

- Modular RF interface support I/F or baseband I/Q radios designed for WiMAX licensed and unlicensed spectrum
- Integrated pair of ADCs (analog-to-digital converters) and DACs (digital-to-analog converters), and a PLL (phase-locked loop) to drive converters
- 10/100 Ethernet MAC with MII interface to external PHY
- External SDRAM and Flash interfaces, test and debug interfaces, and programmable GPIOs (general-purpose I/Os)

Simulation Testbench Gives Green Light for Advanced WiMAX System Development

Cambridge Consultants has developed a WiMAX simulation testbench to support the launch of Aspex Semiconductor's innovative reference code for implementing multiantenna BSs. The software simulates subscriber transmissions, providing an independent testing facility that can be used by developers alongside Aspex's radical 802.16d/e PHY baseband architecture in a familiar, PC-based software development environment. Based on the Linedancer family of processors, Aspex's WiMAX PHY reference code delivers a software-defined radio architecture and support for multi-antenna techniques such as MIMO and beam-forming. This provides wireless OEMs with enormous performance and design flexibility. Written in Matlab, the model simulates WiMAX subscriber transmissions and channel noise, giving system developers the means to begin developing transceiver equipment and to test and verify multi-antenna 802.16e design concepts in the lab. Aspex's fully software-programmable Linedancer processor with its 4096 parallel-processing elements is a key feature of the PHY reference code. The flexible front-end radio architecture allows vendors to deploy dynamically adaptable equipment that can modify its footprint as the subscriber base evolves. This creates a platform that may be software-upgraded with ease to support the evolving WiMAX family of standards, as well as the OEM's own ideas and IP for improved receiver architectures in areas such as antenna diversity. The WiMAX subscriber model simulates an OFDM transmitter. By creating simple scripts defining standard MAC messages, developers can simulate subscriber transmissions to exercise the BS receiver. Aspex also launched its WiMAX Development Kit, consisting of the Accelera PCI-X plug-in card, which implements the WiMAX BS PHY in real time, and the Cambridge Consultants MATLAB testbench.

Fujitsu's WiMAX Work

Fujitsu has developed a cost-effective, fully integrated MAC and PHY mixed-signal baseband processor for BWA applications. This SoC is designed to support frequencies ranging from 2 to 11 GHz in both licensed and unlicensed bands. The processor supports all available bandwidths from 1.75 to 20 MHz. Fujitsu's WiMAX SoC is fully compliant with the IEEE 802.16-2004 WiMAX standard and can be configured to be used in both BS and SS applications. This SoC supports highly efficient adaptive modulation schemes, including 64QAM, 16QAM, QPSK, and binary-phase shift keying (BPSK). When applying 64QAM modulation in a 20-MHz channel and using all 192 subcarriers, the SoC's data rate can go up to 75 Mbps. UL subchannelization is also supported as defined in the standard. Performance enhancement can be realized with the dual reduced instruction set computer (RISC) engines embedded into the SoC. These two processors not only gracefully handle the essential functions required by the WiMAX specification but also allow additional headroom to handle user application software. Fujitsu supports the standards development and compliance programs that are essential to successful broadband wireless deployment. It provides performance-driven WiMAX solutions by leveraging the company's experience and expertise in the networking and communications markets. Fujitsu offers flexible WiMAX SoC and reference designs for WiMAX-certifiable systems to equipment vendors. Fujitsu Microelectronics America (FMA) is shipping an SoC targeting WiMAX BWA equipment for metropolitan area networks (MANs). The MB87M3400 targets BSs and subscriber access equipment, and can be used in equipment carrying up to 75 Mbps of data, Fujitsu claims. Intel recently shipped a similar chip, the Pro/Wireless 5116. Both chips are said to comply with the IEEE 802.16-2004 standard for WiMAX devices. According to Fujitsu, WiMAX will bring cost-efficient, high-quality, fixed broadband connectivity to MAN users. Unlike today's 802.11 MANs, WiMAX MANs will not limit users to LoS connections, Fujitsu says. According to Fujitsu, the MB87M3400 is designed to enable deployment of BWA equipment in licensed or license-exempt bands below 11 GHz. It uses an OFDM 256 PHY that supports channels from 1.75 MHz up to 20 MHz and that can operate in TDD or FDD modes with support for all available channel bandwidths. A programmable frequency selection generates the sample clock for the desired bandwidth. When applying 64QAM modulation in a 20-MHz channel, and using all 192 subcarriers, the SoC's data rate can go up to 75 Mbps, Fujitsu claims. Uplink subchannelization is also supported. The MB87M3400 is based on a RISC processor. The RISC processor implements the 802.16 upper-layer MAC, scheduler, drivers, protocol stacks, and user application software. A secondary RISC/DSP functions as a coprocessor and executes lower-layer MAC functions, Fujitsu says. A multi-channel DMA controller handles high-speed transactions among agents on a high-performance bus. The Fujitsu WiMAX SoC also incorporates radio control and all required analog circuits, the company says, along with various integrated peripheral functions. It uses DES/AES/CCM encryption/decryption engines for the 802.16 MAC privacy sublayer. The chip also includes a memory controller, an Ethernet engine for interfacing to the network, and high-performance DAC/ADC for flexible baseband interface, Fujitsu says. The company says it plans to offer hardware/software reference designs for the MB87M3400 WiMAX SoC for a number of different configurations, including:

- SSs
- SS or BS for HDX (half duplex) FDD or TDD using an external processor
- Full duplex FDD using an external processor

Fujitsu Expands BWA Line

Fujitsu Network Co. Communications, Inc., expanded its broadband wireless strategy. Fujitsu will offer a native mobile WiMAX solution based on the IEEE 802.16-2005 standard, along with a series of Wi-Fi mesh products for carriers, cable operators, utilities, and municipalities to offer turnkey wireless services. The WiMAX portfolio will include WiMAX Forum-certified BSs and end-user devices. Initial Fujitsu WiMAX products will operate at 3.5-, 4.9-, and 5.8-GHz bands with plans to support 700 MHz, and 2.3, 2.5, and 3.65 GHz in the future. The products will feature a 2- to 5-mi service radius in urban/suburban environments, and services up to tens of miles away in LoS applications. Outdoor WiMAX products can be wall-, rooftop-, or tower-mounted. All WiMAX products will be optimized for VoIP services to residential and enterprise users, and will integrate SIP gateway messaging to enable call control and capacity reservation for voice traffic. Voice capacity is not reserved until requested and can be dynamically adjusted while maintaining QoS, thus enabling the optimal use of radio link capacity. Fujitsu already offers a WiMAX SoC and reference designs for WiMAX-certifiable systems. Meanwhile, the Wi-Fi mesh products are based on 802.11a/b/g, and the backhaul radios within them operate within the 5 GHz to 5.8 GHz unlicensed band. They can provide service within 500 yd in 802.11g mode and can be wall-, rooftop-, tower-, pole-, or strand-mounted.

Wavesat's Chip

Wavesat hopes to accelerate the incorporation of its WiMAX controller chips into low-cost and small form-factor CPE through the release of a mini-PCI reference design. The WiMAX mini-PCI Reference Design offers "an essential ingredient to WiMAX mass market adoption," the company says. The Reference Design implements an extended mini-PCI form-factor module based on Wavesat's Evolutive WiMAX DM256 chipset, and includes one mini-PCI WiMAX module, technical documentation, schematics, PCB design gerbers, a bill-of-materials, and six months of technical support, according to the company. The module includes the PHY and low-level MAC functionality as well as the RF circuitry, and supports both HFDD and TDD modes of operation.

Wavesat lists the following key features of the mini-PCI Reference Design:

- Fully supports first round certification WiMAX profile
  - profM3_PMP MAC system profile
  - 3.5-GHz RF interface
  - 3.5-MHz and 7-MHz bandwidth
  - TDD and HFDD modes
  - profC3_20 transmit power class profile
- Meets WiMAX spectral mask and error vector magnitude (EVM) requirement
- Adaptive modulation (BPSK, QPSK, 16-QAM, and 64-QAM)
- Meets all six SUI NLoS channel models
- Patented channel equalization/synchronization algorithms
- Average power requirement — 4.75 W (through mini-PCI interface)
- Size — 3.15 × 2.36 in. (80 × 60 mm)

The company says its WiMAX chipsets, software, and reference designs enable the design of BSs and subscriber units for both licensed and license-exempt radio frequencies, and they support WiMAX 802.16-2004 certification, including forward-compatibility with the 802.16e basic mobility specification.

Freescale Broadens RF Power Transistor Options for WiMAX Base Stations

With seventh-generation high-voltage (HV7) RF LDMOS technology, Freescale Semiconductor (FSL) has achieved the RF power amplifier performance required for use in WiMAX BSs operating in the 3.5-GHz band. This achievement marks the RF LDMOS technology from any manufacturer that has met the challenges. The company plans to continue development of GaAs PHEMT technology that will result in higher-power GaAs devices for use in WiMAX system designs, as well as other applications between 2 and 6 GHz. By offering power transistors in RF LDMOS and GaAs PHEMT technology, the RF solutions support virtually any wireless infrastructure application — with LDMOS performance up to 3.8 GHz and GaAs PHEMT performance up to 6 GHz. Samples of the initial 3.5-GHz LDMOS device are available now. The MRF7S38075H is a 75-W P1dB RF transistor capable of 42 dBm (16 W) average power while meeting WiMAX performance requirements over the 3.5-GHz band. In addition, samples of 40- and 10-W P1dB 3.5-GHz devices are expected in February 2006. These three advanced LDMOS devices round out the existing portfolio of RF power transistors targeting the emerging WiMAX/WiBro bands at 2.3, 2.5, and 3.5 GHz.

Invenova's Protocol Test and Analysis Systems Facilitate WiMAX Certification Testing at CETECOM Labs

Cetecom Labs, the official test lab for WiMAX certification, and Invenova Corporation, a developer of instrumentation, test, and measurement systems for standards-based wireless technologies, announced that Invenova's WiMAX test products are being used in the certification testing of WiMAX products. Cetecom Labs has independently validated the Invenova test systems (Astro8000 series WiMAX Protocol Test and Measurement products) for WiMAX Wave 1 certification testing. Invenova and Cetecom Labs have been engaged in close cooperation in the validation of the WiMAX test suite and test bed. Invenova's Astro8000 series WiMAX Test and Measurement products are designed to benefit WiMAX system vendors and operators by providing them with a comprehensive protocol test and analysis platform. The products support powerful traffic generation and monitoring/analysis capabilities, including full-fledged BS/SS emulation, and provide users fine-grained control over all aspects of WiMAX conformance and system performance testing.

Wavesat and Taiwan-Based Delta Networks Develop Low-Cost WiMAX CPE

Delta Networks, manufacturer of networking equipment, and Wavesat, developer of WiMAX silicon, software, and reference designs, announced a partnership to develop low-cost and small form-factor 802.16-2004-compliant CPE. A hardware/software total solution will be ready for OEMs/ODMs. The new WiMAX CPE design, available from Delta Networks, will integrate Wavesat's WiMAX 3.5-GHz mini-PCI design as well as its proprietary MAC software. Wavesat will assist DNI in integrating the CPE MAC onto Delta Network's modular CPE platform derived from its Wi-Fi product line.

Signal-Creation Software Serves Mobile WiMAX, WiBro

Test-and-measurement giant Agilent Technologies has released signal-creation software for mobile WiMAX and WiBro applications, for its E4438C ESG microwave vector signal generator. Agilent's N7615A Signal Studio for 802.16 OFDMA software creates waveforms that comply with the WMAN-OFDMA physical layer in the IEEE-802.16-2004, 802.16-2004/Cor1/D2 or D3, and IEEE-802.16e/D9 standards. Its ability to create DL or UL subframes in TDD or FDD makes it suitable for testing BS and SS equipment. While working with baseband receiver test and system verification, the N7615A software allows configuration of waveforms for both component and receiver design verification and testing. The software's intuitive GUI (graphical user interface) gives you access to PHY and basic MAC layer parameters, including bandwidth, cyclic prefix ratio (G), sampling factor (n), FFT (fast Fourier transform) size (512, 1024, or 2048), and frame length. Using the software's frame setup parameters, high peak-to-average power ratio downlink or uplink signals can be generated. That can be used to test transmission chain components such as amplifiers. Generating signals for a receiver test is done with automatic generation of correct FCH, DL-MAP, and UL-MAP data. The N7615A Signal Studio for 802.16 OFDMA can create up to 16 incrementally numbered frames/waveforms and can configure frames for downlink, uplink, or both. The software's frame configuration provides for zone and burst allocations, too. Supported zone types include DL-PUSC, DL-FUSC, UL-PUSC, and UL-OPUSC. The software can control signal generator functions remotely through the GUI.

Azonic Systems Unveils WiMAX-Compliant Products

Azonic Systems announced the availability of its WiMAX-compliant MAXGear family of products. The MAXGear WiMAX-compliant family of products includes BSs, SSs, associated radios, and antennas in the 5.8-, 3.5-, and 2.5-GHz frequency bands for both point-to-multipoint and P2P deployments. Azonic Systems' MAXGear products are designed to allow Internet Service Providers and Wireless Internet Service Providers (ISPs and WISPs) to deliver high performance and secure, reliable broadband connectivity to residential and business users by leveraging existing networks and last-mile wireless links, providing uninterrupted access to high-bandwidth applications and real-time online services. MAXGear products will initially offer fixed WiMAX (IEEE 802.16-2004) capability in the 5.8-GHz frequency band. Azonic Systems' unique BS accelerator technology increases BS performance, resulting in higher end-user data rates. Mobile WiMAX (IEEE 802.16e) products will follow pending WiMAX Forum certification.

picoChip Integrates ArrayComm's Network MIMO Software for WiMAX

picoChip and ArrayComm forged an alliance, under which ArrayComm's Network MIMO software will be incorporated into the PHY of picoChip's flexible wireless solution. picoChip will offer this solution as a software option to its customers to add smart antennas and MIMO to their advanced WiMAX BS and SS designs. ArrayComm's Network MIMO software implements all the antenna processing aspects of the WiMAX profiles approved by the WiMAX Forum Mobile Task Group (MTG) for IEEE 802.16e. The ArrayComm solution includes support for MIMO, adaptive antenna systems (AAS), and combined MIMO/AAS modes on both subscriber terminals and BSs. These provide operators the optimized user data rates, cell range, and network capacity they need to meet their business objectives for mobile broadband services. MIMO and AAS, used in combination, increase subscriber data rates, improve cell-edge link budgets, manage interference, and maximize overall network capacity. The result is a significant performance advantage for WiMAX. ArrayComm provides Network MIMO software that integrates with picoChip's WiMAX PHY and picoArray processor.

Atmel Launches 3.5-GHz Chip Line for WiMAX

Atmel Corporation announced its MAX-Link series of transceivers designed specifically for WiMAX applications. The AT86RF535A is a single-chip radio operating at 3.5 GHz with multiple bandwidth options. Additional members of the MAX-Link family are being developed to cover other WiMAX frequency bands and will interface with multiple baseband vendors. These devices combine a low-noise amplifier, power amplifier driver, receive/transmit mixer, receive/transmit filters, voltage-controlled oscillator, synthesizer, receive gain control, and transmit power control — all completely digitally governed. All of the transceivers will provide excellent RF performance with low current consumption and a small die size. The AT86RF535A is available now to select customers. Production volumes will be available early in the second quarter of 2006. Pricing is $18 in quantities of 10,000. Modules incorporating the AT86RF535A transceiver, baseband, and MAC are being added to the road map.

ST Unveils WiMAX Modem Solution

Shortly after the IEEE ratified the new mobile WiMAX standard (802.16e), ST Microelectronics (ST), a supplier of SoC products for the wireless market, announced its turnkey solution for 802.16e BS modems. This new WiMAX offering promises to combine better silicon integration and optimized software libraries. ST's baseband modem combines two quad-MAC DSP cores, each running at

600 MHz, with a 300-MHz ARM926 RISC core, 16 Mb of embedded SRAM memory, and a dedicated channel decoding coprocessor in a single device, demonstrating what ST claims to be the industry's lowest cost-per-channel and highest throughput. According to the company, 802.16e benchmarks have shown that a single STW51000 can address a complete 10-MHz TDD PHY running on the DSPs, as well as the lower part of the MAC running on the ARM926. ST bundles its BS modem SoC with a set of in-house software libraries, including 802.16e software for FDD and TDD modes. The STW51000 is ready for full production. Samples, evaluation boards, tools, and software libraries are available. Delivered in the PBGA 569 package, the device costs $50 in volume orders.

Airspan Demonstrates Its Low-Cost, "Pay-as-You-Grow" WiMAX Base Station

Airspan Networks, Inc., a worldwide provider of WiMAX- and Wi-Fi-based BWA networks and carrier-class VoIP solutions, announced its plans to start shipping MicroMAX-SoC to its customers, initially available in the 3.5-GHz FDD band. Airspan is set to introduce support for the 5.8-GHz TDD and 3.3- to 3.4-GHz TDD bands, followed by a range of other 3.X- and 5.X-GHz bands. The MicroMAX-SoC is Airspan's third AS.MAX BS, the others being MacroMAX and MicroMAX-SDR. MicroMAX-SoC complements Airspan's other WiMAX BSs being optimized for low-density deployment, such as rural areas, in-fill for coverage holes in DSL and cable networks, enterprise solutions, and public safety applications.

Airspan Announces First Mobile WiMAX Device

Airspan Networks, Inc., announced support for mobile WiMAX on its AS.MAX WiMAX product line, and the first details of its revolutionary Mobile WiMAX USB device, called the 16eUSB. According to Airspan Networks, the 16eUSB is the first mobile WiMAX USB device. It is designed to be fully compatible with the IEEE's 802.16e-2005 standard and the WiMAX Forum Mobile WIMAX System Profile, and to support the profile's intelligence with MIMO, beam-forming smart antennas, idle and sleep modes, and handover. As a quad-band device that will operate in all key WiMAX frequency bands, including the 2.3 to 2.4 GHz, 2.5 to 2.7 GHz, 3.3 to 3.7 GHz, and the 4.9 to 5.4 GHz bands, it will allow a user to have access to WiMAX networks virtually anywhere in the world. Airspan also announced support for mobile WiMAX on AS.MAX, its class-leading WiMAX product line. Airspan's high-end AS.MAX BSs, known as HiperMAX and MicroMAX-SDR, will require a "software only" upgrade to enable them to support mobile WiMAX. With the upgrade, the BSs will simultaneously support both 256 OFDM fixed CPEs and SOFDMA mobile WiMAX laptop cards, handsets, and USB devices.

Pactolus SIPware VoIP Deployed Via Satellite and WiMAX by Sawtel

IP voice services provider Pactolus Communications said that its SIPware broadband telephony service is the first to be deployed commercially across a converged satellite and WiMAX ground network. Pactolus made the announcement after satellite and wireless communications company Sawtel chose SIPware to provide voice services to its customers. Pactolus said that this deployment of SIPware provides the industry with a successful model for extending profitable IP services across new networks and multi-network delivery paths. The initial deployment (1,000 nodes creating a 20-mi by 7-mi large cell) makes SIPware available to users on the island of Nassau. Plans are in the works to extend availability to users around the world who — because of accessibility, reliability, and economic barriers — might not otherwise be able to subscribe to IP services.

Alvarion Extends Its BreezeMAX Solution to New Frequencies

The world's leading provider of wireless broadband solutions and specialized mobile networks announced the extension of its BreezeMAX solution to 3.6 GHz with the introduction of the BreezeMAX 3600. Operating from 3.6 to 3.8 GHz and targeted to fixed WiMAX operators in Europe and other countries, the BreezeMAX 3600 enables carriers to offer broadband data, voice, and multimedia services with high performance over wide coverage areas.

Siemens Releases WiMAX Modem

Siemens has released its first WiMAX modem — the Gigaset SE461. The plug-and-play modem is based on the IEEE 802.16-2004 standard and is designed for residential users and small- to medium-sized enterprises. The Gigaset SE461 supports data transfer rates of up to 20 Mbps and can be used to access video-on-demand, video streaming, and VoIP. The device covers frequency ranges of 2.3 to 2.5, 3.4 to 3.6, and 3.6 to 3.8 GHz, enabling it to be used worldwide. The modem supports Microsoft Windows, Mac OS, and Linux, enabling it to network with nearly any other PC. It comes with a close-range antenna designed for desktop use, and an outdoor antenna with a longer range. The company also offers WiMAX BSs and systems to monitor and control WiMAX networks.

CompactFlash Card WiMAX

Runcom has announced the world's first mobile WiMAX Compact Flash card for Pocket PC, according to *PDA Live* (Figure 4.1) [69]. Besides creating a prototype mobile WiMAX (802.16e) transceiver on a CompactFlash card, the Israel-based

Figure 4.1 Runcom's compact flash card for pocket PC. (Courtesy of http://www.dailywireless.org/2006/11/28/compactflash-card-wimax/.)

company signed a collaboration agreement with Microsoft. The software giant agreed to help develop Windows Mobile 5.0 drivers to allow plug-and-play functionality. Then mobile WiMAX CF or USB cards would not need to install or download any drivers.

Runcom's user terminals and BSs comply with the IEEE802.16e-2005 standard for WiBro (the Korean WiMAX variant) and mobile WiMAX. They include the PHY and MAC communication layers. The company claims that its RNA200 ASIC was the first mobile WiMAX-compliant ASIC onto the market, a claim that might find dispute from Sequans, which has several design wins for its SQN1110 mobile WiMAX chip.

GaAs Switches Handle High Power for WiMAX

M/A-COM has announced two RoHS-compliant switches that are optimized for applications that require high power handling, low insertion loss, and high isolation, such as WiMAX or mesh applications. The MASW-007587 DPDT switch is designed to operate from DC to 4 GHz with output power at 1 dB, compression (P1dB) of 40 dBm, typical insertion loss of 1 dB, and isolation of 30 dB. Typical applications include two antenna solutions requiring diversity switching in linear systems that connect the receiver and transmitter to both antennas. The MASW-007588 SPDT switch is designed to operate from DC to 6 GHz with P1dB of 40 dBm, typical insertion loss of 0.7 dB, and isolation of 29 dB. Typical applications include single antenna for transmit/receive switching in linear systems. Fabricated on a 0.5 μm gate-length GaAs process with full passivation, both switches are housed in surface mount 3 × 3 mm PQFN packaging.

Texas Instruments Announces WiMAX Portfolio

Texas Instruments (TI) made a series of announcements regarding its portfolio of WiMAX chips. In addition to collaborations with ArrayComm and Mercury Computer Systems on the development of WiMAX products, the company introduced a new line of digital and analog solutions for WiMAX applications. With ArrayComm, TI announced a collaboration to combine ArrayComm's Network MIMO smart antenna technology with TI's high-performance DSPs on a single reference design. The combined solution, the companies say, will provide operators with twice the data rates and four times the system coverage of current systems, at a reduced cost. With Mercury Computer Systems, TI announced plans to develop the Mercury MTI-203 advanced mezzanine card (AMC) for WiMAX applications. MTI-203 combines three TI DSPs and a field-programmable gate array on a single AMC module.

The company's solution includes the following components:

- Support for fixed and mobile wireless infrastructure applications in multiple frequency bands
- The TMS320TCI6482 1 GHz DSP plus a WiMAX PHY software library for the DSP platform
- A full portfolio of RF products, as well as data converters, up/down converters, and amplifiers
- Collaborations with vendors such as ArrayComm and Mercury to develop reference designs

The offering, which supports the 802.16e standard, includes the TCI6482 DSP, baseband software, and development tools. The system suits both full-sized and "pico" BSs that will serve in roles including mobile access, rural service, cellular backhaul, and last-mile access, according to the company. The TCI6482 provides enough horsepower to efficiently process the WiMAX PHY plus algorithms for FFT/IFFT (FFT/inverse FFT) and MIMO/beamforming, according to TI.

TI Teams with Design Company on WiMAX

TI has announced a collaboration with India-based Tata Elxsi Ltd., the product design arm of the Tata Group, on an end-to-end baseband demonstration system for IEEE 802.16e infrastructure products. Designed to speed time-to-market for mobile WiMAX BS solutions, the system combines both the hardware and software required for system implementation, including a fully integrated MAC, allowing customers to incorporate the complete solution into their own products. TI announced its own 802.16e infrastructure solution for wireless applications, including software, analog, and RF products, to support the emerging mobile WiMAX industry. The design will enable all PHY processing required for a 10-MHz, multi-antenna base band solution with MIMO transmission across various interfaces. The system will incorporate Mercury Computer's MTI-203 advanced mezzanine card for WiMAX, anchored with three TI TMS320TCI6482 DSPs and a supporting compute node to create a WiMAX infrastructure base band solution. The MTI-203 AMC card can plug into serial Rapid I/O-based Advanced Telecom Computing Architecture (TCA) carrier cards, as well as MicroTCA and AdvancedTCA chassis that support Serial RapidIO (PICMG 3.5) across the backplane. The software components, available as a part of this demonstration system, will allow OEMs to select and optimize specific pieces of the design in their own implementation, reducing product development time and allowing them to customize the software and add their own IP.

Proxim Announces WiMAX Family

Proxim Wireless Corporation, a provider of broadband wireless equipment and a wholly owned subsidiary of Terabeam, Inc., has announced that it has launched a family of WiMAX standard-based products that offer service providers, according to Proxim, a compelling cost profile for a high performance wireless product in the 3.5-GHz band. Tsunami MP.16 offers a modular, scalable approach to system deployment. A wider range of service providers, from rural providers requiring less dense configurations to metropolitan providers who need to support more nodes at closer range, will be able to use the WiMAX technology, said Proxim. Proxim announced that its Tsunami MP.11 point-to-multipoint product line had been enhanced with features including WiMAX QoS, roaming with seamless handoffs at speeds up to 200 km/hr and dynamic frequency selection that had already received EN 301-893 v1.3.1 certification. The Tsunami MP.16 3500 is compliant with the 802.16d-2004 WiMAX standard. It operates within the 3.4- to 3.6-GHz frequency band and offers TDD, which is optimal for asynchronous traffic patterns as typically experienced by service providers. The system is comprised of BSs and subscriber units in integrated, outdoor form factors for easy installation.

Nortel Bolsters WiMAX Position with Portfolio Enhancements, New Customers

Nortel is developing a complete portfolio of MIMO-powered WiMAX systems to serve numerous global markets and customer scenarios. Nortel's WiMAX products are designed to allow wireless and wireline carriers, cable providers, media companies, and other ISPs to deliver broadband connectivity to consumer and enterprise users by leveraging existing networks and last-mile wireless links. The portfolio also provides greenfield service providers with newly acquired spectrum to deliver the high-bandwidth promise of WiMAX. Service providers who have recently selected Nortel's WiMAX solution include NEW Energie in Germany, Chunghwa Telecom (CHT) and National Taiwan University in Taiwan, and Telefónica Móviles in México. Nortel and German regional power utility NEW Energie have completed a successful WiMAX broadband service trial. The trial, in the town of Erkelenz in North Rhine-Westphalia, lays the foundations for NEW Energie's commercial launch of WiMAX for bandwidth-intensive wireless services such as live multimedia streams, VoIP applications, and high-speed Internet access. For the trial, Nortel worked with German communications consultant tkt teleconsult to deploy a WiMAX network that allowed NEW Energie to provide broadband wireless connections to a selection of small businesses and consumers at speeds of up to 10 Mbps, equal to the current fastest fixed-DSL services. Nortel also signed an agreement with Chunghwa Telecom to deploy a WiMAX solution in the operator's experimental park to create an environment for testing WiMAX and wireless Mesh integration. In addition, Nortel is deploying a WiMAX trial system at the National Taiwan University campus so that the university can perform field validation and interoperability testing using a variety of devices and multimedia applications. Nortel also completed a trial with the Alberta Special Areas Board (SAB) and NETAGO Wireless for what is expected to be Canada's first commercial WiMAX network. In addition to these and other customer trials, Nortel is responding to increased interest in its WiMAX solution and has expanded its product portfolio to deliver mobile MIMO-enabled WiMAX products in the 1.5-, 2.3-, 2.5-, and 3.5-GHz spectrum bands, establishing one of the most comprehensive global WiMAX and WiBro portfolios in the industry. The products are designed with a flexible architecture that allows for quick rebanding for emerging markets. Nortel is also launching WiMAX demo centers and interoperability labs to include a wide range of device and application partners in their state-of-the-art facilities in Ottawa and Taiwan. In addition, Nortel is working to bridge the digital divide in emerging markets and rural communities through government initiatives designed to bring affordable broadband services to businesses and consumers. Nortel's fixed-WiMAX solution supplied by Airspan achieved the designation of WiMAX Forum-certified, based on the defined FDD system profile operating in the 3.5-GHz frequency spectrum. Nortel's WiMAX solution is expected to show the advantages of WiMAX in delivering bandwidth-intensive, real-time applications on the go in urban settings and how it brings high-speed, broadband connectivity to rural areas.

Alvarion Mobile WiMAX Solution, 4Motion, Targeted for Multiple Markets

Texas Instruments announced that Alvarion has selected the company's portfolio of WiMAX infrastructure technologies as part of its mobile WiMAX solution, 4Motion. Alvarion's BreezeMAX system, the primary building block of 4Motion's radio access network, will leverage TI technology to address the growing demand for mobile broadband wireless technologies, including support for IEEE 802.16e standards, across a broad range of spectrum. These products enable carriers to offer high-performance broadband data, voice, and multimedia services over wider coverage areas. Alvarion's current BreezeMAX WiMAX platform is designed from the ground up according to the IEEE 802.16 standards and uses OFDM technology for advanced NLoS functionality. Its carrier-class design supports broadband speeds and QoS to enable carriers to offer triple play services to thousands of subscribers in a single BS.

Alvarion is the first to provide WiMAX equipment incorporating TI's flexible analog and DSP-based infrastructure technology compliant with the IEEE 802.16e standard, and its BreezeMAX system is well suited to meet the needs of fixed, portable, and mobile wireless broadband applications. Developing products for fixed, portable, and mobile WiMAX markets is a key to success in this growing industry, as Forward Concepts estimates that, by 2009, sales of WiMAX equipment for both segments will total $2 billion. TI announced its complete solution for the WiMAX market based on its TMS320TCI6482 1 GHz DSP, designed for wireless infrastructure applications. The chip is complemented with an advanced software library that reduces product development time while allowing manufacturers to customize the software and add their own intellectual property. TI's flexible solution supports both fixed and mobile applications across multiple frequency bands, enabling equipment manufacturers to create cost-effective system configurations that can be used for multiple broadband wireless applications.

Alvarion Gives a Peek into Mobile VoIP Future

The company has articulated a clear product road map for mobile broadband designed to support not just VoIP but also multimedia IP services of all kinds, including video, over a wireless network that will support ubiquitous broadband connectivity. The more sophisticated type of MIMO that Alvarion is showing provides multiple antennas that can accept and process multiple broadband signals. A complete system includes network systems for handoffs and subscriber management.

Morpho Readies Mobile WiMAX Chip Design

Morpho Technologies has started sampling a licensable hardware and software package for companies designing mobile WiMAX devices. Based on an up-front licensing model, with pricing dependent on volumes and application requirements, the package is targeted at companies looking to add WiMAX support to their existing wireless communication offerings or those planning to develop stand-alone WiMAX products, including handsets, notebook PCs, and portable audio, video, and gaming devices. The integrated 802.16e system solution comprises the recently introduced MS2 PHY Communications Engine, Morpho's SoftPhy software, and the MT 802.16e MAC software. The MS2 reconfigurable communications engine enables Adaptive Algorithm Selection (AAS), which can adapt the PHY algorithms based on channel conditions. This provides better adaptive performance than traditional device architectures. The platform can also be leveraged to implement other air interfaces. Morpho says its "soft," licensable approach can implement an SoC solution in 3 to 6 months, compared to 18 to 24 months typically required for in-house development programs. It adds that the approach offers a significant reduction in risk and can greatly accelerate time-to-market for WiMAX-enabled devices.

Network Evolution with Alcatel 9500 MXC

Alcatel has announced its microwave product — the Alcatel 9500 Microwave Cross Connect (MXC). The Alcatel 9500 MXC enables operators to evolve their networks in line with their business needs without additional external peripherals. The new products offer a flexible architecture ready to transport IP and TDM services via trouble-free migration from legacy networks so that operators are able to maximize the potential of their existing infrastructures — and also maximize return on their investments. The Alcatel 9500 MXC is ideally suited for mobile applications; it features a single indoor/outdoor platform for linking cell sites to the core network for mobile 2G/3G and WiMAX. The platform also offers private operators the dual benefits of higher bandwidth at lower cost and delivers the higher QoS required by metropolitan network operators. Indeed, the integrated multiplexing, cross-connect, and routing capabilities featured in the Alcatel 9500 MXC provide operators — wireless, wireline, and private network operators alike — the flexibility they require. It also affords customers the ability to move to IP at a pace of their choosing, as it smoothes traffic migration with expandable capacity. In North America, the Alcatel 9500 MXC complements ongoing development of Alcatel's existing portfolio of wireless transmission solutions, including the Alcatel 9400 AWY and the industry standard Alcatel MDR-8000.

Telsima Launches Complete WiMAX Solution

Telsima Corporation has announced the launch of its StarMAX line of carrier-grade WiMAX solutions for wireless broadband access. The product range targets operators seeking standards-based, quick time-to-market broadband service deployment for their enterprise and residential customers. StarMAX supports active subscriber mobility management and indoor NLoS SS antenna gains. Telsima provides end-to-end broadband network solutions to enable service delivery at disruptive cost points for the highly competitive telecommunications market. The StarMAX product family comprises a complete suite of WiMAX solutions, including

■ The StarMAX 4100 Series of WiMAX BSs with single- or dual-sector support for several hundred subscribers each, with configuration options that offer support for built-in STC/MRC, GPS, P2P backhaul, or E1 support.

- The StarMAX 2100 Series of WiMAX SSs with three models addressing the residential and enterprise subscribers: StarMAX 2120 — the full indoor NLoS SSs, StarMAX 2110 — outdoor antenna SS with indoor modem, and StarMAX 2150 — outdoor SS with antenna-integrated outdoor modem.
- StarMAX NMS: a GUI-based element management system/network management system that delivers full FCAPS (fault, configuration, accounting, performance, security) functionality.
- StarMAX ProVision: the provisioning and mobility manager, which allows operators to centrally control access, mobility, bandwidth, and QoS for each subscriber.

The StarMAX portfolio supports a range of unique features, including active subscriber mobility management, unmatched indoor NLoS SS antenna gains, integrated P2P microwave backhaul with common Element Management System (EMS), and proprietary RF technology, says the company. As large parts of the world's population get connected to the Internet, Telsima sees WiMAX as the ideal last-mile solution for broadband connectivity, especially in the fast-growing emerging markets that are rapidly growing their telecom networks. Telsima is committed to fulfilling the long promised benefits of BWA by leveraging the benefits of standardization, innovative design, and large market size to deliver disruptive price-performance points. Telsima also offers WiMAX RF simulation to support network planning and to estimate the capacity and coverage of the planned WiMAX infrastructure.

Solar-Powered Streetlights That Deliver Wi-Fi and WiMAX Access Being Tested

Project Starsight is a partnership between Compliance Technology of Fife, Scotland; the London-based sustainable development firm Kolam; the Singapore-based networking company Next-G Systems; and the Abertay Center for the Environment (ACE) at the University of Abertay in Dundee, Scotland. The collaboration has yielded a solar-powered Wi-Fi router/WiMAX router/surveillance camera that may be situated on top of a solar-powered streetlight. The StarSight access point uses a high-gain omni antenna and a high-gain parabolic antenna to offer access and security in a variety of economic regions. It is in use in Cameroon, and there are plans for deployment in India, China, and Morocco. The technology could also offer a power outlet at its base for plugging in VoIP phones, for example.

Azimuth Announces New Wi-Fi and WiMAX Testing Products

Azimuth Systems has announced a number of new products to facilitate accurate testing of Wi-Fi, WiMAX, cellular, and Bluetooth products. The company has rolled out the ACE 400NB MIMO channel emulator for testing Wi-Fi products, as well as the MIMO-ready RadioProof enclosures. The enclosures offer RF isolation to facilitate more accurate testing. The company has also introduced a desktop platform providing Wi-Fi design engineers with a compact solution to meet their testing needs. Three desktop solutions enable testing of standard PC clients, voice- or application-specific clients, and voice-capable infrastructure. Azimuth has also enhanced its W-Series 802.11 test platform with a number of functionality upgrades. The company's STUDIO software is a Wi-Fi data management application that enables the collection, correlation, and analysis of critical test data from multiple sources. STUDIO works in conjunction with the Azimuth DIRECTOR software, which executes test scripts for individual test platforms. The company's products all feature the SmartMotion attenuation system for precise measurement of performance-over-range.

Wavesat and Sanmina-SCI Announce Agreement to Bring WiMAX Mini-PCI to Market

Low-cost and high-quality WiMAX 3.5-GHz Mini-PCI modules are available to OEM/ODMs worldwide. Wavesat and Sanmina-SCI, an EMS company, announced an agreement for production and cost optimization of the WiMAX mini-PCI. The low-cost, small-form factor WiMAX 3.5-GHz mini-PCI modules are available for volume delivery. The WiMAX mini-PCI modules are based on Wavesat's recently launched WiMAX 3.5-GHz mini-PCI Reference Design, and incorporates Wavesat's EvolutiveTM DM256 chipset and MAC coprocessor. Further, the WiMAX mini-PCI modules are fully compliant with the IEEE 802.16-2004 standard and offer easy upgradeability to 802.16e-2005 for basic mobility applications, as well as supporting TDD and HFDD 3.5- and 7.0-MHz bandwidths and modulation up to 64 QAM.

RF Power Detector Handles Wi-Fi, WiMAX Applications

According to Linear Technology, its LTC5533 dual-channel RF power detector is the first in the industry to reach the 11-GHz range, making it suitable for multiband Wi-Fi, WiMAX, and other radio applications. Covering RF applications ranging from 300 MHz to 11 GHz, the dual-channel LTC5533 supports multiple frequencies in one package, as needed for multi-band applications. The device is optimized for power, drawing 500 μA per detector. The LTC5533 contains temperature compensation circuitry designed to provide stable and accurate measurements over the full range of temperature extremes. The device includes buffer amplifiers and is housed in a 4 × 3 mm surface mount package. Key features include two independent temperature-compensated Schottky diode RF peak detectors, 45 dB channel-to-channel isolation at 2 GHz, 300 MHz to 11 GHz input frequency range, –32 dBm to 12 dBm input power range, and 2.7 Vdc to 6 Vdc range. The LTC5533 dual RF power detector is well suited for a range of applications, including dual-band Wi-Fi PA power control, dual-band cellular/WiMAX BS, P2P microwave links, transmit PA forward and reverse power measurements, and low-cost amplitude modulation (AM) detector/receivers.

Adaptive WiMAX Antenna Shown Off

One of the world's first "WiMAX-ready" adaptive antenna systems was unveiled by wireless solutions group Radio Frequency Systems (RFS) at the CTIA Wireless 2006 exhibition. Designed to meet the needs of emerging IEEE 802.16 WiMAX broadband wireless data networks, the new RFS W4A Series antenna system features precision beam-pattern shaping. The new adaptive antenna — which is part of a broad and growing WiMAX suite of solutions from RFS — provides network managers with a powerful tool to ensure optimal data throughput and a reduction in overall cell-to-cell interference across the WiMAX network. Available in 2.5- and 3.5-GHz models (W4A25-90ANV and W4A35-90ANV), the heart of each W4A Series adaptive antenna system is a four-element antenna array. Flexible beam-pattern tailoring is achieved by applying phase and amplitude modulation to each element. As a result, the shape of the beam pattern can be modified in response to changing subscriber traffic and interference sources or as part of a longer-term strategy to ensure optimal data throughput, spectrum use, or network capacity.

TeleCIS Wireless Introduces WiMAX 802.16-2004 SoC Chip

TeleCIS Wireless, Inc., has introduced its TCW 1620 chip, which enables both low-cost, indoor self-installed CPE for fixed WiMAX services and a portable services market before the advent of standardized mobile services. The chip is based on the standard (IEEE 802.16-2004) for fixed WiMAX services that are being rolled out. The chip will enable consumers to buy and install their own fixed indoor equipment — which makes the residential market more viable for carriers — and to also enjoy portable connectivity via PC cards and small USB devices while traveling away from their home or office. The portable capability, in particular, is attractive to network operators because a WiMAX system or network supporting classic last-mile access applications can also support portable operation and hence addresses a much larger market need than does a strictly fixed WiMAX implementation that must be plugged in or bolted to walls. Consumers, particularly the millions around the world accustomed to Wi-Fi-like roaming and portability, also stand to benefit sooner from the higher connection speeds, QoS-enabled applications, and larger coverage area afforded by WiMAX service. The company makes all of this possible via performance enhancements such as MIMO-based techniques, including diversity combining space–time coding on a one-chip design to boost signal gain. Benefiting from the company's experience developing OFDM-based Wi-Fi solutions, the chip provides more than just the WiMAX mandatory compliance features and even more than the WiMAX optional features. By incorporating the company's portfolio of range extension techniques — Rx Technologies — TeleCIS Wireless solutions claims to provide exceptional performance up to 15 dB over competing solutions. In addition, the tightly integrated ASIC has the built-in ability to support a two-antenna (Rx and Tx) MIMO consumer device with a single chip, which is said to deliver high performance in an NLoS environment in a very small form factor and the lowest bill of materials cost for fixed and portable equipment vendors. Evolving to full mobility, the company believes it will continue to lead the market with its second chip, the TCW 2720, delivering WiMAX (802.16e) Mobile/WiBro, Wi-Fi, MIMO, and smart antenna functionality in a single chip designed for handheld devices. This chip will allow end users to connect to the most appropriate network any time and anywhere and provides a solution for WiMAX operators and user terminal device manufacturers as well.

Axxcelera Broadband Wireless Announces WiMAX Certification of Full Duplex FDD CPE

Axxcelera Broadband Wireless, a Moseley Wireless Solutions Group company providing broadband wireless communications products and technologies, announced that it has received the WiMAX Forum Certified seal for Axxcelera's 3.5-GHz ExcelMax Full Duplex FDD CPE SS. The 3.5-GHz ExcelMax platform operates in the 3.3- to 3.8-GHz licensed spectrum. It comprises three different BS architectures: a carrier-class BS chassis, a stackable ultralite base station, and a completely integrated outdoor Access Point. Three different CPE types complement the range of BS products: an outdoor full duplex FDD CPE for VoIP and triple play business customers, an outdoor half duplex FDD/TDD CPE for high-speed Internet and VoIP customers, and a low-cost self-install indoor CPE for residential customers. Broadband users on the ExcelMax system can be centrally provisioned and managed using a scalable carrier grade ExcelMax provisioning and management platform. The ExcelMax platform supports FDD and TDD operation, allowing the use of ExcelMax solutions in different regions of the world where either FDD or TDD spectrum has been allocated. Existing Axxcelera Excel Air customers will be able to upgrade their BSs for WiMAX operation, and future 802.16e operation will be supported in the carrier-class BSs and Access Point configurations.

Handheld Analyzer Offers Fixed WiMAX Test Options

Test equipment maker Anritsu Co. has introduced fixed WiMAX IEEE-802.16-2004 test options for its existing MT8222A BTS Master RF analyzer [2,3]. They render the MT8222A handheld field equipment ready for measuring WiMAX emitters.

The options add RF measurements and demodulation to the BTS Master, joining cable and antenna analysis with interference analysis and spectrum analysis [19]. The unit also provides a power meter and bit error rate tester, and can operate as a channel scanner and power monitor. With the fixed WiMAX options, the BTS Master can serve as a single instrument for anyone responsible for the deployment of WiMAX networks, measuring the transmitted signal strength and signal shape of a selected BTS transmission. The options include familiar channel spectrum, power versus time, adjacent-channel power ratio, and RF summary screens. A demodulator option analyzes OFDM signals and displays detailed measurements for evaluating transmitter modulation performance. The BTS Master's pass/fail mode can also be used with the options. The feature allows a test procedure to be selected, then the BTS Master displays the test results in table format with clear pass or fail indications. Anritsu's Master Software Tools can also be used with the fixed-WiMAX options. This data management and analysis software suite permits custom tests to be created and downloaded into the BTS Master. In addition to fixed-WiMAX analysis, the BTS Master can do W-CDMA/HSDPA and GSM/GPRS/EDGE measurements.

Mobile WiMAX: Rosedale 2

Rosedale 2 is a low-cost SoC that supports IEEE 802.16-2004 and IEEE 802.16e-2005, enabling WiMAX modems for use with fixed or mobile networks. Rosedale 2 is optimized for cost-effective WiMAX modems and benefits from the economics of combined IEEE 802.16d and 802.16e volumes in equipment. The cost effectiveness of Rosedale 2 is further enhanced by its modem designs featuring Ofer-R, Intel's single RF SoC, Wi-Fi/WiMAX multi-band solution. Because it is pin compatible with the Intel PRO/Wireless 5116 wireless modem, Rosedale 2 offers an easy upgrade path for equipment manufacturers. It enables them to design modems with the capability to evolve from 802.16-2004 to 802.16e-2005 with a software update and supports 802.16-2004 and 802.16e-2005 software stacks for flexibility in equipment design, deployment, and applications. Using Rosedale 2-based devices, service providers can choose to immediately deploy a mobile WiMAX network or, in some cases, deploy a fixed-WiMAX network now that can be easily and cost-effectively upgraded to a mobile WiMAX network. Rosedale 2 also gives service providers a path to a Centrino Mobile Technologies-ready network by utilizing the profiles that are expected to eventually be integrated into Centrino Mobile Technology-based notebooks.

Wireless-Enabled Train

The Caltrain commuter rail service [4] has hooked up 16 mi of their track between Millbrae and Palo Alto, California, using WiMAX backbone from Redline, connectivity from Nomad, and in-train Wi-Fi routers from Sensoria to provide speedy connections to commuters while traveling at 79 mph. Tests of the system seemed to work great, with several commuters watching streamed video, pulling large file downloads, and even answering e-mail simultaneously. Now that the technology has been successfully demonstrated, its promoters are planning on building it out across the rest of their line. The future is indeed bright.

LCC Delivers on Its Business Tools Strategy with WiView, a Dynamic Web-Based WiMAX Network Dimensioning Tool

LCC International, Inc., a global leader in wireless voice and data turn-key services, announced the commercial availability of WiView, a comprehensive business planning and dimensioning tool designed to evaluate and estimate the infrastructure requirements and resulting capital and operational expenditures for designing a WiMAX broadband network. WiView is the first to be commercialized in a series of business planning, optimization, and performance tools designed by LCC's Research and Development group. It is the first dimensioning tool on the market dedicated to analyzing WiMAX technology. WiView's proprietary analysis methodologies and dimensioning tools can be utilized in conjunction with services provided by LCC's team of broadband network planning consultants. LCC launched WiView to provide its clients (wireless operators, mobile content companies, equipment manufacturers, and financial analysts) a comprehensive business planning and analysis tool to thoroughly understand the economics of delivering WiMAX services. WiView is a powerful tool that supports the required planning and evaluation of critical elements to bring emerging data, video, and other WiMAX applications and services to market. It represents a major innovation in strategic and business planning. This one-of-a-kind tool can assist clients with evaluation of technology, equipment, and implementation options for fixed and mobile WiMAX broadband networks. WiView's complex analytical program structure allows for examination of the market dynamics, infrastructure requirements, and resulting business case. The tool estimates the network infrastructure required to support specified coverage and capacity requirements, and provides for a variety of "what-if" scenarios to help identify key variables in the business plan. WiView is a Web-based tool that dimensions a network for various WiMAX deployment scenarios and also provides business case analysis. It can be used to analyze the dynamics of fixed or mobile WiMAX deployments and can support greenfield and overlay scenarios. Inputs and results are segmented in various morphological areas such as heavy urban, urban, suburban, and rural. Inputs to the tool are assumptions categorized as marketing (coverage footprint, subscriber counts and usage, etc.), technical (spectrum, channel bandwidth, link budget, WiMAX-specific inputs, etc.), and financial (CapEx, OpEx, etc.). Results include network components such as site counts spectrum requirements, CapEx- and OpEx-based results, as well as financial information including EBITDA, NPV, etc. WiView can be used to perform advanced sensitivity analysis such as "what-if" deployment scenarios, analyze effects of implementing various subscriber usage models, determine spectrum requirements or check effects of spectrum constraints, calculate the minimum number of sites required, and perform several other types of technical and business analyses.

Redline and MARAC Showcase Redline's Indoor "User-Install" WiMAX CPE

RedMAX SU-I indoor plug-and-play modem enables delivery of personal broadband services and rapid deployment of WiMAX networks. Redline Communications, provider of standards-based wireless broadband equipment, announced its RedMAX family of WiMAX products, including the RedMAX SU-I indoor user-installable CPE [5]. Redline's RedMAX SU-I is a user-install, plug-and-play indoor WiMAX modem that delivers personal broadband connectivity to residences and small- to mid-sized enterprises. The SU-I will allow service providers and operators to deliver services quickly, easily add new customers, and realize a return on their WiMAX infrastructure investment. Operating in the 3.3- to 3.5-GHz licensed frequency band and designed to WiMAX Forum Certified specifications, the RedMAX SU-I incorporates an attractive and innovative design with the smallest form factor in the WiMAX industry.

Rohde & Schwarz Adds WiMAX Measurement Solutions

The Vector Signal Generator R&S SMJ100A [6], in combination with the compact Spectrum Analyzer R&S FSL, is a cost-efficient production measurement solution for WiMAX applications offered by Rohde & Schwarz. Internal options allow the performance of tests in accordance with the IEEE 802.16-2004 and IEEE 802.16e-2005 standards. By using the Digital Standard WiMAX R&S SMJ-K49 option, it is possible to generate signals on the physical layer for both mobile and stationary applications. The R&S FSL-K92 option includes all stationary WiMAX applications. For IEEE 802.16e, Rohde & Schwarz currently offers an external solution for the R&S FSL. For the development of WiMAX, Rohde & Schwarz already has the successful high-end Vector Signal Generator R&S SMU200A and the high-quality Signal Analyzer R&S FSQ on the market. The WiMAX package consisting of the R&S SMJ100A and R&S FSL now provides a version that covers all requirements in production. The version for development as well as the one for production can both be remote controlled and have the same user interface, which is truly an advantage. By using the internal R&S SMJ-K49 option, users can generate signals for mobile and stationary applications for the IEEE 802.16-2004 standard, as well as for the current IEEE 802.16e-2005 standard. The new functionalities can be remote controlled via LAN or general purpose interface bus (GPIB). Moreover, the high speed at which frequencies and waveforms are changed means very short throughput time. The R&S SMJ also offers standard-compliant signals for receiver tests and high signal quality when performing amplifier tests. The R&S FSL-K92 option of the Spectrum Analyzer R&S FSL allows users to perform measurements on WiMAX signals in accordance with the OFDM method even without an additional PC. At the moment, users can perform tests on OFDMA signals for mobile applications by using external Windows software. Remote control via LAN is also available. The measurement of modulation quality and all RF parameters such as adjacent-channel power or spectrum masks as well as high measurement speed make the R&S FSL unique in its price class, and significantly reduce throughput time in production.

Sequans and Mitac Bring WiMAX End-User Device to Market

Sequans Communications, a supplier and developer of fixed and mobile WiMAX semiconductor solutions, and Mitac Technology announced their collaboration and the availability of the first of several WiMAX devices Mitac is manufacturing using Sequans' WiMAX fixed and mobile SOCs. T220B, the first unit to become available under the Sequans/Mitac agreement, is a fixed WiMAX (802.16-2004) self-installable desktop unit that provides wireless broadband connectivity at the 3.5-GHz frequency. T220B features switched diversity between four built-in antennas and supports space–time coding (STC) and subchannelization. The RF chip for this device is provided by Sierra Monolithics, one of Sequans' RF partners. Mitac is also developing mobile WiMAX subscriber units built around Sequans' 802.16e-2005 SoCs. The mobile WiMAX units currently under development for release in late 2006 include a PCMCIA card and a desktop unit. The Mitac WiMAX end-user devices are thoroughly tested and proven interoperable with WiMAX BSs using chips from Sequans or others. Sequans has been at the forefront of interoperability testing.

Intel Wows with Dual-Mode WiMAX Chip

Intel Corp. is to announce [8] a client chipset that supports both the fixed and mobile versions of the WiMAX wireless broadband technology. The company is working to make the case for the technology with a chipset road map that targets devices ranging from video games to digital cameras — the idea being that if the clients are there, the carriers will come. The company will unveil Rosedale 2, which has the capability of working both in the 802.16d and 802.16e modes. The chip is meant for use in residential gateways and modems, but the company is also exploring its use in picocell BSs. Intel plans to introduce a single-chip radio called Ofer-R that supports both Wi-Fi and WiMAX.

Virgin Trains May Opt for WiMAX

Travelers on Virgin Trains' West Coast line may be [9] getting Wi-Fi access with WiMAX backhaul. Nomad Digital has emerged as the preferred bidder for the project, which would involve trackside WiMAX base stations connected via DSL and placed every few miles along the route. The WiMAX signal would in turn be relayed to Wi-Fi access points on the trains to provide seamless connectivity for passengers even in tunnels or underground. Nomad Digital is the company behind a scheme already running on the Southern Trains' Brighton Express route from London. Operated by T-Mobile, that service also uses WiMAX for backhaul. Nomad runs similar schemes in the Netherlands and Silicon Valley. As with the Brighton Express service, the Virgin scheme would involve WiMAX coverage backed up with HSDPA for any momentary gaps that might occur. Wi-Fi access has already been made available at some first-class lounges on Virgin's West Coast routes, but this development would be the first time passengers would be able to get connected on board. The service could be extended to Virgin's cross-country service.

Alvarion's BreezeMAX Streams Multimedia Content to Multiple WiMAX Devices Using 802.16e Technology

Alvarion Ltd. announced that its BreezeMAX system is streaming concurrent multimedia content to multiple third-party, end-user devices, showing robust QoS that ultimately enables broadband mobile voice, video, and data services over a single connection. Employing IEEE 802.16e technology, the company is also demonstrating the power of its new 4Motion WiMAX solution, enabled by its BreezeMAX base stations. 4Motion [10] is a complete, end-to-end mobile WiMAX solution incorporating advanced radio technologies, QoS mechanisms, IP mobility core components, and multimedia subsystems, along with subscriber terminals, an OMC, and back-end interfaces. Employing software-defined radio (SDR), beam forming, MIMO, dynamic bandwidth allocation, and scaleable OFDMA technologies, 4Motion and BreezeMAX offer service providers greater coverage, capacity, and flexibility in their mobile WiMAX deployments, along with improved economics.

Wavesat and TI Working on WiMAX Access Card

TI and Wavesat are working on a reference design for a mini-PCI module that will lead to smaller and simpler WiMAX wireless systems [11]. The 5.8-GHz mini-PCI card fits into laptop computers and allows users to connect to the Internet via wireless WiMAX, and the companies plan to have a product commercially available. The reference design would simplify WiMAX design requirements and enable producers to get products to market faster and react quicker to trends in consumer demand. Key features of the design will include 37.5 Mbps data throughput, 10 MHz channel bandwidth, and dynamic frequency selection.

Accton Introduces Low-Cost Mobile WiMAX CPE

Accton Technology has announced the launch of its first wireless broadband modem for operators who are deploying WiMAX networks in the popular 2- and 3-GHz frequency bands [12]. This new series of self-installable CPEs, the WI2400 for operation in the 2-GHz band and the WI3400 for operation in the 3-GHz band, are based on Beceem's MS120 Mobile WiMAX chipset. The CPEs are equipped with two detachable Omni antennas and one optional external antenna. They are easy to install, and allow service providers to address the needs of the fast-growing wireless broadband market. The company said its low-cost WiMAX CPE is a key enabler for the mass deployment of WiMAX networks globally, especially in emerging markets such as India, Pakistan, Southeast Asia, Latin America, Eastern Europe, and the Middle East.

Nokia Introduces Its Flexi WiMAX BS

Nokia announced its Nokia Flexi WiMAX BS, which features a compact size and lightweight design that minimizes space requirements, power consumption, and physical effort to install and run WiMAX networks. It can be installed both indoors and outdoors, and does not require air conditioning. In addition, its modularity allows for easy capacity upgrades as traffic increases. Nokia Flexi WiMAX BS will be commercially available for the 2.5-GHz band and for the 3.5-GHz band [13].

Analog Devices Introduces Series of Clock Generators for WiMAX BSs and Other Telecom Applications

Analog Devices, Inc., has introduced a family of clock generators made to improve the reliability of telecommunications and instrumentation equipment while also reducing size and costs [14]. The clock generator produces a timing or clock signal for use in synchronizing a circuit's operation. It is extremely precise and reliable for applications such as wireless communications and optical networks. Analog Device's single-chip approach replaces a number of discrete components, enabling designers to reduce board space and materials costs. It also improves overall system reliability by diminishing the risks associated with the failure of discrete oscillators. The AD9516 clock IC combines low phase noise clock generation with 14-channel clock distribution at jitter levels below 1 ps. The new series also integrates an integer-N synthesizer, two reference inputs, a voltage-controlled oscillator, programmable dividers, and adjustable delay lines. It offers 14 clock drivers as well, including LVPECL, LVDS, and CMOS. The series is ideal for applications such as wireless and wired infrastructure, optical networks, medical imaging, automated test equipment, and WiMAX BSs. It works for a variety of additional instrumentation that requires low phase noise and low time jitter in the clock path. The AD9526 series has five versions, and each supports a specific frequency range. The AD9516-0 features a VCO that tunes from 2.60 to 2.95 GHz. Other versions cover low frequencies down to 1.50 GHz and 1.90 GHz. Each version may be used with an external VCO of up to 2.4 GHz, and offers six LVPECL outputs, operating up to the maximum VCO rate. All versions also offer four/eight outputs that may be programmed for LVDS or CMOS levels, operating up to 1 GHz and 250 MHz, respectively.

Intel Ships Next-Generation WiMAX Chip

Intel has announced the availability of the Intel WiMAX Connection 2250 — the company's next-generation SoC, which is designed to support mobile networks in addition to fixed networks [15]. According to Intel, the WiMAX Connection 2250 is a dual-mode baseband chip, and, when paired with Intel's discrete tri-band WiMAX radio, the solution is capable of supporting all global WiMAX frequencies. Motorola joins several other telecommunications equipment manufacturers currently expected to deliver Intel WiMAX Connection 2250-based products in 2007.

D-Link Announces WiMAX 802.16-2005 Router

D-Link announced its entry into the WiMAX CPE market with an 802.16e-compliant WiMAX router designed for service providers looking to offer wireless residential service at rates competitive with wire-line technologies [16]. The D-Link WiMAX router combines both WiMAX and Wi-Fi technologies to offer an all-in-one solution for in-house wireless coverage with easy installation and remote management features for service providers. The router is an ideal, cost-effective alternative for delivering a fast and secure broadband connection to consumers who are not reachable by DSL or cable broadband services, according to D-Link. This router supports WMAN and multiple PHY protocols. It supports adaptive modulation — 64 QAM, 16 QAM, QPSK — with up to 5 bs^{-1} Hz spectral efficiency, 1 K FFT, and channel bandwidth up to 20 MHz. Security implementation is based on AES-CCM. Efficient MAC secure data unit (SDU) fragmentation/packing maximizes bandwidth utilization.

Mobile WiMAX Solution Rolls for AWR's VSS Suite

Applied Wave Research, Inc. (AWR) announced a mobile WiMAX solution for the company's Visual System Simulator (VSS) design suite [17]. The software meets the specification defined in the WMAN OFDMA PHY of the IEEE 802.16e air interface for fixed and mobile broadband wireless access systems standard. In addition, it complements the IEEE 802.16d WMAN-OFDM PHY fixed-wireless capability previously released by AWR. The VSS Mobile WiMAX technology enables RF and baseband SoC designers, component suppliers, original equipment manufacturers, user equipment companies, and infrastructure and network equipment providers to design and verify WiMAX-certified products. The software contains all bit-level processing defined in the 802.16e specifications as well as the receiver functionality and the ability to incorporate circuit and RF interactions. A beta version of the VSS Mobile WiMAX software is available immediately, and full production release of the software is available in 2007.

Spirent Introduces WiMAX Testing

Spirent Communications announced a new channel emulation testing solution for WiMAX equipment manufacturers and service providers. The SR550 Wireless Channel Emulator replicates real-world multi-path interference and fading conditions in the lab. The company worked with the WiMAX Forum to develop the functionality for the SR5500, the fifth generation of channel emulation from Spirent. SR5500 covers industry-standard channel models for the key WiMAX operating bands: 2.5, 3.5, and 5.8 GHz.

MIMO Powers Nortel's WiMAX Portfolio

Nortel has unveiled WiMAX portfolio enhancements powered by MIMO technology, which is expected to speed deployment of next-generation, high-bandwidth wireless capabilities. According to the company, the new enhancements are designed to make possible "Internet Everywhere" services such as VoIP, videoconferencing, and interactive gaming. Nortel is also responding to increased interest in its WiMAX solution by expanding its product portfolio to deliver mobile MIMO-enabled WiMAX products in the 1.5-, 2.3-, 2.5-, and 3.5-GHz spectrum bands, establishing one of the most comprehensive global WiMAX and WiBro portfolios in the industry. The products are designed with a flexible architecture that allows for quick rebanding for emerging markets. Nortel is also launching WiMAX demo centers and interoperability labs to include a wide range of device and application partners in their state-of-the-art facilities in Ottawa and Taiwan. In addition, Nortel is working to bridge the digital divide in emerging markets and rural communities through government initiatives designed to bring affordable broadband services to businesses and consumers.

HCL Successfully Integrates HCL WI-Express Solution

HCL WI-Express solution of HCL Technologies Ltd. has been successfully integrated with Wavesat's platform to develop the DragonMAX BSMX-35 product for WITE-LCOM AS. DragonMAX BSMX-35 was developed based on HCL WI-Express — HCL's IEEE 802.16-2004-compliant HMAC (High-level Media Access Controller) software. HCL WI-Express offers chipset designers, OEMs/ODMs, and test equipment manufacturers a standards-compliant, operating-system-abstracted, and thoroughly tested solution to expedite their WIMAX-compliant product development.

Key features of the DragonMAX BSMX-35 include [18]:

- High-speed access with up to 37-Mbps real throughput in the 3.5-GHz WiMAX band at the 10-MHz channel width
- Integrated wide band antenna, which eliminates all external RF-cable, with options for 60 to 90° or 100° sectors
- High-quality Power over Ethernet (POE) for up to 80 m cable
- Available expansion through additional radio port and external N-connector, to provide a repeater link or a WLAN zone
- Professional mounting kit for easy installation on both poles and walls, with azimuth and elevation control
- Support for up to 100 customers per base station unit

Alvarion Enables Voice Services Over WiMAX with BreezeMAX

Alvarion announced the availability of a primary voice service over WiMAX networks enabled by the latest edition of BreezeMAX [20]. Primary voice-over-WiMAX capability is of particular interest to pioneering service providers looking to offer voice services and broadband to areas with little or no existing telecom infrastructure [21]. Alvarion voice and broadband data WiMAX networks can be built quickly and without heavy investments in a complete VoIP implementation, as it can be deployed using the existing TDM infrastructure capacity of V5.2 legacy switches. This is of particular interest to incumbent (ILECs) and competitive local exchange carriers (CLECs), who can now adopt WiMAX as their basic network strategy. Over the past few months, the primary voice services of BreezeMAX have been tested with carriers in Africa and South America, and approved as interoperable with various vendors' Class 5 switches [22]. As a result of these trials, two operators in Africa are leveraging their TDM switches by deploying this BreezeMAX voice and data solution. In addition, operators in Latin America are evaluating the solution for deployment in urban areas to cover unserved areas. Primary voice-over-WiMAX capability is of particular interest to innovative pioneers looking to provide voice services, along with broadband, to areas with little or no existing telecom infrastructure. Alvarion voice and broadband data WiMAX networks can be built quickly and without heavy investments in a full-scale VoIP network, as they can be deployed using the existing TDM infrastructure capacity of V5.2 legacy switches. In addition, the BreezeMAX-integrated voice CPE includes one or two voice lines and battery backup, which works to benefit VoIP network operators with its fast and seamless integration for the residential and SOHO market segment. Commercially available in an outdoor version today, the new CPE will be available as an indoor, self-install version in Q2 2007.

VeriSign Chosen to Secure All WiMAX Devices

VeriSign has been selected by the WiMAX Forum to provide technology that will protect all WiMAX Forum Certified devices from unauthorized access [23]. According to the Forum, the partnership will "create a single, trusted device authentication standard across broadband wireless networks." Accordingly, VeriSign will operate the WiMAX root certificate authority (CA) used to create a single, trusted device authentication standard for WiMAX networks [24]. The VeriSign Custom Device Certificate Service (CDCS) will enable X.509-standard digital certificates to be embedded into all WiMAX Forum Certified hardware devices based on IEEE 802.16-2004 and ETSI HiperMAN 1.2.1 standards (i.e., fixed WiMAX products). According to VeriSign, the use of strong, certificate-based authentication allows service providers to ensure that network access, digital content, and software services can be secured from unauthorized access. VeriSign has met the WiMAX requirements for a PKI Trust Model and can provide scalable, robust PKI trust services to our more than 350 member corporations worldwide.

NexTek Launches Lightning Protection for Wi-Fi/WiMAX

NexTek Inc. announces the development of a new line of SurgeGuard quarter-wave stub lightning protectors [25]. Designed specifically for Wi-Fi and WiMAX applications, the QSS 400 series exceeds 802.11, UNII, ISM, and MIL-STD-202 standards. OEMs have begun installing the QSS 400 series in wireless applications that operate in frequencies ranging from 2.4 GHz to 6 GHz. Devices in the QSS 400 series measure 62.2 (2.45 in.) × 32 mm (1.26 in.) in diameter (with N-connectors). They feature best-in-class performance specifications, including bidirectional protection, low VSWR (1.05 typical), normal and reverse polarity, high RF power, and ultralow let-through. Because of the use of robust construction materials, the maintenance-free QSS 400 series is ruggedized, weatherproofed to IP68 standards, and can withstand multiple strikes, as well as very high transients up to 60 kApk. The QSS 400 SurgeGuard series of lightning arrestors is available in various coaxial connector and gender configurations [26].

Xilinx, AXIS Debut W-CDMA, WiMAX Integrated Radio Card Platform

Xilinx Inc. and AXIS Network Technology announced the availability of CDRSX, a common digital radio system (CDRS) development platform that increases power amplifier (PA) efficiency and reduces capital and operating costs for W-CDMA and WiMAX base stations. The CDRSX development platform consists of the Xilinx W-CDMA and WiMAX digital front-end (DFE) reference designs, and the flexible AXIS Virtex-based development board to provide a power efficient, quick time-to-market route from concept to production for wireless digital radio cards [27]. The platform permits developers to quickly tune the system for optimum efficiency. This provides a huge cost saving as the PA and transceiver stage consume approximately 40 to 60 percent of the base station's total cost. The AXIS CDRSX Development Platform offers OEMs the flexibility to quickly adapt to changes in specification or air interfaces. The platform includes a specially designed board containing RF preamps, ADCs, DACs, a Xilinx Virtex-II Pro FPGA to provide interface support for CPRI, OBSAI, and digital I/Q connectivity and a Xilinx Virtex-4 SX55 FPGA for implementing digital radio signal processing functions, and an operating system for control of the board via an Ethernet connection. The board has two transmit and two receive paths, as well as two additional receive paths for digital predistortion (DPD), and it can support any 20-MHz spectrum in the 400-MHz to 4-GHz frequency range. It is capable of driving the PA from 2 W to 40 W, while providing an effective receiver noise figure per path of 3 dB. The user can set up and control the board using a graphical user interface that enables key signal processing parameters to be displayed and adjusted quickly and easily. The CDRSX Development Platform integrates digital up conversion (DUC), digital down conversion (DDC), and crest factor reduction (CFR) functions from Xilinx, providing an output peak-to-average power ratio (PAPR) of only 5.60 dB for W-CDMA and a reduction of up to 1.57 dB for WiMAX radios. The Xilinx W-CDMA DFE includes a 3-carrier DUC, 3-carrier CFR, and 6-carrier DDC. It provides ~2.5 W of dynamic power consumption, while consuming only 55 percent DSP48 usage in a Virtex-4 SX25 FPGA. The Xilinx WiMAX DFE offers DUC/DDC support for 3.5/7 MHz channels (IEEE802.16-2004) and 5/10 MHz channels (IEEE802.16-2005); CFR and AGC are also supported. The WiMAX DFE is designed to work in UMTS clock subsystem frequencies and only consumes 39 percent DSP48 usage in a Virtex-4 SX25 for a 1 × 1 configuration. The CDRSX Development Platform is available now from AXIS [28].

Quad-MAC CEVA-X1641 DSP Core Targets WiMAX, 3G, Multimedia

CEVA Inc. announced the CEVA-X1641 DSP core. This core features four multiply-accumulate units and extends the performance of the company's established CEVA-X DSP family [29]. CEVA designed the CEVA-X1641 specifically for advanced wireless applications such as WiMAX, WiBro, and 3G Long-Term Evolution. In designing the core, CEVA worked closely with a lead customer that is using the core for WiMAX modems. The CEVA-X1641 also targets advanced multimedia standards such as H.264 and VC1. The CEVA-X1641 uses the CEVA-X instruction set architecture (ISA). It is upward compatible with CEVA-X1620 and CEVA-X1622 dual-MAC DSP cores, enabling CEVA-X1641 licensees to leverage software and components already available for the CEVA-X architecture.

The CEVA-X1641's main features are as follows:

- Four MAC units and twenty-four accumulators (up from two MACs and sixteen accumulators in the CEVA-X1620)
- A 330-MHz worst-case clock speed when implemented in a 130 nm process (the same as the CEVA-X1620)
- A 128-bit data bandwidth (up from 64 b in the CEVA-X1620)
- 8/16/32/40-bit operations (including new video-oriented operations)
- User-selectable, level-one memory sizes totaling up to 128 KB (the memory size is fixed on the CEVA-X1620)

Despite its advances, the quad-MAC CEVA-X1641 is only five percent larger than the CEVA-X1620. According to CEVA, it accomplished this feat by trimming the size of components such as the emulation logic and the memory controller. These optimizations offset the die area needed for new features. Independent benchmarks show that the CEVA-X1620 is one of the fastest licensable cores available. With the introduction of the CEVA-X1641, CEVA may well have taken the speed lead. This will give the core a strong position, particularly considering its relatively small size.

EION Wireless Launches Libra MAX

EION Wireless has launched the Libra MAX product family. The Libra MAX architecture, a versatile platform for WiMAX broadband wireless networks and for integrating EION's IP Intelligence, is an evolution of the field-proven Libra MX family of products purchased by EION from Wi-LAN Inc. [30]. Dual-mode operation, part of the Libra MAX architecture, means operators can roll out industry-standard 802.16-2004 WiMAX interoperable public networks, as well as proprietary Turbo W-OFDM networks when service requirements dictate greater security and performance. The Libra MAX product family includes a range of WiMAX-class base station and SS products with exceptional performance, scalability, and coverage. Operating in the 3.3-, 3.5-, and 3.6-GHz bands, Libra MAX BSs are available in three form factors and provide hot-swappable cards, full card, and power redundancy. The product family also includes a variety of SSs designed to meet customer needs and run network applications such as VoIP, VPNs, Internet access, and others. The architecture is based on the WiMAX Forum Certified Mini-PCI reference design from

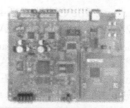

Figure 4.2   WiMax CPE reference design. (Courtesy of http://www.linuxdevices. com/news/NS8538906565.html.)

Wavesat Inc. The Libra MAX platform, based on the Libra MX, is already operating in large-scale network deployments today in the Middle East, Africa, and Russia. The new 3.5-GHz MAX-16 WiMAX Sector Card, ODU, and SSs add industry-standard 802.16-2004 WiMAX to a field-proven platform.

Production-Ready WiMAX CPE Design Runs Linux

Freescale, Celestica, and Wavesat are jointly demonstrating a Linux-based reference design for WiMAX CPE (Figure 4.2). The design features Freescale's PowerQUICC II Pro MPC8323E processor, Celestica's production-ready WiMAX gateway "Solution Accelerator," and Wavesat's Evolutive WiMAX DM256 Mini-PCI module and MAC software. The MPC8323E was designed by Freescale's India-based operation, which also designed the reference design described in the following text, on which Celestica's design is partially based [31].

The Celestica reference design is based on a Freescale-ported 2.6 Linux kernel. The design supports the WiMAX Forum 802.16d-2004 certification (fixed WiMAX) and is "designed for upgradeability" to 802.16e-2005 (mobile WiMAX).

Its features include the following:

- Support for processor- and memory-intensive applications
  - VoIP
  - "Advanced telephony"
  - Parental controls
  - Cryptographic operations
- Supports COTS (commercial, off-the-shelf) backhaul and LAN radios
  - Cardbus ADSL/VDSL/VDSL2, HSDPA, and EVDO adapters
  - Mini-PCI Wi-Fi cards

The MPC8323E is based on an "e300c2" PowerPC core, clockable to 333 MHz. The core was modified by removing the FPU (floating point unit) and adding a second integer unit. Together with a modified multiply instruction, this improves parallel processing efficiency for greater performance, Freescale says.

Additional features include the following:

- QUICC Engine block contains several peripheral controllers and a 32-bit RISC controller that is microcode-programmable for NAT, Firewall, IPSec, and Advanced QoS
- 10/100 Mbps Ethernet
- HSE (hardware security engine) — in models with "E" suffix — processes DES, 3DES, AES, SHA-1, and MD-5
- Asynchronous Transfer Mode (ATM) support up to OC-3 speeds
- Serial ATM
- Multi-PHY ATM
- High-level data link control (HDLC)
- TDM
- Binary synchronous communications protocol (BISYNC)
- UCC can also support USB 2.0 (full/low speed)

Samsung Unveils Wireless Communication Device

Samsung Electronics Co. Ltd. unveiled its latest vision in mobile convergence devices, the SPH-P9000 Deluxe MITs (Figure 4.3). The SPH-P9000 is capable of voice and multimedia data communications through mobile WiMAX technology [72]. The SPH-P9000 is a PDA-sized device utilizing mobile WiMAX and CDMA EV-DO connectivity. Users will have wireless access to the Internet utilizing mobile

Figure 4.3   Samsung wireless communication device. (Courtesy of References 72–77.)

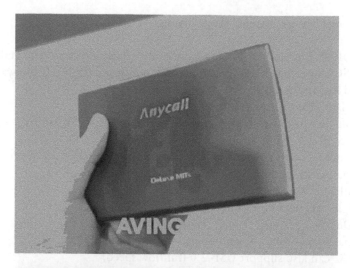

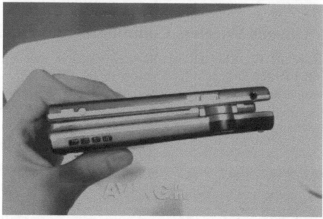

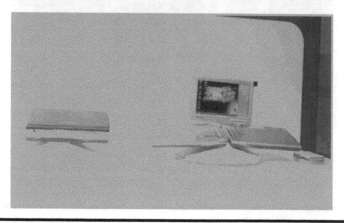

Figure 4.3   (Continued)

WiMAX connectivity. Simultaneously, the CDMA EV-DO technology provides mobile phone connection for voice communication [73]. With Microsoft Windows XP as the operating system, users will find the contents and applications familiar and easy to use. The SPH-P9000 comes with a QWERTY keyboard and built-in digital camera. The 5-in. WVGA screen is designed for movie and document viewing. Storage is based on a 30-GB internal hard drive.

Samsung SPH-P9000 specifications [74–77] are as follows:

- Standard: Mobile WiMAX/CDMA 1x EV-DO
- Camera: 1.3-megapixel camera
- Display: 5-in. WVGA LCD
- 1-GHz (Transmeta) CPU
- QWERTY keyboard
- Bluetooth (Class 1) with BT messenger
- Mini-USB/24-pin connector
- Extended I/O pack
- 2980 mAh/7200 mAh battery
- 30 GB embedded
- Size: 143 × 92 × 29.7 mm
- Weight: 560 g

Samsung's SPH-8100 WinMo Pocket PC with Mobile WiMAX, IMS, and DMB

Samsung's SPH-M8100 Mobile WiMAX slider should force an optical interrupt. Similar to the SPH-P9000 already introduced, this device is part of Mobile WiMAX MITs lineup, only this time in a dedicated IMS-loving handset. IMS support means that this not-a-cellphone handset will not only provide access to content over high-speed mobile WiMAX (WiBro, as it is known in Korea), but it will also feature such SIP-based services as VoIP calls, video conferencing, and "Push-to-All." The handset runs Windows Mobile 5.0 PocketPC and features a 2.8-in. 65-k color, 240 × 320 touch-screen TFT display, MMC micro expansion, and a 2-megapixel camera with another 0.3-megapixel shooter up front for video conferences. It also features T-DMB mobile TV, with both the antenna and stylus tucked neatly away in the case. This handset will do double-duty as a mobile WiMAX modem for laptops [78].

Redline Features WiMAX–Wi-Fi Mesh Network Solution

Redline Communications will unveil a WiMAX–Wi-Fi mesh network solution that combines the Cisco Aironet 1500 outdoor wireless mesh network at WiMAX World USA in Boston, Massachusetts. The solution enables the delivery of fixed and portable wireless broadband services throughout municipal and metropolitan areas. The WiMAX-Wi-Fi solution enables network operators to support advanced communications. Combining Redline's WiMAX Forum Certified RedMAX AN 100U sector controllers and RedMAX Outdoor Subscriber Units (SU-O) with Cisco Aironet 1500 Series APs enables operators to deliver the convenience of Wi-Fi with the QoS levels and manageability of WiMAX. The combined system solution gives operators the ability to cost-effectively deliver wireless, WiMAX, or Wi-Fi Internet access over considerable outdoor distances and in a range of network environments, and to realize revenue opportunities through the rapid provisioning and simplified management of Wi-Fi and WiMAX services [32].

Integrated Tester Checks the WiMAX PHY Layer

LitePoint Corp. has announced the new IQmax test system supporting WiMAX products based on the IEEE 802.16 standard. Based on an integrated vector signal analyzer (VSA) and vector signal generator (VSG) architecture, the single-box IQmax test system can test critical physical layer radio parameters for developers, volume manufacturing tests, and quality assurance (Q/A) stations. The test system supports the IEEE 802.16-2004/WMAN OFDM PHY standard, including all bandwidth and data rate options. The dual RF ports are selectable for either Tx or Rx operation and support the most popular 3.3- to 3.8-GHz frequency band. An optional upgrade to tri-band operation, which adds 2- and 5-GHz frequency bands, may also be available [33]. Included with the system is the IQsignal analysis suite. This GUI-driven software presents the user with all IQmax instrument setup, control, and analysis functions needed to measure the performance of a device under test (DUT). With this tool, many analysis functions are available, including time-domain, RF, and I&Q graphs, frequency spectrogram, power spectral density, constellation diagrams, EVM per symbol or subcarriers and peak, average power levels, and many other functions. To support automated laboratory and manufacturing floor testing, a C++-compatible API is included with the test system, which enables fast non-link-based testing. The IQmax test system is software upgradeable for easy transition to the proposed 802.16e standard or feature enhancements and product upgrades [34].

WiMAX Requires Dedicated RF Test Routines

The original intention of WiMAX was to replace broadband cable networks such as DSL. With the adoption of the 802.16e-2005 standard, broadband mobile radio applications can now also be implemented. This has become possible through extensions at the MAC layer, which handles call setup and data processing. There have also been significant improvements to the physical layer of the standard. As the WiMAX standard continues to evolve, there is a demand for test systems for characterizing and verifying the RF characteristics of communications equipment. Although stationary applications primarily employ the OFDM multicarrier method, mobile applications exclusively use the — expanded — OFDMA method. A major expansion of OFDMA over OFDM is in the number of carriers. In OFDMA, 128, 512, 1024, or 2048 carriers can be used; with OFDM, subscribers are served one after the other. This means that all carriers are assigned to the same subscriber, and the same modulation and power are used in every time slot. With OFDMA, several subscribers are served simultaneously. Several physical carriers are combined into subchannels, and each subscriber is assigned a specific number of subchannels, depending on the bandwidth required. The channel assignment is defined in what is referred to as downlink and uplink maps. Here, channels are assigned to specific subscribers for a specific time [35]. Signal generators are a valuable aid in the development of WiMAX receiver systems. The task is to code the data and the modulation mode for the various subscribers in line with the standard, to distribute the information to the appropriate carriers, and to generate the maps. The development of WiMAX transmit systems, on the other hand, calls for spectrum and signal analyzers. In signal analysis, the carriers have to be reallocated to the respective subscribers in line with the map definitions, demodulated, and results represented in a clear-cut manner. The SMU200A, SMATE200A, and SMJ100A signal generators from Rohde & Schwarz, with an SMx-K49 option installed, can deliver OFDM signals in accordance with the 802.16-2004 standard, as well as OFDMA signals in accordance with the 802.16e-2005 standard. The SMU200A can be equipped with two different baseband modules, fading options, additional noise sources, and two RF paths to generate a wide variety of test scenarios. The latest version of the software allows for the generation of WiMAX multicarrier scenarios with only a single baseband path and RF path in the generator. With the FSQ-K93 option installed, the FSQ signal analyzer will measure WiMAX OFDMA signals directly without requiring an external PC. Analyzing signals from BSs, for example, requires an exact definition of the downlink map. This can be implemented in two ways. The user can enter the required data using a data editor in the analyzer's GUI. Alternatively, an existing configuration can be read from the signal generator. Data to be defined includes, for example, the number of subscribers and the modulation modes, the active subchannels, and the permutation zones. Measurements can be started when the complete set of parameters has been defined, which includes the frequency, the guard interval, the recording time, etc. The measured burst is displayed, and a green bar indicates successful demodulation of the signal. All data relevant to the analysis of the WiMAX OFDMA signal is displayed in a list. The data is listed separately for each subscriber, a feature that is particularly important in OFDMA applications. Data is displayed not only numerically but also graphically, which is very useful in developing WiMAX applications [35].

Aperto Debuts Chassis to Support Both WiMAX Flavors

PacketMax allows card-level support of 802.16d and 802.16e. Aperto Networks introduced a new generation of WiMAX BSs that allow carriers to support a mix of fixed and mobile broadband wireless installations. PacketMax 5000 can be configured with 802.16-2004 (also known as fixed 802.16d) blades or with newer line cards supporting 802.16e-2005. The PM 5000 offers high-gain antennas and all TDD operations, and the mobile version supports full MIMO antenna structures. The 802.16d cards use 256-FFT OFDM, whereas the mobile version uses Scalable OFDMA with FFTs scaling from 512 to 1024 points.The mobile cards support 2.5- and 3.5-GHz operation, and the fixed cards support 2.5, 3.5, and 5 GHz. The PM 5000 chassis is based on the Advanced Computing for Telecommunications Architecture and can support redundant six-sector base stations, redundant four-sector base stations, or a mobile network overlay on a fixed footprint [36].

Agilent Technologies Showcases WiMAX Test and Measurement Performance

Agilent Technologies Inc. announced its newest test and measurement solutions for fixed (IEEE 802.16-2004) and mobile (IEEE 802.16-2005) WiMAX. Spanning the entire WiMAX lifecycle — from R&D and design verification to manufacturing, conformance, and interoperability test — these solutions provide today's engineers with a level of performance and functionality not currently available with competing solutions. Agilent's broad offering for testing fixed and mobile WiMAX comprises a number of premier test solutions [37]. The Agilent Advanced Design System (ADS) environment facilitates design and verification; R&D and conformance-type measurements are covered by the PSA Series spectrum analyzer, 80600-series vector signal analysis software, and ESG vector signal generator. Production-type measurements can be performed with the new MXA and Agilent MXG products. As the most up-to-date, complete, and widely accepted answer to WiMAX R&D, design and verification, production, and conformance, these solutions provide reliable, repeatable, and consistent results across the WiMAX lifecycle. The solutions showcased include WiMAX design and verification, Mobile WiMAX receiver test, and WiMAX signal generation and analysis [38].

Identity Systems Integrated into IEEE 802.16 WiMAX Networks

WiMAX (802.16), both the fixed and mobile flavors, is taking off in a big way all over the world. Sprint rolled out its 4G networks based on this technology in the United States; Rogers Communications and Bell Canada have already rolled out WiMAX in Canada, and so have many firms in Europe, Asia, and Australia. In many cases, WiMAX is blended with Mesh Wi-Fi, BPL technology, and more to form the 4G networks (200 Mbps or more). With these high-throughput networks, the same security challenges faced in the WiMAX space are relevant for Wi-Fi Mesh, BPL, etc., in which physical layer threats (and MAC layer threats), such as eavesdropping of management messages, BS and MS (mobile station) masquerading, management message modification, DoS attack, etc., need to be addressed with multiple layers of AuthN. One of the key value propositions of Identity-enabled NAC (Network Admission Control), (Cisco) and Identity-enabled OAM&P (Nortel) is to address this level of granular AuthN needed for different types of Access Networks and its respective network equipment and user equipment (NE and UE), as well [39,40].

Intel Shows WiMAX, Wi-Fi, Cell Chip with MIMO

In Hong Kong, Intel's point man on wireless demonstrated a MIMO-antenna-based chipset with support for mobile WiMAX (802.16-2005), Wi-Fi (the Draft N flavor that is still in development), and HSDPA —the GSM version of 3G cell data. This was demonstrated as part of a laptop system [41].

Intel Completes Design of Mobile WiMAX Chip

Intel Corp. has announced the completion of the design for its first mobile WiMAX chip, which is expected to find its way into new laptops, handheld PCs, and mobile phones [42]. Together with the company's previously announced single-chip, multi-band WiMAX/Wi-Fi radio, the pair creates a complete chipset called the *Intel WiMAX Connection 2300*. Intel demonstrated a Centrino Duo-based laptop with mobile WiMAX (IEEE 802.16e-2005), 802.11n Wi-Fi, and HSDPA 3G capabilities at the 3G World Congress and Mobility Marketplace in Hong Kong. The mobile processor successfully accessed the Internet at "broadband" speeds over a mobile WiMAX network. Intel provided building blocks for communication servers that deliver enhanced performance, value, and choice for telecommunications equipment manufacturers, and computing tasks. The Intel NetStructure MPCBL0050 single-board computer is the first AdvancedTCA blade server. Also unveiled were the Dual-Core Intel Xeon processors LV 5138 and LV 5128. The fourth product announced is the Intel Carrier Grade Server TIGW1U [43].

New WiMAX Test and Measurement Solution

SeaSolve Software Inc. and National Instruments have jointly announced the release of their fixed and mobile WiMAX RF test and measurement solutions [44]. In an effort to simplify WiMAX test and measurement, the two companies will provide the hardware and software required for the efficient testing, analysis, and troubleshooting of fixed and mobile WiMAX stations and chipsets. SeaSolve's SeaMAX-Fixed and SeaMAX-Mobile signal generation and analysis solutions integrate seamlessly with the NI PXI 5660 RFSA and 5670 RFSG. The software offers analysis of WiMAX transceivers with RF and baseband measurements in accordance with the IEEE 802.16-2004 and IEEE 802.16e-2005 standards. SeaSolve's RF test and measurement capabilities for the NI PXI instruments are designed to help RF engineers, researchers, and wireless device OEMs to efficiently test, measure, and analyze the performance of WiMAX BS and SS transceivers.

RFMD Introduces GaN PAs for WCDMA, WiMAX, and Public Mobile Radio

RF Micro Devices Inc. announced the introduction and sampling of Gallium Nitride (GaN) wideband power amplifier ICs to Tier 1 WiMAX, cellular base station, and Public Mobile Radio (PMR) customers [45]. The new family includes multiple parts, RF 3821 (8 W P1dB WiMAX PA, 2.3 to 2.7 GHz), RF 3823 (8 W P1dB WiMAX PA, 3.3 to 3.8 GHz), RF 3822 (14 W saturated power Public Mobile Radio PA, 100 to 1000 MHz), and RF 3820 (8 W P1dB cellular PA, 1.8 to 2.2 GHz). Both WiMAX power amplifier ICs provide 29 dBm linear output power with 2.5 percent EVM and flat gain of 11 dB across multiple bands. The cellular power amplifier IC provides 27 dBm linear output power with –50 dBc ACPR and flat gain of 13 dB across DCS/PCS/WCDMA frequency bands. The PMR power amplifier IC provides 14 to 12 W saturated output power and flat gain of 11.5 dB with PAE of 65 percent midband at 500 MHz. The designs operate on a 28-V rail and include internal-matching elements to deliver a 50-Ω interface over the band of operation and are packaged in a thermally enhanced AlN package for efficient heat removal. RFMD anticipates that production shipments of the GaN power amplifiers will commence in 2007.

Lattice Ports TurboConcept WiMAX IP to FPGAs

TurboConcept (Brest, France) has ported and tested its TC1000-WiMAX, an 802.16 Convolutional Turbo Code decoder IP core on Lattice's FPGA devices. The core supports all modes of the IEEE 802.16 CTC standard, including OFDM PHY and OFDMA PHY. As part of the deal, TurboConcept becomes a member of Lattice's ispLeverCORE Connection program, and the companies will provide complete systems to designers integrating system-level IP with Lattice's FPGA architectures [46]. The SC FPGA family combines up to 32 3.8 Gbps Serdes channels to support interface protocols, including PCI Express, Serial RapidIO, Ethernet, Fibre Channel, XAUI, and SONET/SDH [49].

Sequans Eyes Verisilicon's Zsp540 Processor for WiMAX Products

Sequans Communications has revealed that it has licensed the ZSP540 core for its mobile IEEE 802.16e WiMAX silicon products. ZSP540 is a member of VeriSilicon ZSP G2 superscalar product family. ZSP540 is a Quad-MAC, Six ALU architecture. The core executes up to four instructions per cycle at frequencies in excess of 400 MHz on 90-nm process technologies, the company claimed [47].

WiMAX Test Set Finds and Solves Design Problems

RSA3408A Real-Time Spectrum Analyzer and RSA-IQWIMAX demodulation and analysis software lets engineers perform time-, frequency-, and modulation-domain measurements to decompose signals and uncover anomalies. It can also generate in-depth analysis for troubleshooting WiMAX devices at the design stage. It is able to capture intermittent or random events, test set [48].

Tektronix Provides World's Most Powerful WiMAX R&D Test Set

Tektronix Inc. announced RSA-IQWIMAX demodulation and analysis software, which is part of a comprehensive test set to find and solve WiMAX design problems. RSA-IQWIMAX software is a new application-specific test tool for characterizing and troubleshooting WiMAX device designs, utilizing a Tektronix RSA3408A Real-Time Spectrum Analyzer, and is the result of a partnership between Tektronix and LitePoint. With RSA-IQWIMAX and the RSA3408A, engineering teams will be able to more quickly detect, diagnose, and resolve design issues, improving time to market for WiMAX end-user products, including consumer electronics, computers, and handheld devices [50]. RSA-IQWIMAX provides spectrum and modulation measurements on OFDM and OFDMA signals in accordance with IEEE 802.16-2004 (fixed) and IEEE 802.16e- 2005 (mobile) WiMAX standards. The RSA3408A captures intermittent or random events that other solutions miss, enabling engineering teams to detect, diagnose, and resolve design issues more quickly. The combination of RSA3408A Real-Time Spectrum Analyzer with RSA-IQWIMAX software is the world's most powerful WiMAX R&D test solution, enabling engineers to perform needed time-, frequency-, and modulation-domain measurements to decompose signals and uncover anomalies, and generate in-depth analysis for troubleshooting WiMAX devices at the design stage. RSA-IQWIMAX analysis software is used on an external PC connected to the RSA3408A by Ethernet or GPIB. Optionally, an engineer may load captured data and analyze the results offline. Test results from the RSA3408A and RSA-IQWIMAX software can be tightly integrated with LitePoint's IQmax(TM) WiMAX Test System to form an integrated end-to-end test solution from R&D through manufacturing test. The single-box IQmax Test System can test critical physical layer radio parameters for developers, volume manufacturing tests, and quality assurance (Q/A) stations at the lowest possible cost. Using Tektronix's RSA-IQWIMAX and the LitePoint IQmax WiMAX Test System, R&D and production teams can share common test algorithms and data formats, reducing production ramp-up time in manufacturing [51]. The Tektronix RSA3408A plus RSA-IQWIMAX and the LitePoint IQmax WiMAX Test System address physical layer test needs from R&D through manufacturing tests. This complements the Tektronix K1297-G35 WiMAX solution, the telecommunications industry's first protocol-monitoring platform for functional testing of WiMAX products that are based on the IEEE 802.16e-2005 standard [70]. The K1297-G35 WiMAX solution for Mobile WiMAX equipment helps bring WiMAX out of the labs and into live networks. The complete offering spans R&D through to deployment [71].

Beceem Introduces Industry's First Mobile WiMAX Wave 2 Terminal Chipset

In a move that continues its leadership in Mobile WiMAX, Beceem Communications (www.beceem.com) made availabile the industry's first baseband and RF chipset that supports all features of the Mobile WiMAX Wave 2 profile. The BCS200 chipset, which includes advanced smart antenna technologies such as MIMO and beam forming plus Beceem's CMOS direct conversion radio, continues to set the industry standard for performance [52]. The BCS200 solution provides significant performance improvements that position Beceem as the leading company to meet the launch requirements of WiMAX service providers focused on Wave 2, such as Sprint Nextel. Key performance benchmarks of the MS120 solution include the following [52]:

- Greater than 25 Mbps total throughput
- More than 25 percent reduction in active power consumption
- Greater than 60 percent footprint reduction, enabling WiMAX integration into space-constraint applications such as mobile phones and consumer electronics

The BCS200 solution builds on Beceem's field-proven MS120 Wave 1 chipset and software that have been used successfully in early mobile WiMAX trials and commercial deployments around the world. As a result, customers will benefit from Beceem's unmatched WiMAX experience, thereby significantly reducing their own development risk, cost, and time to market when launching mobile WiMAX products.

The BCS200 solution consists of the following:

- The BCSB200 baseband chip and associated firmware implements PHY and MAC functionality with minimum processing load for the host processor.
- The BCSR200 direct conversion CMOS radio supporting 2-GHz and 3-GHz designs, as well as dynamically programmable channel bandwidths from 5 MHz to 10 MHz, thereby enabling seamless roaming among all WiMAX networks.
- A complete reference design kit, including driver software and RF calibration tools, facilitates rapid development of mobile WiMAX devices by OEMs and ODMs [53].

LG Readies Mobile WiMAX Devices for Launch

South Korea's LG Electronics Inc. plans to introduce a range of products that support mobile WiMAX technology, the company said. The first products from LG to support mobile WiMAX will be a version of the company's XNote C1 Tablet PC and a PDA (personal digital assistant) based on Microsoft Corp.'s Windows Mobile 5.0 software, said Nam Keehyun, manager at LG Electronics' Digital Media Strategic Planning Department. Mobile WiMAX offers downlink speeds up to 10.2 Mbps, which is expected to increase to 40 Mbps or so by next year. The technology is currently commercially available in South Korea and Japan. The technology is also being tested by operators in other countries and plans are underway to roll out the technology in the United States and China. The XNote C1 with mobile WiMAX will also include support for 3G networks that have been upgraded with HSDPA technology, which allows faster downloads. The new notebook, the KC1 PDA, will offer support for mobile WiMAX and CDMA 2000-1X EV-DO (Evolution Data Optimized). EV-DO is the 3G technology most widely used in South Korea and is also used by U.S. operators [54].

Jacket Micro: Market's First Complete Mobile WiMAX RF Front-End Module

A new product, the M30001, is a highly integrated and performance-optimized WiMAX front end containing all active and passive components required to interface WiMAX transceivers directly to an antenna. Jacket Micro Devices (JMD) has announced it will begin sampling of the device, the market's first complete mobile WiMAX RF front-end module [55]. The single $7 \times 7 \times 1.2$ mm QFN package is seen as ideal for mobile phone, laptop, and consumer electronics applications. The small size of the M30001 allows WiMAX interfaces to be integrated along with other wireless and computing functions into small-form-factor products such as PCI Express, USB, and handsets. M30001 is scheduled for production release in Q2 2007, says the company. The M30001 provides exceptional attenuation in the UMTS transmit and receive bands, making it ideal for cellular environments. Meeting the need for extended range and increased data rates of WiMAX devices, the module delivers 24 dBm output power at 4 percent EVM. It is compatible with MIMO and antenna diversity configurations using a 1×2 architecture [56].

iRiver Preps WiMAX UMPC

South Korea's iRiver is preparing to enter the ultramobile PC arena, the company has said. The prototype device shown sports Wi-Fi, WiMAX, and WiBro connectivity. Little is known about the W10's other specifications, but presumably it is more PC-like than iRiver's media player-cum-PDA, the Disciple D10 and D20, currently only available in the company's home territory. With WiBro built in, the W10 may also not make an appearance outside South Korea. iRiver also showed off its G10 and G20 handheld games devices, and the upcoming hard-disk-based E10 music player. The company confirmed the E10 will also operate as a universal infrared remote control [57].

LG Unveils New WiMAX Communicator

LG Electronics has unveiled a new communicator created using the WiMAX terminal (Figure 4.4). Other features of this communicator, which is yet to be named but is expected to hit the stores in Q2 of 2007, include a touchscreen display, high-speed data transfer standard EV-DO, a 2.0-megapixel camera, microSD card slot, and Bluetooth interface [58].

Aeroflex Measures WiMAX

Aeroflex has announced that it has added significant new wireless test capabilities to its PXI 3000 Series modular wireless test platform to aid the rapid production testing of the most popular consumer mobile devices. Within a single

Figure 4.4   LG Communicator. (Courtesy of http://www.cellphonenews.net/ archives/2006/12/lg_unveils_new_wimax_communicator.php.)

software-definable PXI modular platform, the Aeroflex PXI 3000 Series now includes support for WiMAX OFDMA, 1xEvDO, and HSUPA. With the addition of these new measurement suites, the Aeroflex modular RF test systems now allow testing of cellular, WLAN, and WiMAX in one product, whereas competitive test systems must be configured from numerous instruments, making them more costly, bulky, slower, and harder to integrate. Aeroflex provides signal generation and analysis in a single, configurable platform for testing RF components and wireless devices. With Aeroflex's modular PXI-based manufacturing test systems, customers can protect their investment by rapidly upgrading their test systems via software updates or plug-and-play hardware. Customers can easily add test capability with minimal effort and investment in new equipment and software. WiMAX Measurement Suite, CDMA2000 and 1xEvDO Reverse Link Measurement Suite, and UMTS Uplink Measurement Suite: all of these three new PXI measurement suites are libraries of special functions with both .dll and Visual Basic APIs (application programming interfaces) for use in a broad range of ADEs (application development environments), such as LabVIEW, LabWindows/CVI, Visual Basic, and Visual C/C++. Each measurement suite is supplied with help files, including source code examples, to aid the user in the development of measurement applications. Examples are provided for a variety of ADEs, including Visual Basic 6, LabWindows CVI, and Visual Basic C/C++ [59].

Celestica Joins Freescale and Wavesat to Offer Production-Ready WiMAX Reference Design

CPE manufacturers can now deliver WiMAX-enabled products to market even faster with a production-ready reference design from Freescale Semiconductor, Wavesat, and Celestica. Celestica has joined a preexisting collaboration between Freescale and Wavesat to enhance a comprehensive platform for the rapid creation of WiMAX-enabled products [60]. The optimized solution features Wavesat's WiMAX Mini-PCI module and MAC software, Freescale's MPC8323E PowerQUICC(TM) II Pro processor, and Celestica's WiMAX Gateway CPE Solution Accelerator — a predeveloped platform for customer differentiation in the SOHO, home, and wireless telecommunications infrastructure markets. According to In-Stat, the number of fixed WiMAX subscribers worldwide is projected to reach 16 million by 2010, and the number of mobile WiMAX subscribers is expected to range from 15 million to 25 million. The MPC8323E, which runs the WiMAX MAC software and all applications, was developed by Freescale's India Design Center. The design team also produced a proof of concept that Celestica can leverage to design its own boards and speed development. The solution supports WiMAX Forum 802.16d-2004 certification and is designed for upgradeability to the IEEE 802.16e-2005 standard for mobility in accordance with the WiMAX Forum ETG/MTG profiles. For customers seeking a preengineered, predeveloped solution for compressing product development cycles and driving lower costs, this platform offers numerous benefits, including support for processor- and memory-intensive applications including VoIP, advanced telephony, parental controls, and cryptographic operations; utilization of COTS Mini-PCI WiMAX or Cardbus ADSL/VDSL/VDSL2, HSDPA, and EVDO adapters for maximum network backhaul interconnectivity without incurring unnecessary development costs; compatibility with OTS Mini-PCI LAN options including Wi-Fi(TM) for rapid deployment; and world-class communications processor family road maps that lower customers' cost of ownership [61].

SkyCross Launches New Antenna Products Supporting WiMAX

SkyCross announced a new product line supporting WiMAX. SkyCross pioneered this technology in South Korea with antennas for WiBro, the Korean standard of WiMAX. SkyCross designed and manufactured both the first internal and the first external antennas for WiBro. SkyCross is applying its experience with WiBro in Korea to similar WiMAX networks for last-mile broadband connectivity in other parts of the world. The internal and external antennas in this product family can be used independently or together in the same device to provide better diversity gain for increased reception and broader coverage. The SkyCross antennas for WiMAX standards are applicable to a variety of mobile platforms including PC cards, notebook computers, handsets, and UMCPs (Ultra-Mobile Personal Computers) — these are small tablet PCs for data on the go. SkyCross achieves this flexibility with custom engineering that accommodates the allotted antenna space and other components in these various devices [62]. SkyCross recently announced other product family additions, including mobile video antennas for terrestrial services such as terrestrial digital multimedia broadcasting (T-DMB) and Digital Video Broadcasting–Handheld (DVB-H) [63].

Alvarion Uses Wintegra Solutions for WiMAX Products

Alvarion Ltd. has chosen the WinPath network processor and related software from Wintegra for its next-generation WiMAX products addressing the 802.16e market. The Alvarion BreezeMAX radio access system is the main building block of the company's end-to-end 4Motion mobile WiMAX solution. It integrates Wintegra's silicon to address the demand for mobile broadband while also offering support for WiMAX Forum-based mobile WiMAX solutions over a broad spectrum range. The Alvarion solutions enable carriers to offer high-performance broadband data, voice, and multimedia services. Wintegra's integrated silicon and software solutions are geared toward WiMAX, 3G, and LTE base stations, as well as RNCs, network interfaces, broadband wireless access, and 2G and 3G cell site aggregation and backhaul. The company's fixed and mobile WiMAX solution offers a family of pin- and software-compatible, programmable network processors that may scale from single-sector integrated picostations to multisector BSs, and incorporate advanced antenna technology. Wintegra also offers a software solution to incorporate scheduling, classification, encryption, and QoS features, as well as VLAN marking, payload header suppression, multiple CS layers, IP fragmentation and Generic Router Encapsulation (GRE), and IP-in-IP tunneling. These features are required to meet WiMAX Forum network definitions and also enable rapid integration with next-generation wireless access networks and ASN gateways. The 4Motion end-to-end mobile WiMAX solution offers advanced radio technologies, QoS mechanisms, IP mobility core components, and multimedia subsystems. It features subscriber terminals, an OMC, and backend interfaces, and uses SDR, beam forming, MIMO, dynamic bandwidth allocation, and scalable OFDMA technologies [64].

Intel Ships Next-Generation WiMAX Chip with Support for Mobile Networks

Intel Corp. has announced the availability of the Intel WiMAX Connection 2250, the company's next-generation SoC, designed to support mobile networks in addition to fixed networks. The Intel WiMAX Connection 2250 is claimed to be the industry's first dual-mode baseband chip, and when paired with the company's discrete triband WiMAX radio, the solution is capable of supporting all global WiMAX frequencies. Motorola Inc. currently intends to integrate the Intel WiMAX Connection 2250 into its CPEi 200 series of WiMAX CPE. Motorola joins several other telecommunications equipment manufacturers currently expected to deliver Intel WiMAX Connection 2250-based products. Service providers may benefit from the versatility and faster time to market afforded by the dual-mode support of the Intel WiMAX Connection 2250. Compliance with both the IEEE 802.16-2004 fixed standard and the more advanced IEEE 802.16e-2005 specification for fixed, nomadic, and mobile WiMAX functionality enables the development of CPE that can be deployed in "d" mode and upgraded to "e" mode with a quick over-the-air software upgrade. The Intel WiMAX Connection 2250 is optimized for WiMAX modems and offers flexibility in equipment design, deployment, and application [65].

WiMAX Analyzer

The BumbleBee-EX handheld receiver from Berkeley Varitronics Systems is designed for WiMAX spectrum analysis [66]. The unit measures between 2.0 to 4.0 GHz and 4.9 to 5.9 GHz, which permits it to log 802.16 WiMAX, 802.11b/a/g Wi-Fi, VoIP, Public Safety Band, and Bluetooth RF interference. The instrument comes with a color touchscreen and a water-resistant case [67].

Xilinx Releases Integrated Radio Card Platform WiMAX and W-CDMA

Xilinx has announced the immediate availability of CDRSX, a CDRS development platform that increases PA efficiency for W-CDMA and WiMAX BSs. The CDRSX development platform consists of the Xilinx W-CDMA and WiMAX DFE reference designs and the flexible AXIS Virtex-based development board to provide a route from concept to production for wireless digital radio cards. The platform allows BS OEMs to use PAs to reduce the operating power in the radio head. It permits developers to quickly tune the system for optimum efficiency. This is said to save cost as the PA and transceiver stage consume approximately 40 to 60 percent of the BS's total cost. It offers OEMs the flexibility to quickly adapt to changes in specification or air interfaces [68]. The platform includes a specially designed board containing RF preamps, ADCs, DACs, a Xilinx Virtex-II Pro FPGA to provide interface support for CPRI, OBSAI, and digital I/Q connectivity, and a Xilinx Virtex-4 SX55 FPGA for implementing digital radio signal processing functions, and an operating system for control of the board via an Ethernet connection. The board has two transmit and two receive paths, plus two additional receive paths for digital predistortion (DPD), and it can support any 20-MHz spectrum in the 400- to 4-GHz frequency range. It is capable of driving the PA from 2 to 40 W, while providing an effective receiver noise figure per path of 3 dB. The user can set up and control the board using a GUI that enables key signal processing parameters to be displayed and adjusted quickly and easily. The platform integrates DUC, DDC, and CFR functions from Xilinx, providing an output peak-to-average power ratio (PAPR) of only 5.60 dB for W-CDMA and a reduction of up to 1.57 dB for WiMAX radios. The Xilinx W-CDMA DFE includes a 3-carrier DUC, 3-carrier CFR, and 6-carrier DDC. It provides ~2.5 W of dynamic power consumption, while consuming only 55 percent DSP48 usage in a Virtex-4 SX25 FPGA. The Xilinx WiMAX DFE offers DUC/DDC support for 3.5/7 MHz channels (IEEE802.16-2004) and 5/10 MHz channels (IEEE802.16-2005) — CFR and AGC are also supported. The WiMAX DFE is designed to work in UMTS clock subsystem frequencies and only consumes 39 percent DSP48 usage in a Virtex-4 SX25 for a 1 × 1 configuration.

References

1. http://www.polonix.com/Products/WiMAX.html.
2. http://www.eetasia.com/ART_8800440453_499488_b9f949cd200611.HTM [dated November 6, 2006].
3. http://www.rfglobalnet.com/content/news/article.asp?DocID=%7BAB31B7F3-E09F-42D3-936D-6FC8E880A52D%7D&Bucket=Current+Headlines.
4. http://www.engadget.com/2006/08/07/caltrain-commuter-rail-pulls-wimax-at-79-mph/ [dated 7 August 2006].

5. http://webwire.com/ViewPressRel.asp?SESSIONID=&aId=19338.
6. http://pda.mobileeurope.co.uk/news_wire/news_wire_story.ehtml?o=2391 [dated August 7, 2006].
7. http://www.digitimes.com/systems/a20060926PR205.html [dated September 26, 2006].
8. http://www.eetimes.com/news/latest/showArticle.jhtml?articleID=189601333 [dated June 26, 2006].
9. http://news.cnet.co.uk/networking/0,39029686,49283794,00.htm.
10. http://www.swbusiness.fi/portal/news/?id=14212&area=5 [dated September 28, 2006].
11. http://www.upi.com/Hi-Tech/view.php?StoryID=20060712-111502-3373r [dated July 12, 2006].
12. http://www.digitimes.com/systems/a20061012PR206.html [dated October 12, 2006].
13. http://www.newtelephony.com/news/6ah11152369907.html.
14. http://ipcommunications.tmcnet.com/hot-topics/wireless/articles/3103-analog-devices-introduces-series-clock-generators-wimax-base.htm.
15. http://www.mybroadband.co.za/nephp/?m=show&id=4604 [dated October 18, 2006].
16. http://www.digitimes.com/systems/a20061019PR204.html [dated October 19, 2006].
17. http://www.eetasia.com/ART_8800438808_480500_f9c7e8e3200610.HTM [dated October 24, 2006].
18. http://www.equitybulls.com/admin/news2006/news_det.asp?id=3606 [dated October 25, 2006].
19. http://www.elecdesign.com/Articles/Index.cfm?AD=1&ArticleID=13917.
20. http://www.slipperybrick.com/2006/10/voice-services-alvarion-wimax-breezemax/ [dated October 30, 2006].
21. http://www.alvarion.com/presscenter/pressreleases/9383/.
22. http://www.mobiletechnews.com/info/2006/10/30/131045.html [dated October 30, 2006].
23. http://www.securitypronews.com/news/securitynews/spn-45-20060712VeriSignthe-GotoCompanyforWiMAXSecurity.html.
24. http://www.itwire.com.au/content/view/4952/127/.
25. http://www.wirelessnetdesignline.com/193500132?cid=RSSfeed_wirelessnetdesign-line_wndlRSS [dated October 30, 2006].
26. http://www.eetasia.com/ART_8800439614_499488_13516e6c200610.HTM.
27. http://edageek.com/2006/10/30/xilinx-axis-w-cdma-wimax-radio-card/ [dated October 30, 2006].
28. http://www.eetimes.com/news/latest/showArticle.jhtml?articleID=193501693.
29. http://www.dspdesignline.com/193402983?cid=RSSfeed_dspdesignline_dspdlRSS [dated October 30, 2006].
30. http://www.prnewswire.com/cgi-bin/stories.pl?ACCT=104&STORY=/www/story/10-11-2006/0004449515&EDATE= [dated October 11, 2006].
31. http://www.linuxdevices.com/news/NS8538906565.html [dated November 16, 2006].

32. http://www.newswire.ca/en/releases/archive/October2006/10/c6303.html [dated October 10, 2006].
33. http://www.eetasia.com/ART_8800417596_480300_e10eec8e200605_no.HTM [dated May 12, 2006].
34. http://neasia.nikkeibp.com/dailynewsdetail/004155.
35. http://www.electronicsweekly.com/Articles/2006/10/19/39971/WiMAX+requires+dedicated+RF+test+routines.htm [dated October 19, 2006].
36. http://www.eetimes.com/news/latest/showArticle.jhtml?articleID=193105492.
37. http://webwire.com/ViewPressRel.asp?SESSIONID=&aId=21825 [dated October 9, 2006].
38. www.agilent.com/find/wimax.
39. http://rakesh-rakeshsblog.blogspot.com/2006/11/identity-systems-integrated-into-ieee.html.
40. http://www.techworld.com/mobility/features/index.cfm?featureID=3030&pagtype=samecatsamechan.
41. http://wimaxnetnews/archives/2006/12/intel_shows_wim.html [dated December 6, 2006].
42. http://www.domain-b.com/companies/companies_i/intel/20061208_completes.htm [dated December 8, 2006].
43. http://www.efytimes.com/efytimes/fullnews.asp?edid=16052.
44. http://testinglondon.wordpress.com/2006/12/11/new-wimax-test-and-measurement-solution/ [dated December 11, 2006].
45. http://www.rfglobalnet.com/content/news/article.asp?DocID=%7B7799340D-6E7A-4FDE-8DCB-D2C788D23704%7D&Bucket=Current+Headlines [dated November 27, 2006].
46. http://www.edadesignline.com/196500128?cid=RSSfeed_EDAdesignline_edad-lALL [dated November 27, 2006].
47. http://www.sda-asia.com/sda/news/psecom,id,12393,srn,4,nodeid,4,_language,Singapore.html [dated November 28, 2006].
48. http://www.design-news.org/node/85422.
49. http://www.electronicsweekly.com/Articles/2006/11/29/40256/Lattice+targets+WiMAX+with+turbo+decoder+core.htm [dated November 29, 2006].
50. http://news.thomasnet.com/fullstory/498725/2697 [dated November 6, 2006].
51. http://www.unstrung.com/document.asp?doc_id=111376&WT.svl=wire1_1 [dated November 29, 2006].
52. http://www.primezone.com/newsroom/news.html?d=109754 [dated December 2, 2006].
53. www.beceem.com.
54. http://www.webwereld.nl/articles/44026/itu---lg-readies-mobile-wimax-devices-for-launch.html [dated December 5, 2006].
55. http://www.electropages.com/viewArticle.aspx?intArticle=8050.
56. http://www.bbwexchange.com/pubs/2006/12/14/page1423-382675.asp.
57. http://www.reghardware.co.uk/2006/04/17/iriver_demos_w10/ [dated April 17, 2006].
58. http://www.cellphonenews.net/archives/2006/12/lg_unveils_new_wimax_communicator.php.

59. http://www.unstrung.com/document.asp?doc_id=111042&WT.svl=wire1_1 [dated November 20, 2006].
60. http://edageek.com/2006/11/15/celestica-freescale-wavesat-wimax/.
61. http://www.industrial-embedded.com/news/db/?4618.
62. http://www.wirelessnetworksonline.com/content/news/article.asp?DocID=%7B42A92DC4-24F3-43FD-A606-FAFCE4CD8238%7D&Bucket=Current+Headlines.
63. http://www.mobiletechnews.com/info/2006/11/08/130330.html.
64. http://www.tmcnet.com/Wi-Firevolution/articles/3414-alvarion-uses-wintegra-solutions-wimax-products.htm [dated November 6, 2006].
65. http://www.wirelessdesignasia.com/article.asp?id=3606.
66. http://www.reed-electronics.com/tmworld/article/CA6376471.html.
67. www.bvsystems.com.
68. http://www.asteriskvoipnews.com/wimax/xilinx_releases_integrated_radio_card_platform_wimax_and_wcdma.html.
69. http://www.dailywireless.org/2006/11/28/compactflash-card-wimax/ [dated November 28, 2006].
70. http://www.electronics-europe.de/news_en+M59aa72ca3d5.0.html.
71. http://www.electropages.com/viewArticle.aspx?intArticle=7963.
72. http://www.newlaunches.com/archives/samsung_sphp9000_wimax_pda_puts_umpcs_to_shame.php [dated November 7, 2006].
73. http://news.ninemsn.com.au/article.aspx?id=161504.
74. http://www.mobilephone-review.com/samsung/samsung-sph-p9000-wimax-phone-unveiled-review/.
75. http://www.forbes.com/business/businesstech/feeds/ap/2006/11/07/ap3152259.html.
76. http://www.informationweek.com/management/showArticle.jhtml?articleID=193600742.
77. http://hitechravlik.blogspot.com/2006/11/sph-p9000-samsung-wimax-and-cdma-ev-do.html.
78. http://www.engadget.com/2006/11/08/samsungs-sph-8100-winmo-pocket-pc-with-mobile-wimax-ims-and-d/ [dated November 8, 2006].

Chapter 5

WiMAX Deployment Trends

China's largest listed telecommunications manufacturer and leading wireless solutions provider, ZTE Corp., has announced a trial of its pre-WiMAX kit in Pakistan's capital, Islamabad, through local operator Telecard. Under the contract, ZTE will build a pre-WiMAX trial network comprising one six-sector base transceiver station (BTS) and 17 customer premise equipments (CPEs) for Telecard. The trial will offer telephone services to private residents, dedicated online services for enterprises, broadband services for hotels, and wireless backhaul for Wi-Fi services for Islamabad airport.

Serbia is to receive its first-ever commercial WiMAX network in an agreement announced between leading WiMAX operator VeratNet and ZTE Corporation. ZTE will provide VeratNet with a nationwide WiMAX network that is due for completion by June 2007, serving almost 10 million subscribers with wireless broadband. The first phase of the deployment will be the complete offering of wireless broadband access to business subscribers in Serbia's capital, Belgrade.

Intel-Based WiMAX Deployments Begin

More than 13 carriers from around the globe are now deploying the world's first fixed WiMAX networks to deliver high-speed broadband wireless access to businesses and residences, based on Intel's technologies. Eleven more carriers are preparing to deploy WiMAX networks. Building on the success of WiMAX trials, carriers are rolling out full commercial deployments in cities and in suburban and rural communities, allowing broadband wireless networks to reach locations where previously they were either impossible or too costly for carriers to pursue. New WiMAX carriers include Altitude Telecom (France), AXTEL (Mexico), BEC Telecom, S.A. (Dominican Republic), Dedicado (Uruguay), Globe/Innove (Philippines), Iberbanda (Spain), Irish Broadband (Ireland), SferaNET (Poland), Mikkelin Puhelin Oyj and Savonlinnan Puhelin Oy (Finland), Telgua (Guatemala), Ukrainian High Technologies (Ukraine), and WiMAX Telecom (Austria and Slovakia).

In addition, several carriers are in the process of deploying WiMAX networks that are expected to be up and running soon, including: Americatel Peru S.A (Peru), Call Plus (New Zealand), Chunghwa Telecom Co. Ltd. (Taiwan), DBD Deutsche Breitband Dienste GmbH (Germany), Digicel (Caribbean), Entel (Chile), Ertach (Argentina), Integrated Telecom Company (Saudi Arabia), Next Mobile (Philippines), Taiwan Fixed Networks (Taiwan), and VeloCom (Argentina).

Telabria Launches WiMAX-Class Broadband Service for Data and Voice: Skylink Wireless Network Delivers Symmetric Speeds to 10 Mbps for Residential and Business Customers in Southeast United Kingdom

Telabria, the U.K. regional network operator, has launched its wide area wireless broadband network after six months of intensive trials in Kent, Southeast England. Targeted at both residential and business markets, the Skylink service offers customers symmetric broadband speeds up to 10 Mbps, as well as Voice-over-IP (VoIP) telephone service. Skylink is the first network of its kind in the United Kingdom to offer combined data and voice over a WiMAX-class network to homes and businesses. The Skylink backbone of high-capacity fiber and licensed-band microwave links encompasses over 1,300 sq km (850 sq mi), making it one of the largest next-generation wireless broadband networks in Europe, and brings a whole new class of broadband services to Kent's population of 675,000 households and 60,000 businesses. The initial rollout of Skylink includes the city of Canterbury and the borough of Swale, with additional urban, suburban, and rural areas planned as part of Telabria's ongoing Skylink network expansion. Telabria expects rapid growth of its WiMAX-class network throughout Kent, and plans to expand into other regions.

Tellus Venture Associates Completes WiMAX Feasibility Study for City of Folsom, California: Pilot Project Approved for Implementation

Tellus Venture Associates, in collaboration with Coast2Coast Technologies, completed a study for the City of Folsom, California, that determined a citywide WiMAX system is financially and technically feasible, and would help drive economic development. The conceptual system design and business case evaluation envisioned a low-cost WiMAX system with a multilayered business model that would enable public Wi-Fi access, next-generation municipal and corporate networking solutions, entrepreneurial ventures, and innovative applications for new communities of users, such as healthcare providers. The study recommended establishing a pilot project that would bring together interested organizations to deploy a pre-WiMAX network as a proof of concept for the system itself, as well as for various new technologies.

Siemens to Deliver WiMAX Network for First Commercial Broadband Wireless Access Network in Russia

Siemens and Start Telecom have signed a cooperation agreement for the construction of the first commercial broadband wireless access network in Russia based on the WiMAX technology following the IEEE 802.16-2004 standard. Start Telecom will carry out testing of the Siemens equipment in Moscow and offer commercial WiMAX services to its customers. The Skymax solution offered by Siemens is expected to provide cost-effective broadband wireless access (BWA) for end users, small office/home offices (SOHOs), and small- to- medium-sized enterprises. Siemens claims that the distinctive Skymax feature is high capacity owing to the use of diverse frequency channels (from 1.75 to 14 MHz) with adaptive modulation up to 64 levels. Under the agreement, Siemens Communications will deliver the high-tech SkyMAX solution, including BSs, end devices, as well as a NetViewer monitoring and control system. Start Telecom carried out testing of the Siemens equipment in Moscow and offered commercial WiMAX services to its customers starting in 2006, such as broadband Internet access and data transmission at up to 75 Mbps, video-on-demand, video streaming, or VoIP, with a guaranteed level of quality.

Simply Broadband Ltd. Selects Allgon Microwave for WiMAX Backhaul

Allgon Microwave, a subsidiary of Advantech AMT, has signed a deal with Simply Broadband Ltd. to supply microwave network backhaul solutions for use in their new Swedish metropolitan network. Advantech AMT is the manufacturer of satellite and terrestrial wireless communication equipment, with corporate headquarters in Montreal, Canada. Advantech AMT recently relaunched Allgon Microwave following a trade acquisition. Simply Broadband is launching wireless broadband network services in Uppsala, Sweden's fourth largest metropolitan area. The network will cover the whole region with high-speed mobile Internet access, using a

WiMAX-based solution. Uppsala is the first network covered in Sweden by Simply Broadband, with more regions already in the planning stage. Under the agreement between Advantech AMT and Simply Broadband, Advantech's Allgon Microwave AB will be the exclusive supplier of Ethernet microwave radio communication solutions to Simply Broadband. This will include the unique Allgon Microwave Ethernet LAN-100 product for the network backhaul, as well as a management solution and services for management implementation in the Uppsala project.

A Hundred People to Try WiMAX for BT Belfast and Birmingham

A hundred people are to take part in WiMAX trials in Belfast and Birmingham as BT tests the water for wireless broadband. The United Kingdom's dominant fixed-line telco is collaborating with U.S.-based Navini Networks to carry out the pilots. Navini's WiMAX systems are already being used in Europe, Australia, Asia-Pacific, Africa, and the Americas.

NTT Plans WiMAX Tests

NTT, Japan's largest telecommunications group, plans to test WiMAX technology early. Group companies will work together on trials of WiMAX technology. The tests include measuring data transmission speeds in relation to the location of a handset and whether it is moving or not, optimal parameters for BS allocation, the potential for interference with satellite-based services, and how handovers will work between WiMAX devices and those on other systems such as High-Speed Downlink Packet Access (HSDPA). NTT is currently reorganizing its Internet services, including ADSL and Wi-Fi, under a single NTT broadband platform. The company is taking some infrastructure currently operated by NTT DoCoMo, long-distance and Internet operator NTT Communications, and the NTT East and NTT West local carriers and combining it into a single platform from which group companies can offer services.

Aspen Communications Hopes to Deploy WiMAX to 36 Buildings in Dallas and Offer the Technology to Wireless Broadband Service Providers

Aspen Communications equipped 12 high-rise buildings in the Dallas-Fort Worth area with WiMAX and is offering the wide area solution to wireless broadband service providers. Aspen hopes to have 24 more buildings equipped for its deployment of Gigabit Ethernet, providing up to 1000 Mbps speeds to ISPs. Aspen has connected its network with more than 380 mi of fiber in a solution that includes backhaul, Web access, network service, and WiMAX tower sites in an effort to attract ISPs. Aspen's approach will lower costs for consumers while improving connectivity options for them.

Finnet Group Operators Building WiMAX Network

Alvarion Ltd. and its partner Daimler Finland have deployed two Finnet Group operators to build a WiMAX network using Alvarion's BreezeMAX 3500. Savonlinnan Puhelin (SPY) and Mikkelin Puhelin (MPY) will offer broadband data services to permanent residents and the large influx of summer tourists in the Saimaa Lake District, in the South Savo region of southeast Finland. As part of the government's commitment to "universal broadband," up to 29 percent of funding for the network, known as the eSavo Project, is derived from the various municipalities in the region and the European Union. The Finnet Group consists of 37 telephone-operating companies that focus primarily on local telecommunications services.

Airspan Delivers First Commercial WiMAX Network to Be Built in Russia

Airspan Networks Inc., a leading worldwide provider of WiMAX-based broadband wireless access networks and carrier-class VoIP solutions, has deployed the first-ever Russian WiMAX network for MetroMAX. MetroMAX was established in 2005 by private investors to build and operate an IP-based voice and data network in the Samara region of Russia. More than 3 million people currently reside in the region, which covers approximately 536,000 sq km. Samara is a major oil-producing and refining, light- and heavy-engineering center, with a gross regional product per capita that is more than 30 percent above the Russian national average. Less than 5 percent of Samaran residents currently have access to broadband communications. MetroMAX's goal is to cover the entire region by the end of 2006 with a WiMAX-based system. The initial Airspan deployment is in the largest city, Samara, which has 1.2 million inhabitants. At first MetroMAX will offer its subscribers high-speed Internet access, standard VoIP services, as well as virtual private networks for small- and medium-sized enterprises. It expects to have deployed Airspan's VoiceMAX solution in the network, giving it the ability to offer toll-quality VoIP services as well in a fully integrated network system. KKS Telecom, one of Airspan's principal distributors in Russia, is assisting in the deployment of the MacroMAX BSs and EasyST and ProST customer premise devices in the network.

Start Telecom and Alcatel to Test WiMAX in Russia

Russian telecom provider Start Telecom announced that it has signed a contract with Alcatel to begin field-testing WiMAX wireless broadband equipment in Russia. Under this new agreement, Alcatel will let Start Telecom use its end-to-end WiMAX solution to ensure quick and easy implementation in subscribers' premises. The Alcatel solution includes both BS equipment and indoor CPE. It allows for data transfer speeds of up to 12 Mbps, with potential distances of over 10 km.

Xanadoo Wireless High-Speed Internet Service Launched with Navini Networks: Multiple Premobile WiMAX Deployments Planned throughout Texas

Xanadoo has launched its new wireless high-speed Internet service in Lubbock, Texas, using equipment from Navini Networks. Xanadoo Wireless High-Speed Internet delivers a portable, always-on Internet connection that is revolutionary in its simplicity and convenience. Xanadoo is planning to extend its service to Wichita Falls and Abilene, Texas, in the next few months along with additional Texas markets.

African Broadband Provider Expands Network with Alvarion's WiMAX System

African broadband provider Gulfsat Madagascar has expanded its current network using Alvarion's BreezeMAX WiMAX system. Since 2003, Gulfsat has been providing broadband services to corporate subscribers using Alvarion's BreezeACCESS Orthogonal Frequency Division Multiplexing (OFDM) system operating in 3.5 GHz. The addition of the BreezeMAX network, also operating at 3.5 GHz, is part of the operator's strategy of targeting residential subscribers with greater coverage and increased capacity. As part of the deployment, Gulfsat plans to use Alvarion's BreezeMAX PRO CPE that uses the Intel PRO/Wireless 5116 WiMAX chip.

KDDI Has Successfully Completed Field Trials of Japan's First Mobile WiMAX System in Central Osaka

The trials verified mobile WiMAX functionality in an urban environment, demonstrating practical communication speed along with basic performance and high-speed handover between BSs. The mobile WiMAX system, which was built in accordance with Wire Communications Standard IEEE 802.16e, supports stable, high-throughput communications in nonfixed environments, at speeds of less than 120 km/hr. Each BS covers an area of several kilometers, making the system suitable for providing service in an urban environment. KDDI believes that mobile WiMAX has the potential to become a platform that will complement 3G mobile phone systems in urban areas. The field trials also demonstrated the successful connectivity of mobile WiMAX to "Ultra 3G," and of Ultra 3G to EV-DO and ADSL, among others. In addition, the trials successfully demonstrated a seamless handover between WiMAX and EV-DO — the first in the world. An Ultra 3G trial system also connected the WiMAX system to an multimedia domain (MMD) application server via an IPv6 network. With these trials, KDDI successfully tested services that can only be found on an Ultra 3G platform, including interoperability on both fixed and mobile networks, such as mobile WiMAX, and automatic selection of the most suitable network for various user functions, such as exchanging picture and sound files. KDDI aims to commercialize mobile WiMAX in the future and will continue to carry out various performance tests, including simultaneous multiterminal connectivity and trials with adaptive arrays. The company has just completed field trials of the technology in an area around the city of Osaka to assess how mobile WiMAX performs in an urban environment.

KDDI also put the technology under the spotlight to measure the high-speed handover between BSs, which it said is satisfactory at speeds of up to 120 km/hr. The operator also demonstrated handover between mobile WiMAX and 3G variant EV-DO. In addition, the Japanese operator is working on a system that will choose the right radio technology — cellular, Wi-Fi, or mobile WiMAX, for example — depending on what activity the user is carrying out at the time.

Crowley Data to Launch WiMAX

Crowley Data, Poland, has launched the country's first WiMAX network, using equipment supplied by Redline. The new network will be rolled out in the city of Krakow, and is expected to become available to business customers. Expansion to other cities is expected in coming months. Crowley is a leading provider of data transmission services, voice, and Internet access services in Poland, targeting primarily the business and government sectors.

True Employs WiMAX in Broadband Growth Strategy

Thailand's largest high-speed Internet provider, True Corp., has found a strategy to increase its broadband user base to 600,000, up from its current level of 350,000, and double its annual broadband turnover to THB5 billion ($128 million). True is focusing on five key business areas to attract more clients and boost revenues: wireless broadband access via WiMAX, VoIP telephony, international gateway facilities, Internet security, and autobackup connection services for businesses. The company is currently testing a WiMAX network in Nakhon Ratchasima and plans to extend coverage to ten provinces, with prices expected to be equivalent to its basic ADSL service charges. True also intends to introduce new low-cost VoIP packages.

Aperto Sets Up WiMAX Center in India

Aperto Networks, which builds WiMAX BSs and subscriber units, is opening a development center in India to speed development of its WiMAX-Forum-Certified™ and WiMAX-class products. Aperto said that Videsh Sanchar Nigam Ltd., an Indian communications services provider, has completed deployment of Aperto's PacketWave, a multiservice broadband wireless system, across 65 cities in India.

TVA, Samsung Start WiMAX Tests

Brazilian cable TV company TVA Sistema de Televiso and Korean electronics company Samsung have begun testing WiMAX wireless communications in Sao Paulo. The objective of the project is to sell not only WiMAX access but also the applications that will sit on top of the service, TVA said. The companies will carry out tests for data transfer of up to 3 Mbps per user, for use from both fixed and mobile devices, testing also for moving access at up to 120 km/hr. Samsung will produce the communication towers, software, and a line of end-user devices designed specifically for this service.

The idea is for notebooks and PDAs to be used for connection and, eventually, devices with convergent communications such as cell phones. In Brazil, the frequency band assigned for WiMAX is 3.5 GHz. TVA plans to offer the service using its multi-channel multipoint distribution service (MMDS) license that it currently uses for providing paid television services.

Intel Goes WiMAX in Saudi Arabia

Intel's operations in Saudi Arabia have achieved a regional first by adopting WiMAX technology to support their communication needs through Integrated Telecom Co. (ITC) WiMAX network in Saudi Arabia. ITC, the second licensed data services provider in Saudi Arabia, has started the deployment of its unique WiMAX network infrastructure. All of the company employees in Riyadh will now use the fixed WiMAX infrastructure (IEEE 802.16-2004) on a 3.5-GHz frequency provided by Saudi-based data service provider ITC, which has linked the office with the

Internet backbone of local ISP Nesma Internet. The office's WiMAX setup uses an Intel-enabled CPE, delivering on-demand access to high-speed Internet broadband services and connecting to the wireless LAN in the office. Riyadh aims to become the first Middle East city to integrate wireless capabilities through WiMAX, and the Saudi government began issuing fixed WiMAX (IEEE 802.16-2004) licenses on a 3.5-GHz frequency recently, the first Middle East country to do so.

Axtel Orders WiMAX Equipment for 17-City Expansion

Mexican telco Axtel has contracted Canadian equipment vendor SR Telecom to provide it with OFDM products as part of its expansion of its wireless broadband network to 17 new cities. The value of the deal is $10 million. Axtel said it will spend $150 million on expanding its services in 2006.

BSNL Launches WiMAX Trial

Indian telco BSNL has rolled out trial WiMAX-based Internet services in ten cities using Motorola equipment, according to the *Business Standard*. BSNL says it is testing WiMAX services at speeds of up to 10 Mbps in Bangalore, Chennai, Kolkata, Pune, Hyderabad, Ahmedabad, Hissar, Pinjore, Rohtam, and Panipat. If successful, the trials will be extended to other regions.

WiMAX Deployment in China

picoChip has signed a development partnership agreement with WTI-BUPT (Wireless Technology Innovation Institute, Beijing University of Posts and Telecommunications), China. WTI-BUPT will use picoChip's WiMAX reference designs and PC102 processor within its research programs, and the two organizations will work together to develop commercial WiMAX systems optimized for the special needs of the Chinese market. WTI-BUPT will also be investigating TD-SCDMA implementations for 3G based on picoChip technologies.

WiMAX Trials in United Kingdom

Intel has teamed with the Science Museum in one of its first U.K. trials of WiMAX. The company will be showcasing real-world demonstrations of WiMAX in three different usage models. Two are based on Alvarion's BreezeMAX — one in a business environment with a demo from the Science Museum, and one in the digital home, which is being demonstrated at Dolby Laboratories European headquarters.

A rural location demonstration is also scheduled with an example from Brighton-based Wi-Fi service provider MetraNet.

Irish Broadband Expands Its Network Using Alvarion WiMAX and Broadband Wireless Systems

Alvarion Ltd., has delivered over $4 million in additional equipment to Irish Broadband. This network expansion enables Ireland's leading, innovative wireless broadband service provider to nearly double its subscriber base by expanding its network coverage in Dublin and to eight other major cities in Ireland and Northern Ireland. To enable rapid growth and serve the full range of potential customers from residences and SOHOs to medium and large businesses, Irish Broadband is deploying broadband wireless equipment in both licensed and license-exempt frequency bands, including Alvarion's BreezeMAX 3500, the worldwide leading WiMAX system BreezeACCESS VL, and WALKair 3000 systems. This latest order makes Alvarion Irish Broadband's largest broadband wireless equipment supplier. As part of its network expansion plans, Irish Broadband and Intel announced a major initiative for the immediate rollout of WiMAX networks using BreezeMAX, which uses the BreezeMAX PRO, the world's first CPE that uses the Intel WiMAX chip, to eight of Ireland's major urban centers. Included in the WiMAX launch are the cities of Athlone, Arklow, Carlow, Ennis, Kilkenny, Letterkenny, Newbridge, and Wexford.

Duo Focuses on WiMAX

U.K.-based picoChip has turned to Cambridge Consultants to develop reference designs for the emerging 802.16e mobile WiMAX standard. Many view the mobile flavor of WiMAX as potentially more lucrative than the fixed flavor [1]. The technology could become the de facto fourth-generation cellular implementation, delivering broadband service to mobile users. Such a service could be a compelling offer everywhere, whereas fixed WiMAX may win major business only in regions in which service providers have not already deployed wider broadband. The partnership between picoChip and Cambridge Consultants will deliver designs for both the base station and the client sides of the wireless link. The two claim that the software-centric nature of the implementation will minimize risks associated with deploying a product based on any emerging standard. The plan is for the design to be field-upgradable to meet tweaks in the standard's development. The partners also claim that it will allow designers to add system functions — for instance, moving to multiple-input, multiple-output (MIMO) or smart-antenna technologies. Indeed, picoChip also just signed a partnership with ArrayComm to add that company's MIMO technology to picoChip's physical-layer portfolio. The mobile

WiMAX reference designs will rely on picoChip's picoArray silicon. The massively parallel multiinstruction, multiple-data architecture delivers an array of DSP cores to the communication task.

American Packet Solutions Provider Verso Technologies Has Completed a Trial of Voice over Internet Protocol (VoIP) Telephony on a WiMAX Platform

VoIP over pre-WiMAX has been successfully tested in a trial in South Africa utilizing solutions supplied by Verso Technologies and Saab Grintek Technologies, according to the companies. The trials involved Wi-Fi-compatible PDAs obtaining access to the public switched telephone network (PSTN) via customer premise gateways. Backhauling of WiMAX technology to the existing Telkom South Africa Infrastructure was accomplished through customer premise gateways. Verso's Class 4 and Class 5 soft-switching and gateway technologies were used to deploy the test.

Airnet Deploys WiMAX Networks

Airnet NZ Ltd., Hawke's Bay leading wireless Internet service provider, began deploying WiMAX technology throughout its local network. Airnet breaks new ground in the New Zealand communications industry as it works with Intel to deploy one of the country's first WiMAX networks. Airnet is one of around 20 carriers worldwide who are collaborating with Intel to deploy WiMAX technology.

NEW Energie and Nortel Complete WiMAX Trial

Nortel Networks and German regional power utility NEW Energie have successfully completed a WiMAX broadband service trial. The pilot, held in the North Rhine-Westphalia town of Erkelenz, lays the foundations for the commercial launch of a WiMAX service that will offer high-bandwidth applications such as live multimedia streams, VoIP, and Internet access at speeds of up to 10 Mbps. NEW Energie expects to launch in areas with little fixed broadband coverage, and will target small business and home users first. For the trial, Nortel worked with German communications consultant tkt teleconsult to deploy a WiMAX network that allowed NEW Energie to provide broadband wireless connections to a selection of small businesses and consumers at speeds of up to 10 Mbps, equal to the current fastest fixed DSL services.

NEW Energie expects to launch new broadband wireless services, based on Nortel WiMAX technology, to areas that have little fixed broadband coverage. The pilot installation in Erkelenz also showed the user-friendliness of a potential

WiMAX service. Users were able to simply plug-and-play the small indoor WiMAX modem into their computer. The flexibility of the service also allowed for users to automatically update the speed and cost of their specific wireless connection to a level that suited their usage profile.

Airspan Claims First Aussie WiMAX Deployment

Broadband wireless equipment manufacturer Airspan Networks has made the first deployment in Australia of equipment certified by the WiMAX Forum. The deployment took place during the Melbourne Grand Prix, with the help of Intel Corp. According to Airspan, Intel Australia approached the Grand Prix Corp. to propose the use of a WiMAX wireless data connection to link medical specialists trackside with their counterparts at the Alfred Hospital. Airspan's AS.MAX equipment was then deployed to provide high-speed broadband connectivity from the racetrack to the hospital, over a distance of 3 km. An AS.MAX MacroMAX BS was placed on the top of a building adjoining Albert Park and two Airspan ProST WiMAX subscriber units were deployed at the trackside trauma center, providing connectivity for laptop computers and portable x-ray systems. Airspan's EasyST, claimed to be the world's first self-installable WiMAX-Forum-Certified modem, was also used trackside. The Airspan Networks EasyST and ProST both incorporate Intel's ProWireless 5116 chip.

Airspan claims this was also the first time WiMAX technology had been operated anywhere in the licensed 3.5-GHz spectrum in Australia. That spectrum was loaned to Intel, Airspan, and the Grand Prix Corp. for the duration of the event by Unwired Australia, which owns rights to WiMAX spectrum in Australia's capital cities, and is gearing up for commercial WiMAX services on a larger scale in the future. Unwired uses proprietary Navini technology for its customer access but has made much of its plans to upgrade to Navini mobile WiMAX equipment. Airspan gear is used for backhaul from its Navini BSs. According to Airspan, its equipment used for the Grand Prix is software upgradeable to the mobile WiMAX standard.

Wagga to Get WiMAX Trial

Austar and SP Telemedia have announced Wagga residents will get the WiMAX technology. According to a report by *The Australian*, the first commercial trials will include Wagga, because of the aggregate demand, but other regions will be close behind. The grand plan is to roll out the Austar network across 55 regional centers covering some 750,000 regional homes. Some noncommercial pilots of the new technology have already been held in Australia, including an Intel showcase at the Formula One Grand Prix in Melbourne, where it demonstrated sending x-rays from a trackside medical center at the Grand Prix circuit to the Alfred Hospital.

Synterra Launches Moscow's First Commercial WiMAX Service

Russian alternative telco Synterra has launched a commercial WiMAX network for business users in Moscow [87]. The network is the first in operation in the city, according to the company's marketing department. Synterra plans to invest around $3 million in network development in Moscow and a further $4 million in surrounding areas. WiMAX subscribers numbered several hundred at the launch, with Synterra targeting several thousand corporate clients. Synterra comprises Komet, RTComm.Ru, and Telecom Center companies. Synterra plans to expand coverage of its WiMAX network in Moscow to 95 percent from the current 80 percent, the company said [110]. The company plans to increase the number of WiMAX BSs by 50 to 60 percent, Synterra said. The BSs are connected to the company's fiber-optic network, which is over 2000 km long, the company said. Synterra launched its WiMAX network in April 2006.

Intel Invests in U.K. WiMAX Venture

Intel Capital is putting $25 million into a joint venture with ISP Pipex Communications to promote the use of the long-range wireless broadband technology WiMAX. The fruit of the union, to be named Pipex Wireless, will provide WiMAX access to homes, businesses, and public sector organizations in the United Kingdom's metropolitan areas. London and Manchester will be the first cities to see a WiMAX deployment from the new company, in 2007. Pipex Wireless plans to roll out WiMAX in the United Kingdom's top eight population centers during 2008 and hopes to eventually sell its services in the top 50 metropolitan areas. Pipex Wireless already has a license to operate WiMAX services in the 3.6-GHz band. The license is an inheritance from Pipex Communications, which started trials for the technology in the Stratford-on-Avon area.

Telecom Cook Islands Ups Internet Speeds, Plans WiMAX Tests

Telecom Cook Islands (TCI) has launched a residential ADSL service on the island of Rarotonga, offering consumers two new packages. "Broadband Home Standard" provides data speeds of 128 kbps with a 700-MB download limit, although "Broadband Home Plus" offers a 256-kbps connection and 2 GB of prepaid usage. The domestic ADSL service will be restricted to slower speeds between 8 a.m. and 6 p.m. to give priority to TCI's business customers. Wi-Fi Internet access is currently provided by TCI at six hot spots on the island, and work is continuing to expand availability. TCI is also planning to hold WiMAX trials in the near future.

Bell Canada and Rogers Launch WiMAX Service

Inukshuk Wireless, a joint venture between Bell Canada and Rogers Communications, has launched a new WiMAX broadband service and plans to expand it nationwide. The Sympatico High-Speed Unplugged service — available in parts of Montreal, Toronto, Edmonton, St. John's, and Whitehorse — is expected to cover two-thirds of Canada within three years. The 3-Mbps service is priced at Can$60 per month and requires a Can$99 modem with a two-year service contract. A 512-kbps-per-second option is available at Can$45 per month.

Intel, Suburban Telecom Sign MOU

Intel signed a memorandum of understanding (MoU) with Nigeria's Suburban Telecom Limited as part of efforts to accelerate the deployment of the Wireless Internet Network (WIN) project around the Federal Capital Territory. The project is geared toward providing affordable and reliable broadband wireless Internet not only in Abuja but also in other states in Nigeria. Under the program, which has the backing of the Federal Capital Development Authority, Intel will provide technological support for Suburban's Abuja Digital Initiative that includes the wireless Internet network project known as CT Access currently being deployed in Abuja.

Both companies will also collaborate in the digital inclusion initiative being sponsored by Intel, to provide affordable connected personal computers in Nigeria, Internet access, and software. In specific terms, Intel will provide hardware solutions that address the challenges faced in the deployment of personal computers (PCs) in Nigeria such as affordability and use in the rural environment; provide curriculum-based digital content using the school learning and teaching technologies; provide advise on WiMAX deployment, as well as explore other opportunities to collaborate with Suburban on other digital initiatives, including the Computers for All Nigerians Initiative (CANI) and rural connectivity programs.

On its part, Suburban Telecom is expected to provide broadband Internet connectivity using appropriate technologies including WiMAX to homes, schools, and offices in Abuja and other parts of the country. Suburban had launched Nigeria's first citywide wireless Internet network project in Abuja under a public–private partnership initiative with the Abuja Investment and Property Development Company (AIPDC), a venture in which the Federal Capital Territory Authority has a 20 percent stake. The initiative has since grown from 20 hot spots at inception to 30 hot spots.

Intel Bets on Brazil

The chip giant Intel's venture capital arm has set up a $50 million fund to invest in Brazil's tech economy. Intel's venture capital division plans to invest $50 million in Brazilian companies, a decision that reflects the country's growing appetite for technologies. IntelCapital has invested roughly $35 million in 13 Brazilian companies, including Digitron, TelecomNet, and Neovia, since 1999. The $50 million pot signals the growing importance of South America's largest economy as an emerging market for Intel's computer and wireless chips.

Intel plans to spread the money among a variety of companies, from software and hardware developers to content and service providers. The focus, though, is to promote a greater use of PCs, Internet, and wireless services, including WiMAX.

Samsung Invests $20 Million in WiMAX Startup

Samsung Ventures America, the U.S.-based venture capital investment arm for Samsung Venture Investment Corp. (SVIC), has invested more than $20 million in C-round funding in broadband wireless chipset company Beceem Communications Inc. Beceem contributes to the IEEE 802.16e standards effort and has helped define the first mobile WiMAX profile for the WiMAX Forum.

Airspan Successfully Completes WiMAX Demonstration in Sri Lanka

WiMAX System enabled the first-ever broadband wireless video and voice call from Colombo to Galle, at an Intel Event. Airspan Networks announced that it has successfully completed a live demonstration of its AS.MAX WiMAX solution in Sri Lanka. Airspan's AS.MAX product family has been designed for indoor, self-installable deployment of CPE, an essential requirement of operators for the economic rollout of broadband wireless. The EasyST is the first product of its type to fully enable indoor plug-and-play WiMAX services. The product family became commercially available in the third quarter of 2005. The products give businesses and consumers uninterrupted access to a rich variety of high-bandwidth applications, such as networked gaming, streamed digital music, TV, videoconferencing, and other real-time services. Fixed WiMAX is expected to deliver end-user data rates greater than 1 Mbps.

WiMAX Trial Slated for Auckland

Auckland-based specialty ISP Natcom is to roll out a WiMAX trial in Auckland and is looking for a few businesses to test the service. The Natcom is also one of three Kiwi foundation service providers for the high-powered, brand-new IPStar satellite broadband service. Natcom says its trial is open to small- and medium-sized business customers who want both Internet cost savings and "a standard and speed of service at a quantum leap from their existing wired or wireless service." A few other trials by different operators are also scheduled. CallPlus has said it is testing the technology, and BCL is said to be looking at it, according to the NZPA, which also noted that Wellington-based New Zealand Wireless has plans to run a trial.

Globetel to Install WiMAX Network in 30 Russian Cities

Globetel Wireless, a subsidiary of Globetel Communications, has entered into an agreement to install wireless communications networks in 30 cities throughout the Russian Federation, providing broadband, VoIP, and digital enhanced cordless telecommunications (DECT) technologies. Russian company Internafta will pay Globetel Wireless for the installation of the networks in Russia's 30 largest cities, beginning with Moscow and St. Petersburg. In October 2005, Globetel demonstrated its Hot Zone 4010 equipment, which will form the backbone of the wireless networks, to members of the Russian government and the telecommunications and technology establishment. Globetel Wireless will manage the networks and maintain a 50 percent shareholding. Globetel plans to roll out the network in three phases (ten cities per phase) over the next 27 months.

Clearwire Launches VoIP over Its WiMAX Network

Clearwire, the broadband wireless provider, began offering a residential VoIP service over its network. The service was jointly developed with Bell Canada. Features include a local phone number within Clearwire's market, unlimited local and long-distance calling within the United States and Canada, competitive international calling rates, call forwarding, enhanced call forwarding, caller ID, voice mail, voice mail to e-mail, three-way calling, caller blocking, and international call blocking. The first market launch is in Stockton, California. Clearwire is using a WiMAX-class access solution developed by its wholly owned subsidiary, NextNet Wireless. The service operates at FCC-licensed 2.5-GHz frequencies in all of its U.S. markets. Clearwire sends its signal wirelessly from a transmitter on top of a cell tower to a specially developed receiver modem. Clearwire is currently providing wireless Internet service in 27 metro markets, covering more than 200 cities and towns in Alaska, California, Florida, Hawaii, Idaho, Minnesota, Nevada, North Carolina, Oregon, Texas, Washington, and Wisconsin in the United States, as well as Ireland, Belgium, Denmark (under the Clearwire name with Danske Telecom), and Mexico (via MVSNet).

Plans Announced for North America's Commercial Mobile WiMAX Deployment

At the annual CTIA WIRELESS 2006 trade show, Samsung Telecommunications America (Samsung) unveiled its plans to work with regional service provider Arialink to deploy the first commercial mobile WiMAX network in North America. Samsung plans to provide its suite of WiMAX-ready products, as well as installation, training, and product support, enabling Arialink to commercially launch mobile WiMAX in Muskegon County, Michigan. Samsung will be the exclusive provider of mobile WiMAX services for Arialink in the Muskegon County region and is slated to be the first technology solutions provider to deploy commercial mobile WiMAX in North America. Samsung has enacted similar trials and plans for mobile WiMAX deployment in Europe and Asia.

Samsung's suite of WiMAX-ready products ushers in the age of converged services delivered from a single, IP-based network. Home, business, and vehicular applications can include VoIP, video telephony, multimedia messaging and conferencing, location and telematic services, broadcast, and multimedia push-and-demand services. Mobile WiMAX will drive revenue through delivery of broadband services to rural and suburban locations not accessible by current technology, as well as creating broadband "hot zones" in more densely populated areas. This project will fulfill Arialink's commitment to provide network services to underserved areas and to enhance broadband service choices throughout Muskegon county. The state of Michigan is providing financial backing for the project as part of the Digital Divide Investment Program. Samsung believes that Muskegon County's pilot network and eventual regional deployment of mobile WiMAX will have larger implications.

TFN Sets Up Largest Experimental WiMAX Network in Taiwan

Taiwan Fixed Network (TFN), one of the four operators of fixed-line telecommunication services in Taiwan, announced the establishment of an experimental WiMAX network in the eastern Taipei metropolitan area, the largest of its kind in Taiwan. Through technological cooperation with Intel, the experimental WiMAX network consists of 2 BSs and 150 CPE sets supplied by U.S.-based Airspan Networks, according to TFN. One BS has been set up in the government-developed Nankang Software Park, with the other established beside a high-rise office/factory mixed-use building, TFN indicated.

With embedded Intel Pro/Wireless 5116 chips based on the IEEE 802.16-2004 standard, the CPEs will be installed in buildings, the first indoor WiMAX CPE model in Taiwan, TFN pointed out. Within a radius of 1 to 3 km from a WiMAX BS, the indoor CPE can reach a download speed of up to 75 Mbps, TFN noted. The connection between WiMAX CPEs and corresponding BSs is intended to be a wireless substitute for fixed-line ADSL or cable modem networks, a so-called "last-mile solution," TFN emphasized. TFN will offer the 150 CPE sets for one year of free wireless access to the Internet to enterprises stationed in the software park and the high-rise building, TFN indicated. With three to five CPE sets allocated to a company, depending on its size, 30 to 50 enterprises can enjoy the free service, TFN added.

Russia's Enforta to Invest $50 Million in WiMAX Networks

Russia's Prestige-Internet, operating under the Enforta brand, plans to invest over U.S. $50 million in the construction of WiMAX networks in 28 cities in Russia, according to the company. The construction is expected to be completed in two years. The company currently operates WiMAX networks in Novosibirsk and Ryazan and plans to launch its networks in 12 more cities, adding that the 12 cities do not include Moscow or St. Petersburg. The company plans to build the networks itself; however, it may consider buying existing networks from other companies. Investments are expected to be made by Sumitomo Corporation and Baring Vostok Capital Partners (BVCP). Prestige-Internet, founded in 2003, is controlled 100 percent by the Netherlands' Enforta BV. Sumitomo Corporation and BVCP jointly own 75 percent in Enforta BV.

Pacnet, Intel to Trial WiMAX in Singapore

Singapore's ISP, Pacific Internet (Pacnet), has signed an MOU with Intel to work toward Singapore's first WiMAX wireless Internet infrastructure [140]. Under the agreement, the companies will conduct studies and market trials to better understand market needs and behaviors in Singapore. They plan to launch the trial for selected customers and intend to release a number of education white papers during the process. Through their collaboration, Intel and Pacnet hope to boost wireless adoption in Singapore and the greater Asia-Pacific region. The companies plan to develop a highly interoperable network, so that a variety of devices can access it. In addition to benefits for individuals and businesses, Pacnet and Intel expect the WiMAX network to be especially beneficial for public safety and emergency situations. For example, a police officer in Singapore could access a database within a moving vehicle.

Siemens Installs First WiMAX Network in Latin America

Colombian broadband provider Orbitel has launched its WiMAX network and has started taking orders for the service [2]. The plans range from $39 to about $325. The network will offer speeds of up to 2 Mbps. The network is now live in Cali, but will soon be made available in 14 other cities. The network uses Siemens' WayMAX gear. Fixed wireless technologies — of all flavors — are finding a home in emerging markets, especially those with limited legacy infrastructure. All in all, Siemens will cover 15 Colombian cities with WayMAX@vantage for Orbitel to provide the company's customers with broadband Internet access, featuring data rates of up to 2 Mbps. The network supports data-intensive services such as high-quality video streaming to laptops.

Turbonet Deploys Aperto Solution for WiMAX in Turkey

Turbonet, a wireless Internet service provider (WISP) in Turkey, has deployed Aperto Networks' Packetwave WiMAX-class broadband wireless solution for trial in Istanbul [3,4]. Turbonet has been awarded a test license by Turkey's regulatory authorities and is field-testing Aperto's end-to-end 3.5-GHz WiMAX-class solution, which includes an array of BSs, subscriber equipment, and an element management system. Aperto is also providing technical support in the execution of the trial. Aperto Networks helps service providers deliver wireless voice and broadband by building WiMAX BSs and subscriber units.

Chunghwa Telecom Launches First WiMAX Network in Taiwan with Redline's RedMAX Products

Chunghwa Telecom, the largest telecommunications service provider in Taiwan, has successfully completed the first phase of its WiMAX and Wi-Fi access network in Taiwan. The WiMAX connections have been established using Redline Communications' RedMAX products, for a complete WiMAX system. Chunghwa Telecom is using Redline's WiMAX-Forum-Certified RedMAX BS (AN-100U) and RedMAX Outdoor Subscriber Unit (SU-O) to connect multiple Wi-Fi zones in urban centers throughout Taiwan. M-Wave Technology Corporation, a Redline-Certified Partner, is managing the network planning and implementation. Prior to rolling out their network, Chunghwa Telecom conducted an exhaustive review of WiMAX products and other available technologies, including wireless mesh networks. Redline's RedMAX family of WiMAX products proved to be the best choice for delivering the speed and performance required for a citywide deployment and will enable Chunghwa Telecom to easily expand their network and support more users over time.

Yozan Conducts WiMAX Feasibility Test in Hokuriku Region of Japan

Yozan has set up a WiMAX feasibility test with a broadband transmitting station in the Hokuriku region in Japan [5]. Hokuriku is typical of mountainous regions in which it is difficult to implement WiMAX infrastructure. Two BSs were set up in the elementary school and the forestry cooperative, and from there 40 access points were set up to residential houses via WiMAX. Security cameras were set up on strategic points checking up on children going to school. Disaster prevention graphics including flooding will also be sent via WiMAX. The Ministry of International Affairs and Communication, Ishikawa Prefecture, has implemented the WiMAX feasibility test in an effort to alleviate the digital divide and revitalize the rural area for young people and attract new companies to set up business. Yozan is working on a trial with America's Tropos Networks and the Tropos Wi-Fi mesh network. Yozan uses a WiMAX 4.9 GHz as backhaul for the nomadic front end using Wi-Fi and mobile WiMAX on IEEE 802.16e, respectively, as it is becoming popular worldwide.

Deutsche Breitband Dienste Deploys Airspan's AS.MAX Products in Germany

Airspan Networks Inc. announced the signing of an agreement with Deutsche Breitband Dienste GmbH (DBD) of Germany for the deployment of Airspan's AS.MAX family of WiMAX products [6]. To date, DBD has placed orders for 400 BSs under the agreement. DBD, Germany's first and largest WiMAX operator, provides broadband access services using Airspan's WiMAX technology in the 3.5-GHz band, for both residential and enterprise customers. DBD's largest deployment is in Berlin, where thousands of subscribers enjoy the freedom of wireless Internet at competitive prices. This deployment leverages Airspan's AS.MAX MacroMAX BS and EasyST CPE, which include support for advanced features, such as uplink subchannelization, and 802.16 nRTP, RTP, and UGS QoS service classes. DBD is also one of the first operators to deploy Airspan's VoiceMAX technology on a WiMAX network. VoiceMAX gives operators the ability to deliver carrier-grade VoIP services through a software suite that provides VoIP admission control, which controls the user experience of VoIP calls over WiMAX and Wi-Fi networks. VoiceMAX enables a wireless operator to prevent network congestion and prevents data traffic from degrading voice quality as the network is loaded with IP traffic. With VoiceMAX, DBD can guarantee high-quality and consistent voice services to its subscribers at all times.

MTI Wireless Edge to Exhibit WiMAX, Wi-Fi, and RFID, ETSI-Compliant Flat Panel Antenna Solutions

MTI announced that because of the continued strong demand for their flat panel antenna solutions, covering the most relevant frequencies in Europe, MTI is actively seeking new business opportunities via distributors and representatives from East European countries and to further expand their distribution channels in East Europe. MTI has a large selection of antenna solutions for WiMAX, Wi-Fi, and RFID in all applicable frequency bands, as well as an Integrated Enclosure Antenna (IEA) solution.

Plain Sailing at WiMAX Telecom

The Swiss-based wireless broadband operator WiMAX Telecom says it has set a new record for live video transmissions over a WiMAX network. The firm, which has operations in Austria, Slovakia, and Croatia, transmitted images over a distance of

40 km from a yacht competing in the World Sailing Championships in Austria. The yacht was moving at 12 knots while sending the live video feed via the WiMAX network.

Intel's WiMAX Debuts at Sundance

Fresh Voices dove into Intel's digital entertainment zone at the Sundance Film Festival to find out what Core Duo and WiMAX can do in a home theater. In a local venue, Intel showed off its WiMAX-based broadband wireless network, built in collaboration with Alvarion and Mountain Wireless. The network, covering 55 mi, reached an area from Salt Lake City to Park City. To showcase how the new dual-core chipset powers the network, Intel streamed a live film premier to an audience at a remote ski lodge.

Samsung Invests in WiMAX Chip Developer

Samsung's venture capital investment subsidiary, Samsung Ventures America, was the primary investor in a $20-million round of financing for WiMAX start-up Beceem Communications. The U.S.-based company claims to be the leading provider of chipsets for WiMAX technology. With this new round of capital, Beceem will accelerate its chipset product development with the goal of becoming the first company to deliver a chipset that is fully compliant with the new mobile WiMAX standard. The company has reportedly demonstrated its prototype chipsets to leading telecom equipment manufacturers. Beceem was founded in 2003 in Silicon Valley to offer semiconductor solutions to the wireless broadband market. The company is a contributor to the IEEE 802.16e standards effort and is a member of the WiMAX Forum.

Venezuela Gets Mobile WiMAX Technology from Samsung

Samsung will be deploying the innovative mobile WiMAX technology in the South American country of Venezuela. Samsung has gone into collaboration with the Venezuelan pay-TV and telecommunications operator Omnivision C.A. With the network established, Omnivision plans to start offering service in Caracas. Further, as they expand their network, seven of the major cities of the country would be covered under this program. The expansion of the network is expected to take around three years. This agreement to establish a mobile WiMAX platform in Venezuela comes after Samsung signed a similar deal with TVA Sistema de Televisao SA in Brazil. They are aiming for a trial launch of their services in this country.

Bangalore-Based Sloka Telecom Makes Low-Cost WiMAX and 3G Equipment

A Bangalore-based start-up is rolling out indigenously developed wireless BSs. The latest entrant into the Indian products arena, Sloka Telecom, has plans to supply wireless infrastructure products in WiMAX and 3G, such as BSs, for the Indian and international markets.

Nigeria: NetnearU Partners Intel on WiMAX Deployment

NetnearU, one of the leading wireless Internet Service Providers with state-of-the-art technology in Wi-Fi deployment, has entered into partnership with Intel, the global chip manufacturer to set up Wi-Fi hot spots across the country. The company is venturing into the new territory through the deployment of WiMAX technology with Intel, to lower the cost of Internet access in the country. The company has already taken delivery of its first Alvarion WiMAX equipment and will deploy it in Lagos. Under the agreement, Intel is expected to provide hardware solutions that address the challenges faced in the deployment of PCs in Nigeria, such as affordability and use in the rural areas. It would also provide NETnearU advice on WiMAX deployment and also explore further opportunities to collaborate with NETnearU on the digital inclusion initiatives such as Computer for All Nigerians Initiative (CANI), Wireless Without Worry (WOW), and rural connectivity. NETnearU is, however, expected to provide broadband Internet connectivity, using appropriate technology including WiMAX, to homes, schools, and offices in Nigeria and also explore other opportunities to collaborate with Intel on other digital inclusion initiatives.

NTC Allocates WiMAX Spectrums in Thailand

Operators have applied for wireless broadband Internet licenses in Thailand [7]. Telecom companies can provide WiMAX wireless broadband Internet on the 2.5- and 3.5-GHz spectrum bands. The 5-GHz spectrum, which is commonly used for WiMAX in other countries, will not be made available at this stage. The 2.5- and 3.5-GHz spectrums had already been allocated for WiMAX use by the Frequency Allocation Panel, which was dissolved after the NTC was established. Shin Satellite, True Corp PLC, and TOT PLC stand to be the first telecom operators to develop WiMAX as they already own the available spectrums and have used them for their existing businesses. ShinSat owns the 3.5-GHz spectrum; True's pay-TV operator, UBC True, owns the 2.5-GHz spectrum; and TOT owns the 2.4-GHz spectrum, which falls within the range of the spectrums to be made available.

Mobile WiMAX Deployment Gets Under Way in Puerto Rico

Islanet Inc. has launched its Volare premobile 802.16e WiMAX residential service using the company's network infrastructure and licensed 2.5-GHz EBS channels [8,9]. Islanet is a provider of commercial wireless Internet and data services in Puerto Rico. The Volare service was deployed using the Ripwave MX system from Navini Networks, which offers plug-and-play broadband wireless access solutions for commercial premobile WiMAX deployments. The Volare service was launched in greater Mayaguez (a city on the island's western coast) and already provides high-speed wireless Internet access to more than 600 subscribers. It is now available countrywide, with plans starting at $19.95 per month for plug-and-play activation. The modem and service are available anywhere within the coverage area, and there is no need for a cable or phone line.

Fujitsu Unveils WiMAX Strategy Encompassing Silicon, Systems, and Services

Fujitsu Network Communications and Fujitsu Microelectronics America Inc. have articulated a comprehensive WiMAX strategic vision that includes development of every major component in the WiMAX network, including silicon solutions, electronic devices, radio access network solutions, professional services, and backhaul infrastructure solutions [121]. Backed by the Fujitsu global presence and leadership in the development of next-generation networks, the Fujitsu WiMAX solution will allow carriers to work with one strategic partner for broadband wireless networks, helping them offer the leading-edge services that consumers are demanding for any time, anywhere voice, video, and data communications. The new Fujitsu WiMAX product line includes two models of BSs for indoor or outdoor use. These BSs include a very compact radio frequency (RF) unit with world-class high-efficiency RF amplifiers and a high-performance, compact baseband (BB) unit. The system is based on the ratified IEEE 802.16-2005 standard and the WiMAX Forum definition of mobile WiMAX. By integrating industry-leading intellectual property for multiple antenna technologies such as MIMO into these new systems and leveraging its world-leading digital predistortion (DPD) amplifiers, Fujitsu is providing the highest-performance, comprehensive WiMAX solution that easily scales to meet the demands of the rapidly expanding broadband wireless access market. The Fujitsu-fixed WiMAX SoC was an integral part of the first BS to be WiMAX-certified in January 2006. In June 2006, Fujitsu announced its road map for delivery of WiMAX mobility silicon solutions, and in September 2006 Hopling Technologies announced its plan to partner with Fujitsu to bring Linux-based WiMAX reference boards to market. Fujitsu Network Life Cycle Services are an integral part of the network solution. These services are available to help carriers create and extend their WiMAX footprint by utilizing planning services such as RF engineering, site acquisition, and site preparation [128]. When carriers are ready to build their network, Fujitsu offers a full line of deployment services, which include installation and test/turn-up services, as well as backhaul and back-office connectivity provisioning. Carriers can also opt to have Fujitsu monitor and maintain their wireless network with network operations center (NOC) services and provide network statistics, so that the inner workings of their network are fully visible to carriers. Full maintenance and support is also available 24/7, with rapid deployment of on-site technical assistance personnel and spares management as needed. Fujitsu has formed key regional partnerships to augment development efforts and meet specific requirements of carriers around the world. In North America, for example, Fujitsu has partnered with two broadband wireless access leaders — Airspan Networks for WiMAX solutions and BelAir Networks for Wi-Fi mesh solutions.

Navini Supplies WiMAX in Sweden

SB Broadband in Sweden announced that they have launched a network using pre-WiMAX 802.16e equipment from Navini Networks [10]. The network will be deployed in the rural area of Sodermanland, in the southwest of Sweden, and will cover nine municipalities. SB Broadband will use its licenses for the 3.5-GHz spectrum for providing the service, according to the company's press release.

Aircel Launches WiMAX

Indian mobile operator Aircel, a subsidiary of Malaysia's Maxis Communications, has launched WiMAX services in Chennai and is rolling out wireless broadband networks in Bangalore. Aircel has received requests from Indian IT majors such as Intel, TCS, Infosys, and Wipro to provide a WiMAX facility to their employees so that they can work out of homes in case of emergencies [11]. Aircel has launched wireless Internet services through WiMAX technology in Bangalore, after Chennai. According to Aircel, the company is identifying and deploying Wi-Fi hot spots throughout the city, with indoor and outdoor points backhauled with WiMAX. Internet services at these hot spots would be enabled through prepaid cards integrated with payment gateways for online registration, and subsequently activated using the authentication, authorization, and accounting (AAA) mechanism. Aircel has enabled WiMAX-based Internet connectivity at the Palace Grounds, the venue of the four-day (Asia's largest) IT event beginning October 28, 2006, to enable exhibitors and business delegates to get a first-hand experience of the technology. The company was also in the process of WiMAXing Vidhan Soudha, the state's Secretariat that houses the Assembly and the Council, and adjacent buildings belonging to the state government. The company had recently launched WiMAX in Chennai [12] with 90 percent coverage across commercial areas in Chennai and has already enabled wireless connectivity for SME and enterprise clients through WiMAX, based on 802.16d standards, at a speed range of 2 to 10 Mbps. This would help the end user to stay connected to the Internet and intranet with high uptime, the company said. It currently provides mobile cellular services in Tamil Nadu, West Bengal, Orissa, Assam, North East, and Jammu and Kashmir [13].

Urban WiMAX Plans London Launch

U.K. ISP Urban WiMAX plans to launch London's WiMAX service in 2007 [125]. The service will be aimed at small- and medium-sized enterprises that need to be able to upload high volumes of data to the Internet. The company is looking to raise an additional $5.7 million in funding. According to TeleGeography's GlobalComms Database, in March 2006 Urban WiMAX announced plans to launch trials of what it describes as "the United Kingdom's first true WiMAX services" in London, based on the 802.16d standard, as opposed to the so-called pre-WiMAX technology. The trial began in April 2006 and allows users to access the service for free, ahead of a planned commercial launch. Urban WiMAX claims the service will cost 30 to 50 percent less than the rival's equivalent speed wholesale SDSL service.

WiMAX in the United Kingdom

WiMAX trials are now taking place in the United Kingdom, offering high-bandwidth broadband connectivity via wide area wireless [126]. Milton Keynes has become the first major town in the country to benefit from wide area coverage via WiMAX wireless broadband technology. The Milton Keynes rollout will initially provide around 500 businesses and homes with long-range wireless access speeds of up to 10 Mbps, powered by five BSs. The project is a collaboration between ISP Pipex and the city's local authority, and, if successful, will be extended across the whole city.

Nortel Tests Uplink Collaborative MIMO 4G WiMAX Technology

Nortel Networks conducted testing of the Uplink Collaborative MIMO technology standard, which could potentially allow wireless operators to serve twice as many mobile broadband customers with the same number of cell sites [127]. If implemented properly, this WiMAX-based technology would let carriers significantly boost subscription revenues without an increase in capital investment.

Uplink collaborative MIMO creates a technological disruption that offers revolutionary improvement in wireless network capacity and provides a clear path to 4G mobile broadband — of which WiMAX is the first technology.

Microsense to Offer WiMAX Solutions

WAN and Wi-Fi solutions provider Microsense announced its readiness to offer end-to-end WiMAX solutions across India. Microsense has also developed flexible authentication and billing systems for WiMAX networks for providing service to individuals and enterprises, a company statement said. Pune and Bangalore were the front-runners for providing citywide broadband wireless access, launched by the respective government authorities. Both the cities are in advanced stages of preparedness, it said. Microsense has successfully completed the RF blueprint for WiMAX and Metro Wi-Fi deployment in Pune, along with Intel and the Pune Municipal Corporation. The company has also been short-listed by the government of Karnataka as its top vendor for the Unwire Bangalore initiative, it said [14,15].

DSat Providers Consider WiMAX Return Path

DirecTV and Echostar's Dish Network are considering the emerging WiMAX long-range wireless technology as a means of providing a return path for interactive services and on-demand applications. The two companies are exploring the possibility of launching a joint-venture wireless service to support a high-speed return path in an effort to better compete with on-demand services that are now widely available on digital cable.

Inukshuk Announces Availability of National Wireless Broadband Network

Inukshuk Wireless Inc. has announced the completion of the initial phase of its new wireless broadband network, with service available in 20 centers across Canada. Built in conjunction with Bell Canada and Rogers Communications, the Inukshuk network is one of the largest of its kind in the world. This next-generation IP wireless network based on pre-WiMAX standards enables portable megabit services, allowing subscribers to access the Internet and other applications such as VoIP, video streaming, and a variety of data applications. The total investment of the partnership between Bell and Rogers is expected to reach $200 million by 2008, covering over 100 urban and rural areas. The initial phase of the network covers over 5 million households and 40 percent of the population and is now available in 20 areas across Canada, including the Greater Vancouver Area, Victoria, Red Deer, Calgary, Edmonton, Whitehorse, the Greater Toronto Area, Barrie, London,

Windsor, Kitchener-Waterloo, Hamilton, Ottawa, Gatineau-Hull, Quebec City, the Greater Montreal Area, Charlottetown, Halifax, Fredericton, and St. John's. The network leverages existing cellular towers of both Bell and Rogers, wirelessly connecting customers to the Internet and providing secure data transmission over the licensed spectrum. The new technology is also being deployed in the United States and Mexico, and Inukshuk expects Canadian users to have access to an extensive North American broadband footprint in the future.

Austar and SP Telemedia for Rural WiMAX

Australian pay-TV provider Austar has teamed up with IP network operator SP Telemedia, which offers services under the Soul brand name, for the delivery of wireless broadband services to rural areas. Austar is building out a WiMAX broadband wireless network to 750,000 homes in 25 outlying regions by the end of 2007. Under the new alliance, the network will utilize SP Telemedia's extensive IP-based network for backhaul and switching services, and Internet connectivity. Austar says the $50 million project will deliver "true broadband" services to rural customers currently limited to Internet speeds of up to 256 kbps.

BellSouth to Unveil Add-Ons for Wireless Broadband

BellSouth, a powerhouse of the landline, is eyeing more ways it can send services through the sky. BellSouth is investigating WiMAX technology as an inexpensive way to provide high-speed Web services in areas where its wired network has been damaged, degraded, or not yet built up.

Iliad's IFW Unit to Offer WiMAX Access to Free Users

According to Telecompaper, Iliad's wireless in the local loop (WiLL) subsidiary, IFW is to offer WiMAX services to over 1.6 million broadband customers currently signed up to Iliad's ADSL service provider Free. The trial WiMAX service will be based on Alvarion 802.16d infrastructure and will enable Free broadband subscribers to gain wireless Internet access in the majority of France's metropolitan areas, once they have installed IFW-compatible software and equipment.

Aperto Raises $26 Million for Its WiMAX Systems

Aperto Networks, a start-up based in Milpitas, California, raised $26 million in venture funding for its WiMAX BSs and subscriber units. The company currently claims more than 200 customers in 65 countries. The new Series E follow-on financing round brings the company's total capitalization to $120 million. The financing round was led by GunnAllen Venture Partners with significant participation from existing investors, including JK&B Capital, Canaan Partners, Alliance Ventures, Innovacom, JAFCO, and Labrador Ventures.

Milwaukee Schools Tap WiMAX for Families

Officials from the Milwaukee Public Schools are looking to extend Internet access into the homes of students and staff members through the use of an emerging WiMAX wireless broadband technology. If successful, Milwaukee's deployment of the technology would be one of the first in the nation by a school system. The program is part of a growing trend among school systems nationwide to bring Internet service into the homes of all students and educators. Similar programs have mostly used dial-up service as a means of providing free Internet access to students. Also, a low-bandwidth solution such as dial-up does not usually permit students and teachers to take advantage of the Internet's full potential as a teaching and learning tool, which requires the use of graphics, video, sound, and other programs too large to be downloaded efficiently via a dial-up connection. Milwaukee plans to deploy a WiMAX system, using television channels that the Federal Communications Commission has allocated for educational purposes. The channels — or 2.5-gigahertz (GHz) frequencies — have been used to broadcast educational programs into classrooms in a one-way exchange of information, but the WiMAX system would provide for a two-way exchange of data, officials say.

WiMAX to Be Launched in Belarus

WiMAX data transmission network has been launched in a test mode to check electromagnetic compatibility of WiMAX and other Belarusian communication networks. Ericsson has supplied the equipment for the Belarusian WiMAX network. At present, Beltelecom is the only operator providing WiMAX services. WiMAX will be available throughout the country.

ADC, Aperto Team for Worldwide WiMAX

ADC and Aperto Networks have entered a partnership agreement to market, sell, and install carrier-grade WiMAX broadband systems and solutions for potential service-provider buyers on a global basis. Under an original equipment manufacturer (OEM) deal, Aperto Networks of Milpitas, California, will supply its range of WiMAX-Forum-Certified product lines — including BSs, service platforms, and software portfolios — to Minneapolis-based ADC, as it addresses WiMAX market opportunities among voice, data, and multimedia service-provider customers. Aperto's PacketMax systems and technology — said to be compliant with the Advanced Open Telecom Platform (ACTA) standard — will make its way into the broad Digivance line of wireless LAN, convergence platform, distributed antenna systems, and ClearGain amplifiers marketed by ADC's Active Infrastructure Business Unit. The companies said their deal will result in a new system, the Digivance WMX 5000, a 12-sector coverage, high-density traffic offering aimed at licensed and license-exempt bands, and positioned to drive down both capital expenditure and operating expenditure costs for operators of Internet Protocol (IP) intensive point-to-point and point-to-multipoint networks. ADC and Aperto, which have customers in 140 and 65 countries, respectively, also are likely to coordinate, direct, and conduct third-party channel sales activities to address worldwide markets.

Alcatel, Samsung Team on WiMAX

Alcatel and Samsung have agreed to cooperate on interoperability between Alcatel's mobile WiMAX infrastructure based on the IEEE 802.16e standard (referred to as WiBro in Korea) and Samsung's mobile WiMAX terminals. This strategic cooperation will allow both companies to accelerate the introduction of mobile WiMAX (WiBro) solutions for the global market. The interoperability tests will target the introduction of a fully interoperable mobile WiMAX solution. This will enable the worldwide audience to access the high-speed broadband services from a mobile device at multimegabit speeds as a complement to fixed and mobile networks.

Wireless Provider Alvarion Targets Africa

Wireless broadband provider Alvarion Ltd. has gained traction in the African market, with recent deals in Ghana and Madagascar. Ghana Telecom, that country's incumbent carrier, has announced that it will be using Alvarion's eMGW — a point-to-multipoint fixed wireless system — to offer data and voice services to SOHO and residential users. It will also build a broadband wireless network in Accra, Ghana's capital, to provide broadband data and toll-quality voices services. Alvarion's eMGW system supports Internet services, corporate network access, and carrier-class telephony in a single system. It includes a "hybrid-switching" architecture that uses both circuit and packet switching to maximize spectrum and equipment utilization. African broadband provider Gulfsat Madagascar will expand its current network, using Alvarion's OFDM system operating in 3.5 GHz. The company's strategy is to target residential subscribers, with greater coverage and increased capacity. Initially, this network will offer broadband services to residential subscribers in the capital city of Antananarivo.

Southern Europe Set to Receive First Premobile WiMAX Commercial Network

Codium Networks, an independent integrator specializing in "WiMAX-driven" network solutions, has announced that it will use equipment from Navini Networks to deploy a broadband wireless network in southeastern Spain. Thousands of subscribers will receive service via the new network. Providing portable, non-line-of-sight high-speed Internet access with plug-and-play activation and retail friendly distribution, Navini's products deliver personal broadband to customers. Navini's Ripwave provides the access technology, and the backhaul is supplied by InfiNet Wireless Radio Router P-P Solution.

Telsima's Indian Dream

Telsima Corp., a leading developer of converged network solutions, has announced the commencement of its manufacturing operations from India. Telsima sees huge potential for affordable broadband services, and has pioneered the use of WiMAX-based solutions that will enable operators to deploy non-line-of-sight broadband wireless services in both dense urban and rural locations in India. The company also plans to enhance its Sales and Support Center in Gurgaon, India. Telsima plans to achieve more than 50 percent of its sales from India.

Russia's Sibirtelecom Launches Pilot WiMAX in Three Cities

Russian regional telecommunications operator Sibirtelecom has launched pilot WiMAX projects in the cities of Tomsk, Novosibirsk, and Irkutsk. In addition to the development of WiMAX networks, Sibirtelecom is also developing Wi-Fi networks, aiming the two services at various market segments. Although its WiMAX and Wi-Fi networks are under construction, it may acquire some companies operating such networks. Sibirtelecom also plans to start offering IPTV services in the cities of Barnaul and Tomsk and to expand its cable TV services in Irkutsk. The company has started offering IPTV services in Novosibirsk. Sibirtelecom provides a wide range of telecommunications services, including fixed-line, mobile, and Internet services, in the Siberian Federal District. Russian government-controlled telecom holding Svyazinvest owns 50.67 percent of Sibirtelecom.

WiMAX Pilot Planned for Cyberjaya

Multimedia Super Corridor Malaysia (MSC) caretaker Multimedia Development Corp. (MDeC) signed an agreement with U.S.-based Air Broadband Communications Inc. Under the agreement, Air Broadband will lay out WiMAX infrastructure to cover

Cyberjaya. This will be a pilot project. The Universal Service Provision (USP) program is aimed at providing telecommunications services to unserved and underserved areas and communities in the country.

Bermuda to Benefit from WiMAX Deployment

Bermudan telecom company North Rock Communications plans to launch a high-speed wireless network based on WiMAX technology. The new service, tentatively named North Rock Max, will be rolled out in a phased approach and will complement the company's existing wireless networks on the island. North Rock Max will offer both Internet access and voice telephony with unlimited local calling, and will begin to replace Wi-Fi over the next few years. North Rock Communications launched its original fixed wireless service for the corporate community in January 2000, with residential services following in June 2002. In September 2004, the company became the only alternative to incumbent telco BTC when it began offering customers a local phone line.

SAMSUNG Commercializes WiMAX Service in the Croatian Market

Samsung Electronics Co. Ltd. has teamed up with Croatia's fixed operator H1 to roll out WiMAX to the Croatian market. The two companies entered a strategic partnership during the process of introducing the latest telecommunication equipment to the Croatian market. Samsung will be providing the Croatian market with the equipment and technologies for its upcoming friendly user trial service. The friendly user trial service will begin in Split, Croatia's second largest city, followed by nationwide availability soon thereafter. The WiMAX trial in Croatia is considered to be historical, as it will be the first actual commercialization of the 3.5-GHz frequency in the European market [145]. The standard WiMAX frequency in the European market is 3.5 GHz, and is expected to expand greatly following the fulfillment of the contract between Samsung and H1.

PeterStar Launches WiMAX Campaign

Russian alternative telco PeterStar has launched a WiMAX network in Kaliningrad. The St. Petersburg-based operator aims to follow up the launch by extending the network to other Russian cities. The company reported that it has invested $1.2 million in infrastructure in Kaliningrad, including a metropolitan fiber-optic and copper cable network spanning 80 km.

Abu Dhabi's Wateen Teams Up with Motorola

Wateen Telecom, the Abu Dhabi Group's latest communications venture in Pakistan, has signed a contract under which Motorola will be the primary designer, supplier, and planner of Wateen's wireless broadband voice and data network throughout Pakistan.

SR Telecom Expands WiMAX Distribution Network

SR Telecom Inc. has signed a Sales Cooperation Agreement with Sagem Communication, a member company of SAFRAN Group. Sagem is a major force in the mobile and broadband communication industries and will market and resell the SR Telecom symmetryMX line of WiMAX products. With this agreement, Sagem and SR Telecom will build on their joint marketing efforts to deliver field-proven, carrier-class WiMAX-based, broadband access solutions. The combined efforts will focus on telecommunications service providers across Europe and Africa.

WiMAX in Porto Alegre

The government of Porto Alegre — capital city of Brazil's most southern state, Rio Grande do Sul — plans to invest $1.5 million in building a WiMAX network. Coverage will extend to most public buildings such as state offices, schools, and health centers. The city's own government IT and communications company, Procempa, will be in overall charge of the rollout, which will see 28 connection points established, and 350 such points when the network is eventually fully deployed.

AT&T Goes beyond Convergence

Real-time network analysis, WiMAX, and a host of emerging technologies are on AT&T Corp.'s mind these days. AT&T has set up WiMAX trials for the rural, suburban, and urban markets — in Alaska; Middleton, New Jersy; and Atlanta, respectively. The Atlanta trial involves 3.5-GHz licensed spectrum and should begin customer trials in the fourth quarter of 2005, AT&T said.

BellSouth Expands Georgia WiMAX Service

The company said that it has installed a third radio tower in Athens, which will expand the availability of the service. Besides Athens, BellSouth has also launched WiMAX service in Palatka, Florida, and New Orleans. BellSouth does not require that wireless broadband subscribers also subscribe to their standard voice service, although the company does offer discounts for the service to its wireline customers as well as Cingular Wireless subscribers. BellSouth is a co-owner of Cingular.

Company Launches WiMAX Service in Uganda

Uganda is the first East African country to make use of WiMAX technology. So far only South Africa and Egypt have made limited use of the technology. Infocom is a sister company to Celtel Uganda, and the company is planning to take the technology to other African countries.

Mexican Axtel to Invest $150 Million after Intel Deal

Mexican telecom firm Axtel has invested $150 million on improvements that include building Latin America's first network, using a new wide access and fast wireless Internet technology. Axtel signed an agreement with the world's top microchip maker, Intel Corp., to use its WiMAX technology for the first time in the region.

ITC Starts Saudi WiMAX Delivery

This multimillion dollar project, which is being implemented by Integrated Telecom Company (ITC), will be the first such network in Saudi Arabia to be based on WiMAX technology. The network will be installed using a turnkey solution from Intracom and IP solutions from Cisco and will be based on WiMAX technology from Redline Communications.

Greece's Intracom in Cooperation Agreement with U.S. Axxcelera Broadband

Greek defense and technology company Intracom said it entered into a strategic cooperation agreement with U.S.-based Axxcelera Broadband Wireless. Intracom said it will now be able to offer WiMAX technology in addition to its own IEEE technology for telecom customers in Europe, the Middle East, and Africa.

Payless Communication Holdings Inc. Targets Acquisitions for Wireless VoIP over Wi-Fi and WiMAX

Advance Technology Solutions (ATS) Inc. will manufacture and distribute innovative technologies such as Softswitches, VoIP, Wi-Fi/WiMAX, and IPTV devices for residential and commercial use. Integrated Telecom Services (ITS) Inc. will file for its CLEC license so it can offer local, long distance, dial-up Internet, and DSL services to both residential and commercial customers on the West Coast of the United States. ITS will also offer VoIP services on the West Coast and offer ATS's product line. ITS will also deploy IPTV in the near future with various partners in the telecom and entertainment industry.

Pactolus Drives WiMAX-Delivered VoIP Carrier Services

Pactolus Communications Software, a developer of Class 4/5 SIP-based IP voice services, has introduced support for WiMAX delivery of its SIPware Services Suite and customized applications based on the RapidFLEX Service Creation Environment (SCE). Pactolus' WiMAX support aids service providers in their quest to deliver services — such as primary line VoIP, audioconferencing, and real-time prepaid voice services — to new customer populations, regardless of their current degree of last-mile transport access. The company also supports WiMAX delivery of customized and new innovative services based on its SEC. The product aims at helping operators integrate 3G and VoIP primary line services for bundling to consumer and business customers. It also focuses on assisting service providers to extend and enrich the service profitability potential of their WiMAX investments and strategies. Many cellular and wireless Internet service providers (WISPs) are using WiMAX to reduce backhauling costs, extend coverage throughout rural areas, support consumer usage of VoIP-IM services, such as Skype and GTalk, and bring new bandwidth efficiencies and range to urban wireless coverage.

Redline's WiMAX Products Chosen for Major Broadband Network in Saudi Arabia

Redline Communications Inc.'s RedMAX family of WiMAX products will be deployed with Cisco Systems Inc.'s IP solutions, part of the $22.2 million first phase of a major IP network implementation in Saudi Arabia. INTRACOM Middle East, a multinational information and communications technology solutions provider, will incorporate RedMAX in a countrywide communications network for ITC, a licensed data service provider in Saudi Arabia.

VIA NET.WORKS Starts Operations in Zurich and Geneva

VIA NET.WORKS (Switzerland) Ltd. will be carrying out WiMAX pilot operations in Zurich and Geneva [129]. The planned areawide covering of WiMAX will be supported by Chinese companies. VIA NET.WORKS is conducting negotiations with Chinese carriers and investors to acquire WiMAX concessions in other European countries and set up WiMAX networks. VIA NET.WORKS is already the sole European provider with direct IP data connection to China. VIA NET.WORKS has been dealing with WiMAX technology since the beginning of 2004. The planned setup of an areawide WiMAX network in Switzerland and other European countries will be carried out in cooperation with Chinese investors, engineers, and telecommunications providers.

Networkplus Offers Islandwide WiMAX Coverage

As expected, Mauritius should be the first nation in the world fully covered by a WiMAX network. Only outlying islands will not be included in the network built by Networkplus. In 1989 Mauritius became the first country south of the equator with a cellular mobile network (TACS). In 2004 the island featured Africa's first UMTS network. On the 2nd of June, 2005, only five days after the license had been issued, Networkplus started its WiMAX network, "Nomad," for business users. Some two months later, individual consumers could sign up as well.

BellSouth Offers WiMAX to Ravaged Gulf Coast

As more evidence that it is embracing WiMAX as a key strategy for delivering broadband, BellSouth will extend the wireless high-speed service to customers in Hurricane-Katrina-devastated Gulfport and Biloxi, Mississippi. The former regional Bell operating company said the pre-WiMAX service will feature downstream speeds up to 1.5 Mbps. The firm has installed a similar service in some Georgia communities and has offered the service to businesses in New Orleans. The two largest former RBOCs — Verizon Communications and AT&T (formerly, SBC Communications) — have been using fiber for advanced broadband communications.

Alcatel to Deliver WiMAX Network to Netia for Broadband Wireless Access in Poland

Alcatel has signed a cooperation agreement for the construction of a broadband wireless access network in Lublin, one of the largest cities in south-east Poland, based on the WiMAX technology. Netia is Poland's largest alternative provider of fixed-line telecommunications services. This announcement reinforces Netia's plans to provide telecommunication services, based on WiMAX technology, in Poland. Under the agreement, Alcatel will supply, install, and integrate an end-to-end WiMAX solution, enabling Netia to carry out testing WiMAX in the Lublin area by providing a representative panel of users with broadband wireless access to the Internet and data transmissions with a guaranteed level of quality.

Airspan Announces Completion of Large Connectivity Project in the Dominican Republic

Airspan Networks Inc. has completed deployment of a large-scale rural connectivity network under the Dominican Republic's Rural Public Telephony Phase II Project and has initiated commercial operations. The project, which was developed under the auspices of INDOTEL, was installed and is being operated by BECTEL, and has benefited over 1,750 communities in 18 provinces in the country. Users of the new network can make and receive local, national, and international calls, using a network based on fixed and mobile wireless technologies that also give Internet access and VoIP service. Townships in the provinces of La Altagracia, Hato Mayor, María Trinidad Sánchez, Monseñor Nouel, Monte Cristi, Peravia, Valverde, La Vega, San Cristóbal, San José de Ocoa, Santiago, and Santo Domingo have already benefited from the project.

Digicel Ramps Up Caribbean Services, Plans WiMAX Expansion

Digicel will offer wireless services in Haiti and Trinidad and Tobago. The company also conducted a WiMAX broadband pilot project in the Cayman Islands and plans to expand WiMAX offerings into Barbados and Jamaica.

KT and Alcatel to Partner on Mobile WiMAX

Alcatel and KT announced a partnership to accelerate the adoption of mobile WiMAX based on the IEEE 802.16e standard. They will also set up a center to perform interoperability tests between WiBro and mobile WiMAX solutions. WiBro's earlier time to market is an opportunity for vendors and operators to assess what mobile WiMAX could be like for real, what deployment constraints would occur, and what kind of applications would be the most attractive using the technology.

Nortel to Build WiMAX Network in Canada

Nortel will build a WiMAX Network in Canada to equip rural areas with high-speed wireless broadband access and increase economic activity [122]. The Alberta Special Areas Board (SAB) has selected Nortel to build the first commercial broadband wireless access network in Canada, based on the WiMAX IEEE 802.16-2004 (fixed WiMAX) standard. The SAB is collaborating with NETAGO Wireless to bring wireless broadband services to rural Albertans. The WiMAX network will operate in the 3.5-GHz spectrum band and be made available to roughly 80 percent of SAB residents by the end of summer 2006. This WiMAX network will support the goal of bridging the digital divide through affordable broadband wireless Internet services to users located in rural areas of Alberta. The new WiMAX network will also extend the service area of the Alberta SuperNet Project to approximately 4200 government, health, library, and educational facilities in 429 communities across Alberta. The WiMAX network will equip SAB residences and businesses with fixed broadband wireless access at data rates between 1 and 3 Mbps, which is comparable to cable-broadband and DSL connections. The high-speed capabilities will support sophisticated broadband services such as e-mail, high-speed Internet access, multimedia applications including streaming video and music, VoIP, and other real-time business collaboration services. The network will also support video surveillance and remote telemetry.

Natcom Tests WiMAX in Auckland

Natcom has begun testing its WiMAX Airthernet service in Auckland and is seeking trial customers to check the viability and quality of the service. The trial is open to small- and medium-sized business customers. Interested companies can register their interest online. Airthernet is the brand name for Natcom's new wireless broadband services. Natcom says the service is for those who want Internet cost savings and a leap from their existing wired or wireless service.

VCom Signs Major WiMAX Agreement with MRO-TEK to Supply Wireless Broadband Equipment Across India

VCom Inc. has been selected by Bangalore, India, headquartered MRO-TEK Ltd. to supply VCom's WiMAX-ready BSs and CPE to serve market needs for WiMAX technology in India. Subsequent to achieving domestic regulatory approvals for India and compliance, MRO-TEK will offer VCom's 3.3- to 3.4-GHz WiMAX-ready products domestically in India under the MRO-TEK brand label via a multiyear supply agreement totaling $10,000,000. This supply agreement represents one of the largest commitments to WiMAX technology in the South Asia region to date and recognizes VCom's design leadership for WiMAX, the surging demand for broadband in India, and India's rapidly advancing economic growth. The agreement also opens the door for other VCom products, including an expanded WiMAX product family, to be added over time, based on market demand.

Sydney to Get Business WiMAX Network

Wireless broadband carrier Access Providers has announced it will build a WiMAX-based network in Sydney with exclusive focus on business customers. Access Providers plans to deploy the new network and connect customers by 2007. The company claims this will be the first WiMAX network to be built in Australia, based on the fixed WiMAX standard, 802.16-2004, ratified by the IEEE.

WiMAX Network Planned for Finland

Omnitele has been contracted by two local Finnet group telephone companies, Mikkelin Puhelin and Kajaanin Puhelinosuuskunta, to carry out the radio network planning of two extensive WiMAX implementations. Mikkelin Puhelin, in cooperation with Savonlinnan Puhelin, is building broadband wireless access to rural areas in Finland. The network will be built over WiMAX technology and will consist of almost 100 WiMAX BSs in an area of 10,000 sq km, covering around 50,000 summer cottages.

Sprint Casts Its Lot with WiMAX

Sprint Nextel Corp. announced that the carrier will adopt the 802.16e mobile WiMAX standard as its 4G broadband technology, partnering with Intel Corp., Motorola Inc., and Samsung. Sprint will deploy WiMAX gear to leverage its 2.5-GHz spectrum holdings, which covers 85 percent of the top 100 U.S. markets. The plan is to conduct trials with commercial releases expected in 2008 [130]. The rollout will complement, not replace, Sprint's existing EV-DO network.

Fujitsu Unveils Mobile WiMAX SoC Solution

Fujitsu Microelectronics America has come out with a mobile WiMAX system-on-chip (SoC) solution. The integrated one-chip MAC and PHY mixed-signal baseband SoC is designed to optimize performance and power consumption using Fujitsu's 90-nm process technology, and is suited for PC cards and mobile devices [131]. The Fujitsu mobile WiMAX SoC is fully compliant with the IEEE 802.16e-2005 mobile WiMAX standard. The mobile WiMAX SoC will be designed into subscriber systems that will be deployed along with 802.16e-2005-compliant BSs in supporting end-to-end mobile wireless networks. Engineering samples will be available in 2007. Fujitsu plans multiple releases. Its initial release will provide the broadband SoC to deliver MIMO Wave 2 certification compliance. Second and third releases will follow to support full mobility, VoIP, and multimedia applications over mobile appliances.

Poland's Netia Selects Alvarion's Broadband Solution

Netia, a leading competitive Polish telecommunications provider, has selected Alvarion's BreezeMAX 3600 for a 20-city WiMAX deployment in Poland [16]. An extension of Alvarion's market-leading BreezeMAX solution operating from

3.6 to 3.8 GHz, the BreezeMAX 3600 is targeted at WiMAX operators in Europe and other countries where that frequency is available, and enables carriers to offer broadband data, voice, and multimedia services with high performance over wide coverage areas. As a customer of Alvarion's MGW solution for multiresidential voice and data services, Netia began this WiMAX deployment in 20 additional cities on receiving the nationwide license. Netia is one of four Polish carriers who received the nationwide WiMAX license.

Ultranet2go Spreads WiMAX across Mexico

Mexico is the latest country to hop on to the WiMAX bandwagon. Ultranet2go has covered a large chunk of the country with mobile broadband wireless service [17]. Using Navini Networks' Ripwave MX gear, the company says that some 3.2 million POPs (points of presence) will encompass areas from Puebla to Veracruz to Aguascalientes. Ultranet2go says that Tampico, Matamoros, Xalapa, Coatzacoalcos, Cuernavaca, Chilpancingo, and Iguala could also be covered eventually.

Redline's RedMAX™ Products Chosen for First WiMAX Network in Northern Pakistan

MyTel is to make advanced voice and broadband services accessible to millions of people and businesses [18]. MyTel has begun its RedMAX deployment in the city of Peshawar, and will expand its WiMAX network to an additional 13 regions in northern Pakistan. The network will improve the delivery of voice and broadband services to its existing customers and extend its network to reach more businesses, residents, and municipal organizations. The Redline RedMAX and wireless IP transport products being deployed for the MyTel project are being provided through SARCORP, a Redline Certified Partner in Pakistan.

India Designates WiMAX Frequencies

India's Department of Telecom (DoT) has short-listed four frequency bands to allocate spectrum for WiMAX services. The frequencies include 2.5 to 2.69 GHz, 3.4 to 3.6 GHz, 2.3 to 2.4 GHz, and 700 MHz. According to *The Economic Times*, the DoT has requested the Department of Space (DoS) to release 95 MHz in the 2.5- to 2.69-GHz band, for 3G and WiMAX. In the 3.4- to 3.6-GHz band, the DoT is seeking to release 150 MHz for WiMAX. In the 700-MHz band, the DoT is seeking to designate 40 MHz for rural WiMAX applications, the report said [132].

Racsa: WiMAX to Launch in Costa Rica

Costa Rican state-run ISP Racsa is to launch a WiMAX pilot project in the San José neighborhoods of Escazú and Santa Ana. The initial system will have a range of 8 km, and Racsa will install additional BSs, eventually aiming for coverage of the entire metropolitan area [19]. According to previous reports, Racsa plans to invest $5 million to provide citywide wireless Internet coverage in the capital San José and in the city of Heredia. Racsa is also looking at Wi-Fi and power line communications (PLC) technology as alternatives for expanding Internet access in the country. Racsa has 46,000 residential access clients and 7,000 corporate clients. The total includes 27,000 cable modem clients.

Nortel Powers Commercial WiMAX Network

Greece is getting its first commercial WiMAX network, as per an agreement between Craig Wireless and a Nortel-backed joint venture. A 4-city rollout is planned for Athens, Heraklion, Patras, and Thessaloniki [133]. At launch, the network will support Craig's Internet Everywhere services, which includes VoIP, videoconferencing, and interactive gaming. UniNortel, a joint venture between Nortel and Unisystems, has been contracted to deliver a WiMAX-ready solution. The network, which the companies say will mark Greece's first commercial WiMAX network, will be powered by a Nortel WiMAX product. Craig will expand the reach of the network to other cities and areas in Greece next year. The goal, according to the companies, is to deliver high-speed services to areas of Greece that have limited or no broadband access. The wireless access provider also believes mobile WiMAX is a good fit for Greece and will work with Nortel to deliver the technology to more rural areas of Greece in the future [133].

WiMAX Ready to Go National in the United States

WiMAX will be a reality for mobile surfers in the United States, supplementing rather than replacing Wi-Fi and fast cellular networks, according to a top U.S. analyst. Clearwire aims to build a U.S.-wide network from its current 29 metropolitan areas and patchy rural test beds [20,150]. Clearwire also has networks in Denmark, Belgium, Ireland, and Mexico, run through partners. As the standards for WiMAX are not yet set, these networks currently use pre-WiMAX technology developed by NextNet. U.S. operator Sprint has also announced plans to build a nationwide WiMAX network, and Intel will include WiMAX chipsets alongside Wi-Fi in its future notebooks. WiMAX will eventually provide data transfer speeds of 10 Mbps and higher, making it ideal for rich media. But Clearwire's vision also includes VoIP services.

Entel Launches Chile's First Commercial WiMAX Network

According to local reports quoted by BNamericas.com, Entel has launched the first commercial WiMAX network in Chile following initial investment of $5 million [134]. The first stage of the project involved deploying 22 BSs between the northern city of Arica and Puerto Montt in the south. Entel General Manager Richard Büchi told reporters that the company plans to spend $15 million on stage two by expanding the network to more locations and reaching 500,000 mobile data users by 2010.

Softbank and Motorola Ink WiMAX Deal

Motorola said that it has signed an agreement with Softbank for the deployment of a 2.5-GHz WiMAX trial network in Tokyo [21]. Motorola will supply an end-to-end trial system, including access points, an access network, and prototype WiMAX mobile handheld devices. Softbank Corp. provides mobile communications, fixed-line voice and broadband services. The company acquired the third largest mobile operator in Japan, Vodafone KK. Softbank currently has more than 20 million wireline and wireless customers in Japan.

C & W Testing WiMAX

Cable & Wireless has created new possibilities for its customers such as sending video or multimedia messages over a variety of devices. In an effort to reinforce its commitment to stay in the forefront, Cable & Wireless has recently been testing WiMAX, a technology for deploying wireless broadband. For the last 40 years that Cable & Wireless has been doing business in the Cayman Islands, it has stayed abreast of changes in communication technology. As the demand for wireless Internet access increased, Cable & Wireless continually invested in Wi-Fi and now looks forward to seeing how the test of the less-established WiMAX works for a portion of its customers. Cable & Wireless was the first company in the Cayman Islands deploying pre-WiMAX technologies after Hurricane Ivan [135]. The primary focus was to temporarily restore Internet services to remote areas as quickly as possible. Cable & Wireless also deployed hot spots throughout the Cayman Islands for convenient Wi-Fi connectivity. Wi-Fi hot-spots are available at 19 locations across all three Islands, with new locations coming online continually. Cable & Wireless also has numerous retail outlets consisting of its own stores and partner agents that sell the broadband offerings. C & W Broadband DSL on the fixed network offers customers such benefits as a free spam and virus filter, fastest plans for the best price, and 24/7 customer support. Cable & Wireless's steadfast commitment to providing the most secure and reliable Internet products will continue, and the trial of WiMAX will simply be one more technology in its sophisticated network. The testing schedule for the investment and the introduction of WiMAX will occur over a 12-month period. Meanwhile, Cable & Wireless continues to maintain its position as market share leader in mobile and Internet services in the Cayman Islands [135].

Kingdom of Tonga to Offer WiMAX through Alvarion Platform

Tonga Communications Corporation has chosen the BreezeMAX 3500 solution from Alvarion Ltd. to provide WiMAX services to the Kingdom of Tonga. The islands' national operator, Tonga CC, plans to overlay its existing GSM network with WiMAX to offer broadband data services to the citizens of Tonga. The Kingdom of Tonga, the last remaining Polynesian monarchy, is made up of about 100,000 residents, who inhabit 42 of its 170 islands. The islands are spread over 700,000 sq km in the south Pacific, and have thousands of visitors each year.

Paper: Orbitel to Install 30 WiMAX BSs

Colombian long-distance operator Orbitel plans to expand its WiMAX coverage to the capital Bogotá through an initial deployment of 30 BSs. The Bogotá expansion could eventually require 150 BSs. Orbitel invested $10 million in 2006 in network expansions [22]. By 2007, the company expected to have WiMAX service in 12 major Colombian cities with 10 percent of its revenue coming from such services. The expansion started in the city of Cali, where Orbitel is using the Way-MAX@vantage solution supplied by German equipment manufacturer Siemens. Orbitel owns one of three national WiMAX licenses that have been awarded in Colombia.

Vietnam's First WiMAX Service to Be Tested in October

Vietnam launched its first WiMAX broadband network on a trial basis in northern Lao Cai province [123]. The project, jointly carried out by Intel, the Vietnam Data Communication Company (VDC) of the Vietnam Post and Telecommunication Group (VNPT), and the U.S. Agency for International Development (USAID), will provide Internet and VoIP services to people in the province. A BS and nearly 20 hot spots will be installed in many places in Lao Cai province such as schools, clinics, post offices, Internet cafes, hotels, and offices [124,144].

Ertach Expands WiMAX Networks

Argentine broadband provider Ertach has extended its WiMAX networks in the provinces of Buenos Aires and Tucumán, according to BNamericas. The company claims to have invested nearly $200,000 to migrate two nodes in the cities of Bahía Blanca and San Miguel de Tucumán to WiMAX [23]. The wireless broadband technology will allow connections of 4 Mbps in a radius of 20 km from the center of each city. BNamericas recently reported that Ertach's goals during 2006 include expanding its national backbone with an investment of $10 million, implementing a communications network for Buenos Aires province, and increasing WiMAX penetration.

Freescale, Wavesat Partner on WiMAX CPEs

Freescale Semiconductor and Wavesat Inc. are collaborating to provide reference designs for WiMAX-enabled CPEs targeted at both residential customers and small- to medium-sized businesses. The residential CPE reference design adds a wide range of functionality to the typical CPE, including wireless, voice, and video, as well as everything from a print server to a media server. The CPE includes a Freescale MPC8323E PowerQUICC II Pro processor, a DSP for VoIP capabilities, and interfaces, including a four-port Ethernet switch and two Mini PCI slots — one for a Wi-Fi LAN, and the other for a WAN over WiMAX [136].

Intel and NDS to Collaborate on Protected WiMAX-Based TV Multicast

Intel Corporation and NDS Group PLC has launched a trial system to demonstrate TV and video services for fixed WiMAX technology. Intel and NDS are also to collaborate on industry and market development activities. The companies will engage in demonstrations to service providers and the industry to show how WiMAX can offer more than broadband access with pay-TV services. Companies intend to enhance the system to support the 802.16e standard in the future and to make sure that security requirements protect the interests of content providers in an aim to demonstrate pay-TV services delivery over mobile WiMAX to Intel-based PDA and notebook devices [137].

Angkor Net Launches WiMAX in Cambodia

Singapore-based VoIP company Media Ring launched its Angkor Net ISP in Cambodia. Angkor Net is the first ISP in Cambodia to offer WiMAX wireless broadband services [138]. Media Ring hopes that WiMAX services can improve the low Internet penetration rate in Cambodia. Wireless services allow Angkor Net to offer broadband Internet speeds without installing telecom infrastructure. These savings can be passed along to Cambodian users to boost Internet take-up. Upon launch, Angkor Net has 90 percent WiMAX coverage in Phnom Penh. Angkor Net is the ISP brand of Cambodia Data Communication (CDC), a joint venture between Media Ring and Cambodia-based Anana Computer. Media Ring holds 40 percent of CDC, with Anana holding the remaining 60 percent.

Telsima Wireless Solutions Attain WiMAX Forum Compliance

Telsima Corporation announced that its StarMAX 4120-3.5-GHz WiMAX BS and the StarMAX 2140-3.5-GHz subscriber station have passed WiMAX compliance and interoperability testing standards. The products are now officially WiMAX-Forum certified [139]. Telsima, a developer of WiMAX-based broadband wireless access and mobility solutions, offers a portfolio consisting of WiMAX BSs and subscriber stations. Products are made for indoor, outdoor, and semi-outdoor use, and support 2.5-, 3.3-, and 3.5-GHz frequency bands. The company also offers the Network Management Software and Provisioning Manager, as well as the TRUFLE mobility management solution. The TRUFLE solution offers subscribers basic mobility within OFDM-based WiMAX networks, which enables reconnection and IP session conservation when a user is in range of another BS. When used with the Telsima D+E–DualMode BSs, the TRUFLE solution enables operators to offer basic mobility services based on WiMAX. It also offers a migration path 802.16e-2005 while preserving operators' existing infrastructure investments.

Alvarion Launches Mobile WiMAX for United States

Alvarion Ltd. has released premobile WiMAX gear for the 2.3- and 2.5-GHz frequency bands to address the North American market [24]. The BreezeMAX 2300 and BreezeMAX 2500 products will be shipped, beginning late 2006. Built to the IEEE 802.16e standard, BreezeMAX is a third-generation OFDM platform with advanced non-line-of-sight functionality. Already available as a certified radio access BS for the fixed version of WiMAX, BreezeMAX is deployed in more than 180 installations in 80 countries. BreezeMAX 2300 and 2500 are part of the company's mobile WiMAX solution 4Motion, an end-to-end WiMAX solution, incorporating QoS mechanisms, IP mobility core components, and multimedia subsystems along with subscriber terminals, an NMS, and northbound and back-end interfaces. It is designed to employ software-defined radio, beam forming, MIMO, dynamic bandwidth allocation, and scaleable OFDMA technologies, the company said.

Alcatel to Build First WiMAX Network in Estonia with Elion, a TeliaSonera Subsidiary

Alcatel announced that it has been selected by Elion Enterprises Ltd., part of Telia-Sonera, a leading telecommunications company in the Nordic and Baltic region, to deploy a commercial broadband wireless access network in Estonia [25,28a,28b]. Initial deployment has been completed in Tallinn and the surrounding areas, and the system will be for commercial operation. This WiMAX network will enable Elion to provide additional users with broadband access to high-speed Internet and data transmissions with a guaranteed level of quality. Under the terms of the agreement, Alcatel will supply an end-to-end WiMAX solution, including BSs and CPE.

Wavesat, Siemens Collaborate on WiMAX Platforms

Wavesat and the Microwave Networks Division of Siemens are collaborating on WiMAX-Forum-Certified platforms based on the IEEE 802.16-2004 standard and in compliance with WiMAX Forum interoperability profiles [26]. The two companies are conducting interoperability testing between Siemens' WayMAX@vantage BS and CPE, based on Wavesat's WiMAX 3.5-GHz Mini-PCI design and DM256 chipset, and now offer WiMAX-Forum-Certified solutions.

Airspan Announces Addition of 5.8-GHz Frequency Band to Its MicroMAX BS Product

Airspan Networks Inc. has commenced shipments of its MicroMAX BS in the 5.8-GHz frequency band [27]. With this announcement, Airspan introduces MicroMAX in the 5.8-GHz TDD WiMAX profile. The company will add MicroMAX frequencies in the 3.3- to 3.4-GHz TDD band. With this latest addition to its portfolio, Airspan offers customers the best cost-performance profile in a WiMAX BS in both licensed and unlicensed WiMAX-supported frequencies. Airspan first announced the launch of its MicroMAX BS in March 2006 in the 3.5-GHz FDD band. The BS is based on the high-performance SQN2010 WiMAX-Certified BS system design of Sequans, and was the first cost-optimized, pay-as-you-grow WiMAX solution available in the marketplace. It offers service providers and network operators a unique value proposition of very high performance at an affordable price point. The MicroMAX is Airspan's third AS.MAX BS, the others being MacroMAX and HiperMAX-Micro. MicroMAX complements the larger WiMAX BSs by being optimized for lower-density deployment, such as rural areas, in-fill for coverage holes in wireless, DSL, and cable networks, enterprise solutions and public safety applications.

Nortel Teams Up with Runcom to Deliver MIMO-Powered Mobile WiMAX Technology

Nortel and Israel-based Runcom Technologies have yielded a collaboration focused on technologies that overcome transmission interruptions and delays that disrupt the real-time quality essential to new high-bandwidth applications [141]. This new technology, MIMO, is the focus of Nortel and Runcom's development efforts and is an advanced antenna technology that is used both in transmission and receiver equipment. The Nortel/Runcom collaboration is expected to deliver MIMO-enabled mobile WiMAX (802.16e) devices. Because Nortel's MIMO technology is able to accommodate several input and output paths simultaneously, it can deliver three times the speed and efficiency at one-third the cost, compared to competing WiMAX solutions that use alternative technologies. Using the Runcom MIMO chipset, Nortel will deliver leading WiMAX solutions that meet future market requirements.

Du Runs WiMAX Tests before Its Year-End Launch

At Dubai, Du, the country's second-largest telecom operator, races to meet WiMAX launch deadline and is also testing out next-generation technologies. Du might use the network to provide mobile telecommunications and high-speed Internet that are accessible through mobile phones, handset devices, and computers [142].

Comstar UTS Eyes WiMAX

Russian telco Comstar Unified Telesystems (Comstar UTS) has revealed plans to construct WiMAX networks in 16 regions. A *Prime Tass* report, which cites business daily *Kommersant*, says the firm is looking at rolling out wireless broadband networks in cities with over one million inhabitants where it already has operations or affiliates [143]. Comstar is already building a trial WiMAX system in Moscow and has now applied for spectrum in the 2.5- to 2.7-GHz range.

Samsung Sets Out Plans for WiMAX Worldwide

Telecommunications and digital convergence technologies manufacturer Samsung plans for WiMAX development and deployment in Asia, Europe, and the Americas. Samsung said the latest additions to its product portfolio are two elements that will be used to support the IMS/WiMAX solution: radio access station (RAS) and access control router (ACR). The standard RAS — built for large-scale deployments — features a smart antenna that uses the 802.16e interface protocol to provide broadband data rates of up to 30 Mpbs per sector, supporting three to six sectors. RAS is also available in a mini version, capable of 20-W power output and small enough to mount on ceilings, walls, or poles. Samsung's ACR contains IP-based radio access network architecture based on the IMS core network. It enables mobility to be efficiently managed using a centralized control structure. ACR also facilitates seamless wireless connectivity, minimizing both handover latency on Layer 2 over air, and bearer path switch delay. Both products — the RAS and the ACR — are core elements of Samsung's IMS-network-based WiMAX platform, designed to deliver high-speed services such as voice, videoconferencing, and instant messaging to rural and suburban locations not accessible by other technologies. Samsung said its WiMAX solution also will create broadband "hot zones" in more densely populated areas. The company is now working with telecommunications providers around the globe to deliver wireless high-speed broadband services capable of voice, data, and video at speeds up to 75 mph with a 20- to 30-Mpbs data rate. Samsung said it is allying with Korea Telecom in South Korea, Sprint Nextel in the United States, TVA in Brazil, KDDI WBB in Japan, and BT in Great Britain, and recently partnered with Telecom Italia to successfully demonstrate WiBro capabilities. Samsung noted that mobile WiMAX makes possible a broad range of converged services, delivered from a single IP-based network, including:

- VoIP
- Video telephony
- Multimedia messaging and conferencing
- Location and telematic services
- Multimedia push and demand services

To help drive these applications, Samsung now is promoting two WiBro phones — the H1000 clamshell and the M8000 smart phone — and a PCMCIA card that can be used in laptops and Tablet PCs.

FPGAs Address Emerging WiMAX Market Requirements

WiMAX product development is an ideal match for the advantages of an FPGA approach. The programmability of FPGAs provides a proven future-proofing strategy for developers having to deal with the rapidly evolving standard and product requirements. In addition, WiMAX applications are demanding from a performance and feature standpoint, and Platform FPGA offerings such as the Xilinx Virtex-4 and Spartan-3 families offer system-level solutions that include embedded processors, high-performance DSP engines, and a full suite of customizable IP.

Air Broadband to Use Fujitsu WiMAX SoC

Air Broadband has selected Fujitsu's WiMAX SoC for its new wireless IP switch-router implementations for WiMAX ACR and BSs. Air Broadband's wireless IP switch-routers, which are based on IEEE 802.11 WLAN and IEEE 802.16 WiMAX, provide fast layer 2 and layer 3 roaming and scalability in multicell networks, enabling real-time applications and management capabilities. The implementations for PiMAX ACR and BS provide the IP mobility, multivendor base-station compatibility, wide scalability, and per-flow QoS (MCSQ) improvements needed for WiMAX deployment.

Forty Kilometers with WiMAX — New Transmission Record in Wireless Broadband Internet over Water

WiMAX Telecom Group, the multinational operator of WiMAX services in Europe, transmitted live pictures of the World Sailing Championships on the Neusiedler-see, in Austria, via its wireless broadband Internet connection. It set a new record transmitting live video at ranges of up to 40 km, and from moving vessels. The experience gained will be of use to WiMAX Telecom in extending its network in the coastal region of Croatia. This is an important achievement of interest not only to boat owners and yachtsmen. WiMAX Telecom also took on a sporting challenge of a special kind at the World Sailing Championships on Austria's Neusiedlersee. From a yacht moving at 12 knots, pictures of the World Sailing Championships were streamed live — and over a distance of 40 km, thus beating all previous forecasts about the range of WiMAX technology. This technology will be of increasing importance for transmission from all moving vehicles in the future. Ships in coastal waters will benefit greatly. Even at a distance of 40 km from the shore, they will be linked via the Internet and hence be reachable for sending messages or for VoIP telephony. WiMAX is an extremely inexpensive alternative to expensive, satellite-supported communication solutions.

RF Transistors Meet WiMAX BS Demands

With its seventh-generation high-voltage (HV7) RF LDMOS technology, Freescale Semiconductor has achieved the RF power amplifier performance required for use in WiMAX BSs operating in the 3.5-GHz band. Freescale's achievement marks the first time RF laterally diffused metal oxide semiconductor (LDMOS) technology from any manufacturer has met these challenges. Freescale, which already offers a portfolio of 12-V GaAs pseudomorphic high electron mobility transistor (PHEMT) products, plans to continue development of high-voltage GaAs PHEMT technology that will result in higher-power GaAs devices for use in WiMAX system designs, as well as other applications between 2 and 6 GHz. By offering power transistors in RF LDMOS and GaAs PHEMT technology, Freescale's RF solutions support virtually any high-power wireless infrastructure application — with LDMOS performance up to 3.8 GHz and GaAs PHEMT performance up to 6 GHz. WiMAX systems use a 64 quadrature amplitude modulation (QAM) OFDM signal. The MRF7S38075H is a 75-W P1dB RF transistor capable of 42-dBm (16-W) average power, while meeting WiMAX performance requirements over the 3.5-GHz band. These three advanced LDMOS devices round out Freescale's existing portfolio of RF power transistors targeting the emerging WiMAX/WiBRO bands at 2.3, 2.5, and 3.5 GHz. Although advanced HV7 LDMOS devices complement 12-V GaAs PHEMT devices for 3.5-GHz WiMAX applications, the new high-voltage GaAs devices currently under development will operate up to 6 GHz. This makes them an excellent choice for WiMAX and other wireless applications operating in this frequency range. With an operating voltage above 20 V, the GaAs devices will achieve output powers as high as 100 W, while still meeting the stringent demands of digitally modulated systems.

Indonesia Gets National WiMAX Network

Aperto Networks and PT. Citra Sari Makmur (CSM), one of Indonesia's largest telecommunications operators, have announced they will expand the existing deployment of Aperto's WiMAX-class multiservice broadband wireless systems to cover a wider area across Indonesia. The deployment will take place in stages and will involve a transition to the latest family of Forum-certified products from Aperto. CSM uses the network primarily to deliver broadband wireless services to Indonesia's financial services and banking sector. The network supports legacy frame relay applications, VPN, Internet access, leased line, and telephony services. But the CSM also provides data, voice, and multimedia services to hotels, enterprises, and high-end residential customers across various cities in Indonesia.

Singapore Plans to Make Itself a Mega Wi-Fi Hot Spot

According to reports, Singapore is in the process of launching a nationwide Wi-Fi network that will let users receive a network connection to the Internet from virtually anywhere [28a,28b]. The mega Wi-Fi network will be based on WiMAX, which is a high-speed, reliable, and robust wireless standard being pushed by Intel and other companies. At the moment, Singapore already has a countrywide Wi-Fi network setup. For every square kilometer of the country, there is one public hot spot already in place.

Unwired, Mitsui Cooperate on Global WiMAX

Mitsui will invest between 5 to 8 million Australian dollars (US$3.8 to 6 million) in Australian wireless broadband carrier Unwired. The two companies have also agreed to work together on developing mobile WiMAX infrastructure and applications [29]. The two companies have also undertaken to share information to facilitate their working together on the development of mobile WiMAX and on mobile applications to be used by Internet and mobile phone users, on mobile WiMAX and mobile phone networks around the world. Unwired, which reportedly has plans to move to mobile WiMAX when commercialized, has also committed to sharing expertise and to training Mitsui staff on its network, technical, and marketing aspects of wireless broadband.

WiMAX Boxes Hit New Zealand

Siemens provides Alvarion kits to TelstraClear and other operators [30]. TelstraClear says that Si is one of a number of products the company will be testing for deployment in the small business market. Siemens has received initial shipments of new Alvarion WiMAX CPE suitable for home and office use. Availability of such equipment suggests that WiMAX services from telcos and ISPs will almost certainly be launched. The key features of the Alvarion BreezeMAX Si equipment are self-install and the ability to work indoors without an external aerial. The Si supports connection speeds of up to 18 Mbps, and QoS. It has some routing capability but is really a bridge type of product. It has an Ethernet port that can connect directly to a PC and, in its next version, it will have voice ports. Although the Si is being supplied initially to Siemens' Alvarion customers, this is the type of equipment one will expect to see sold by service providers and in retail stores for expanding WiMAX services to homes and businesses.

Redline System to Be Used for WiMAX Deployment on Oil Rigs in Gulf of Mexico

Redline Communications announced a multipoint WiMAX network deployment at sea. Redline, a provider of broadband wireless equipment, will deploy a system to be used by Pemex to establish high-speed WiMAX connections on board 11 off-shore oil rig platforms in the Gulf of Mexico [31]. Pemex, a major Mexican oil company, owns 11 oil production platforms located up to 10 mi offshore from Ciudad del Carmen, Campeche. The platforms span an average of 6 mi between each platform. The new 3.4-GHz WiMAX network uses double redundancy components and systems at all points in the network so that environmental interference is minimized, as this could significantly impact data throughput and link reliability. The Redline RedMAX family of WiMAX solutions features a carrier-class Red-MAX BS with support for voice, video, and prioritized data traffic, which enables long-range, high-capacity wireless broadband networks. Products also include the RedMAX indoor subscriber unit and outdoor subscriber unit, which are designed for enterprise and residential services. The RedMAX management suite offers operators the ability to monitor and control the network for high service availability.

Hopping Aboard the Mobile WiMAX Bus

With a mobile WiMAX service about to soft-launch in Seoul, one of South Korea's biggest telecom carriers, KT, demonstrated the mobile Internet service to reporters [32]. The service is being promoted under the brand name WiBro. WiBro technically refers to a Korean-developed technology that was folded into the IEEE 802.16e mobile WiMAX specification. Trials of the service began in April 2006, and a limited commercial service will kick off. The initial service covers a single area in downtown Seoul, three areas south of the Han River in the city's IT valley, and the suburb of Bundang. A subway line and two expressways from Seoul to Bundang also have coverage. About 150 BSs support the service now, and this is expected to expand to between 700 and 1000. At that time, the full commercial service will launch in Seoul and nine other cities, according to KT's plans. KT says the service should deliver up to 1 Mbps to users travelling as fast as 120 km/hr (75 mi/hr). If KT and SK Telecom, which is also planning to launch a service, can deliver for a cheap, flat monthly fee, they could provide an attractive consumer alternative third-generation data service. They offer similar data rates but are relatively expensive.

Carrier-Class WiMAX Solution

The MOTOwi4 portfolio of wireless broadband solutions has a new member [33]. The carrier-class WiMAX network, supporting both 2.5 and 3.5 GHz, is an 802.16e solution that uses advanced antenna techniques to provide greater coverage range and building penetration. It is based on its carrier access point architecture, an all-IP fully distributed peer-to-peer architecture that reduces the amount of equipment needed. These carrier-class WiMAX access points feature a combination of MIMO antenna techniques and software-defined radios (SDR) that, along with the IP architecture, provide flexibility in network deployment and enable operators to choose among many third-party vendors to add applications and services. MOTOwi4 is a portfolio of wireless broadband solutions and services that create, complement, and complete IP networks.

Mobile WiMAX Goes Mini

Asserting that current macrocell architectures are insufficient for meeting the demand of emerging wireless broadband systems, OFDMA-gear vendor Adaptix, is releasing a suite of third-generation WiMAX equipment based on more numerous and more dense microcell layouts [34]. Designed to address the market for high-bandwidth applications beyond voice, using smaller cell footprints, the new BX-3000 Micro BSs and SX series of mobile terminals are based on the IEEE 802.16e-2005 standard for mobile WiMAX, but are easily adapted to support future forms of broadband, including MIMO systems, as well as the 3rd Generation Partnership Project's (3GPP) Long Term Evolution (LTE) standard, both of which are likely to use OFDMA as their underlying networking technology. The Adaptix system, by contrast, is designed for mobile carriers that need to get the highest performance in terms of bandwidth in the most cost-efficient and spectrally efficient manner. Concentrating on mobile WiMAX, as opposed to the earlier, fixed 802.16d standard, Adaptix has developed a virtual BS setup that comprises the compact BS plus as many as three outdoor RF antennas that will, for instance, enable flexible installation options for buildings.

Intel Installs Wireless WiMAX Internet in Amazon Island City

Intel has created a WiMAX network for and donated computers to the 114,000 residents of Parintins, Brazil [35]. A boat transporting 60 desktop computers for computer labs at two schools pulled into the island city's port. Intel launched wireless Internet access with the company's WiMAX technology, using a satellite link to beam bandwidth to a place where even electricity is hard to come by. Intel's World Ahead Program, which promotes the use of computers in public areas in developing countries, bankrolled the installation of a WiMAX tower and five spots in the city of Parintins where students, teachers, and doctors will now have fast Internet connections for the first time. Parintins, about 1,600 mi north of Brazil's industrial and financial hub of Sao Paulo, is home to more than 114,000 people but has no roads linking it to other cities; so the only way to get there is by boat or airplane. Like many places around Latin America's largest country, Internet connections are limited to spotty and expensive dial-up links. One of the biggest challenges in Parintins for the Santa Clara, California-based chipmaker was a lack of electrical power at the schools, a hurdle Intel overcame by working with the local government. Intel also is eying spots in the Middle East and Africa to set up WiMAX infrastructure.

Implementing WiMAX Using a Software-Configurable Processor

WiMAX has garnered widespread support because of the efficiency it promises to bring to wireless last-mile digital communications applications [36]. This wireless building block, however, is a fast-moving target that continues to change and adapt as SDR gains acceptance and market share. Not only do these new techniques give rise to new algorithms and standards, they stress the capabilities of traditional processors and hybrid-based architectures. As a consequence, 802.16 SDR cannot be adequately implemented using fixed architectures such as fpgas and assps. By abstracting hardware as software, software-configurable processors achieve the same throughput as fpga and high-end dsp-based architectures, while extending overall programmability and flexibility to enable developers to support evolving standards in a timely fashion. The 802.16 WiMAX specification contains a rich set of options and requirements to address a wide range of wireless deployments for multiple applications and markets. To support the evolving standards, a programmable solution is needed that can easily address real-time computational requirements. Stretch software-configurable processors address compute intensity by uniquely enabling developers to convert C/C++ functions into custom instructions. These instructions can perform multiple operations, operate on multiple data, and execute in a highly pipelined fashion, to deliver tremendous software acceleration. Software-configurable processors abstract hardware to the degree that developers can write application and algorithmic code in C so that a single development environment results in hardware and software optimized together.

MobiTV to Demo HD via WiMAX

MobiTV demonstrated live HD content delivered over a pre-mobile WiMAX network at the CTIA Wireless IT & Entertainment show in Los Angeles [37]. The mobile-TV provider said the real-time demonstration will showcase its service running over Navini Networks' Ripwave MX equipment to both fixed and mobile CPE, providing attendees with a preview of several proof of concepts.

First WiMAX Transmission in Latin America

Eight cameras and a 40-person team worked to send pictures to the Internet. At Santiago de Chile, in the exhibit of the Red Bull Formula 1 racer, the first live transmission via WiMAX for Latin America was demonstrated [38]. The final check-out was done on 27th October, 2006, to ensure the signal could be picked up by eight cameras and directed on board a digital TV mobile truck, which transmitted video on IP. The picture could then be seen by thousands of cybernauts. It took weeks to make the technical preparations. Making the footage available online means that it will always be available to users, who will then not have to depend on a fixed programming schedule as in the case of traditional TV broadcasting.

Motorola to Develop Mobile WiMAX Chipsets

Motorola, Inc., has announced a strategic initiative to develop mobile WiMAX chipsets for the company's next-generation WiMAX devices [39]. Motorola's initial chipset will focus on core 802.16e mobile WiMAX functionality supporting voice, video, and data for low-power mobile applications in handsets and modules. These first chipsets are scheduled to support commercial Motorola WiMAX devices in 2008, for carriers in North America, Japan, and around the world, including Sprint and others. Motorola is working with its silicon vendors on the overall fabrication of the chipsets.

Taiwan Market: NCC Finalizes WiMAX License Plan

Taiwan's National Communications Commission (NCC) finalized its plan to release nine six-year operating licenses for WiMAX wireless broadband services in March–June, 2007. There will be three 90-MHz radio frequency bands available for WiMAX operation in the northern, central, and southern regions of Taiwan, creating nine combinations with a corresponding nine licenses [40]. In 2007, the WiMAX Forum will hold its member conference along with a large international WiMAX exhibition in Taiwan in October [41].

Airspan's WiMAX VoIP Testing Successful

Airspan Networks provides fixed and wireless voice and data systems worldwide, including VoIP solutions and WiMAX systems [42]. Airspan's WiMAX-Forum-Certified AS.MAX platform, was deployed using an experimental license in the 3.5-GHz band from a main Kiva Networks location to multiple areas around the downtown Cherry Creek business district in Denver, Colorado. The purpose was to test fixed broadband data and VoIP service, over WIMAX. In addition to testing VoIP over WiMAX, the firms also tried out portable nomadic service utilizing Airspan's self-installable EasyST subscriber terminal. The AS.MAX product family includes WiMAX BSs, backhaul solutions, and CPE, which not only provides a solution, but eliminates the truck roll typically required for a wireless deployment by virtue of its indoor, self-installable WiMAX CPE, EasyST, Airspan's all-indoor subscriber terminal. It has a sister product, the indoor/outdoor ProST, which requires professional installation. The AS.MAX platform offers multivendor interoperability, decreasing CPE costs, self-installable products, and a target of enabling and supporting inexpensive, ubiquitous broadband wireless access. The system is based on radio technology, which provides a wide coverage area, high security, and resistance to fading. They can be quickly and economically deployed, making them a viable alternative to, or replacement for, traditional wired networks.

German WiMAX Pilot Successful

The town of Erkelenz in North Rhine-Westphalia helped lay the foundations for the German regional power utility NEW Energie's commercial launch of WiMAX for bandwidth-intensive wireless services, such as live multimedia streams, VoIP applications, and high-speed Internet access [43]. The WiMAX pilot, according to a release from Nortel, used German communications consultant tkt teleconsult to deploy a WiMAX network that allowed NEW Energie to provide broadband wireless connections to a selection of small businesses and consumers at speeds of up to 10 Mbps, equal to the current fastest fixed DSL services. NEW Energie expects to launch new broadband wireless services based on Nortel WiMAX technology in the second quarter of 2006 to areas which have little fixed broadband coverage. WiMAX is a next-generation technology that uses advanced wireless transmission techniques to bridge the last-mile connection between an operator's network and a user, eliminating the need for fixed copper or cable in the ground. The pilot installation also showed the user-friendliness of a potential WiMAX service. Users in Erkelenz were able to simply plug and play the small indoor WiMAX modem into their computer, said the release. The flexibility of the service also allowed for an individual to automatically update the speed and cost of their specific wireless connection to a level that suited their usage profile.

Algeria Becomes the Arab World's WiMAX Pioneer

WiMAX is commercially available in Algeria, although several operators in many Arab countries have started testing the service [44]. Smart Link Communication (SLC) has deployed WiMAX to provide broadband wireless services in Algeria. SLC's goal is to build a wireless broadband backbone covering the national territory, to develop the metropolitan broadband networks, and to set up an independent new generation telecom infrastructure. SLC launched the first national multiservices network. The deployment of this network makes it possible to develop services based on broadband wireless access, VoIP, and virtual private network (VPN-IP MPLS). Algeria's tough and mountainous terrain makes it an ideal candidate for wireless connectivity solutions.

Chunghwa Combines Wi-Fi and WiMAX

Chunghwa Telecom has announced that it has begun the process of creating a nationwide wireless broadband network in Taiwan by linking its Wi-Fi hot spots with WiMAX technology [45]. The Taiwanese telco has chosen Redline Communications to supply WiMAX equipment, which offers wide-area broadband coverage, whereas the Wi-Fi hot spots will offer improved data speeds in high-usage areas.

WiMAX Interest from Over a Dozen Companies in Sri Lanka, Reports Regulator

More than 12 companies have responded to Sri Lanka's Telecommunications Regulatory Commission's (TRC) offer of nationwide WiMAX operating licenses in the 3.5-GHz frequency band. The regulator will initially set the tariffs for any services launched, as part of a government initiative to provide Internet connectivity to remote areas at very low costs. The response has been overwhelming, and the intention of TRC is to have the major cities covered by WiMAX [46]. So far, the watchdog has assigned test WiMAX frequencies to incumbent fixed line provider Sri Lanka Telecom (SLT), which could deploy an islandwide WiMAX network after gaining regulatory approval. SLT is initially aiming to roll out WiMAX in metropolitan areas including Colombo, Kandy, and Galle.

WiMAX Products Hit U.S. Market

The first products based on the WiMAX broadband technology have finally hit the U.S. market after many delays in setting standards. Red Herring says the products, from Aperto Networks, Redline Communications, Sequans Communications, and WaveSat, add credibility in the United States for the technology, which already has a growing market in Eastern Europe, South America, and the Middle East. These first products are only for the fixed standard for stationary wireless connections.

APERTO Unveils WiMAX Solutions Ecosystem

Aperto Networks unveiled a comprehensive partnering program dedicated to advancing WiMAX by offering a wide range of leading-edge solutions and turnkey services for network operators looking to capitalize on WiMAX opportunities. Participants in Aperto's WiMAX Solutions Ecosystem (WiSE) program, which includes more than 50 of the WiMAX industry's leading companies, align with Aperto Networks in five key areas [47]:

- Enabling technology partners to provide the latest advances in baseband, radio, element management, provisioning, and applications delivery technologies for WiMAX subscriber and infrastructure solutions. Intel, Fujitsu, Sequans, and others have worked with Aperto to establish the foundation for PacketMAX fixed and mobile solutions.
- PacketMAX interoperability takes WiMAX-Forum-Certified products to the next level. WiSE partners can certify that their subscriber and infrastructure equipment works optimally within Aperto's award-winning Packet-MAX architecture. Aperto leads this effort through coordinating three levels of interoperability testing and system integration. Aperto has completed interoperability testing between PacketMAX BS and multiple third-party subscriber units.
- WiMAX applications enable service delivery to the WiMAX end user and are dedicated to ensuring that operators can profitably deliver these services that their customers demand. Allot Communications, Veraz Networks, ADC,

Telco Systems, and other WiSE partners have joined with Aperto to ensure high-quality, end-to-end service delivery over WiMAX. Sample applications include managed VoIP, municipal and mesh networking, video delivery, and advanced operations and business support.

■ Tools and services partners complement PacketMAX by offering unique training, network planning, or turnkey services that are required to design, install, operate, and maintain the network throughout its life cycle. WiSE members include EDX Wireless, DoceoTech, and a network of WiMAX experts and system integrators.

■ Channel partners make up the distribution network that provides PacketMAX and related value-added solutions and services in local markets, globally. Operators can select WiSE partners carrying the Aperto-Certified logo — putting the highest level of WiMAX competency and PacketMAX experience to work on their projects. Aperto has over 50 such partners across the globe.

Comsys Presents Mobile WiMAX/Cellular Convergence

Comsys Communication and Signal Processing has presented ComMAX, its baseband processor for mobile Internet convergence. Comsys is in a unique position to drive mobile Internet convergence through its background and knowledge of both 3GSM cellular and mobile WiMAX (IEEE 802.16e) technologies. Building on its mature cellular baseband solutions, currently enabling multimillion handsets in the market, Comsys develops its 4G product offerings [48]. Integrating both mobile WiMAX and Cellular technologies into a single baseband processor, the ComMAX SoC provides a converged mobile WiMAX/Cellular solution targeting manufacturers of multimode terminals. Addressing the service similarities between 3GSM and mobile WiMAX, ComMAX provides extensive power and cost savings at both chip and handset levels, and is a cost-effective path toward seamless 4G services. The processor and accompanying reference designs are expected to be available in the market during 2007.

Nokia Bets Big on Mobile WiMAX Tech

Nokia is set to launch the first WiMAX-capable mobile in 2008. The company is also ready to offer its services as a technology partner to Indian cellular operators wishing to set up WiMAX networks [49]. Currently, Nokia has a portfolio of over twenty 3G (third generation) handsets and now plans to make several handsets of the NSeries category capable of tapping into a WiMAX network for broadband Internet. Tablet devices, such as Nokia N770, are expected to be among the first devices to support WiMAX. As the country jogs into the wireless Internet era, with Pune, Bangalore, and Chennai getting WiMAXed, the need for such devices will increase. Nokia is betting on mobile WiMAX to take off in India, with operators seeing a huge demand for wireless broadband. Partnering with Intel, the firm is helping accelerate the development, adoption, and deployment of standards-based mobile WiMAX technology across the world [50]. It hopes to partner with those service providers who are without cellular spectrum licenses but who want to offer mobile broadband in their portfolio in India. Nokia's Flexi WiMAX BS is the latest addition to its suite of products for WiMAX. Others include Radio Access, Unified Core Network, and NetAct Operations Support System. The Nokia Flexi WiMAX BS will be available for the 2.5-GHz band at the end of 2007, and for 3.5 GHz in early 2008.

Intel Merging Wi-Fi with WiMAX

The chip giant is working hard to put both wireless broadband technologies on one chip. Putting the two technologies on the same chip will allow consumers to switch between local hot spots and the regional network. Delivering chips that consume less and less power is critical for Intel's success. The company is promoting a new category of computers called "ultramobile" PCs, which fall between laptops and smart phones.

Eighty-One-Percent of WiMAX Networks Built with Alvarion Equipment According to Sky Light Research

According to Sky Light Research, Alvarion's 2005 WiMAX market share was 81 percent of all deployments worldwide. Since its launch in mid-2004, Alvarion's BreezeMAX system has been successfully deployed in over 180 installations in more than 80 countries, including with carriers such as T-Com (Germany), Entel (Chile), Iberbanda (Spain), and Kenya Data Networks (Kenya). In 2003, Alvarion was the first company to partner with Intel to work together to incorporate Intel's 806.16-2004 chips into the company's systems. Since then, Alvarion has led the WiMAX industry with numerous milestones [52]:

- Launched a WiMAX system — BreezeMAX 3500 in June 2004
- First to offer a commercial WiMAX CPE, BreezeMAX PRO, using the Intel PRO/Wireless 5116 broadband interface chip
- First with a commercial self-installable WiMAX CPE, BreezeMAX Si, paving the way for portable and nomadic services
- First to demonstrate 4Motion, an end-to end mobile WiMAX solution based on IEEE 802.16e-2005, to provide personal broadband services any time, anywhere

- Several industry awards, including IEC's InfoVision and WCA's Best Technology Foresight
- Certification of BreezeMAX and successful interoperability of its mobile WiMAX solution, 4Motion, with end-user devices embedded with a WiMAX chip

France-Based Maxtel Offers Affordable "AnyMAX" WiMAX System

To address the growing need for WiMAX solutions, particularly in municipal deployments, France-based Altitude Telecom and motorways operator APRR have teamed up to form a consortium called Maxtel, which offers an affordable system for wireless broadband [53]. Maxtel's AnyMAX system uses devices attached to street lamps that coordinate with a WiMAX BS to cover a townwide or citywide zone. The system draws power from the street lamps. Maxtel noted that installation of AnyMAX BSs needed to cover a city the size of Paris can be achieved in fewer than three months.

Heathrow Express Gets WiMAX Access

The Heathrow Express train service becomes the latest to offer a wireless Internet service to its passengers, following on from GNER and Virgin. Users will be able to connect to the service via a WiMAX backhaul, which offers a greater range than standard 802.11 Wi-Fi signals, with fixed repeaters along the line [54].

Web Access in Cars Hits the Road

Automotive PCs will connect through regular cellular phone signals [51,55]. Makers expect the in-car systems to eventually move to WiMAX — high-powered Wi-Fi that blankets broadband access across cities — over the next few years.

Towerstream Offers High-Availability Pre-WiMAX Solution to Boston Businesses

High-availability T1+ businesses are guaranteed to receive 99.999 percent availability 24 hours a day, 7 days a week, and 365 days a year. Customers who purchase the Hi-Vi T1+ product are assured their service will have less than a minute of downtime per month. Any additional service interruptions will be covered under the terms of the SLA agreement, and customers will be credited the appropriate amount pending on the length of the outage, if one ever occurs [56]. Towerstream is able to offer the Hi-Vi T1+ by providing customers with two separate T1 connections, each pointing at different BSs around the city. By doing this, Towerstream provides true last-mile redundancy to its customers in need of a reliable broadband service. This, combined with Towerstream's redundant wireless ring architecture in the sky, gives customers a complete wireless broadband solution.

Alcatel, C-DOT Open WiMAX Reality Center

The first WiMAX IEEE 802.16e-2005 laboratory in India brings experts together to test and build preintegrated customer-specific solutions. Alcatel and C-DOT, the Indian government's telecom technology development center, announced the official inauguration of the new WiMAX reality center in Chennai. This is the first lab of its scale entirely dedicated to WiMAX IEEE 802.16e-2005 technology in India. Hosted at the C-DOT Alcatel Research Center, a global broadband wireless R & D center, with 51 percent owned by Alcatel and 49 percent by C-DOT, this laboratory will bring together experts from across India, who will test and build preintegrated customer-specific solutions. It will serve as a showcase of broadband wireless access for rural, urban, and suburban regions in India, at a time when the Indian regulatory body, TRAI, has just made its recommendations to the Department of Telecom regarding WiMAX frequency allocation, a C-DOT statement said [57]. The WiMAX reality center includes an end-to-end architecture — comprising BSs, WiMAX Access Controller (WAC), and CPEs — which demonstrates the benefits of the WiMAX IEEE 802.16e-2005 standard and showcases residential and business usages with VoIP, high-speed Internet access, and multimedia applications such as IPTV, mobile TV, and video streaming.

Chennai Goes WiMAX

Chennai will be WiMAX-enabled. Aircel Business Solutions is implementing the project. The project has been in the beta trial stage. With trials conducted successfully over a period of twelve months, the system is already functional in 70 percent of the city. Over 200 SMEs in Chennai are already using WiMAX. The remaining 30 percent will become operational. Once the system successfully kicks off in Chennai, Aircel Business Solutions will deploy WiMAX across 44 cities including Delhi, Bangalore, Pune, Ahmedabad, Coimbatore, Hyderabad, etc., by 2008 [58].

Wavesat Receives Strategic Investment from SK Telecom

Wavesat announced it has completed a significant round of funding led by SK Telecom. The financing round, which also included participation from existing investors, will be used to accelerate the introduction of Wavesat's upcoming UMobileTM family of full-mobility WiMAX/WiBro solutions for the cellular handset market. This will complement Wavesat's existing leadership products for the fixed and nomadic (laptop) WiMAX markets, enabling Wavesat to provide best-in-class solutions for each WiMAX segment [59]. The funding round is expected to take Wavesat to profitability and followed a very successful year in which Wavesat grew revenue by nearly 300 percent, formed strategic partnerships with several industry leaders, received more than 30 design wins worldwide, and secured WiMAX Forum Certification for its WiMAX product portfolio. Wavesat provides a full range of standards-based integrated circuits, software, and development platforms supporting WiMAX 802.16-2004 certification and designed for upgradeability for basic mobility. Featuring the industry's only WiMAX Mini-PCI card and chosen by ODMs and OEMs worldwide, Wavesat's WiMAX portfolio provides effective wireless connectivity for a wide range of network sizes and coverage from urban to rural applications. Wavesat provides solutions for each WiMAX market segment, including the following:

- Fixed (access points, backhaul, DSL extensions) using its 802.16-2004 OFDM solutions
- Nomadic (high-speed connectivity for laptop mobility) with its 802.16-2005 OFDM EvolutiveTM products
- Full mobility (cellular applications) with its upcoming 802.16-2005 sOFDMA UMobileTM WiBro/WiMAX product family

WiMAX Broadband Debuts in Wellington

WiMAX wireless broadband is now available in Wellington, courtesy of junior telco Nzwireless, which has invested more than $1 million setting up a network of BSs covering the cbd and part of Lower Hutt. Nzwireless has been trying out WiMAX for six months with dozens of customers [60]. It is offering the service, which it will initially market to business customers, with 2-Mbps download and upload speeds, and a 10-Gb data cap for $80 a month, plus tax, and a $500 installation fee. A 3-Mbps plan costs $125, and for an extra $25 a month the customer gets unlimited usage [61].

Baramati Pilots Intel's WiMAX

Baramati (near Pune) has become the first town to get WiMAX services in India. The pilot project has been deployed by Intel along with Aircel and the Maharashtra government, on the 3.3-GHz frequency, over 20 and 6 km. It will be available in Baramati and four neighbouring towns and will allow bandwidth speeds of up to

512 kbps [63]. Research firms Maravedis and Tonse Telecom have predicted that India will have 13 million WiMAX subscribers by 2012 [62,64].

Samsung and TVA to Bring Mobile WiMAX Service to Brazil

Samsung Electronics and TVA Sistema de Televisao S.A Brazil signed a contract to commercialize the mobile WiMAX platform in the city of Curitiba, Brazil. TVA plans to commercialize mobile WiMAX services in Curitiba first [65]. Access will the be extended to other Brazilian cities. Samsung will supply BSs and other system hardware and mobile WiMAX modems initially and, in the near future, provide PCMCIA cards and terminals for service portability. Samsung has already begun to deploy this mobile WiMAX platform in Venezuela and will bring this platform to Brazil, Latin America's largest market. The mobile WiMAX platform offers wireless high-speed data communications on the move, complying with the IEEE 802.16e standard. In addition to mobility and portability, the WiMAX platform also brings low-cost data transmission to Brazilian users.

More WiMAX for SA

South Africa's telecom regulator ICASA has opened a public consultation period into the award of further licenses that can be used for WiMAX wireless broadband services. ICASA is inviting comments regarding the procedures and criteria for offering new concessions. Three firms — Telkom, Neotel, and Sentech — already hold licenses covering the 3.5-GHz band, although Sentech and WBS/iBurst have spectrum in the 2.6-GHz range. Local Web site MyADSL reports that 60 MHz of spectrum is still available at 3.5 GHz, and 126 MHz is free at 2.6 GHz [66].

Windows Mobile to Gain Plug-and-Play WiMAX

Runcom Technologies signed a collaboration agreement with Microsoft to develop Windows Mobile compatible drivers for its WiMAX chipset, with the goal of making mobile WiMAX a mass market technology with plug-and-play capabilities. Runcom contends that users should be able to connect Windows Mobile 5.0 devices to WiMAX networks simply by inserting a mobile WiMAX Compact-Flash or USB card, such as Runcom's RNE200 CF card, without downloading or installing drivers [67]. The company says its proprietary OFDMA technology, integrated into the new IEEE 802.16e standard for mobile wirelessMAN, offers seamless communications capabilities to standard mobile devices. The company builds PHY- and MAC-layer silicon for user terminals and BSs that comply with IEEE 802.16e-2005 WiBro and mobile WiMAX applications, it adds [68].

TVCable Chooses Airspan for WiMAX Expansion

Ecuador's largest cable TV operator, TVCable, has awarded Airspan Networks a contract for the expansion of its WiMAX network in the 3.5-GHz frequency band. The first phase of the network implementation has been installed, and WiMAX-based services are already commercially available in Guayaquil. Future network expansions are being planned for countrywide WiMAX coverage [69].

Brasil Telecom Plans Mobile WiMAX Network

Brazil's third largest fixed line operator Brasil Telecom Participações (BrT) plans to implement a mobile WiMAX network in the southern cities of Porto Alegre and Curitiba, BrT said in a statement. Consumers in these cities will be able to use the Internet without losing their connection while on the move, with mobile devices such as mobile phones, laptops, or PDAs [70]. Brazil already has some 250 WiMAX networks in operation, or in a test phase, but most are on a fixed or nomadic system, which does not allow the same degree of mobility. BrT is controlled by Citigroup.

Aperto Unveils Mobile WiMAX Strategy

Aperto Networks has unveiled its strategy of supporting a wide range of deployment options for network operators looking to capitalize on the IEEE 802.16-2004 fixed and IEEE 802.16e-2005 mobile WiMAX standards. Aperto's mobile WiMAX offering is based on an extension of Aperto's industry-leading PacketMAX architecture, including the PM5000, the first BS to be certified by the WiMAX Forum. Aperto has adapted PacketMAX to accommodate the mobile WiMAX standard through 802.16e-2005-compliant radio controller modules and software selectable subscriber units, allowing spectrally efficient colocation of the equipment, based on the fixed and mobile WiMAX standards, or an elegant migration from fixed to mobile WiMAX [71]. With advanced technologies such as MIMO, antenna diversity, and space-time coding (STC), the PacketMAX platform will evolve to yield even greater link budgets to enable more effective communications for WiMAX users, no matter where they are located, whether at the office, at home, or on the move. PacketMAX will also include multiple BS form factors for mobile WiMAX, such as single-sector, multisector, and pico-cell BS, allowing network operators to optimize their deployments.

VSNL Hopes to Launch WIMAX

Videsh Sanchar Nigam Ltd. plans to launch WIMAX services if the required spectrum becomes available [72]. At present, the company is testing WIMAX. VSNL has partnered with Aperto networks, developer of the world's most advanced WiMAX BSs and subscriber units, to deploy multiservice broadband wireless systems.

Australia Deploys Commercial WiMAX

Airspan Networks Inc. announced a successful deployment of Australia's commercial WiMAX solution with regional carrier Buzz Broadband in Queensland, Australia [73]. Buzz Broadband is a locally based carrier and ISP operating in the cities of Bundaberg, Maryborough, Hervey Bay, and Childers. As an existing Airspan customer, Buzz Broadband has deployed broadband wireless services to date using Airspan ASWipLL systems for its 22 BSs and backhaul links. It is now expanding that network with Airspan's WiMAX products to deliver telecommunications services throughout the region, as a viable broadband alternative to incumbent Telstra for 150,000 people in and around its service area. Buzz Broadband has begun deployment of Airspan's AS.MAX equipment for the provision of broadband data and VoIP services to its customer base. To ensure that admission control and priority number (emergency) calls can be supported in accordance with service-level agreements (SLAs) with its customers, Buzz Broadband will apply Airspan's VoiceMAX as part of the broadband access network, working in parallel with the quality of service (QoS) requirements of the 802.16 WiMAX Forum standard. Buzz Broadband has significant licensed spectrum holdings in the 3.4-GHz band, which further ensures that its customer SLAs can be offered and met. Airspan's AS.MAX solution will be rolled out across a 30,000 sq km region of Queensland, where Buzz Broadband holds 3.4-GHz licenses, providing high-speed broadband and VoIP connectivity at distances exceeding 30 km from the base-station sites. Initial deployments will consist of MicroMAX BSs, Airspan's low-cost high-performance WiMAX-Forum-Certified BS, which will be linked to Airspan's WiMAX-Forum-Certified ProST and EasyST subscriber units. The EasyST is the world's first self-installable WiMAX-Forum-Certified modem. The EasyST and ProST both incorporate Intel's ProWireless 5116 chip. Airspan's solution is the first WiMAX-Forum-Certified solution to be used in permanent commercial service in Australia, according to a release from Airspan [73]. It is also the first time a WiMAX-Forum-Certified technology offering commercial services has been operated anywhere in the licensed 3.4-GHz spectrum in Australia.

Alcatel and ACCA to Expand 802.16e WiMAX Trials to Urban Areas in Japan

Japanese communication service company ACCA Networks and French equipment manufacturer Alcatel have announced the successful completion of WiMAX trials in the suburban area of Yokosuka Research Park, and say they now plan to expand the tests to include the urban area of Yokohama city [74]. ACCA will be the first provider in Japan to conduct 802.16e-2005 WiMAX verification testing in both suburban and urban areas, allowing it to ascertain the respective characteristics of both types of areas. Alcatel has provided ACCA Networks with its 9100 Evolium WiMAX end-to-end radio solution, including BSs, wireless access controller, operation and maintenance center, as well as indoor CPE mobile terminals and integration services. The trial, operating in the 2.5-GHz frequency band and based on the Universal WiMAX IEEE 802.16e-2005 standard, marks an important step toward offering commercial services in Japan [78].

WiMAX Service Comes to Chicago

Towerstream brought WiMAX to Chicago [75]. Although not exactly Clearwire, the WiMAX company will be launching its pre-WiMAX broadband Internet service in Chicago, just as interest in the technology heats up to the point of being scalding to the marketplace. Sprint/Motorola/Intel made a $4 billion bet on WiMAX technology. The Towerstream WiMAX network will serve business users in the Chicago metro area, according to Towerstream. The company has said that its Hi-Vi T1+ service offers 99.9 percent reliability — that's a might lofty claim. Following on the heels of this claim, Towerstream advertises that its customers will experience less than a minute of downtime per month. Towerstream's Hi-Vi T1+ service is already available in select markets right now, including New York, Los Angeles, Chicago, San Francisco, Greater Boston, and Providence and Newport, Rhode Island.

WiMAX Blows into Nevada

AT&T has launched WiMAX in Pahrump, Nevada, which is located about 60 mi outside Las Vegas, and which may be most famous for being featured on a recent episode of NBC's Studio 60. AT&T is using equipment from Soma Networks, which it calls "WiMAX-ready" because it has not yet been certified. The equipment is designed for the mobile WiMAX standard, 802.16e-2005, although AT&T is using it in a fixed mode in Pahrump [76]. The carrier is marketing the Pahrump WiMAX network as "AT&T Yahoo! High-Speed Internet" with downstream speeds up to 1.5 Mbps and upstream speeds up to 384 kbps. The service is priced at $29.99 a month, with the required equipment offered free after a rebate.

Siemens to Supply Equipment for WiMAX Network in Ryazan

Siemens and New Telecommunications operator have signed a contract for building a WiMAX-based wireless broadband network in Ryazan. Accordingly, Siemens will provide WayMAX equipment certified by the WiMAX Forum, which includes BSs, subscriber terminals (Gigaset SE461 modems), SURPASS hiT 7020 interface converter, routers, and network management and monitoring subsystems. The operator will provide last-mile broadband access for end users, home offices, and small and mid-sized companies [77].

Clearwire Unwires Seattle as WiMAX Gains Steam

Fixed wireless Internet service provider Clearwire Corp. launches services in Seattle [80]. The Seattle launch brings Clearwire's high-speed Internet service deployments to 31 markets, covering more than 8 million potential subscribers, and currently serving about 162,000 actual subscribers [79]. Clearwire controls between 12 and 198 MHz of spectrum in markets, covering 210 million potential customers across the country. The company's service uses a proprietary, pre-WiMAX technology and offers an alternative to DSL and cable connections. Interestingly, Clearwire recently launched a mobile WiMAX trial in Oregon. Depending on the level of success Clearwire experiences during its mobile WiMAX trial, the ISP could shift into the mobile wireless arena, offering voice, data, and video, using mobile WiMAX technology.

TW-Airnet Deploys Airspan MicroMAX Network in Taiwan and Planning for MultiCity Deployment of WiMAX

TW-Airnet of Taiwan has chosen Airspan's MicroMAX family of WiMAX products to launch WiMAX-based services in Taiwan [81]. TW-Airnet is part of the Chunghwa United Telecom Group (CHUT) of companies, which was founded in 2000 to further the development of Taiwan's telecom technology industry. As an innovative leader in the industry, CHUT adopted wireless technologies in 2002, and today has the broadest wireless broadband coverage among telecom operators in Taiwan. TW-Airnet provides customers with wireless Internet access, ADSL, and the MOD system, a home entertainment set-top box with home-banking service capabilities. Focused on enhancing its leading position in Internet service and broadband access, TW-Airnet has selected Airspan for deployment of a WiMAX network in the 5.8-GHz band in 11 Taiwanese cities. TW-Airnet will use Chu-I Enterprise as its technology integration partner on this project. The initial deployment in Kinmen Island and Taichung City commenced in the first half of 2006. Airspan's WiMAX products and services will be a key component of TW-Airnet's broadband wireless architecture. By selecting Airspan's MicroMAX BSs, TW-Airnet will be able to deliver new and innovative Internet access, VoIP, and multimedia services to its customers with greater speed. TW-Airnet will also improve its operational and capital expenditure efficiencies while advancing the network technology and service control that the company and its customers need for long-term business success. Airspan first announced the launch of its MicroMAX BS in March 2006 in the 3.5-GHz FDD band. The BS is based on the high-performance SQN2010 WiMAX-Forum-Certified BS system design of Sequans, and was the first cost-optimized, pay-as-you-grow WiMAX solution available in the marketplace. It offers service providers and network operators a unique value proposition of very high performance at an affordable price point. In October 2006 Airspan introduced MicroMAX in the 5.8-GHz TDD WiMAX profile. The company will add MicroMAX frequencies in the 3.3- to 3.4-GHz TDD band. The MicroMAX is Airspan's third AS.MAX BS, the others being MacroMAX and HiperMAX. MicroMAX complements the larger WiMAX BSs by being optimized for lower-density deployment, such as rural areas, in-fill for coverage holes in wireless, DSL, and cable networks, enterprise solutions, and public safety applications [81].

Proxim Wireless Tsunami Product Line Deployed to Support Africa's Malawi Interbank MalSwitch Initiative

Tsunami.GX90 full-duplex point-to-point Ethernet bridges and Tsunami MP.11 point-to-multipoint products have been deployed by Malawi Switch Centre Limited (MalSwitch), a subsidiary of the Reserve Bank of Malawi, to support and deliver wireless banking services to the state capital, the commercial capital, and unwired rural areas [82]. This backbone is the cornerstone of the MalSwitch initiative to provide E-commerce services beyond urban areas. The backbone has been designed and deployed by Business Connexion, a leading integrator of wireless networking systems and Proxim Platinum Partner. Malawi is a small, highly populated land-locked African country of approximately 12 million people. Its economy is predominantly agricultural-based, with over 80 percent of the population living in rural areas. The Tsunami.GX90 links span almost 187 mi (300 km) linking the state capital, Lilongwe, with the commercial capital, Blantyre. The 45-Mbps full-duplex backbone supports voice and data for MalSwitch commercial customers. Along the backbone, services are redistributed by Proxim MP.11 wireless access links to rural communities. The towns served join the backbone to access banking services in either Lilongwe or Blantyre. Proxim's Tsunami family of wireless Ethernet bridges provides a variety of plug-and-play solutions to the growing demand for transparent, reliable, and economical high-speed network interconnectivity. With a wide variety of performance options ranging from 24- to 216-Mbps aggregate throughput, Tsunami.GX links allow network planners to select the optimum solution for their specific application. Drawing on Proxim's leadership in WiMAX, the Tsunami MP.11 point-to-multipoint products have been developed as a platform to enable WiMAX capabilities for license-free frequency bands. Available in indoor and outdoor models, the MP.11 Series is capable of supporting converged video, voice, and data transmission in fixed and mobile applications [82].

IRAQTEL Selects Redline to Establish Iraq's First WiMAX Network

Redline Communications and IRAQTEL will deploy the first WiMAX network in Iraq using Redline's WiMAX-Forum-Certified RedMAX products. Vision Valley, a specialist in systems integration, network design, and implementation, will provide its regional expertise to ensure the network is effectively established [83]. IRAQTEL will deliver advanced voice and broadband services to thousands of businesses and residents throughout its region via the Redline network. IRAQTEL will begin its RedMAX deployment in Basrah, and will expand its WiMAX network to include additional regions across Iraq. The Redline solution will enable IRAQTEL to quickly and cost-effectively establish broadband wireless networks to deliver the voice and broadband services its enterprise and government customers need and extend its network to reach more businesses, residents, and municipal organizations [84].

Urban WiMAX to Raise £35 Million to Fund Expansion of U.K. Network

Wireless broadband network operator Urban WiMAX plans for a £35 million fund-raising to finance a national roll-out for its WiMAX wireless broadband service. The London WiMAX service launched fully in January 2007. Urban WiMAX has also suggested that it might pursue acquisitions of companies holding WiMAX licenses and other wireless broadband operators, as a way of expanding its fledgling business [85].

Middle East Sees Another Mobile WiMAX Trial in Lebanon

Globalcom Data Services (GDS), an ISP, has selected communications solutions provider Alcatel to conduct the first IEEE 802.16e-2005 WiMAX trial in the Middle East. The trial is expected to help GDS assess the capacity of WiMAX prior to its commercial deployment in Lebanon. Alcatel will supply its 9100 Evolium WiMAX end-to-end radio solution, to include BSs, wireless access controller, and operations and maintenance center. It will also provide GDS with indoor CPE [86]. According to Alcatel, its solution will offer broadband wireless Internet access at a burst rate of up to 12 Mbps. GDS is intending to introduce broadband access across Lebanon by the end of next year, with service provided through DSL and WiMAX.

Alcatel to Make First Latin America WiMAX Deployments

Alcatel expects to make its first WiMAX deployments in Latin America in the first quarter of 2007. Spanish telecom group Telefónica has awarded Alcatel a contract to upgrade its broadband infrastructure in Latin America [88]. Alcatel is involved in more than 40 major triple-play deployments and more than 40 network transformation projects worldwide.

Airspan Selects Wavecall for Fixed and Mobile WiMAX Network Deployments

Airspan Networks Inc. has made its final selection of 3-D ray-tracing propagation models for use in its fixed and mobile WiMAX network deployments. Wavecall SA of Switzerland will supply its WaveSight 3D model to Airspan for all RF modeling of WiMAX products in urban areas. Airspan will use the model to plan the mass deployment of WiMAX in urban and suburban environments [89]. WaveSight was chosen for its prediction accuracy, which is measured as a reduction in calibrated model standard deviation. Other factors contributing to the selection were Wavecall's responsiveness, positive customer support, and seamless integration of WaveSight into the planning tool deployed by Airspan. Significantly, the WaveSight 3D model is suitable for all types of propagation environments (pico, micro, and macrocells). Also, WaveSight uses well-known and open-format interfaces. Presently, Airspan is using Ericsson's Planet EV and Wavecall's WaveSight to carry out 3-D radio planning for large WiMAX network deployments in the United Kingdom, Japan, Australia, Malta, and the United States [89].

Intel Unveils WiMAX Network in Rural Egypt

Working with Egypt's government, business, and education leaders, Intel Corp. has installed a WiMAX network to connect two public schools, a healthcare center on wheels, a municipal building, and an E-government services kiosk in rural Oseem, Egypt. Intel also donated and installed computers in the mobile health center and PC labs at the two schools, the company said [90]. Intel aims at bringing PCs to developing countries in an effort to promote the use of technology in rapidly growing regions of the world.

Germany WiMAX Licenses Awarded

Germany's telecom regulator Bundesnetzagentur has awarded three nation-wide and two regional WiMAX licenses at the end of a three-day auction, which raised €56.07 million ($73.37 million). Luxembourg-based Clearwire Europe and

German operators Deutsche Breitband Dienste and Inquam Broadband acquired the nationwide licenses, paying €20 million, €16.5 million, and €18 million, respectively. Italian MGM Productions Group paid €1.2 million for one regional license, whereas German ISP Televersa paid €342,000 for two regional licenses [91].

India's First Certified WiMAX Network Deployed

Aperto Networks announced that BSNL, telecom service provider in India, has begun rolling out Aperto's carrier-grade, WiMAX-Forum-Certified products. The deployment of PacketMAX BSs and subscriber units across six cities and four rural areas in India comes as a result of Aperto's successful bid [92]. The six initial cities getting the WiMAX equipment are Kolkata (in West Bengal), Bangalore (in Karnataka), Chennai (in Tamil Nadu), Ahmedabad (in Gujarat), Hyderabad (in Andhra Pradesh), and Pune (in Maharastra). The deployment will also cover four rural districts in the state of Haryana. The WiMAX network will enable BSNL to offer enterprise customers a wide range of value-added, high-bandwidth data communications services, such as MPLS, VPN, leased line, and Internet access, as well as VoIP, telemedicine, E-education, E-governance, and E-commerce in remote areas. BSNL will be deploying Aperto's PacketMAX 5000 BSs. BSNL will also be deploying Aperto's PM 300 subscriber units, along with Aperto's WaveCenter EMS Pro, the element management system.

Alvarion Unveils Converged WiMAX Wi-Fi Solution

Alvarion is expanding its portfolio with the introduction of two new converged solutions that combine Wi-Fi functionality with WiMAX and pre-WiMAX products. Specifically, the company unveiled BreezeMAX WI2 and BreezeACCESS WI2. The goal of the new solutions, according to Alvarion, is to advance personal broadband services by providing a cost-effective, converged network that combines Wi-Fi portability for IEEE 802.11b/g devices with WiMAX quality of service (QoS). The WI2 solutions each include an outdoor Wi-Fi access point (AP) with integrated power module capable of connecting to various commercial power sources, either a BreezeMAX or BreezeACCESS VL unit for backhaul and network management software [93].

WiMAX @ Fiji

Alvarion will deliver a BreezeMAX solution to Fiji International Communications (FINTEL) to enable the company to offer WiMAX data services to the businesses and residents of the Fiji Islands [93]. The wireless services will initially be launched in the capital city of Suva, according to Alvarion.

Max Telecom Selects Proxim Wireless for WiMAX Equipment

Max Telecom has selected Proxim Wireless' WiMAX product line and network management system to build a broadband wireless network serving Bulgaria's domestic and business customers [94]. Max Telecom will initially deploy Proxim's Tsunami MP.16 WiMAX BSs in the major cities of Sofia and Plovdiv, with a view to achieving national coverage in 2007. The company plans to offer its customers a broad portfolio of services that support triple-play Internet access, VoIP, and video streaming.

Nortel Expands WiMAX, Ethernet Reach

Nortel and Chunghwa Telecom will build the first WiMAX network in Taiwan, driven by a local government under the Mobile-Taiwan project. The network will be in the northeastern county of Yilan [95]. Nortel is also teaming with Toshiba Corp. to provide a wireless trial for the Japanese government, using WiMAX platforms. The trial is for mobile high-speed broadband services in the northern Tohoku region. The project is part of Japan's goal of having broadband connectivity for all its citizens by 2010. Nortel is providing WiMAX BSs, based on the IEEE 802.16e standard, in both Taiwan and Japan. On the Ethernet side, Easynet Belgium and the Joint Universities Computer Centre of Hong Kong are using Nortel's Metro Ethernet networking technology to enable businesses and students to connect to Internet services and configure WANs for local and international communications [118].

Agni to Roll Out Dhaka WiMAX Network Based on Motorola System

ISP Agni Systems has begun a phased deployment of WiMAX technology, supplied by Motorola, to provide wireless broadband access in Bangladesh's capital Dhaka, and plans to roll out the service gradually to other cities [96]. Commercial services are expected to start in 2007, and the entire network is expected to be completed by mid-2008. Phase one of the deployment will be a fixed outdoor solution using Motorola's Access Point 100 series system. Phase two, expected to start in the third quarter of 2007, will involve an upgrade to an 802.16-2005 mobile WiMAX system using Motorola's WiMAX Access Point (WAP) 400 series system [97].

Grand Rapids, Michigan, to Partner with Clearwire to Provide WiMAX-Based Wireless Broadband

The city of Grand Rapids, Michigan, its consultant, and its partners have selected Clearwire to construct a privately owned and operated wireless broadband network that will offer mobile, portable, and nomadic data service throughout the city's

45 sq mi [98]. With networks in 33 markets covering more than 370 cities and towns in the United States, this is the first time that Clearwire has partnered with a municipality to build a network of this type. Clearwire's network in Grand Rapids is also expected to include WiMAX/Wi-Fi hybrid hot spots that involve the placement of numerous Wi-Fi hot spots in strategic locations throughout the city. However, what is of special interest is that the city has mainly opted for WiMAX rather than Wi-Fi for its citywide network [99]. The city also expects that deployment of the robust Clearwire WIMAX network will provide an economic development tool to attract and retain business, reduce the digital divide, improve city service delivery and reduce the cost of government, facilitate wireless technology use for citizens and visitors, and create a seamless wireless infrastructure to attract and retain young professionals — all without a burden on taxpayers. In a program designed to provide digital inclusion, Clearwire will provide discounted service of $9.95 per month to up to 5 percent of the total household count in Grand Rapids for qualifying low-income citizens to be administered by a nonprofit agency yet to be determined. To better serve visitors and occasional users, free Wi-Fi hot spots will be provided throughout the city for visitors and occasional users.

Oki, Huawei to Collaborate on Mobile WiMAX

Oki Electric and Huawei are going to collaborate in the mobile WiMAX business to the telecom carriers in Japan [100]. Oki will begin providing Huawei's mobile WiMAX Series products to telecom carriers in Japan in the fiscal year ending March 2008. Oki will also provide its products globally with the support of Huawei. Mobile WiMAX can be used, for example, for higher-speed mobile communication among 3G mobile phone users in the metropolitan area, or to enable those living in suburban areas — where laying out fiber lines or ADSLs can be difficult — to access services through a wireless system [101]. With this collaboration, Oki hopes to provide total solutions to telecom carriers in Japan. It will offer network equipment such as WiMAX BSs and BS control equipment for infrastructure, built-in terminals, and PCMCIA card terminals. It will also offer services to evaluate, adjust, and improve equipment, as well as to provide maintenance service from its offices located throughout Japan. As a value-added reseller (VAR), Oki will customize Huawei's mobile WiMAX products for telecom carriers in Japan. Oki will also develop its own WiMAX–Wi-fi converter, WiMAX communication module for embedded systems, and indoor BS solutions such as pico cells. For BS solutions, in particular, Oki plans to develop solutions with support from Huawei. Huawei, on the other hand, will develop applications and customize products based on Oki's marketing information, to promote mobile WiMAX products suited to Japan [100].

Intel Demonstrates WiMAX Connection 2300 for Laptops

Intel announced design completion of its first mobile WiMAX baseband chip. Combined with the company's previously announced single-chip, multiband WiMAX/Wi-Fi radio, the pair creates a complete chipset called the Intel WiMAX Connection 2300, Intel Corp. said. Intel showed an Intel Centrino Duo mobile-technology-based notebook with mobile WiMAX (IEEE 802.16e-2005), Wi-Fi (IEEE 802.11n), and high-speed downlink packet access (HSDPA) 3G capabilities, successfully accessing the Internet at broadband speeds over a mobile WiMAX network [102]. Accordingly, the completed design of the Intel WiMAX Connection 2300 brings Intel a step closer to an integrated wireless system-on-chip that will help drive WiMAX adoption by maximizing useable space in mobile devices. As laptops become smaller, for example, they will have limited space for new technologies. Integration also helps enable ubiquitous connectivity on ultramobile PCs, consumer electronics, and handheld devices that have significant size constraints for the number of cards or components. Intel plans to sample the WiMAX Connection 2300 chipset, both card and module forms, beginning in late 2007.

India to Enter Broadband, WiMAX Manufacturing

India will soon see the advent of broadband and WiMAX manufacturing. The recently merged Alcatel–Lucent alliance has decided to utilize India for manufacturing broadband and WiMAX equipment through a transfer-of-technology and contract manufacturing arrangement with state-owned ITI [103]. This will happen at the ITI plant at Naini Tal in Uttar Pradesh. The ITI plant in India will be used by Alcatel–Lucent for telecom equipment manufacturing. Alcatel already has a tie-up with ITI for manufacturing of GSM towers, BSs, and 3G equipment at ITI's Rae Bareli and Mankapur plants. Alcatel and the Centre for Development of Telematics (C-DoT) are jointly developing WiMAX equipment in Chennai, where they run a global R&D center lab. The CPE developed in this center are set for field trials in January 2007. The pilot projects for WiMAX will be conducted in Chennai with BSNL, in Mumbai with MTNL, and in one city each in Japan and Mexico.

Siminn to Launch Iceland's First WiMAX Network

Iceland's fixed line incumbent Siminn (Iceland Telecom) has launched the country's first commercial WiMAX network following the successful trial of the service in the Grímsnes area. Siminn claims the pilot was so successful that commercial

WiMAX services have been offered to customers living in Grímsnes as well as other outlying areas [104].

Viettel to Test WiMAX

Viettel, the telco wholly owned by the Vietnamese military, has announced a trial offer of WiMAX mobile broadband service in the city of Hanoi. The pilot network of ten base transmitter stations (BTS) will have a capacity of around 3000 subscribers and will offer speeds of up to 10 Mbps within a 32-km range of a BTS [105]. Viettel won a year-long trial WiMAX license from the regulator, the Ministry of Post and Telematics (MPT), in March 2006, along with Vietnam Post and Telecommunications Corporation (VNPT), the Vietnam Television Technology Company (VTC), and FPT Telecom Joint Stock Company (FPT Telecom). VNPT began testing a WiMAX service in the northern province of Lao Cai in October 2006.

Maxis Selects Alcatel for WiMAX Field Trial

Alcatel–Lucent and Maxis Communications Berhad have signed an agreement to conduct a WiMAX trial of a Universal 802.16e–2005 WiMAX solution. The field trial is an important step toward offering commercial services and satisfying growing demand for wireless broadband access, especially in residential areas in Malaysia [106].

Buzz Technologies Signs Wi-Fi/WiMAX Agreement with Thai Military for Wireless ISP Services

Buzz Technologies Inc. announced it has signed an agreement with the Thai Military Lanna Center, Chiang Mai, The Third Army Region [107]. Buzz Technologies will supply the following to test with the intention to purchase secure online communications: Wi-Fi/WiMAX, instant messaging (IM), voice and video, short message service (SMS), MMS alert services, secure dedicated Web browser, and a selection of Buzz Hardware devices to troops deployed in the field and to provide coverage to military bases.

Fujitsu Bets Big on WiMAX

Fujitsu wants to get back into the wireless race in North America by being a major U.S. player in the race to build high-speed wireless broadband WiMAX networks [108]. Fujitsu announced a whole new line of WiMAX products covering every major component in the WiMAX network, including silicon solutions, electronic devices, radio access network solutions, professional services, and backhaul infrastructure solutions. The company presented two new high-performance BSs designed for indoor or outdoor use. So far, Fujitsu has invested tens of millions of dollars in WiMAX technology.

Alvarion Concentrates on WiMAX

Alvarion is selling its cellular mobile unit to LG Wireless for $15 million in cash and the assumption of certain liabilities. Alvarion is unloading the unit to focus more of its efforts on WiMAX. Alvarion believes the cellular mobile business is a good fit for LG Wireless and views the deal as being in the best interests of shareholders. Going forward, all of Alvarion's revenues will be attributed to its broadband wireless access (BWA) business. Alvarion reports that it has more than 100 commercial deployments and 120 active WiMAX trials up and running [109].

picoChip Engineering Center Builds WiMAX Chipsets for Chinese Broadband Wireless Alliances

picoChip has announced a significant expansion in its global presence, with the establishment of a new development center in Beijing, China. The new operation complements the company's existing development site in Bath, United Kingdom. picoChip also has an engineering facility in Shenzhen and sales office in Shanghai as part of its commitment to the Chinese market [111]. This expansion builds on the base provided by picoChip's established relationships and local operations. These include a highly productive partnership with WSPN-BUPT (Wireless Signal Processing and Network Lab, Beijing University of Posts and Telecommunications), focused on developing wireless systems based on TD-SCDMA and commercial WiMAX systems optimized for the Chinese market. A similar collaboration with the Institute of Computing Technology (ICT) of the Chinese Academy of Sciences (CAS), a world leader in network software and protocol stacks, has already produced software technology that is in use by picoChip's customers worldwide [111]. picoChip has been working in China since early 2003, when it established a partnership — in the form of a joint development center — with Millennium Meshwork Data Systems (MMDS).

Alcatel Taps Sequans to Develop Low-Cost WiMAX CPE

Sequans Communications announced its cooperation with Alcatel to bring Universal WiMAX 802.16e-2005 to high-growth economies. The cooperation will enable the production, starting Q2 2007, of low-cost end-user devices based on

Sequans' chips and tailored to the growing need of broadband access in developing countries. This will allow end users with low average income to benefit from broadband services at an affordable price [112]. Alcatel's leadership in advanced antenna technology combined with Sequans' leadership in feature-rich, high-performance WiMAX silicon lowers the overall cost per user of WiMAX networks by significantly improving coverage and capacity and enabling cost-optimized CPE. Sequans' SQN1110 mobile WiMAX chip for end-user devices features the industry's lowest power consumption, drawing a mere 350 mW of power, and delivers a throughput of more than 10 Mbps. It is suitable for the development of the full range of subscriber WiMAX devices, including indoor and outdoor CPE, PCMCIA cards, PDAs, multimedia devices, and multimode handsets [113].

Network Equipment Makers Eye Mobile WiMAX Products in 2007

A number of Taiwan-based network equipment makers, including Gemtek Technology, Accton Technology, and Zyxel Communications, are expected to begin commercial shipments, although in small volumes, of mobile WiMAX products in 2007, as many market sources have indicated. Demand for 802.16e-compatible mobile WiMAX is picking up now as more telecom service providers are building their mobile WiWAX infrastructure, bypassing the fixed-type WiMAX systems [114]. Gemtek shipments of mobile WiMAX CPE products topped one million units in 2007. Accton started trial production of mobile WiMAX CPE products, including WiMAX network cards and WiMAX modems, in 2007, and Zyxel began production of its mobile WiMAX devices at that time also [114].

India's BSNL Pairs with Intel on WiMAX

Indian state-owned service provider Bharat Sanchar Nigam Ltd. (BSNL) is teaming with Intel Corp. in a bid to deploy the country's first WiMAX-based wireless broadband and telecom service. The companies expect to sign a technology agreement soon, according to a report from New Delhi in *The Financial Express* [115]. The pact could give BSNL an edge over potential rivals in offering WiMAX services. Private companies currently offering broadband services in India include Bharti Airtel Ltd., Reliance Communications Ltd., and Tata Teleservices Ltd., which together have about 850,000 subscribers. BSNL is in the process of conducting trials on mobile services using WiMAX. Intel is conducting WiMAX trials in a dozen Indian cities. Another state-owned communications firm, Mahanagar Telephone Nigam Ltd., is conducting two pilots in the country. Further, privately owned Videsh Sanchar Nigam Ltd. is deploying multiservice wireless broadband systems from Aperto in 65 Indian cities [115].

Fitel Tests WiMAX

Taiwanese PHS mobile operator First International Telecom (Fitel) says it is setting up a trial WiMAX network in Taipei. The initial phase will see up to 30 BSs installed across the city, although it will be commencing its trial with just 5 BSs in the east of Taipei. Funding for the project is coming from the government's Mobile Taiwan (M-Taiwan) program, reports *DigiTimes* [116]. Fitel estimates that it would take around 200 BSs to provide full WiMAX coverage of central Taipei, and up to 700 to cover the whole Taipei metropolitan area. Nortel will be supplying the first five BSs, with Motorola contracted for another five. The remainder will come from one of these two firms or from Alcatel, Fitel says.

Sumitomo Electric Networks Elects Starent Networks Mobile WiMAX Access Solution

Starent Networks Corp. announced that Sumitomo Electric Networks Inc. (Suminet) has selected the Starent Access Service Network Gateway (ASN-GW) and Home Agent (HA) as key elements of its mobile WiMAX solution. Starent Networks will deliver its access-independent ST16 Intelligent Mobile Gateway with ASN and HA services to Suminet as the access component of Suminet's end-to-end mobile WiMAX offering [117]. The companies are already working toward an initial field trial with a mobile WiMAX operator in Japan. The ASN Gateway concentrates subscriber traffic from BSs. Its primary responsibilities are providing mobility services to mobile IP-aware and simple IP subscriber access devices and processing of subscriber control and bearer data traffic. The ASN Gateway connects to a home agent, which acts as the anchoring point for a subscriber session as the subscriber moves through the network. The Starent ST16 platform offers deployment flexibility by enabling both services to be integrated on the same chassis for lower operational expenditures or distributed on separate nodes in cases where mobility between different access technologies is desired. Major and emerging operators in Japan have already begun initial trials of mobile WiMAX. Several additional operators have applied for field trial licenses. In addressing this market, Suminet will leverage more than 20 years of experience providing technology solutions to customers. Suminet has a significant number of key customer relationships, which will be the primary targets for their end-to-end mobile WiMAX network solution.

Redline Introduces WiMAX Products

Redline Communications launched its RedMAX WiMAX products for the 3.3- to 3.5-GHz frequency band. The introduction of the 3.3- to 3.5-GHz RedMAX products enables operators across the Asia Pacific region to access Redline's proven

WiMAX solutions to deliver the broadband services that their customers need [119]. The 3.3- to 3.5-GHz RedMAX products are now being deployed by several operators in India and Vietnam and will be commercially available in the first quarter of 2007. The new RedMAX products join Redline's complete WiMAX-Forum-Certified systems that are being tested and deployed by more than 75 operators in 39 countries. The RedMAX products will include the AN-100U BS, SU-I indoor subscriber unit, and SU-O outdoor subscriber unit. The Redline's RedMAX family of WiMAX solutions is a system that receives the WiMAX-Forum-Certified mark for conformance to the WiMAX performance and interoperability standards. The carrier-class RedMAX BS (AN-100U) supports voice, video, and prioritized data traffic, enabling long-range, high-capacity wireless broadband networks. Redline's WiMAX products also include the RedMAX SU-I indoor subscriber unit and SU-O outdoor subscriber unit designed for enterprise and residential services. The Red-MAX Management Suite enables operators to monitor and control the network, ensuring high service availability. Redline is maintaining its WiMAX leadership with the expansion of its RedMAX family to include products for additional frequency bands, applications, and standards [119].

Radio Makes Room for WiMAX

WiMAX will work best in the UHF spectrum between 300 MHz and 3 GHz. That would exclude AM, FM, and VHF TV. There is no question that broadband technology is beginning to change broadcasting as we know it. The eventual deployment of widespread WiMAX availability also will change it. WiMAX may eventually supplant some of the broadcast services way down the road [146]. Developments may alter the broadcasting landscape, but radio's strengths will keep it viable.

Synterra Takes WiMAX to Kursk

Russian wireless broadband operator Synterra has completed construction of its WiMAX network in the city of Kursk. *Prime Tass* reports that the new network incorporates three BSs, which is sufficient to cover around 80 percent of the city territory [120]. The initial capacity is for 1500 customers. Synterra already has a WiMAX network in Moscow; the Kursk system is its first in a regional capital. It holds licenses in the 2.5- to 2.7-GHz band in Moscow, the Moscow region, and 16 other regions.

WiMAX Takes Wings in India

WiMAX is just the kind of leapfrog technology that makes sense in emerging telecom markets such as India and China. Certified WiMAX took a big step forward in India when local incumbent Bharat Sanchar Nigam Ltd. rolled out fixed wireless networks in six Indian cities and offered high-bandwidth connections to corporate customers. The cities where networks would be rolled out include Kolkata (in West Bengal), Bangalore (in Karnataka), Chennai (in Tamil Nadu), Ahmedabad (in Gujarat), Hyderabad (in Andhra Pradesh), and Pune (in Maharastra). California-based Aperto is a key supplier for a 65-city fixed wireless network being built by another local phone company, VSNL. The network will eventually be extended to 200 cities [147]. In addition to these networks, Intel has WiMAX trials planned for Mumbai, New Delhi, Pune, and Bangalore. Similar to Intel, Alcatel is also aggressively pushing WiMAX in India. Indian ISP DishNet has fixed wireless networks deployed (or under development) in eight cities and is targeting consumers. Nokia will start selling WiMAX gear in 2007, and Motorola is also planning to jump into the fray, according to local media reports. According to a report by research firms Maravedis and Tonse Telecom, India will have 13 million WiMAX subscribers by 2012. The demand for wireless broadband gear is going to add up to about $4.5 billion by 2012.

WiMAX in Formula One Cars

F1 racing supremo Bernie Ecclestone is effectively holding up F1's adoption of WiMAX for use in racing cars [148]. A BMW Sauber team member, sponsored by Intel [149], said that it would be extremely useful to have the ability to receive the larger amounts of data that WiMAX could permit. The trouble is, that at aertain race circuits, the radio signal becomes too weak to be received by the teams. The negotiations are at a delicate stage because of this problem.

References

1. WiMAX wireless broadband: Fixed-flavor questions abound, mobile lurks. EDN, March 31, 2005, p. 44, www.edn.com/article/CA512128.
2. http://gigaom.com/2006/07/07/orbitel-launches-wimax-in-colombia/.
3. http://www.digitalmediaasia.com/default.asp?ArticleID=16341.
4. http://www.techtree.com/techtree/jsp/article.jsp?article_id=74301&cat_id=579.
5. http://www.japancorp.net/Article.Asp?Art_ID=13149 [dated August 29, 2006].
6. http://www.marketwire.com/mw/release_html_b1?release_id=161484 [dated September 11, 2006].
7. http://nationmultimedia.com/2006/10/25/business/business_30017035.php.
8. http://www.techweb.com/wire/networking/193402237 [dated October 25, 2006].
9. http://voipforenterprise.tmcnet.com/feature/service-solutions/articles/3241-islanet-launches-residential-wimax-service-puerto-rico.htm [dated October 25, 2006].
10. http://www.wisoa.com/site/2006/10/27/wimax-launch-from-navini-in-sweden/ [dated October 27, 2006].
11. http://infynews.blogspot.com/2006/10/infosys-working-with-aircel-to-provide.html [dated October 28, 2006].

12. http://www.sda-india.com/sda_india/psecom,id,102,site_layout,sdaindia,news, 13120,p,0.html [dated October 28, 2006].
13. http://www.telegeography.com/cu/article.php?article_id=15061&email=html.
14. http://www.newkerala.com/news4.php?action=fullnews&id=43210 [dated October 30, 2006].
15. http://news.monstersandcritics.com/india/article_1216215.php/Microsense_to_unwire_Bangalore_with_WiMAX [dated October 30, 2006].
16. http://www.ynetnews.com/articles/0,7340,L-3294676,00.html [dated August 23, 2006].
17. http://wearables.engadget.com/2006/08/07/ultranet2go-spreads-wimax-across-mexico/ [dated August 7, 2006].
18. http://www.newswire.ca/en/releases/archive/August2006/10/c4927.html [dated August 15, 2006].
19. http://www.cellular-news.com/story/18500.php.
20. http://www.vnunet.com/vnunet/news/2163856/wimax-ready-national [dated September 8, 2006].
21. http://www.telegeography.com/cu/article.php?article_id=13594&email=html.
22. http://www.cellular-news.com/story/19468.php.
23. http://www.telegeography.com/cu/article.php?article_id=13448&email=html.
24. http://www.xchangemag.com/hotnews/6ah495423.html.
25. http://www.webwire.com/ViewPressRel.asp?aId=21392.
26. http://www.xchangemag.com/tdhotnews/6ah10121353.html [dated October 10, 2006].
27. http://www.marketwire.com/mw/release_html_b1?release_id=170455 [dated October 10, 2006].
28a. http://www.telegeography.com/cu/article.php?article_id=14587&email=html.
28b. http://www.dailytech.com/article.aspx?newsid=3979.
29. http://www.digitalmediaasia.com/default.asp?articleID=17794 [dated August 28, 2006].
30. http://m-net.net.nz/home/task,read/page,1/category,5/article,567/ [dated August 23, 2006].
31. http://www.tmcnet.com/wifirevolution/articles/2811-redline-system-be-used-wimax-deployment-oil-rigs.htm.
32. http://www.cio.com/blog_view.html?CID=22567 [dated June 29, 2006].
33. http://neasia.nikkeibp.com/neasia/004538.
34. http://www.unstrung.com/document.asp?doc_id=98008&WT.svl=news1_1 [dated June 26, 2006].
35. http://www.usatoday.com/tech/wireless/2006-09-20-intel-wimax-amazon_x.htm?POE=TECISVA [dated September 20, 2006].
36. http://www.cieonline.co.uk/cie2/articlen.asp?pid=1104&id=11931.
37. http://www.multichannel.com/article/CA6370524.html?display=Breaking+News.
38. http://english.ohmynews.com/articleview/article_view.asp?at_code=370942&no=326810&rel_no=1.
39. http://www.eetimes.com/news/latest/showArticle.jhtml?articleID=192400121 [dated August 29, 2006].
40. http://www.digitimes.com/telecom/a20061026A2006.html [dated October 26, 2006].
41. http://www.digitimes.com/telecom/a20061201PD202.html [dated December 1, 2006].
42. http://news.tmcnet.com/news/2006/05/12/1648392.htm [dated May 12, 2006].
43. http://www.govtech.net/magazine/channel_story.php/99207 [dated April 15, 2006].

44. http://www.cellular-news.com/story/17069.php.

45. http://www.telegeography.com/cu/article.php?article_id=13232&email=html.

46. http://www.telegeography.com/cu/article.php?article_id=13196&email=html.

47. http://www.wimax.com/commentary/news/wimax_industry_news/aperto-unveils-wimax-solutions-ecosystem [dated December 4, 2006].

48. http://home.businesswire.com/portal/site/google/index.jsp?ndmViewId=news_view&newsId=20061204005567&newsLang=en.

49. http://www.moneycontrol.com/india/news/technology/nokiawimaxcapablemobile/nokiabetsbigmobilewimaxtech/market/stocks/article/254205/1.

50. www.thehindubusinessline.in.

51. http://www.asteriskvoipnews.com/wimax/wimax_for_cars.html.

52. http://www.skylightresearch.com/.

53. http://www.tmcnet.com/wifirevolution/articles/2149-france-based-maxel-offers-affordable-anymax-wimax-system.htm.

54. http://techdigest.tv/2006/11/heathrow_expres.html.

55. http://www.technewsworld.com/story/54037.html.

56. http://www.earthtimes.org/articles/show/news_press_release,17707.shtml [dated November 7, 2006].

57. http://www.ciol.com/content/news/2006/106110805.asp [dated November 8, 2006].

58. http://bothack.wordpress.com/2006/11/03/chennai-goes-wimax/ [dated November 3, 2006].

59. http://www.ccnmatthews.com/news/releases/show.jsp?action=showRelease&searchText=false&showText=all&actionFor=620149 [dated November 6, 2006].

60. http://www.stuff.co.nz/stuff/0,2106,3851969a28,00.html [dated November 6, 2006].

61. http://www.geekzone.co.nz/TheBartender/1670.

62. http://www.business-standard.com/common/storypage.php?autono=263657&leftnm=8&subLeft=0&chkFlg= [dated November 3, 2006].

63. http://cities.expressindia.com/fullstory.php?newsid=207903.

64. http://www.rediff.com/money/2006/nov/03intel.htm.

65. http://www.phonemag.com/index.php/weblog/read_more/20061109samsung_and_tva_to_bring_mobile_wimax_service_to_brazil/ [dated November 8, 2006].

66. http://www.telegeography.com/cu/article.php?article_id=15284&email=html.

67. http://www.windowsfordevices.com/news/NS2314387608.html [dated November 8, 2006].

68. http://www.theunwired.net/?itemid=3449.

69. http://www.telegeography.com/cu/article.php?article_id=15307&email=html.

70. http://www.cellular-news.com/story/20388.php [dated November 13, 2006].

71. http://www.wirelessdesignasia.com/article.asp?id=3657 [dated November 15, 2006].

72. http://infotech.indiatimes.com/Tech_News/News/VSNL_hopes_to_launch_WIMAX_in_6_months/articleshow/414343.cms [dated November 12, 2006].

73. http://www.govtech.net/digitalcommunities/story.php?id=102410 [dated November 16, 2006].

74. http://www.telegeography.com/cu/article.php?article_id=15427&email=html [dated November 17, 2006].

75. http://www.thewirelessreport.com/2006/11/17/wimax-service-comes-to-chicago/ [dated November 17, 2006].

76. http://www.wirelessweek.com/article/CA6393023.html.
77. http://www.ospint.com/text/d/3488725/ [dated November 16, 2006].
78. http://www.telecompaper.com/news/article.aspx?id=148670&nr=&type=&yr=2006.
79. http://rcrnews.com/news.cms?newsId=27769 [dated November 15, 2006].
80. http://seattle.bizjournals.com/seattle/stories/2006/11/13/daily18.html?surround=lfn.
81. http://www.marketwire.com/mw/release_html_b1?release_id=185105 [dated November 15, 2006].
82. http://www.marketwire.com/mw/release_html_b1?release_id=183095 [dated November 14, 2006].
83. http://www.newswire.ca/en/releases/archive/November2006/18/c6275.html.
84. http://www.telegeography.com/cu/article.php?article_id=15465&email=html.
85. http://www.itpro.co.uk/networking/news/98312/urban-wimax-to-raise-35m-to-fund-expansion-of-uk-network.html [dated November 20, 2006].
86. http://www.bbwexchange.com/pubs/2006/11/20/page1423-283753.asp [dated November 20, 2006].
87. http://www.cellular-news.com/story/20558.php [dated November 22, 2006].
88. http://www.bnamericas.com/story.jsp?sector=2&noticia=373405&idioma=I [dated November 22, 2006].
89. http://www.tmcnet.com/wifirevolution/articles/4164-airspan-selects-wavecall-fixed-mobile-wimax-network-deployments.htm [dated December 18, 2006].
90. http://www.edn.com/index.asp?layout=article&articleid=CA6400848&ref=nbednn enews&industryid=2282 [dated December 18, 2006].
91. http://www.telegeography.com/cu/article.php?article_id=15922&email=html [dated December 18, 2006].
92. http://www.rfglobalnet.com/content/news/article.asp?DocID=%7B3772B90B-A3FF-4443-A957-DFFB2746F05F%7D&Bucket=Current+Headlines [dated December 18, 2006].
93. http://www.wirelessweek.com/article/CA6397714.html [dated December 6, 2006].
94. http://www.telegeography.com/cu/article.php?article_id=15744&email=html [dated December 6, 2006].
95. http://www.xchangemag.com/articles/501/6ch614263356388.html [dated December 6, 2006].
96. http://www.telegeography.com/cu/article.php?article_id=15748&email=html [dated December 6, 2006].
97. http://www.cio.com/blog_view.html?CID=27206 [dated December 5, 2006].
98. http://www.govtech.net/digitalcommunities/story.php?id=102746.
99. http://www.unstrung.com/document.asp?doc_id=112476&WT.svl=news2_1 [dated December 8, 2006].
100. http://www.digitalmediaasia.com/default.asp?ArticleID=20326 [dated December 7, 2006].
101. http://www.convergedigest.com/Wireless/broadbandwirelessarticle.asp?ID=20086.
102. http://laptoping.com/intel-wimax-connection-2300.html [dated December 9, 2006].
103. http://economictimes.indiatimes.com/articleshow/748769.cms [dated December 9, 2006].
104. http://www.telegeography.com/cu/article.php?article_id=15832&email=html.
105. http://www.telegeography.com/cu/article.php?article_id=15836&email=html.

106. http://malaysianwireless.blogspot.com/2006/12/maxis-selects-alcatel-for-wimax-field.html.
107. http://www.bbwexchange.com/pubs/2006/12/11/page1423-377384.asp.
108. http://www.forbes.com/technology/2006/11/22/fujitsu-intel-nttdocomo-pf-guru-in_nh_1122unwiredpportfolio_inl.html.
109. http://www.wirelessweek.com/article/CA6394404.html [dated November 22, 2006].
110. http://www.telegeography.com/cu/article.php?article_id=15538.
111. http://www.bbwexchange.com/pubs/2006/11/27/page1423-286860.asp [dated November 27, 2006].
112. http://www.bbwexchange.com/pubs/2006/11/28/page1423-287464.asp [dated November 28, 2006].
113. http://www.tmcnet.com/wifirevolution/articles/3790-sequans-alcatel-bring-universal-wimax-high-growth-economies.htm [dated November 28, 2006].
114. http://www.digitimes.com/systems/a20061128PD206.html [dated November 28, 2006].
115. http://www.eetimes.com/news/latest/showArticle.jhtml?articleID=196600227 [dated November 29, 2006].
116. http://www.telegeography.com/cu/article.php?article_id=15679&email=html [dated December 1, 2006].
117. http://www.tmcnet.com/usubmit/2006/10/10/1963645.htm [dated October 10, 2006].
118. http://www.digitimes.com/telecom/a20061205PR203.html [datedDecember 5, 2006].
119. http://www.zdnetindia.com/cstech/voip/reviews/stories/164600.html [dated December 13, 2006].
120. http://www.telegeography.com/cu/article.php?article_id=15895&email=html [dated December 15, 2006].
121. http://www.indiaprwire.com/pressrelease/computer-networks/20061026847.htm.
122. http://www.techworld.com/mobility/features/index.cfm?featureid=2896&pagtype=all [dated October 26, 2006].
123. http://www.thanhniennews.com/business/?catid=2&newsid=21556.
124. http://english.vietnamnet.vn/tech/2006/09/617170/ [dated 29 September 2006].
125. http://www.telegeography.com/cu/article.php?article_id=15058&email=html.
126. http://www.itpro.co.uk/networking/features/96729/wimax-in-the-uk.html.
127. http://www.teleclick.ca/2006/10/nortel-tests-uplink-collaborative-mimo-4g-wimax-technology/ [dated October 30, 2006].
128. http://www.ferret.com.au/articles/zz/view.asp?id=2187.
129. http://www.vianetworks.com/.
130. http://www.xchangemag.com/hotnews/68h812460.html [dated August 8, 2006].
131. http://www.digitalmediaasia.com/default.asp?ArticleID=16431.
132. http://www.eetimes.com/news/latest/showArticle.jhtml?articleID=193001507 [dated September 18, 2006].
133. http://www.wirelessweek.com/article/CA6369184.html [dated September 6, 2006].
134. http://www.telegeography.com/cu/article.php?article_id=14470&email=html.
135. http://www.caycompass.com/cgi-bin/CFPnews.cgi?ID=1015219 [dated August 1, 2006].
136. http://www.wi-fiplanet.com/news/article.php/3621921 [dated July 24, 2006].
137. http://www.indiantelevision.com/headlines/y2k6/may/may74.htm [dated May 6, 2006].
138. http://www.digitalmediaasia.com/default.asp?ArticleID=15213.

139. http://www.tmcnet.com/wifirevolution/articles/2931-telsima-wireless-solutions-atta-wimax-forum-compliance.htm [dated October 4, 2006].
140. http://www.channelnewsasia.com/stories/singaporebusinessnews/view/204733/1/.html [dated April 24, 2006].
141. http://biz.yahoo.com/prnews/061010/to425.html?.v=5 [dated October 10, 2006].
142. http://archive.gulfnews.com/articles/06/10/15/10074955.html.
143. http://www.telegeography.com/cu/article.php?article_id=14908&email=html.
144. http://vietnamnews.vnagency.com.vn/showarticle.php?num=03BUS231006 [dated October 23, 2006].
145. http://www.bbwexchange.com/pubs/2006/12/04/page1423-368693.asp.
146. http://www.rwonline.com/pages/s.0048/t.553.html [dated December 13, 2006].
147. http://gigaom.com/2006/12/14/in-india-wimax-takes-wings/ [dated December 14, 2006].
148. http://www.f1newstoday.com/blogit/2006/12/16/wimax-in-formula-one-cars/ [dated December 16, 2006].
149. http://www.theinquirer.net/default.aspx?article=36410.
150. http://www.asteriskvoipnews.com/wimax/clearwire_pushes_wimax_to_the_big_time_go_craig_go.html.

Chapter 6

WiMAX — A Revolution

Worldwide Telecommunications and Communications Markets at $197.6 Billion in 2005 Are Anticipated to Reach $446.9 Billion by 2010

Research and Markets [2] has added "Worldwide Telecommunications and Communications Market Opportunities, Strategies, and Forecasts," 2005 to 2010 to their offering. The worldwide telecommunications markets are set for extraordinary growth, doubling from $123 billion in 2004 to $282 billion by 2010. Communications represents an opportunity for expansion of economies. Internet-based communications systems are vastly improving the efficiency of the supply chain for the largest 5000 companies worldwide. The combination of voice, video, and data on a network makes people more efficient. More information can be communicated, not in real-time, but is available as people need it. Messaging systems play a significant role in passing information asynchronously, just in time. Underdeveloped countries use communications to achieve trading and exchange of goods. As people have portable communications devices, they want more goods and can make an economy emerge where there was none before. The uncertainty in the telecommunications markets has been resolved. Digital, IP, and Ethernet will replace all other protocols. The convergence of networks is to IP, the Internet, and Ethernet. It works seamlessly; it is reliable, resilient, and fast. Now the issue is how fast the TDM networks will be replaced by the new technology. Wireless is everything. Third-generation base stations promise to coexist with WiMAX 802.16 base stations in metro environments. Worldwide telecommunications and communications equipment market forecasts and shipments in dollars analyses indicate strong growth in very large existing markets. Markets at $197.6 billion in 2005 are anticipated to reach $446.9 billion by 2010.

The Promise of WiMAX Long-Range Wireless

WiMAX requires a tower, similar to a cell-phone tower, which is connected to the Internet using a standard wired high-speed connection. But as opposed to a traditional Internet service provider (ISP), which divides that bandwidth among customers via wire, it uses a microwave link to establish a connection. The current IEEE wireless standard dictates that WiMAX will provide a service range of up to 50 km and also be able to provide broadband transmission speeds of about 75 Mbps. This is, in theory, about 20 times faster than most commercially available wireless broadband. Currently, tests are being conducted worldwide in more than 75 cities. Apart from greater range, WiMAX is more bandwidth efficient. Ultimately, WiMAX may be used to provide connectivity to entire cities and incorporated into laptops to give users an added measure of mobility. Because WiMAX does not depend on cables to connect each endpoint, deploying WiMAX to an entire high-rise, community, or campus can be done in a matter of days, resulting in significant workforce savings. Although it has been stated and shown that portable WiMAX is a service that can be offered now, it is also clear that, down the road, full mobility is in the future for WiMAX. Indeed, it is the lure of the one billion cellular handset market (that is driving WiMAX adoption); the portable gaming device and portable DVD and TV players are all end-user devices that would benefit from true broadband connectivity. Fully mobile broadband wireless is significantly more difficult than just delivering voice and a few hundred kbps. It is expected that the superior efficiency, advanced MAC, and an all-IP design will help propel mobile WiMAX to the forefront of the race to 4G.

WiMAX Set to Usher in the New Era of Wireless Broadband

WiMAX was available in 2006 for commercial deployment. The infrastructure requirements are backhaul to feed wireless networks and base stations. The spectrum uses both licensed and unlicensed bands. WiMAX is a strong contender for high-mobility enterprise applications. As the cost of WiMAX approaches that of Wi-Fi, WiMAX becomes the next generation of wireless broadband technology. WiMAX targets multiple-site mass metropolitan applications. WiMAX is a lot like Wi-Fi, but unlike Wi-Fi's 200-m range, WiMAX has a reach of 25 to 30 km, offering a way to bring the Internet to entire communities without having to invest billions of dollars to install phone or cable networks. WiMAX can deliver favorable cost, reach, security, and usability. During the aftermath of Hurricane Katrina in the U.S. Gulf Coast, the communications infrastructure collapsed, except for WiMAX, putting a spotlight on market opportunities for broadband wireless systems for all major metropolitan areas. UTStarcom equipment was used in combination with WiMAX switches to achieve connectivity. Within 5 hr of the arrival of graduate students with a wireless network after Hurricane Katrina struck the Gulf Coast, anyone with a laptop at the hospital where the network was installed could send e-mail, surf the Web, and send instant messages. With an Internet telephone, they could make and receive calls over the connection, which is similar to a low-priced DSL link.

WiMAX Adoption to Rise, DSL to Gain Ground

According to a Prévision-SITM Annual Telecom Forecast 2007 release, WiMAX will be adopted as a backhaul technology (Figure 6.1). WiMAX is expected to come in a big way and make way for pilot testing [3,12]. WiMAX rollouts are expected in the second quarter of 2007, subject to spectrum clearances.

According to prediction, WiMAX will be the preferred "new" technology to be implemented by operators in the next year. WiMAX rollouts will occur in the second quarter of 2007, subject to spectrum clearances. Large operators and new players will enter this segment, using this technology as an alternate to terrestrial networks for triple-play services. The opening of 2.3- and 2.5-MHz bands will further boost mobile WiMAX. The most populous region of the world, which at present contributes around 40 percent of the total mobile subscribers, is expected to cross a personal one billion mark in 2007.

With few exceptions, various operators who are planning, or are in the process of deploying, WiMAX networks in North America, South America, Asia, and Europe were upfront about one question: What new applications will drive WiMAX forward? What will people do with these networks that they cannot do today? Although not particularly satisfying, the simply answer is, "nothing." 3G provides a data pipe supporting VoIP, video streaming, gaming, Web browsing, etc. So, too, will

- Mobile subscriber base set to reach 2.9 billion mark by the end of 2007. We expect six markets, especially China, India, Russia, the United States, and Brazil, to account for more than 50 percent of the total net additions in 2007.
- The difficulty of the mobile operator business model formed on high subscriber acquisition costs (principally handset subsidies), high churn levels and falls in the price per minute of mobile voice telephony.
- The rapid evolution of the Mobile Virtual Network Operator (MVNO) concept and operators' realization that a wholesale strategy can, in some cases, be more profitable than a retail business.
- The impact of IP, in particular, Web-based alternate service providers is rapidly driving down the price of voice telephony. One thing is clear—mobile voice prices are on the slide.
- The Walled Garden Approach of mobile operators in Europe will see a significant change forced by premium content operators.
- The telecom industry is moving away from a royalty-based model to an open source-based model.

Figure 6.1   Pathbreaking global trends for 2007. (Courtesy of http://www. expresscomputeronline.com/20061030/market07.shtml and http://wireless federation.com/news/wimax-adoption-to-rise-ds/-to-gain-ground.)

WiMAX. WiMAX, however, if it lives up to its claims, will be faster, cheaper, and deployable in a broader array of devices. The result should be a better experience. It may even drive usage on particular applications. None of these applications, however, is likely to be revolutionary.

Would-be WiMAX operators should take note [4]. WIMAX may promise new wireless functionality, but they cannot count on radically new applications when justifying a deployment. Luckily, they can — over time — count on performance boosts that should make these applications more appealing and profitable.

Sprint Says WiMAX is 4G

A lot of people are enthusiastic about having an "Internet anywhere" experience. WiMAX-based 4G networks will make possible pervasive, immediate, visual interactions that will make for a better, and more humane, world. A mobile WiMAX network, with the bandwidth to support voice and video, will make closeness possible. WiMAX creates a 10-fold improvement in the price per bit. That is made possible by the fact it uses a wider channel [5]. WiMAX chips benefit from the economies of price/performance known as Moore's Law, compared to the older code division multiple access (CDMA) technology. The result: WiMAX is one-tenth the cost per bit of CDMA. Sprint's plan is to have 100,000 points of presence enabled with WiMAX service by the end of 2008. The network will be an overlay on the company's existing CDMA EV-DO 1x cellular net. Subscribers will be able to use either network, depending on coverage and services, through network cards and eventually through integrated wireless interfaces. A related development will be interfaces that combine both 802.11 wireless LAN and 802.16e mobile WiMAX chips. These combined chipsets will be common. Sprint's subscribers will be using indoor access radios to connect to the WiMAX net. The goal is to make this connection extremely simple to use. Initially, many users of the Sprint network will connect via PCMCIA cards with mobile WiMAX chipsets. Because the availability of truly pervasive multimegabit wireless Internet will be a powerful attraction, Sprint is talking to consumer electronics companies, including Sprint's WiMAX partners Motorola and Samsung, persuading them to integrate WiMAX into their devices, such as putting WiMAX in a TV set, and putting it in printers.

WiMAX Challenges 3G

In the United States, WiMAX has gained significant momentum. Its standardization is complete, vendor and operator ecosystems are expanding, and the hype is getting louder, often justifiably so. Figure 6.2 shows the result of asking the participants "Has your business considered investing in WiMAX?" Beyond the hype and theoretical discussion, Pyramid Research [6] looks at real-world examples of

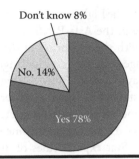

Figure 6.2 WiMAX opinion survey. (Courtesy of http://www.pyramidresearch. com/.)

pre-WiMAX deployments and reviews practical issues such as time to market, business models and pricing, device availability, economics of scale and spectrum availability, with an emphasis on a number of key questions, most notably, can WiMAX challenge 3G? Pyramid Research [6] surveyed about 100 operators to get their views, investments plans, expectations, and concerns in regard to WiMAX. With 78 percent of the surveyed operators considering an investment in WiMAX, they believe the promise of WiMAX is compelling and the technology warrants further examination. The result is an in-depth, case-study-based analysis about the viability of WiMAX, and the potential threat it poses to 3G. Key questions answered by the operators include:

■ Does mobile WiMAX perform better than 3G?
■ Will mobile WiMAX be cheaper than 3G?
■ How will mobile WiMAX IPR affect the 3G value proposition?
■ Which players have the best case for deploying mobile WiMAX?
■ What is the current operator perception of mobile WiMAX? What do operators believe is the primary driver for its success?
■ What is the largest obstacle?
■ Where are the most attractive opportunities for mobile WiMAX?
■ How will spectrum availability, licensing procedures, market competition, and technology time to market impact certain markets?
■ What is the size of the WiMAX opportunity in key sample markets (France, India, Mexico, and the United States)?

WiMAX Market Projections

WiMAX technology is entering a rapid growth phase, as service providers are now able to buy WiMAX-Forum-Certified equipment, reports In-Stat [7]. The number of worldwide subscribers reached 222,000 in 2006 and is forecast to grow to

19.7 million by the end of 2010, the high-tech market research firm says (Figure 6.3a). Most of those subscribers are in the Asia-Pacific region. Almost all subscribers are using a fixed service today, with the exception of those in South Korea. Although WiMAX faces many challenges, the biggest challenge still comes from competing technologies and services, says In-Stat. WiMAX will have difficulty competing in areas that already have established broadband services. WiMAX will need to provide a demonstratively superior service to win customers from the incumbent provider. Much of WiMAX's early success will come from underdeveloped regions of the globe, says In-Stat. In-Stat expects sales of 802.16e equipment to quickly overtake those of 802.16d [7].

Recent research by In-Stat found the following:

Although 3G users account for a low percentage of mobile phone users overall, current 3G users are more likely to use the multimedia capabilities of handsets, with increased levels of messaging, gaming, watching video, and downloading new content for personalization of handsets. Those "early adopters" provide interesting insights about what mobile usage patterns WiMAX service providers will need to address and the network challenges associated with them. Siemens surveyed

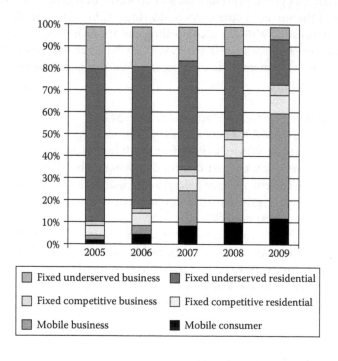

a

Figure 6.3 WiMAX market projections. (Courtesy of http://www.dailywireless. org/2006/11/15/wimax-market-projections/ and In-Stat.)

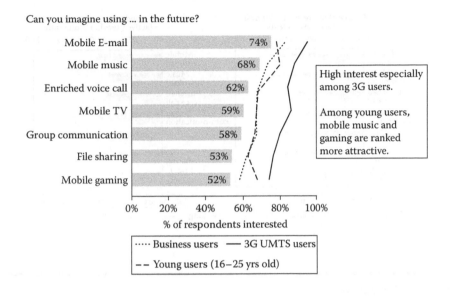

Can you imagine using ... in the future?

b

Figure 6.3 (Continued)

over 5300 mobile communication subscribers in eight countries about innovative wireless applications and their expectations with respect to the content and functionality of these applications (Figure 6.3b). A few trends are clear: mobile music and e-mail access on a mobile handset are among the most popular applications, as shown in Figure 6.3b [8].

Not surprisingly, subscribers to 3G services are significantly more likely to capture and transmit video with their devices than their counterparts on 2G networks (Figure 6.3c). This is reflective of the superior transmission capability of 3G networks and the fact that video capture is a standard feature of 3G devices. Higher consumption of data services is also reflected in a proportionately higher propensity to download ringtones and games. Survey data from the fourth quarter 2005 shows that 3G subscribers are about twice as likely to download a ringtone and between three and four times more likely to download a game [8].

Since the first launch of 3G networks, data services such as multimedia messaging, ringtone and wallpaper downloads, and Web connectivity have flourished in the marketplace. More recently, new services such as location-based services, mobile TV, and mobile commerce, which require high-speed data network capabilities for satisfactory user experience, are also gaining traction in the marketplace. These types of services are now offered by many of the operators with 3G networks. Considering that mobile operators are faced with decreasing average revenue per unit (ARPUs),

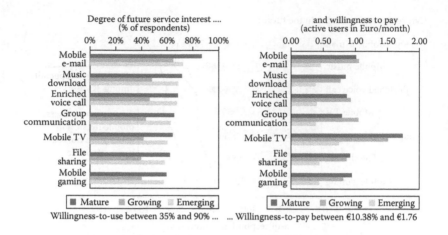

c

Figure 6.3 (Continued)

those new value-added services represent a crucial revenue stream. In fact, data services already represent 20 percent of mobile operators' overall revenues. Maravedis believes that this proportion will continue to grow. However, these new opportunities come with new challenges. Bandwidth-hungry and real-time applications such as VoIP will require the optimization of mobile networks to sustain quality-of-service (QoS) [8]. It is no surprise that WiMAX service providers privilege the performance of the access network when considering equipment from vendors. The following table (Figure 6.3d) summarizes the results of a survey of WiMAX service providers. Even though these carriers identified lower equipment cost as their top

Highest priority	Better throughput/QoS	Better coverage	Lower equipment cost	Interoperability/ flexibility	Ease of installation
1	33%	0%	47%	13%	13%
2	7%	40%	13%	27%	13%
3	27%	33%	13%	7%	20%
4	20%	20%	27%	20%	7%
5	13%	7%	0%	33%	47%
Total	100%	100%	100%	100%	100%

d

Figure 6.3 (Continued)

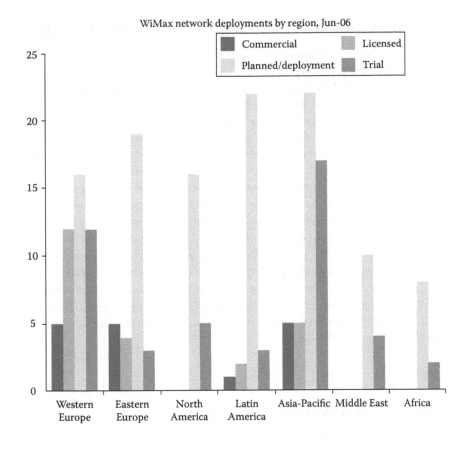

WiMax network deployments by region, Jun-06

Figure 6.3 (Continued)

priority, more throughput and increased coverage were very important selection criteria, more so than interoperability.

Respondents were also asked whether they would offer mobile services if current systems were mobile-capable. Most answered yes, but expressed concerns about their country's regulations as well as additional capital expenditure required. To support mobility would require increased infrastructure. The priority is to offer limited mobility and portability. Operators will need to deploy this infrastructure before offering mobility. There is still a long way to comprehend fully the ever-evolving trends in mobile applications from location-based services to file sharing. According to Maravedis, the WiMAX industry will benefit from the lessons learned from early 3G adopters [8].

Over 200 Operators Planning WiMAX Deployments

Sprint plans to build a nationwide wireless broadband network. Operators around the world have been putting WiMAX technology through its paces for some time. There are more than 200 operators listed in TeleGeography's WiMAX Market Tracking database that are either planning WiMAX rollouts or have already deployed trial or commercial systems (Figure 6.3e) [9]. Announcements of new deployments come almost daily. The aforementioned figure highlights that most networks are being planned and tested in the Asia-Pacific region. Africa's adoption of the technology has been improving, with numerous networks planned as a result of deregulations and the prioritization of the telecom sector, which has opened the door to competition, investment, and the hope for low-cost advantages promised by WiMAX. Spectrum availability will obviously play a key role in the spread of WiMAX technology. Moving forward, operators worldwide will be looking for regulators to help clear the way for WiMAX by ensuring that sufficient spectrum is offered, and at frequencies that support the development of global roaming. According to consultant Senza Fili, there will be 15.4 million WiMAX subscribers in 2010, 41 percent of whom will be based in the Asia-Pacific region. The consultant said the region's demand for portable and mobile services will spur the uptake of the mobile flavor of WiMAX.

Service Providers' Challenges and Expectations Regarding Fixed WiMAX

WiMAX and cellular broadband provide a pathway to "personal broadband." WiMAX ushers in the opportunity for DSL, cable, and cellular operators to provide a single, extensible IP/SIP platform for delivery of wireless communications that include triple-play IPTV, Internet access, and VoIP phone service. As WiMAX evolves to full 4G mobility, it will be capable of providing a full set of services when combined with local area DSL, cable, or fiber optics. WiMAX is the first major effort to develop a framework for the long-term evolution of 4G technologies. WiMAX operators providing DSL replacement will face the same challenges as current ISPs providing broadband Internet access. WiMAX must offer a tier of services to satisfy multiple classes of users [10]. WiMAX continues to be one of the most talked about and highly anticipated technology developments in the wireless industry [13,14] — a sector that has seen more than its share of well-hyped initiatives in recent years. In terms of hype cycles, WiMAX may actually be eclipsing some of the industry's earlier "savior" technologies, primarily because it is viewed as a linchpin for the future convergence of wireless and wireline networks, in addition to promising advancement for broadband wireless services and applications [11].

Mass Adoption of WiMAX Is Possible in Developing Countries with Minimal Infrastructure

WiMAX is likely to become popular in geographical pockets as it offers significant benefits to developing countries with poor existing infrastructure. However, success of this technology in the developed world depends on a number of factors. From the time of the invention of the radio, the future of technology has been wireless. The benefit of eliminating wires has led to the development of radio, satellite communication, cell phones, and, eventually, Wi-Fi. This commoditization was responsible for the wide adoption of the technology, leading to cheaper products and a rise in usage. WiMAX received a boost when Intel began marketing it in full swing in early 2004. Looking to cover entire cities with Wi-Fi, Intel decided to install a large number of access points, but the general consensus was that management of these access points would be a difficult task. Internet access had to evolve as a carrier technology and the company started working on unlicensed spectrums. By mid-2006, Intel was widely promoting the WiMAX Forum and was making strategic investments in companies that had the potential to become market leaders in this segment through its venture capital division. Despite the hype, WiMAX products have just recently entered the market. The mobile version went on the market in 2007, when the first products were certified. The deployment of equipment must be initiated for WiMAX to get the momentum. This is important to bring the cost point lower and help it compete with other technologies. Companies have invested heavily in competing technologies, as they have an interest in seeing these technologies succeed. Competition with other technologies is an inhibiting factor. WiMAX at the moment has some advantages over these technologies, but not in all areas. The mass media often refers to WiMAX as the next generation of Wi-Fi, but the real question is whether WiMAX will replace Wi-Fi as a preferred access medium. The short answer is no. The two technologies will coexist. WiMAX is likely to succeed as a technology because it has a standard, which means lower prices, more competition, and the ability to take over the market. In addition, the developments in Asia-Pacific related to the economy and booming industries are likely to increase demand for this technology.

WiMAX is changing the way operators approach their broadband network strategies, and is opening up opportunities for equipment manufacturers to work together to develop innovative and profitable solutions [15]. The international market research group (http://www.imriresearch.com./) also forecast that the worldwide WiMAX equipment market would continue to expand rapidly, with a five-year compound annual growth rate (CAGR) of about 139 percent between 2005 and 2009, when it thinks the market can reach $1.6 billion. Siemens said its WayMAX@vantage product line, which consists of a base station, modems, and routers, has passed the WiMAX Forum testing. Infonetics Research says that, from an almost nonexistent market in 2004, worldwide WiMAX revenue surged 759 percent in 2005, hitting $142.3 million.

Wi-Fi–WiMAX Mesh Solution Benefits

Cost-effective wireless mesh networks answer the growing demand for ubiquitous Internet access for both urban and rural environments. Operators can quickly install mesh access points from street lights, power poles, or other public infrastructure to generate immediate revenue from both WiMAX and Wi-Fi customers.

NextWeb and QRA Survey Pre-WiMAX Service Users: Customers Indicate Solid Approval of Fixed Wireless Service

NextWeb, California's largest fixed-wireless ISP for business, and Quality Resource Associates (QRA) Inc., a leader in primary market research, studied customer attitudes regarding pre-WiMAX business Internet service. Over 85 percent of customers who responded to the survey indicated that fixed wireless broadband service is at least as good (33 percent), and for many, better (49 percent), than their previous (usually DSL or wireline T1) service, indicating the broad market appeal of this emerging alternative to wireline Internet service. Nearly half (48 percent) of those surveyed said they were "familiar" with the emerging WiMAX standard. NextWeb has been a member of the WiMAX Forum since late 2004, and is actively implementing pre-WiMAX technology in its carrier-class fixed wireless broadband network.

Other findings include the following:

- Almost half (47 percent) of the customers surveyed said they chose the fixed wireless broadband solution because it would save their companies money. This demonstrates that the value proposition for fixed wireless — cost savings, quicker installation, and better support — is well understood by business Internet customers.
- A majority (60 percent) of customers said they considered the NextWeb service as a direct alternative to wireline Internet service, such as T1, and 65 percent said they had T1 or some type of broadband service prior to NextWeb. Far from simply using wireless as a backup, many businesses now trust fixed wireless as their primary Internet connection.
- Regarding VoIP, a significant percentage of customers (44 percent) say they are planning to implement VoIP, with over 60 percent of those planning to implement in six months or less.

WiMAX Future in Balance, Claims Report from OECD

In a wide-ranging report, the Organisation for Economic Cooperation and Development (OECD), an international trade body, has highlighted spectrum, regulatory, industry, and security issues that may hinder the take up of the next-generation broadband wireless network [116]. The OECD said much of the wireless technology's success depended on spectrum availability and allocation. The report also highlighted that WiMAX could raise serious privacy and security concerns by enabling wireless surveillance over long distances without consent, as well as public safety issues. The report has been seen as a blow to supporters of WiMAX, which has been talked of as the next step up from Wi-Fi and 3G mobile networks.

Muni Wi-Fi/WiMAX Great for Gaming

As more and more cities have Wi-Fi and/or WiMAX clouds deployed, more people will be able to access the Internet at broadband speeds for low or no cost. The upcoming ubiquity of wireless broadband access will usher in an era of 80 percent and 90 percent Xbox Live, Nintendo Wi-Fi, and PlayStation 3 Hub connect ratios.

Game developers who had been ignoring online functionality will rush to add it. Those who have been doing it for years will be sitting pretty in the leadership position.

Companies that provide services which require broadband access will also benefit. Massive Inc. will be able to place ads more effortlessly into a greater number of games, for instance. Newly connected gamers will be able to download Nintendo's back-catalog of games. Software that enables tethering of multiple broadband connections will make the digital distribution channel viable for multi-GB downloads, improving the viability of the digital distribution business model.

World of Warcraft Will Break 20 Million Subscribers

Some negative side-effects will result as well. The nation will need to learn to cope with an outbreak of massively multiplayer online game (MMOG) addiction as unsophisticated gamers learn to cope with this particularly addictive style of game. Viruses will leap from PSP to PSP or even from PSP to Nintendo DS, bricking everything in their wake. Parents will fail to keep up with the speed of technology and will (as always) underparent, exposing their children to sexual predators who will use the new networks in sophisticated ways. And gamers who have heretofore been big fish in small ponds will learn what true competition is like. Tens of millions of new gamers will be competing for the same leaderboard spots currently vied for by mere hundreds of thousands of gamers. The impacts of these networks will extend far beyond gaming, of course. Still, gamers are in for a wild ride.

Asia-Pacific to Represent Majority of WiMAX Market

Although WiMAX faces several key challenges in the Asia-Pacific market, its subscriber base will grow from more than 80,000 in 2005 to more than 3.8 million by 2009, reports In-Stat [54]. In 2009, Asia-Pacific WiMAX subscribers will account for 45 percent of the world total, the high-tech market research firm says. Issues that may hamper the adoption of WiMAX networks in the region include spectrum regulation that varies significantly across countries and competition on mobility from other technologies, said In-Stat.

In-Stat also found the following:

- South Korea is estimated to contribute more than 40 percent of the regional WiMAX equipment revenue in 2009, followed by China with 34 percent and Japan with 17 percent.
- South Korea will also boast the highest WiMAX service revenue in 2009, because of its sophisticated broadband content/application industry, which results in higher ARPU.
- By 2009, Asia-Pacific WiMAX equipment spending will account for $1,988.2 million.

Also, according to In-Stat, WiMAX has excellent prospects for expanding the market for fixed, portable, and mobile broadband access. WiMAX's advantages in cost, flexibility, and portability will also allow its providers to take market share from operators using proprietary wireless or wireline technologies, the market research firm found.

A recent In-Stat report suggested that the aggressive forecast relies on subscriber units, currently about $500, falling to less than $100 by 2010. Although traction in the 802.16-2004 market will be important, the real success of WiMAX will depend on the much larger 802.16e market, said the research firm. In addition, 802.16e offers new and existing mobile operators performance and economical improvements over existing 3G technologies, especially in its ability to deliver ARPU-attractive, multimedia services, according to the In-Stat report.

WiMAX Said to Complement Wi-Fi, 3G

Both fixed and mobile WiMAX will complement, not compete with Wi-Fi and 3G cellular data, according to a study by market research firm Forward Concepts. According to the study, fixed 802.16d systems can provide backbones for Wi-Fi hot spots where DSL or cable is unavailable or impractical. When emerging 802.16e provides a mobility WiMAX capability, it will augment the Wi-Fi infrastructure, which will remain dominant for several years.

WiMAX Market Opportunity

Based on its ability to reduce costs and increase efficiency within the enterprise environment, analysts forecast significant growth for the WiMAX standard. According to Visant Strategies, the number of worldwide WiMAX users is expected to grow from virtually nothing in 2005 to 14.9 million users in 2009, creating over $13.8 billion in service revenues from this segment. According to this study, WiMAX will gain a major share of the broadband wireless access market by 2009 because of the wide support it has obtained from leading equipment vendors.

WiMAX Vendors Look to Mobility

WiMAX equipment and component makers have made steady progress on fixed wireless broadband products but look eagerly to a future mobile WiMAX. Industry participants gathered at the Wireless Communications Alliance's WCA International Symposium and Business Expo in San Jose, California to discuss this subject.

WiMAX Important to Cellular Operators

Both fixed and mobile WiMAX will be important to cellular operators to help them relieve congestion from their cellular data networks and to prepare for data technologies beyond 3G, a study by ABI Research claims. The study noted that mobile WiMAX will eventually form part of cellular providers' networks, alleviating network congestion in urban areas. Providers will use it to offload part of the data traffic. At the same time, WiMAX is becoming a stepping-stone to 4G mobile services, which will be based on related technologies, the study said.

WiMAX to Be Used by 7 Million in 2009

U.S.-based research firm Parks Associates has said that the number of people using the wireless standard will grow. It is expected that industry will then back the technology, and will begin to look more closely at developing hardware for deployment.

Survey Reveals Predictions for Breakthrough WiMAX Applications and Keys to Adoption

As interest continues to build for WiMAX, industry participants report that interoperability and last-mile data connectivity will be leading factors in accelerating the technology's widespread adoption. In a survey conducted by Motorola Inc. and Trendsmedia, 45 percent of respondents predict that the ability to achieve seamless mobility through interoperability among various devices and networks will be the "tipping point" to WiMAX success. Motorola and Trendsmedia conducted the survey with attendees from WiMAX World.

WiMAX Fever Intensifies

WiMAX is one of the fastest-growing emerging sectors within the world's telecom industry, with the global market potential estimated to be worth up to $1 billion in 2007 and $4 billion by 2010, according to recent research from analyst firm Maravedis. Motorola has been gearing up for a WiMAX offensive on a global scale, as it is expected that interoperability and last-mile data connectivity will be leading factors in accelerating the technology's widespread adoption. Motorola announced an alliance with chip giant Intel to advance the use of mobile WiMAX and also unveiled its MOTOwi4 product line of fixed and mobile broadband infrastructure.

WiMAX Spectrum More Economical than 3G

The price paid per hertz for WiMAX spectrum is as much as 1000 times lower than for 3G spectrum, according to another report from Maravedis titled "Spectrum Analysis — The Critical Factor in WiMAX versus 3G." This white paper provides an in-depth review of the economics of spectrum for both 3G and WiMAX around the world. The low cost of BWA/WiMAX spectrum compared to 3G is a clear driver for service providers to enter the field of wireless services with WiMAX. The much lower cost of WiMAX/BWA spectrum has resulted in a high number of licensees, with a total of 721 license holders being awarded for BWA/WiMAX against 106 licensees for 3G, according to the report.

Maravedis' latest research also revealed that, unlike 3G licenses, the BWA/WiMAX licenses awarded across the world are essentially regional licenses. North America is a perfect example of a situation where 100 percent of its WiMAX/BWA licenses are regional. In Europe and the CALA region, the proportions are 78 and 71 percent, respectively. The report also suggests that most regulators have not kept pace with the progress of technology that makes fixed–mobile convergence a reality. Whether it is fixed applications with CDMA technology or mobile applications with WiMAX, the two fields are converging and will be competing for a share of the one billion mobile subscribers market.

New Products and Key Deployments Accelerating WiMAX Growth

By 2010 the worldwide WiMAX market is forecast to reach $3.5 billion, when it will account for 4 percent of all broadband usage. This growth will be driven by new equipment from a growing list of hardware suppliers and an increasing number of WiMAX trials and deployments. These are some of the key findings from a new research report: "WiMAX: Ready for Deployment?" published by IDATE, a research, consulting, and education firm specializing in wireless communications. This new report provides a comprehensive analysis of the current state and future prospects of the market built around WiMAX technology. Other key findings include the following:

- WiMAX has attracted many leading equipment manufacturers and component suppliers. Many are also forming strategic partnerships. Alcatel and Intel have implemented a dedicated WiMAX program. Nokia, which views WiMAX as a complement to 3G, has partnered with Intel to incorporate WiMAX into future handsets. Other key suppliers include Airspan Networks, Alvarion, Aperto Networks, Fujitsu, Motorola, Navini, Nortel, Proxim, Redline Communications, Sequans, SR Telecom, Wavesat Wireless, and Wi-LAN.
- WiMAX systems and services are being evaluated/deployed in suburban business districts that lack high-quality DSL access; in urban markets to compete against DSL and broadband cable; by wireline carriers and ISPs to compete with integrated operators' converged fixed-mobile offers; and by mobile carriers to overcome 3G network saturation and transition to 4G. These service providers include Altitude Telecom, AT&T, BT, Clearwire, France Telecom, Iberbanda, Korea Telecom, Monaco Telecom, Telekom Austria, TelstraClear, Towerstream, Verizon, and Yozan.
- On a worldwide basis, WiMAX systems can be deployed in a large number of licensed and unlicensed frequency bands. However, delays in allocations and licensing by regulatory agencies, coupled with a lack of a common worldwide frequency band for WiMAX use, may slow market development.

WiMAX Opens Range of Design Options

Analysts agree that standardization under the WiMAX banner — providing equipment vendors with a unified front and access to off-the-shelf silicon — will prove important in driving the fixed wireless market forward. As a brand, WiMAX promises to do for last-mile broadband Internet access what Wi-Fi did for WLANs. But there are important differences between the two, primarily, the necessity for WiMAX equipment builders to use flexible architectures to maximize their potential market without having to create multiple incompatible designs.

The Future Is Bright for Mobile WiMAX

Mobile WiMAX might be better than the rest, but it faces a mighty climb in Europe, according to a report. Mobile WiMAX wireless broadband technology, working under the IEEE standard 802.16e, offers Wi-Fi bandwidth with a cellular range. The 802.16e standard's supporters are pitching the technology's supremacy over other cellular broadband technologies, with issues like lower latency, more bandwidth, and a large vendor support base, but time to market is really the issue here, according to IDC EMEA Emerging Technologies Research.

Wireless Data's Future? 3G, Wi-Fi, WiMAX Combo

With wireless service providers and equipment manufacturers attempting to sort out the future course of mobile broadband data, some say the "right combination of 3G, WiMAX, and Wi-Fi" will be needed to achieve the most success. WiMAX will have an important role to fill as the move to wireless multimedia grows, according to Rysavy Research and Datacomm Research Company. According to the report, WiMAX can succeed, but only if vendors execute their plans perfectly. In mobile markets, WiMAX operators must employ low-cost, high-density base station architectures to deliver superior capacity and in-building penetration. Also, CDMA wireless technologies will dominate mobile technology for the next several years, but these 3G systems still will not be able to meet the demand. With two billion wireless subscribers already active, Rysavy noted that no single network technology can solve all market needs. Thus, pressure will build to implement additional solutions, including Wi-Fi and WiMAX. The two latter technologies, however, are often not embraced by traditional service providers. The only way to support more broadband users is to offload multimedia traffic onto mobile broadcast networks and to employ more densely deployed wireless networks, whether they be 3G, WiMAX, or Wi-Fi, the report stated.

WiMAX Poised for Global Domination

WiMAX is threatening to replace GSM and even W-CDMA as the most interesting wireless communications technology for semiconductor companies. The importance of the wireless broadband access technology to chip suppliers is increasing as new GSM mobile phone deployments start to decline and W-CDMA shows only a steady rollout, according to speakers at the IEEE MTT-S International Microwave Symposium in San Francisco.

WiMAX — the Catalyst for Broadband Wireless Access in Asia-Pacific

New analysis from global growth consulting company Frost & Sullivan, "WiMAX Growth Opportunities in Asia-Pacific," reveals that revenue in the WiMAX services market — covering 12 major Asia-Pacific economies — is forecast to total

$165.3 million by the end of 2006 and could reach $5.4 billion in 2010. The increased activities surrounding BWA spectrum allocation in Asia-Pacific in 2005 and 2006 have brought about the resurgence of WiMAX. The low broadband subscriber penetration and teledensity in the region are major drivers in the deployment of WiMAX. In comparison to Europe and North America, the Asia-Pacific region is expected to be a more suitable test bed for WiMAX, given the lack of telecommunications infrastructure, low broadband penetration, and geographically dispersed population.

Unlike the trends that are sweeping across the global cellular market, cellular subscriber growth in the Asia-Pacific region is poised to see continued double-digit growth in the next three years, according to Frost and Sullivan. Given the markets' infancy and the vast population base, India and Indonesia are likely to fuel a significant portion of the growth. The implementation of "lifetime validity" in India, as well as the ongoing network expansion into rural areas in developing cellular markets, will further help sustain the mobile industry's high growth in the region. Although the growing popularity of prepaid services has been a major driver of subscriber growth in the region, the influence of the low-end market is likely to be more pronounced in the coming years. Factors contributing to the growth of the low-end market include the launch of low-cost entry-level mobile handsets, the move into rural areas for long-term sustainable growth, the continuous price cuts in call rates, and the introduction of affordable flat-rate pricing plans.

WiMAX Equipment Sales Up 48 Percent in 1Q 2006

Although relatively small, the WiMAX equipment market surged in the first quarter of 2006, with revenue jumping 48 percent, to $68.3 million, according to Infonetics Research's quarterly WiMAX and Outdoor Mesh Network Equipment report. Annual revenue is forecast to reach $1.7 billion by 2009 [1]. The increases are mostly because of mounting shipments of WiMAX CPE units, indicating that service providers with WiMAX networks are driving subscriber growth. Surges in the WiMAX market are forecast to continue as WiMAX evolves from a fixed-only solution to both fixed and mobile solutions.

1Q 2006 highlights [1]:

- About 62 percent of total WiMAX revenue comes from CPE, 38 percent from base stations; by 2009, this shifts to 79 and 21 percent, respectively.
- Worldwide outdoor wireless mesh access node revenue increased 22 percent to $46 million, and unit shipments increased 25 percent.
- About 30 percent of WiMAX equipment comes from EMEA, 26 percent from North America, 26 percent from Asia-Pacific, and 18 percent from CALA; deployments in EMEA are mostly in Eastern Europe, Africa, and the Middle East, indicating that the strong early market for WiMAX is in developing countries.

Fixed WiMAX to Shrink

A report from Juniper Research predicts that the number of fixed WiMAX subscribers will grow from 1.3 million in 2006 to 8.5 million in 2011. However, the advent of certified mobile WiMAX equipment in 2007 will lead to many subscribers adopting mobile WiMAX instead of fixed WiMAX. Fixed WiMAX is expected to primarily serve as a last-mile connection for fixed wireless broadband access to homes and businesses. There are also plans for it to be used as a backhaul solution for cellular, Wi-Fi mesh, and Wi-Fi hot spot networks. The initial growth for fixed WiMAX is expected to occur largely in developed regions because of the high number of pre-fixed WiMAX installations. But in due course countries/regions in the "developing world" like China, India, and South America will see a larger growth owing to low broadband penetration levels, as per the prediction. Mobile WiMAX will complement rather than compete with 3G mobile services, however. Operators' billion dollar 3G investments will not be affected by mobile WiMAX. Instead, they will use mobile WiMAX as either a filler or complementary network to existing 3G provision. Mobile WiMAX will also see large adoption in fixed wireless services initially, and so will affect fixed WiMAX take up. Unlike 3G, which has a large voice component, mobile WiMAX will be primarily data driven, according to Juniper Research.

WiMAX Gains Momentum, Competes with DSL

For a technology that has established itself in broadband communications, WiMAX is positioned on the forefront of the competition, says a report from TelecomView. According to TelecomView, the WiMAX network market is expected to gain 88 million subscribers, accounting "for $43 billion in system spending by 2011." According to the study, business cases show that WiMAX will be competitive with fixed DSL services where copper loops are in place. However, WiMAX is the only choice where copper is not available. According to the release, the report also finds that up to a quarter of the subscribers in this forecast will be using a converged service that combines fixed and mobile WiMAX by 2011.

TelecomView study also predicts WiMAX to be significant in the mobile market. WiMAX will become an important tool of mobile carriers for providing high-speed wireless services. The new, emerging carriers will use WiMAX as their base technology for voice and high-speed data services, whereas many established carriers will use it to provide higher-speed services and to lower their costs. TelecomView's new report, "Broadband Strategies for the Mobile Market," analyzes the market for WiMAX in mobile networks with forecasts through 2011, along with a business case that illustrates the benefits of a WiMAX architecture in high-speed mobile networks.

Study: WiMAX to Control Broadband Wireless

A new study from Senza Fili says WiMAX soon will dominate the fixed broadband wireless market, but its future in mobile is not as clear. In its report, titled "Fixed or Mobile WiMAX? Forecasts and assessment for the transition from 802.16-2004 to 802.16e WiMAX," Senza Fili says 802.16e — the version of WiMAX that supports mobile access — will be the clear winner over 802.16-2004, which only supports fixed services. The former's performance meets the requirements of both fixed and mobile service providers and creates the economies of scale needed to drive equipment prices down. Even though it will not be available for a year or more after 802.16-2004, the report predicts that nearly 60 percent of WiMAX subscribers will be using 802.16e by 2010.

However, the report also suggests that mobile operators with 3G networks will not be the first to adopt WiMAX. New and established service providers that are eager to enter the mobility and portability market but do not have cellular spectrum will drive WiMAX adoption, the report said. By 2010, there will be 15.4 million WiMAX subscribers worldwide, generating $16.5 billion in service revenues, the researchers predict.

Asia-Pacific to Hold 44 Percent of WiMAX Market by 2009

As per the latest market research report "WiMAX Market Forecast (2006–2010)" by RNCOS, the subscriber base in the Asia-Pacific region is expected to cross the 80,000 mark in 2005 and swell to over 3.78 million subscribers through 2009. WiMAX subscribers in the Asia-Pacific region would constitute 44 percent of the worldwide subscribers by 2009. The implementation of WiMAX networks may be hindered by the regional variations in spectrum regulations and competition from other new emerging mobile technologies. According to the report, South Korea is expected to provide the highest regional WiMAX equipment income of 41 percent in 2009, followed by China at 33 percent and Japan at a mere 18 percent. High ARPU, resulting from a large subscriber base developed by competitive wireless service providers will assign the highest WiMAX service revenue to South Korea in 2009.

WiMAX Gets Real

WiMAX is well on its way, according to a report from ABI Research. The firm noted that with the announcement from the WiMAX Forum that some companies' equipment has successfully passed the "first wave" of WiMAX certification for 802.16-2004, WiMAX is finally starting to get real. Aperto Networks' PacketMAX

5000 base station, Redline Communications' RedMAX AN-100U base station, SEQUANS Communications' SQN2010 SoC base station solution, and Wavesat's miniMAX CPE solution are all now certified as first-wave approved. There is a long queue of companies waiting to undergo the same certification process. Then, they can proceed to "wave two," covering security and QoS, and when they too are certified, we can expect to see larger numbers of products actually reaching the market, according to ABI Research. At that stage, the firm said, the market will begin to widen, and real interest will emerge from wireless ISPs in deploying certified fixed WiMAX solutions, rather than the proprietary systems that have been available for some time. In fact, ABI Research noted that several initial deployments of pre-WiMAX networks are under way across the globe, including a growing number from Latin America.

Schools Give WiMAX and Wi-Fi Top Marks

Schools are turning to wireless networks — especially WiMAX — as a more cost-effective way of providing Internet access to more locations. As a result, global spending on mobile and wireless by education authorities will rise from $827 million last year to a healthy $6.5 billion by 2010, according to predictions from Juniper Research. This figure includes the spending on handheld and portable wireless devices, hardware, software, and services. The research house said independent wireless networks capable of interoperating with 2G and 3G systems are "central to the mobile future of education." Wi-Fi has been widely used for the past four years by major educational institutions for wireless broadband campus networks, and the greater power of WiMAX will make it attractive as well. Spending on mobile and wireless software will reach $987 million in 2010, and hardware spending will reach $825 million, according to the prediction. Portable and handheld devices will form the largest component of overall expenditure on mobile and wireless systems in education — sales of more than 12 million units will generate revenues of $2.756 billion by 2010, the research company estimates.

WiMAX Chipset Market Faces Much Uncertainty, Says In-Stat

WiMAX technology promises to satisfy a strong demand for mobile broadband, but competing technologies are significant threats, reports In-Stat. Despite much uncertainty in this market, the market research firm foresees the value of the WiMAX chipset market could reach as high as $950 million by 2009 (Figure 6.4). A report by In-Stat found that the WiMAX chipset market has a relatively small number of players, despite the tremendous hype around WiMAX. Intel and Fujitsu launched WiMAX PHY and MAC system-on-a-chip (SoC) solutions, along with

Geographic breakdown: WiMAX chipset revenue forecast (US$ m)		
Region	2005(e)	2009(f)
North America	2.76	227.45
EMEA	3.53	208.49
Asia Pacific	2.76	398.03
CALA	2.10	113.72

Figure 6.4   WiMAX chipset revenue forecast. (Courtesy of In-Stat.)

start-ups Sequans and Wavesat, the research firm indicated. Signal processing specialist picoChip also powered the market for macro base-station chipsets with its software reference designs, the research firm added.

Report Says Telecoms Are Primed for Major Rollouts of WiMAX

Telecom network operators are convinced that WiMAX will have a positive impact on their ability to deliver new services, and most expect to see deployment of WiMAX in commercial networks by the end of 2007, according to results of a worldwide survey of service provider professionals conducted by Heavy Reading, Light Reading Inc.'s market research division. "Service Provider WiMAX Deployment Plans," the latest report from Heavy Reading, presents full results and analysis of an invitation-only survey gauging not only service provider perceptions of WiMAX, but also their plans to incorporate the new broadband wireless technology into their own networks. A total of 262 service provider professionals, representing more than 175 different network operators worldwide, participated in the survey. "Service provider respondents overwhelmingly view WiMAX as a technology that will have at least some impact on the future of telecom networks, and a solid majority expect it to have a major impact," the report states. "Less than 2 percent of the 262 respondents categorized WiMAX as offering 'more hype than hope,' although nearly 60 percent said WiMAX would have a major long-term impact on telecom networks and services. These results clearly show that WiMAX developers have succeeded in making a strong case for their technology, and that service providers are expecting WiMAX to have a place in future network designs."

Positive attitudes toward WiMAX and its role in telecom networks cut across all service provider types. For every type of service provider included in the survey, more than 50 percent of respondents said WiMAX would have a major long-term effect on networks and services. The carrier respondents most bullish about WiMAX's prospects were those from long-distance operators (69.1 percent of whom said WiMAX would have a major long-term impact), Bell companies (68.8 percent), and operators of conventional wireless networks (68.4 percent).

The evaluation process for WiMAX is already well under way, and the next 12 to 18 months will be critical in determining how many carriers make investments in WiMAX and how extensive those investments will be. A majority of respondents say their company is now evaluating WiMAX, and almost all of the rest say their company is likely to take a close look at the technology once it matures — which most expect to occur in the next year and a half. The vast majority of respondents expect to see commercial WiMAX service launched within the next two years. Nearly 40 percent of respondents expect commercial WiMAX service to be available this year, and more than 80 percent anticipate it by the end of 2007. Wireless technologies such as the IEEE WiMAX standard 802.16 could be an appealing option for emerging Latin American wireless markets because it is economical and enjoys wide coverage, according to handset and accessories distributor InfoSonics.

RNCOS Research: WiMAX to Constitute a Major Share of Wireless Broadband Market

WiMAX is all set to hit the fixed access market for the time being, although the basic and full mobility WiMAX is the goal for the year 2010. The kind of enthusiasm that WiMAX has aroused among businesses as well as individuals is not just for the wired version of the technology; wireless WiMAX is where most of the silicon and large-scale equipment makers seem to be more interested in investing. Setting up a broadband connection through DSL includes heavy installation charges. WiMAX, on the other hand, is a comparatively less expensive alternative to DSL, as it does not require any modem or cables to get a WiMAX connection. The maintenance cost is also reduced with a WiMAX connection.

According to the market research report titled "WiMAX Market Forecast (2006–2010)," published by RNCOS, it is predicted that "WiMAX and other emerging high-speed wireless technologies will capture more than 42 percent of the wireless broadband business over the next few years, whereas 3G will have to content with less than 59 percent of the market in 2009." The report covers every significant aspect of WiMAX technology such as the latest WiMAX market trends, the standards followed, the spectrum allocations, and its functioning and implementation, etc. The report also covers various benefits of WiMAX technology such as performance, coverage, and so on. Discussing the future market scope for WiMAX, the report estimates that "The comparatively better performance and flexibility of WiMAX will enable this technology to take over the high-speed wireless segment in the next 3 years. Though 3G will be important for its mobility, WiMAX will directly compete with DSL." The report suggests that approximately half of the world consumer market will be captured by the wireless networking standard 802.11n in the next 2 to 3 years. According to the report, WiMAX will be the most popular standard in the coming years.

Wi-Fi to Hold Its Own against WiMAX "Past 2009"

WiMAX's popularity will explode over the next three years, according to Infonetics, but it is not going to come close to Wi-Fi for a while. Revenues from WiMAX equipment are set for impressive growth, analysts report, but will continue to lag behind those from Wi-Fi. Research company Infonetics predicts WiMAX will reach revenues of $142 million (£81.7 million) this year, shooting up to $1.6 billion by 2009.

Although the milestone is an important one for long-range broadband technology, revenues from WiMAX pale in comparison to those from Wi-Fi, which jumped 10 percent year on year to reach $2.4 billion. Infonetics expects the Wi-Fi market to be worth $3.9 billion before the end of the decade, largely driven by the enterprise segment, which will see a 120 percent jump in revenue between 2005 and 2009.

Mobile WiMAX Adoption Will Lag behind Fixed

WiMAX, although ready to emerge strong in the broadband wireless market, may struggle to take hold in the mobile space, according to a report by Senza Fili Consulting. Despite the struggle of mobile WiMAX, the report predicts that the adoption of the new version of WiMAX that supports mobile and fixed access — 802.16e — will start to overtake adoption of 802.16-2004, which only supports fixed services.

WiMAX Equipment Tops $142 Million in 2005, Surging to $1.6 Billion in 2009

From an almost nonexistent market in 2004, worldwide WiMAX equipment revenue surged 759 percent in 2005, hitting $142.3 million, according to Infonetics Research's quarterly WiMAX and Outdoor Mesh Network Equipment report.

Infonetics forecasts that the worldwide WiMAX equipment market will continue expanding rapidly, with a five-year unit CAGR of 139 percent between 2005 and 2009, when the market will reach $1.6 billion.

Outdoor wireless mesh access nodes, currently used primarily by municipal authorities to provide broadband coverage, represent a modest but rapidly growing wireless segment, totaling just under $110 million in 2005 (up 1114 percent from 2004).

Market Highlights

■ For the quarter, WiMAX revenue topped $46 million in 4Q 2005 and units reached 33,000, boosted by certification of WiMAX products late in the year.

- In 4Q 2005, 47 percent of total WiMAX revenue was from base stations and 53 percent from CPE.
- In 2005, 42 percent of WiMAX equipment was from North America, 30 percent from EMEA, 24 percent from Asia-Pacific, and 4 percent from CALA; North America has been the pioneering region for WiMAX deployment; strong growth is expected in Asia-Pacific in coming years.

Mobile and Fixed WiMAX to Overshadow Fixed-only 802.16-2004 WiMAX by 2010

WiMAX will quickly dominate the fixed broadband wireless market, but its success in the mobile arena will be slower and more difficult to achieve, according to "Fixed or Mobile WiMAX? Forecasts and Assessment for the Transition from 802.16-2004 to 802.16e WiMAX," according to Senza Fili Consulting. Despite this, 802.16e — the version of WiMAX that supports mobile access — will be the clear winner over 802.16-2004, which only supports fixed services. Its superior performance meets the requirements of both fixed and mobile service providers and creates the economies of scale needed to drive equipment prices down. Even though it will not be available for a year or more after 802.16-2004, 57 percent of WiMAX subscribers will be using 802.16e by 2010.

WiMAX offers both fixed and mobile access over the same infrastructure, opening the way for a new personal broadband service that gives users continuous broadband Internet access at home, at work, and while they are on the move. By 2010, there will be 15.4 million WiMAX subscribers worldwide, generating $16.5 billion in service revenues. In 2010, 41 percent of subscribers will be in Asia-Pacific countries. WiMAX's success will depend on the availability of 802.16e WiMAX-Certified products in 2007 and on a substantial price reduction for portable and mobile subscriber units, which Senza Fili Consulting forecast to decline to the $140 to $190 billion range by 2010.

Over 750,000 BWA/WiMAX Subscribers in Brazil by 2010 — Report

There will be 768,000 accumulated BWA/WIMAX subscribers in Brazil by 2010, of whom two-thirds will be using WiMAX, according to the latest report from leading research firm Maravedis. The Brazilian players anxiously awaited the new 3.5-GHz auction that started in 2006. Bidders either expanded their current coverage areas or entered the WiMAX arena. Moreover, positive regulatory changes in the 2.5-GHz band opened the WiMAX market starting in 2007.

Maravedis predicts that the most active players will be companies with deep pockets such as Telemar, Brazil Telecom, Embratel, and Telefonica, which are thoroughly testing the technology and crafting their business plans. Maravedis' latest research also reveals that Brazil remains a very price-sensitive market. Demand for broadband services is exploding, but both service providers and residential end users demand very-low-cost CPE (in the $100 range) before they will fully adopt WiMAX. So far, the demand for broadband wireless services has been mainly driven by high-end corporate and government users.

New Developments Boost WiMAX Growth

Despite regulatory hurdles and the absence of a common worldwide frequency band, the WiMAX market is expected to hit $3.5 billion by 2010 and account for 4 percent of overall broadband usage. According to Alexander Resources, market growth will be fueled by developments on the supply side as equipment manufacturers and component suppliers form strategic partnerships with each other and even establish dedicated WiMAX programs. Also, the lack of high-quality DSL access in some suburban business districts will encourage WiMAX deployment. Even in urban areas, the technology is expected to compete with DSL and broadband cable.

BT — WiMAX to Go Rural FIRST

BT has hinted that broadband wireless WiMAX technology may get its first U.K. deployment through rural areas instead of urban ones. The news follows successful trials, although not without some problems: BT's researchers took WiMAX to four remote locations in the United Kingdom to test it in the most severe weather conditions over the most testing terrain. Seventy-three percent of wireless broadband users in rural areas expressed "extreme satisfaction" with the service.

WiMAX Subscribers to Reach 13 Million in India by 2012

There will be 13 million WiMAX subscribers in India by 2012, according to Maravedis Research and Tonse Telecom, which partnered to produce a new research report entitled "India Broadband Wireless and WiMAX Market Analysis and Forecasts 2006–2012." The Indian telecom sector operates in a volume-driven market. If WiMAX is to succeed, it will only be on the premise of huge volumes and not small deployments, the report said [16].

Report: Equipment Units Falling behind WiMAX Growth

In spite of the potential of WiMAX, Strategy Analytics urged caution that equipment shipments are not likely to reach tens of millions of units a year until after 2010 [17]. The report was underscored by a second-quarter earnings announcement from Alvarion Ltd., which has shipped the most WiMAX gear to date. During the company's second quarter, which ended June 30, 2006, Alvarion said its WiMAX solutions sales reached $17 million. Alvarion's CPE is based on Intel's Rosedale chip. The company said it has more than 100 active WiMAX trials under way.

Broadband Internet Access Market Expanding

Analysts predicted a 60 percent rise in the wireless broadband Internet access market in 2006 compared to 2005, stating that the market would reach $80 million, a survey by iKS-Consulting showed [18]. Industry observers agreed that the wireless broadband market would expand its share of the Internet market by almost one percentage point to 6 percent in 2006, and would continue its growth into 2007 and 2008. Also, a rise is forecast for pre-WiMAX and WiMAX wireless broadband Internet networks. As of mid-2006, pre-WiMAX and WiMAX technology covered only 5 percent of the wireless broadband access market. However, its share rocketed, and hit 20 percent of the total broadband Internet market in Russia in 2007, and is expected to be dominating the market by 2009 or 2010.

Russian Wireless Broadband Market Up 61 Percent Since January

The Russian wireless broadband market saw a 61 percent increase in the first half of 2006, reports Cellular News, quoting market research firm iKS-Consulting [19]. According to iKS-Consulting, there were 35,000 wireless broadband users as of July 1, 2006, up 8,000 users since January 1, 2006. iKS-Consulting attributes the jump to an increased demand for wireless Internet access, low development of wireline infrastructure, and the emergence of new operators on the market. Wireless broadband made up less than 8 percent of the wireless market and about 5 percent of the entire market. Currently, the wireless broadband technology of choice is Radio-Ethernet, or IEEE 802.11 wireless technology, although the research firm expects WiMAX to become more popular in the upcoming years. Approximately 100,000 households use combined broadband technologies, where providers offer wireless technologies in the "last mile" and wireline technologies in the "last meter."

The stage is now set for major players in the fields of wireless mobile communications, information technology, and media entertainment to challenge for leading roles in next-generation mobile networking (NGMN) converged wireless broadband [20]. The broadband data that comprises the entertainment and information programs, and increasingly richer mobile communications are fundamentally similar — the bytes and packets of data are becoming organized around IP/SIP and differ primarily in bandwidth and degree of quality needed to satisfy the applications, voice, or video entertainment. The overriding requirements drive the use of most effective wireless broadband systems and similar sets of technologies and network delivery methods. WiMAX has developed upon the IEEE 802.16 framework standard for wireless broadband systems based on MIMO-OFDMA and other advanced technologies. Over the past several months, this set of technologies has become recognized as the wireless platform technology for NGMN, or 4G. The overriding motivation for such a shift is the requirement to deliver increasingly higher bandwidths at reasonable cost. Such a shift must deliver a large improvement to justify the cost of starting on a new upgrade path that makes prior generations incompatible and, sometimes, obsolete. The fields of wireless have contributed to each other along their increasingly convergent paths of development. Both tracks have been enabled by the field of high-speed, highly integrated semiconductors, and design capabilities and component developments. The Wi-Fi/WiMAX track has benefited from an open, competitive market and development environment to see rapid sales growth and uptake of new technologies.

IEK: Taiwan WiMAX Industry to Generate NT$110 Billion by 2012

The Industrial Economics and Knowledge Center (IEK) of the government-sponsored Industrial Technology Research Institute (ITRI) estimates that Taiwan's WiMAX industry will generate NT$110 billion ($3.3 billion) by 2012, according to the Chinese-language *Economic Daily News* (EDN). The value of the industry is expected to grow to NT$10 billion in 2009, from NT$850 million in 2006, the paper quoted IEK as saying, adding that companies such as Zyxel, Foxconn Electronics, Accton Technology, and MediaTek have already started investing in the segment [21].

MobiTV Backs WiMAX

On the heels of Sprint [22] Nextel's decision to go with WiMAX as its 4G technology of choice, MobiTV threw its support behind the technology, saying it is committed to offering advanced mobile television and media delivery services over WiMAX networks [23]. As part of its commitment to the technology, MobiTV says it is "investing heavily in research and technology development." The company's overarching goal is to deliver a compelling video user experience that seamlessly blends technologies. MobiTV says it supports a technology-agnostic approach to mobile television. MobiTV inked a content deal with AT&T to deliver its television service over AT&T's Wi-Fi network. It made its support for WiMAX official by announcing plans to use the technology for its new network, using the 2.5-GHz spectrum. Sprint was MobiTV's first mobile television customer in the United States. In addition to Sprint, MobiTV delivers mobile video services to Cingular Wireless and Alltel in the United States; Bell Canada, Rogers, and TELUS in Canada; 3 and Orange in the United Kingdom; and America Movil in Latin America. Earlier in 2006, the company surpassed the 1 million subscriber mark.

Among the applications coming in for testing at the end of 2007 and stated for commercial release in 2008 using WiMAX technology by Sprint and its partners — Motorola, Samsung Electronics in South Korea, and Intel — could be the following [24]:

- Video-on-demand and other video services: Consumers will be able to watch the movies or TV shows they want, where they want, on phones, laptops, or other devices.
- Media sharing: The network is so robust that moms will be able to shoot movies of their kids playing soccer and then e-mail them to friends and family from the sidelines.
- Superfast downloads: Music and video files will be downloaded in seconds rather than minutes.

WiMAX offers broad coverage in metro areas, but also promises affordable coverage in rural areas.

Pushing Past Trials, WiMAX Footprint Grows

WiMAX stands poised to graduate from trial islands of service to a true broadband-access alternative for subscribers [25]. To date, 25 percent of Seoul, South Korea, is covered by an expanding WiBro service. No wonder, then, that Intel Corp. decided to plow $600 million into Clearwire Corp., a WiMAX carrier start-up in the United States. Motorola Inc. has also invested close to $300 million in Clearwire. Such large, high-profile investments "could cause a chain reaction," said ABI Research Inc. The crucial step where investment may prove important is in moving WiMAX from its current backhaul and municipal base to a ubiquitous broadband service capable of interworking with global Internet and cellular networks. To date, carrier exploitation of the existing 802.16d fixed WiMAX technology has largely come in two areas: as a backhaul service for cellular, operating as an alternative to T1 lines or point-to-point fiber links; or in conjunction with Wi-Fi meshes to provide tiered mesh services in larger metropolitan areas. If the optimistic market analyses are correct, WiMAX could nab nine million subscribers worldwide by 2009, not counting infrastructure applications in cellular backhaul. Thanks in part to South Korea's familiarity with WiBro, an early pre-WiMAX service, close to half of those subscribers will be in Asia. The popularity of mobile WiMAX lies in part in the flexibility of implementation. The February 2006 profiles of WiMAX services specify five frequency options: 2.3 to 2.4 GHz, 2.35 to 2.36 GHz, 2.496 to 2.69 GHz, 3.3 to 3.4 GHz, and 3.4 to 3.8 GHz. Many other options at 5 GHz and above are being considered, although most developers are avoiding the microwave ranges specified in 802.16a.

The WiMAX industry is accelerating in the Asia-Pacific region, but technology and business uncertainties remain, reports In-Stat. The total APAC market, including WiMAX CPEs, WiMAX base stations, and WiMAX commercial services, but excluding the non-radio-access part of total WiMAX solutions, was valued at $106.4 million in 2006, and that figure will grow to $4.3 billion in 2011, the high-tech market research firm says. According to another piece of research by Frost and Sullivan, WiMAX has been widely accepted in the region compared to broadband wireless access (BWA) and Wi-Fi. The firm said that while BWA has not been able to make a remarkable progress owing to lack of standardization and poor interoperability, WiMAX on the other hand has generated much interest as the next evolutionary data-voice enabler. The added mobility and greater range that WiMAX offers over its predecessor, Wi-Fi, and its ability to provide greater bandwidth over 3G networks, further strengthen its appeal. Ultimately, the fate of WiMAX is likely to be determined by its correct positioning and strategic mix; either complimentary or complementary to existing technologies. Asia-Pacific is expected to be a more suitable test bed for WiMAX, given the lack of telecommunications infrastructure, low broadband penetration, and geographically widespread population, said Frost and Sullivan. According to In-Stat, trial network deployments are in progress in at least 13 Asia-Pacific countries. Many service providers in developing countries such as India, Thailand, Philippines, and Indonesia have shown great interest in setting up WiMAX networks and extending telecommunication services coverage to underserved places. In-Stat said equipment vendors, including chipset makers, CPE makers, and system solution providers, have to act very quickly to adopt the latest technical specifications and optimize their equipment performance in real environments.

WiMAX Attracts Giants

Global media and Internet companies, including News Corporation and Yahoo, are eyeing WiMAX as a new media alternative to traditional mobile networks and fixed-line broadband [26]. The technology already has the support of pay-TV group Austar and Sydney-based broadband company Unwired. It is also being given close consideration by the Australian Federal Government, which is preparing to hand out $1.1 billion in funds for regional broadband networks that will be eventually used for video services as well as Internet and voice. Close to 70 submissions for the funds were received. Broadband technologies such as WiMAX help satellite-based pay-TV groups such as Austar and Direct TV in the United States — in which News Corp., publisher of *The Australian*, holds an interest — provide the so-called triple-play of video, Internet, and voice services. News Corp. Chief Rupert Murdoch has long toyed with wireless networks and it was reported in the United States this week that he may purchase a stake in the WiMAX group Clearwire. In Japan, the broadband alliance between Softbank and Yahoo also announced a WiMAX trial network. New media groups such as Yahoo, Microsoft, and Google are increasingly moving into access technologies that have traditionally been the purview of telecommunications companies. Now, bigger media groups such as News are exploring the idea. Microsoft and Yahoo recently added Internet-based voice services to their popular messaging service, which between them has more than 30 million users around the world.

WiMAX Cell Phones Edge Closer to Reality

An elaborate antenna technology needed for sending and receiving WiMAX signals has been a big drain on a mobile device's batteries. Although the telecommunications industry has now settled on final specifications for WiMAX, including provisions for power efficiency, manufacturers are still exploring ways to build the energy-efficient chips needed to make consumer WiMAX devices viable. Power-saving chips are paving the way for superbroadband handheld devices. WiMAX-enabled handhelds would be able to access greater bandwidth than traditional cellular networks, allowing faster streaming media and Internet downloads. Moreover, WiMAX phones using VoIP might drop fewer calls and keep working up to 50 km away from base stations, compared with 16 km for cellular networks and Wi-Fi's mere 100 m. Some phones already come equipped with a Wi-Fi chip and can access local Wi-Fi hot spots, in addition to cellular networks. But Wi-Fi coverage is spotty — although WiMAX signals beamed from central towers could blanket entire metropolitan areas. In addition, WiMAX signals can carry 70 Mbps of data — more than three times the roughly 20 Mbps from Wi-Fi, and far outperforming the 300 kbps on cellular networks. So far, only a handful of businesses in large U.S. cities are taking advantage of WiMAX technology, using equipment installed before the recent standards were finalized. Now large companies, including Intel, Alcatel, and Qualcomm, are pushing to develop WiMAX-compliant base station and chipset technologies. Similar to most chips for cell phones, WiMAX chipsets have two halves: one sends and receives radio signals, the other processes those signals. Unlike cellular chipsets, which can access only a narrow band of the radio spectrum, often making downloads slower, WiMAX chipsets are designed to tune into and process broader swaths of the radio spectrum. Collecting and processing more of the radio spectrum requires more power, though, because more frequencies must be sorted through. In addition, most WiMAX equipment uses an antenna technology called MIMO, which uses more than one antenna to simultaneously collect and send more information over greater distances, and power-hungry signal processing algorithms are needed to sort through the information collected via MIMO connections. The power problem is even more formidable for manufacturers who want to build chips for multiband WiMAX phones for use in different parts of the world. Each region, such as the United States and Asia, is setting aside a different portion of the spectrum for WiMAX, and accessing multiple bands usually requires a separate chip for each band. Most chipmakers are solving the problems of power consumption in WiMAX chips by using smaller transistors that require less voltage to turn on and off. Additionally, algorithmic methods are being used to efficiently code and decode information onto radio waves, relieving some of the power consumption burden from MIMO. To reach even greater efficiencies, engineers want to move more functions from the processing chip onto the radio chip. Other companies, including Texas Instruments and Intel, are also working on the concept, which would reduce the amount of data that needs to be shuttled between the two chips, thus saving power. Integrated mobile WiMAX technologies will be needed, says WiMAX Forum, to provide reasonably priced products that also have faster data access — without sapping batteries. Consumers are buying more "smart" phones capable of Web browsing, for instance, and WiMAX is becoming attractive to existing wireless providers because it could encourage even more use of digital data services, where the providers often charge by the kilobyte.

WiMAX Interest Soars in Japan

According to NTT DoCoMo, WiMAX can cover an area of up to 50 km in radius with a single base station and can offer data rates as high as 75 Mbps. Performance in early trials suggests that actual WiMAX performance will fall below these targets, but will still be far superior to Wi-Fi. Motorola and Softbank revealed plans to test a WiMAX wide area wireless networking service in Tokyo [27]. The two companies are the latest to join Japan's rapidly growing WiMAX sector, in which at least four trials have been announced or are under way. Motorola will provide a complete trial system, including access points, a back-end access network, and prototype WiMAX mobile handheld devices. Softbank will use this to measure the effectiveness of WiMAX as a wireless broadband technology. Motorola plans to use multiantenna WiMAX access points to boost performance closer to theoretical limits. Softbank operates a five million subscriber broadband Internet service in cooperation with Yahoo Japan. Yozan, Japan's first commercial WiMAX service provider, began service with a hybrid WiMAX and Wi-Fi in Tokyo. Yozan claims to have deployed more than 100 base stations, mostly in Tokyo, with another 300 under construction. In common with South Korea, another early adopter of WiMAX, all Japan's WiMAX operators are mobile phone service providers. According to research firm In-Stat, the Asia-Pacific market for WiMAX hardware and services will be worth $106.4 million during 2006, and will expand rapidly to $4.3 billion in 2011.

WiMAX Spectrum Owners Launch WiSOA

The WiMAX Spectrum Owners Alliance (WiSOA), launched at an inaugural meeting in Paris, is the first global organization composed exclusively of owners of WiMAX spectrum [28]. The founding members are Unwired Australia, Network Plus Mauritius, UK Broadband, Irish Broadband, Austar Australia/Liberty Group, Telecom New Zealand, WiMAX Telecom Group, Enertel, and Woosh Telecom. The driving concept behind WiSOA is to focus on the issues specific to those who are actually building businesses around WiMAX. The aim, then, is to put forward a perspective that is fundamentally different from that of most 3G operators.

Roaming is one of the critical success factors for any network seeking to be a global standard, and WiMAX is no exception. So far, the main roaming activity has centered on the pre-WiMAX WiBro system, with the formation of the WiBro and Mobile WiMAX Community (WMC) by leading Asian operators plus Covad [29]. Now a new alliance has burst on the scene, spearheaded by another hotbed of early WiMAX activity, Australasia. Inaugurated in Paris, the WiSOA has set itself an ambitious target of connecting a billion users (though in an unspecified time frame). It limits its membership to companies that own licenses and operate WiMAX or pre-WiMAX services, in contrast to a previous, defunct attempt at creating a roaming group — the WiMAX Global Roaming Alliance (WGRA) — which was largely based around license-exempt WISPs. The contrast reflects the shift of the WiMAX movement away from such markets and toward carrier-class, licensed-band deployments, but the fading of the WGRA does not detract from the merits of its objectives. The WiSOA's founder members contain four from Australasia — Unwired Australia, and Austar Australia, Telecom New Zealand, and Woosh Telecom — plus WiMAX Telecom of Austria, Enertel from the Netherlands, Network Plus Mauritius, UK Broadband, and Irish Broadband. All these were early adopters of broadband wireless networks, and many are now migrating these to fully standardized WiMAX, which will enable relatively straightforward roaming, technically speaking at least. The members signed their first international WiMAX roaming agreement, covering all WiMAX frequency ranges. This agreement acted as the backbone of a future global network. A further 12 members are on the point of joining the alliance, it claims, with Reliance Telecom of India likely to head the queue. The WiSOA will act as the enabler and coordinator of roaming agreements between different WiMAX members, in a similar way to some alliances formed for Wi-Fi hot spots and metrozones, notably the Wireless Broadband Alliance. It points out that roaming revenues in the GSM world amount to $25 billion a year. It will work with the WiMAX Forum, but has a more specific remit, which it may feel the forum has not prioritized — to accelerate roaming deals and, in so doing, to ensure that the value of licensed spectrum is fully realized by both government bodies and investors [30].

Telecom and Woosh have recently joined a fledgling group for owners of WiMAX radio spectrum. The spectrum owners' group focuses on the spectrum between 2.3 and 2.5 GHz and between 3.4 and 3.5 GHz. Other members include Unwired Australia, UK Broadband, and Austar Australia [31]. Similar groups exist for owners of CDMA and GSM cellular spectrum.

WiMAX Trial Performance Exceeds Expectations, Pipex Wireless

Pipex Wireless has successfully completed the latest phase of its WiMAX trial in Stratford-upon-Avon. Working with wireless solutions provider Airspan Networks, the trials have tested Pipex Wireless' WiMAX-based broadband services in a number of locations, with uplink speeds being particularly impressive [32]. Performance has been evaluated using both indoor and outdoor antennas, powered by Intel Rosedale chipsets, with the trial showing that WiMAX can deliver near-symmetric services in most environments. This will mean that businesses and home users will benefit from being able to send content such as e-mail attachments and large files at the same speed as typical broadband downloads. Speeds in excess of 2 Mbps up and down have been achieved indoors at a range of 1.2 km from the base station with no direct line of sight. Drive tests using the indoor antenna in a vehicle at various distances from the base station have shown symmetric speeds of 5 Mbps. Speeds of 10 Mbps down and 9 Mbps up have been achieved to external antennas at the test house at 1.2 km from the base station. Longer-range tests with external antennas have achieved 6 Mbps down and 4 Mbps up at a range of 6 km from the base station.

Fixed WiMAX Sales to Peak in 2007: Mobile WiMAX to Kick Off Deployment

Fixed WiMAX sales hit their peak and then leveled off in 2007, whereas mobile WiMAX started to see deployments during the same period. The crossover point between the two will be late in 2008. Performance, power consumption, and cost requirements for WiMAX ICs become much more challenging on the mobile platform. MIMO will be required, which means increased circuitry; thus, IC vendors will have to trade off MIMO performance for die area, power usage, and price [33].

WiMAX Equipment Market to Exceed $2 Billion by 2009

WiMAX has excellent prospects of increasing the business for a secure, handy, and movable broadband gateway. WiMAX's benefits in price, adaptability, and movability will also permit its suppliers to seize a stake in the market from proprietors utilizing patented wireless or fixed-line technologies, the state-of-the-art market research company RNCOS declares [34]. The main challenges to WiMAX technology will be global coordination of spectrum, enough to permit companies to manufacture instruments worldwide at greatly reduced costs at the WiMAX equipment market. WiMAX technology outshines the various long-established wireless or fixed-line applications, with its advantages in flexibility, movability, and price. Therefore, the WiMAX service providers simply outsmart the established wireless speculators in the area of market stake.

WiMAX — The Best Personal Broadband Experience

Global roaming among the service providers of WiMAX technology will enable subscribers to access multiple networks via the same device but through one single and familiar interface. Global roaming will become a critical feature of mobile services offered and will lure subscribers and help generate added revenues [35]. If service providers provide access to their partners with the help of roaming agreements similar to the existing ones for mobile networks, they can get the desired footprint in the market without building a broad infrastructure [36]. WiMAX technology is optimized mainly for high-throughput and real-time applications of data. This technology can be easily deployed in both greenfields on which operators depend entirely for edge infrastructure, as well as complementary networks that network operators integrate within their networks for enhancing the capacity and throughput according to the need of delivering true mobile broadband service (Figure 6.5). A profitable model is offered by wireless WiMAX broadband networks to service providers. So, they can deploy several value-added services and get additional streams of revenue. Also, the added cost of packaging new services with the existing ones is comparatively low, as operators enjoy a good rapport with subscribers. They can leverage current branding, marketing, and customer service operations for supporting their new services [36].

Fifteen Million WiMAX Users by 2009

Reseach and Markets' latest report predicts 15 million WiMAX users worldwide by 2009 [37]. Some of the key findings indicate that most WiMAX projects are still in the trial phase. Although North America leads the world with the largest number of WiMAX licenses, regions with high broadband penetration will see slow WiMAX

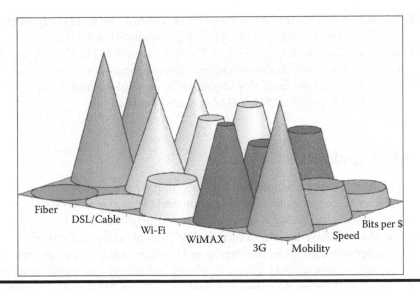

Figure 6.5   WiMAX relative to other broadband technologies. (From The Implications of WiMAX for Competition and Regulation, OECD document [dated March 2, 2006].)

adoption, whereas areas with low and scattered broadband penetration rates will see the most growth. This is evident in the latest deals by Israel-based Alvarion, one of the leading wireless broadband equipment providers to ISPs and network providers in places like Poland, Mexico, and several African countries.

The report "WiMAX — A Market Update (2006–2007)" discusses the various aspects of the WiMAX technology [38]. The report gives an overview of the current WiMAX market. It explains the standards followed for spectrum allocations and the market operations. It also talks about the implementation scheme of WiMAX as a technology. It addresses the various drivers of WiMAX, such as performance, coverage, etc., that are pushing the implementation of this technology.

The key findings are [38,42]:

■ Most of the WiMAX deployments around the world are still in a trial phase, providing only high-speed Internet service, but in the future, the largest markets for WiMAX will be for mobile applications.
■ The number of worldwide WiMAX users is forecast to reach 14.9 million in 2009, creating over $13.8 billion in service revenues for the WiMAX market.
■ WiMAX is expected to gain a major share of the broadband wireless access market by 2009 because of the wide support it has obtained from leading equipment vendors.
■ The Asia-Pacific region has the largest share in terms of WiMAX subscribers, attributed to large population and emerging economies in the region.

- Regions such as Eastern Europe and Latin America are increasingly adapting to WiMAX technology because of a lower broadband penetration level.
- In more developed regions such as Western Europe, WiMAX adoption has been slow due to the high levels of broadband penetration.
- North America is by far the leading region in terms of the number of WiMAX licenses, with a total of 394 WiMAX license holders.

WiMAX Rollouts

As of July 2006, WiMAX service had been tested in more than 50 countries worldwide. At least 12 countries already have commercially deployed WiMAX service. Many more markets had WiMAX service in the early deployment or planning stages [39]. Intel and Motorola have invested a total of $900 million in the U.S.-based wireless broadband operator Clearwire. Intel has agreed to pump $600 million into the firm, which currently offers services using proprietary technology developed by its subsidiary NextNet Wireless. Motorola, meanwhile, will pay $300 million to acquire NextNet and take a stake in Clearwire [40]. Russia's Start Telecom says it plans to begin the rollout of a WiMAX wireless broadband network.

WiMAX Poised for Big Growth, Says Semico Research

According to Semico, WiMAX is poised do for broadband what cellular has done for phones — make broadband mobile. Semico believes that WiMAX will become part of a number of networks, providing broadband wireless access in rural areas, offering backhaul services, offloading data traffic, and making broadband mobile, the firm said [41]. Semico's most recent WiMAX forecast, which includes both base stations and CPE, found that the market is poised to grow from 6000 units in 2005 to nearly 4.3 million units in 2010, a compound annual growth rate of more than 268 percent. The forecast is featured in the firm's study entitled, "WiMAX, Wireless Expands its Boundaries."

WiMAX Boom in Latin America

WiMAX, the wireless broadband technology, is set for a boom in a region with traditionally low Internet rates. Latin America, which already is seeing strong Internet growth, is expected to see a further boost thanks to the introduction of WiMAX, experts say [43]. Whereas operators in Europe are seeing WiMAX as a useful technology to reach areas that traditional DSL technology cannot cover, such as remote and rural areas, operators in Latin America see WiMAX as a way to reach a larger audience. Many smaller operators and start-ups also see the technology as a way to enter the broadband market as DSL prices are seen as too expensive for the majority of Latin Americans. The cost of broadband in Latin America is relatively high. WiMAX technology, which uses radio signals rather than copper or cable for connections, is less costly to install than traditional broadband, and thus will eventually become less expensive for the end user, experts say. Latin America is expected to see the number of wireless broadband and WiMAX subscribers go from 273,460 this year to 2.5 million in 2012, according to a forecast by Maravedis. The macroeconomic environment is fairly robust at this time — Latin American currencies are doing well, commodity prices are high, and so the price of a PC is now relatively low. These factors are driving the demand for broadband services, and will eventually boost WiMAX, says Pyramid Research.

Brazil

Brazil, already the largest broadband and Internet market in South America, is seen as the leading market for WiMAX, and Mexico is considered to have strong potential down the road. Other countries with good potential include Argentina, Chile, Colombia, and Peru, experts say. Brazil had a total of 22 million Internet users last year, according to an estimate from the International Telecommunications Union (ITU). That is by far the largest number in Latin America. However, it only represents 12 percent of the population, which means Brazil lags behind countries like Mexico, Chile, Peru, and Uruguay in penetration rates. There are only 3.3 million broadband subscribers in Brazil, according to an estimate for 2006 by Price Waterhouse Coopers. And of the total, only a few have what is considered true broadband, according to TelComp (the Brazilian Association of Competitive Telecom Service Providers). Those with transfer rates of 2.5 MB only represent some 0.2 percent of the Brazilian population.

Argentina, Chile, and Colombia

In Argentina, another key market, local operator Ertach expanded its WiMAX network to cover Tucuman and Bahia Blanca, following services launched in Buenos Aires. In Colombia, Orbitel (one of the country's three long-distance operators) expanded its WiMAX coverage to Bogotá after launching in Cali. And in Chile, Entel (one of the top telecom operators) recently launched WiMAX.

Steady Growth Forecast for WiMAX

A study by Juniper Research forecasts that the total number of mobile WiMAX subscribers will grow from 1.7 million in 2007 to 21.3 million in 2012 — following the initial release of certified equipment planned for early 2007 [44]. The report forecasts higher growth in developing regions, where operators are looking at leap-frogging 3G and adopting OFDMA-based mobile WiMAX standards. Developed regions like South Korea and Japan are expected to see a reduced adoption rate toward 2010 owing to the markets reaching saturation point in terms of mobile penetration. Because of the ability of mobile WiMAX to serve mobile, as well as fixed wireless subscribers, Juniper Research believes that mobile WiMAX will be adopted across both markets.

Other highlights and findings of the report include the following [44]:

- The global market for mobile WiMAX equipment, including base stations and CPE equipment, is estimated to reach $2.53 billion by 2012.
- Juniper Research predicts that mobile WiMAX services will be primarily data driven, and that the voice services market will be less than 10 percent of the total mobile WiMAX services market in 2012.
- North America will be one of the largest markets for mobile WiMAX voice services and is expected to come up to 32 percent of the total worldwide market in 2012.
- Juniper Research has identified a greater interest among OEMs in a dual-mode WiMAX–Wi-Fi product rather than a dual-mode WiMAX–3G solution.
- Fixed Internet providers are more comfortable with using mobile WiMAX as a fixed wireless solution, rather than competing with incumbent mobile carriers [45].

Mobile WiMAX has transitioned from being a hyped technology to being a ratified standard with a realistic certification timeline [47]. Apart from it being a cheaper alternative to 3G, the litmus test of mobile WiMAX lies in the upcoming operator trials, which would establish its performance in the real world, the report said. The report specifically looks at the need for mobility, the emergence of any time, any place broadband, also known as *personal broadband*, and how mobile WiMAX fits in with the personal broadband concept. Some WiMAX services, like many Internet sites, will be advertisement-supported, with consumers paying extra for premium WiMAX services [46].

Vendors Begin to Introduce WiMAX Infrastructure Gear

WiMAX got the push it needed when Intel, Motorola, Nokia, and Nortel Networks announced plans to roll out WiMAX equipment for consumer and service providers [48]. Commitment from established vendors means WiMAX could become a mainstream wireless broadband technology in the next two years. Motorola has rolled out its first line of WiMAX consumer gear, a wireless modem that connects a customer's computer to a WiMAX service provider. The company is offering units that can be mounted outdoors to provide service outside and a device that can be used inside a home or office. Motorola says it will make the devices available for trials later this year. They should be widely available in the first half of 2007. The early products have some limitations. The WiMAX modems are too large to fit inside computers, so early users would not have much mobility. But, Motorola is developing mobile WiMAX chipsets that will be used in its cell phones and smartphones, which means people could connect to a WiMAX network as they roam about town. The phones with WiMAX chipsets will be launched in 2008 by telecom carriers in the United States, Japan, and other countries. So far, Sprint is the only major U.S. carrier with plans to sell Motorola's WiMAX-enabled phones. The carrier says it will spend up to $3 billion over the next two years to build out its WiMAX network.

Nokia also made a leap into mobile WiMAX by unveiling its Flexi WiMAX base station, designed for service providers who want to provide wireless broadband services to subscribers. The first base station will be commercially available at the end of 2007 for the 2.5-GHz band, which is used in the United States. Nokia will follow with base stations that support the 3.5-GHz band, which is not available in the United States, and WiMAX-capable mobile devices in 2008. Service providers are getting more options when it comes to putting up WiMAX base stations. Intel rolled out a package of hardware and software platforms that base station makers can incorporate into their towers to speed deployment of WiMAX networks. Intel's NetStructure WiMAX Baseband card is small enough for space-constrained environments and consumes less power than traditional cellular technology. Intel says its technology can be upgraded if standards change to support new features and functionality. The hardware is designed to handle both 802.16d (fixed) and 802.16e (mobile) WiMAX standards. The first software release will support fixed WiMAX, followed by an upgrade to mobile WiMAX in 2007. Telecom equipment maker Nortel rolled out a portfolio of mobile WiMAX technologies for service providers, including base station transceivers, network gateways, antennas, mobile subscriber stations, and management systems [50]. The technology is based on Multiple Input, Multiple Output technology, known as *MIMO*, which uses multiple antennas for improved performance. The equipment will let service providers offer services like mobile video, VoIP, streaming media, file sharing, and electronic payment for goods over the Internet on mobile devices [51]. Intel has been one of the biggest advocates of WiMAX, along with many start-ups that have ventured into this space. But new products from Motorola, Nokia, and Nortel — large equipment vendors that are experts at selling gear to service providers — are a sign that WiMAX is ready for wide deployment. "Operators now see it as more viable technology," says Forrester Research, and they are more confident about it with support from the main vendors [48]. We could always look forward to Apple's hardware line-up, including their new iTV device, adopting fixed WiMAX in the second half of 2007 [49].

Yankee Group: Standards Vital for Mobile WiMAX Adoption Will Become Reality in 2008

Yankee Group predicted that adoption of mobile WiMAX standards will become a reality in 2008. In its report, Yankee Group predicts that in the future, more devices and applications will be developed using 802.16e-based technology, but that wireline operators will want to wait for the full spectrum of capabilities before investing in WiMAX. A crucial challenge task for vendors is clarifying whom the technology benefits, and why service providers should invest in it, the report said [52].

Some of the opportunities and challenges for mobile (802.16e) WiMAX include the following.

(802.16e) Opportunities [53]

- Device development and applications: More devices and applications will be developed to utilize WiMAX mobile access.
- Established markets: Wireline operators will want to wait for the full spectrum of capabilities before investing in WiMAX, which means that "e" is the best fit.

(802.16e) Challenge [53]

- Defining customer segments and targeting them: It is crucial for vendors to clarify just whom this technology will truly benefit, and why the service providers will want to invest in the technology.

Lack of Telecom Infrastructure Drives WiMAX Adoption in Asia-Pacific: Report

Research and Markets has released its "WiMAX Growth Opportunities in Asia-Pacific," which provides an overview of the status of fixed and mobile WiMAX deployment in the region along with key market drivers, constraints, trends, vendor profiles, and regulatory conditions. The report concludes that the low broadband subscriber penetration and teledensity in the Asia-Pacific region are major motivators of WiMAX deployment [55]. Compared to Europe and North America, Asia-Pacific is expected to be a more suitable test bed for WiMAX, given the lack of telecommunications infrastructure, low broadband penetration, and geographically widespread population. The report also adds that broadband wireless access (BWA) solutions have suffered either an early demise or slow adoption because of the lack of standardization and poor interoperability. Worldwide interoperability for WiMAX, on the other hand, has generated much interest as the next evolutionary data–voice enabler. The added mobility and greater range that WiMAX offers over its predecessor, wireless fidelity (Wi-Fi), and its ability to provide greater bandwidth over 3G networks further strengthen its appeal, the report said [55].

WiMAX Edges into the Mainstream

Sprint Nextel made the headlines in August 2006 with the announcement that it is to splash out $4.5 billion on a nationwide wireless WiMAX network to be built over the next couple of years. As expected, it will be used as a high-bandwidth, mobile network that will leapfrog 3G in terms of its videoconferencing and fast data transfer capabilities. WiMAX equipment sales hit $142.3 million in 2005, according to California-based research house Infonetics, with a five-year unit combined annual growth rate forecast at 139 percent between 2005 and 2009 [56]. As a last-mile connection to the Internet, fixed WiMAX can offer a number of advantages over a leased line or DSL alternatives. In some buildings in large cities, there is no copper available to provide DSL and a T1 line can take too long to get up and running. A WiMAX connection can, in theory, be installed by mounting a dish in a matter of hours. The evidence from users here is that where it is available it works well and is cheaper than more conventional connection methods. WiMAX is an interesting last-mile solution, but it also looks extremely attractive as a WAN technology to link buildings on a campus or offices on different sides of a city. Of course, if two offices have WiMAX links to the Internet, it is possible to set up a VPN between the two, but some WiMAX ser-vice providers, like the Canada-based Redline Communications, sell equipment that enables high-speed point-to-point connections over distances of several miles, and a theoretical range of about 50 mi [56]. The cost of a WiMAX link is surprisingly low. Redline's AN80 Ethernet bridge devices, for example, cost $4000 per pair, providing a 10-Mbps data link. If you factor in the cost of running a cable from the roof of the office to the data center and a support contract of about $600 per year, it is pretty clear that a WiMAX setup replacing a single T1 leased line could pay for itself in about a year [56]. Redline's devices, and probably most others as well, provide basic DES encryp-tion, which makes the WiMAX connection at least as secure as an unencrypted leased line. With additional hardware, this can be enhanced to government-grade crypto. Any other appliances, such as caches, compressors, or wide area file system (WAFS) devices, that can be used on conventional WAN links can also be connected to the WiMAX devices. But it is hard not to conclude that the economics of WiMAX looks tempting. A 10-Mbps WAN for $600 a year, with an initial investment of $4,000 plus installation, or a T1 Internet connectivity for half the price of a leased line, with the option of turning it up to 5 Mbps when necessary? It sounds good. There is no reason to expect a WiMAX connection to be less reliable than a T1 from your telco, and the weather really would not make any appreciable difference to your connection. If your connectivity bills are getting too high or you want more flexibility in the bandwidth available to you, WiMAX is certainly worth looking into [57].

There Will Be Few Opportunities for WiMAX Operators to Make Strong Financial Returns: Analysys

Early business cases from the WiMAX community show attractive financial returns in a variety of deployment environments, but modeling with more realistic assumptions shows that there may be very few situations in which WiMAX has a secure long-term business case, according to a new report "The Business Case for WiMAX" published by Analysys [59], the global advisers on telecom, IT, and media.

Key findings from the new report include the following [58]:

- Although emerging countries have low penetration of fixed network infrastructure and services, the business case for WiMAX will still be difficult. Low disposable incomes, low penetration of PCs, and the growing strength of cellular services will limit the returns.
- In principle, there is an opportunity to make a healthy profit from WiMAX in rural areas of developed markets unserved by DSL or cable services [60]. However, with fixed operators rapidly extending the reach of DSL, these opportunities are likely to be few in number and limited in size.
- Head-to-head competition with fixed broadband services in developed markets would require a spectacular performance by a WiMAX operator to overcome the growing capabilities and services on offer, such as IPTV. WiMAX would encounter fierce competition from DSL services offered by a wide array of major consumer brands using their own networks, wholesale services, and local loop unbundling (LLUB).

This new report models the business case for WiMAX in a number of potential deployment scenarios, including a developing market urban area, a developed market urban area, and a developed market rural town. It identifies the critical factors that will make or break the business case for WiMAX in these environments as illustrated by a variety of case studies and market data [75].

Motorola CTO Bets on WiMAX to Connect the "Disconnected"

Motorola CTO believes a quarter of the next billion people that would be connected over mobile networks would be from the emerging markets of India and China. She is betting on 4G and WiMAX technologies to connect and empower India, especially its rural segments. It would be a mobile device that would bring Internet to the masses, rather than a wired device like the PC, she stresses, adding that wireless broadband access is how WiMAX will play the role of enabler. Even though Wi-Fi can be used for providing connectivity in relatively smaller areas, for a wider area like the rural sector, WiMAX is the most cost-effective. It uses a different kind of air interface and is more spectra-efficient than 3G technologies. There is a traditional evolution of cellular technology, that is, from 2G to 2.5G and 3G, or GSM to CDMA to HSPDA and EvDO, among others. However, for developing countries like India, it makes sense to bypass 3G and move over to 4G, she said [61].

Mobile WiMAX: Back to Basics

If there is one safe assumption about mobile WiMAX, it is that the technology would not languish as a niche player. Why? It is not simply because a few hundred vendors and service providers have a good deal of money and reputation riding on this technology. It is also because, even if mobile WiMAX does not live up to all of its backers' lofty ambitions, it is clearly shaping up to be a viable choice for mobile broadband. To help CIOs and IT managers sort through their options, this edition of *Unstrung Enterprise Insider*, entitled "Mobile WiMAX: Who's Doing What," looks at vendor plans, when the technology will be commercially available, and what enterprises can expect in terms of throughput, coverage, roaming, and device selection [62]. This is important because, although the first WiMAX-Forum-certified user devices are likely to debut sometime in the second half of 2007, it will take at least another year before the technology starts to become a viable option for most enterprises.

Corporate End Users to Represent the WiMAX "Sweet Spot"

Mobile corporate use is anticipated to dominate the projected WiMAX market of $49 billion by 2012. WiMAX presents an emerging opportunity for many telecom players, both from established incumbents as well as bold start-ups aiming to compete head on in the broadband wireless access market [63]. In developing strategies and targets for sustainable business models, NSR [64] predicts that the sweet spot of demand within the next five years rests with enterprise end users for corporate-based applications. The so-called road warrior, a highly mobile enterprise user, is expected to present the largest market opportunities for WiMAX in terms of the subscriber base. In revenue terms, the corporate base, which includes fixed and mobile/nomadic users, should likewise garner the highest revenue streams. NSR does recognize that consumer markets, which include the younger set and college students, are "wildcards," such that high adoption of WiMAX services could come as a tremendous market boost. A device such as an integrated 'iPod/Gaming Unit' that is WiMAX-enabled could hit the marketplace and send demand skyrocketing. NSR predicts a healthy market for WiMAX equipment and services globally. From a combined revenue base of $1.1 billion in 2007, the market is forecast to reach close to $49 billion by the end of 2012, for cumulative revenues of over $132 billion within a five-year time frame. Key end-user groups include mid- to high-level corporate users and the road warrior, with healthy niches that include government users, young urban professionals, and rural users [63,64].

If WiMAX Can Gain a Loyal Customer Base with Revenue Projections, the Cellular Companies Will Merger Quickly with Them: Face-Off — 4G versus WiMAX versus Wi-Fi

Moving from 3G to 4G should simplify making applications available to mobile users because of the faster data rates. This will make the middleware used to adapt applications for the slower speed of wireless systems obsolete. The availability of a complete IP-based service with the security of a VPN (Virtual Private Network) to the mobile end user will be a major benefit. The access to the network will be continuous. The face-off between 4G versus Wi-Fi versus WiMAX will be a globally adopted network of shared applications, resources, and standards meeting a minimum delivery requirement of VoFi, broadband, and multimedia services to all 4G-enabled end users. The best in performance will be the solution of choice. If WiMAX can gain a loyal customer base with revenue projections, the cellular companies will quickly merge with them [65].

WiMAX IPOs on the Horizon

For WiMAX operators, product suppliers, and software vendors, the technology represents a huge opportunity to shake up the telecom market, one that Clearwire and NextWave are hoping investors will be quick to appreciate [114,115]. On December 18 and 19, 2006, two wireless upstarts, NextWave and Clearwire, filed to go public with the Securities & Exchange Commission. Both companies hope to make their fortunes with WiMAX. Market researcher Gartner's Gartner Dataquest expects the North American WiMAX services market to increase from 30,000 connections in 2006 to 21.2 million by 2011 [114,115].

WiMAX for Rural America

Discussions about WiMAX availability, particularly in rural America, often raise more questions than they answer. However, some answers can be inferred from the comments of these seasoned independent operators. All of the carriers we spoke to are positive about the promise of WiMAX. However, their experiences in the crucible of broadband wireless have taught them to be conservative. This is no bad thing in terms of positive public perception of the technology. However, it probably means they will be slow to adopt technology for the sake of technology. Clearly, reliability, cost savings, and the business case will rule the day. These are everyone's primary market drivers. Existing gear, both licensed and unlicensed, is getting the job done for carriers that are aggressively deploying, but carriers always look for improved solutions. In the United States, the biggest opportunities probably lie in the laps of Sprint and Clearwire. What is very uncertain is how aggressive their strategies will be. For rural customers, it seems clear that those markets are least likely to be early recipients of major carrier deployments. Will that leave rural America bereft of WiMAX service? Perhaps. If vendors launch comprehensive lines of product, what previously happened may recur. Smaller, independent carriers will continue to aggressively roll out gear (mostly unlicensed) in the rural markets while steadily adopting WiMAX into the mix. Clearly, no one seems to be waiting on new devices to deploy. There is tons of demand, and smaller carriers are rolling out service as fast as they can [119].

WiMAX, the Future of Wireless Networks

AUSalliance, the combination of Unwired, Austar, and Soul, says it will use WiMAX technology and claims that this will offer services equivalent, and in many cases better, in price and performance to the most popular Asymmetrical Digital Subscriber Line (ADSL) offerings [120]. One of the big arguments made in the favor of WiMAX becoming a viable broadband option is the economies of scale [117]. Many proponents of the technology believe that global standards at certain specific ranges of frequencies could allow chip makers access to a big market that justifies spending millions on developing silicon. Most mobile phone developers are acknowledging the importance of the greatly anticipated WiMAX networks. A simple fixed WiMAX radio running in unicast, assuming 40 Mbps per channel, might support all of two high-definition television (HDTV) simultaneous sessions at 19 Mbps (assumes no special compression techniques) [118]. Why stay with cable when you can grab it from the air onto your own home network? Why stay at home when your laptop with the right external card can be your TV/phone/data source anywhere? They can do it cheaply, too. WiMAX will be less expensive to build out nationally than any wired method. You do not have to bring fiber to the house when you have video coming through the air. Samsung has clearly stated that in their opinion WiMAX is the future of wireless networks. Motorola seems to agree by predicting that 2007 will be the year of WiMAX, when an increasing number of commercial launches of Wimax networks is expected [121–123].

2007 Will Be the Year of WiMAX

With 2006 coming to a close, Motorola predicts 2007 will be the year WiMAX will begin entering the mainstream with growing consumer awareness and anticipation, and with an increasing number of commercial launches of mobile WiMAX networks [124]. With industrywide support, performance, and cost advantages, WiMAX is clearly well positioned to play a pivotal role in the evolution of future broadband wireless networks on a global scale. Last year, IEEE ratified the standard behind mobile WiMAX 802.16e-2005, and fixed WiMAX-Forum-Certified products have been deployed. Chipset manufacturers have announced or launched silicon that will support mobile WiMAX functionality in devices and CPE.

It May Well Be WiMAX versus 3G: Frost & Sullivan

According to the recent new analysis from Frost & Sullivan titled "World Wi-Fi and WiMAX Chipsets Markets," WiMAX is emerging as a direct competitor to 3G [125,126]. This development is being attributed to the introduction of mobility into the WiMAX road map, as well as the expensive rollout of 3G services in many areas of the world. This concern is more prominent in the Asian region. The combination of 2.5G, such as EDGE, with WiMAX could be seen as a far less expensive business model compared to the 3G deployment model. The Frost & Sullivan analysis reveals that the revenue in this WiMAX chipsets industry totaled $18 million in 2005 and is projected to reach $257.3 million in 2008. The introduction of products based on WiBro and the demonstration of their performance will serve to boost the "mobile WiMAX" industry.

Users and Vendors Make WiMAX Plans

Vendors of WiMAX wireless technology and services predicted that the emerging technology will vastly enhance wireless bandwidth at a fraction of the current cost. U.S. carrier Sprint Nextel announced a $3 billion investment in WiMAX in the coming years and, according to Sprint, WiMAX will yield a tenfold improvement in cost and performance per megabits per second compared to the cost of infrastructure and operations for its cellular network. Sprint has not revealed whether it expects to charge businesses or consumers for WiMAX services. Nortel Networks showed a cellular base station transceiver for mobile wireless that it plans to sell to carriers in 2007. The display included a promotional sign promising three times the speed of current wireless networks at one-third the cost [66]. There are efforts going on to connect WiMAX through cars. With added WiMAX bandwidth, Zipcar (United States) might be able to install a Wi-Fi access point in each car to allow a user to access the Internet via a handheld device or laptop. American Wireless Broadband

(AWB) is set [66] to begin trying out a WiMAX transceiver from Motorola in apartment buildings in Itasca, Illinois. The Chicago-based wireless ISP is already working with Motorola in a test of Broadband over Power Line Technology being used by ten apartment dwellers in the same Itasca complex. That service has worked successfully for the past two months, offering up to 12 Mbps of throughput. TowerStream is already including precertified WiMAX equipment in the Boston area. Clearwire has announced a WiMAX trial in Portland, Oregon, in partnership with Motorola and Intel. That trial will last through 2007, according to a statement from Intel. It is also backing Pipex's trial of WiMAX in Milton Keynes, United Kingdom.

WiMAX Is the Bell of the Wireless Ball

After years of occasional hype, both fixed and mobile WiMAX are finally here. There are real products, installations [68], and customers [67]. The convenience of mobility is clearly going to be a core driver for WiMAX going forward, just as it has been for cellular. Motorola has exhibited its mobile WiMAX equipment. There were many chip vendors, including Beceem, Intel, Runcom, and Texas Instruments. This is the most important segment of the WiMAX market to watch; these components and the reference designs sold by their vendors will largely define WiMAX products, in much the same way that Wi-Fi chips define their products. Much progress on many fronts is being made relating to WiMAX. It is expected that a massive uptake of WiMAX in Asia is possible in 2007 and significant progress will be made in the United States beginning in 2008. Still, the biggest variable in the success of WiMAX is the competitive scenario. The cellular community is going to respond to WiMAX in a big way. They have to, or they risk losing customers, and perhaps not just for data services but for voice as well [77]. This situation is going to spawn one of the most memorable battles in the history of wireless technology and, ultimately, benefit users with low prices, greater availability, and higher performance [67].

Gemtek Expects WiMAX CPE Shipments to Top One Million Units in 2007

Taiwan-based network-equipment maker Gemtek Technology expects its shipments of WiMAX CPE products to total one million units, or 20% of projected global shipments, in 2007 [69]. As indicated, in terms of sales value, Gemtek's shipments of WiMAX devices will amount to NT$3 billion ($91 million) in 2007. For 2007, the company anticipates its revenues to grow over 30 percent from the NT$16 to 16.5 billion projected for this year. In addition to WiMAX devices, IP set-top boxes (STBs) and integrated access devices (IADs) will also be among the major export items in 2007, with expected shipments of 1.5 to 2.0 million units and sales of NT$6-8 billion.

WiMAX Poised for Rapid Growth Despite Major Challenges, Says In-Stat

WiMAX technology is entering a rapid growth phase, as service providers are now able to buy WiMAX-Forum-Certified equipment, according to research firm In-Stat. Worldwide subscribers are forecast to grow to 19.7 million by the end of 2010, In-Stat indicated, adding that most of those subscribers are in the Asia-Pacific region. Almost all subscribers are using a fixed service today, with the exception of those in South Korea, the firm said [70]. According to In-Stat, although WiMAX faces many challenges, the biggest challenge still comes from competing technologies and services. WiMAX will have difficulty competing in areas that already have established broadband services. WiMAX will need to provide a demonstratively superior service to win customers from the incumbent provider. Much of WiMAX's early success will come from underdeveloped regions of the globe, according to In-Stat [70].

In-Stat expects the mobile version of WiMAX to quickly overtake the fixed version and power the technology's future growth, in spite of hurdles presented by regulatory uncertainty and spectrum availability [72]. Although WiMAX is entering a period of rapid growth, the high-speed data technology will enjoy even more rapid growth in future months and years as the technology's mobile version takes off, according to a report issued by In-Stat. Most subscribers currently use WiMAX 802.16d, the fixed wireless version; In-Stat expects 802.16e, the mobile wireless version, to quickly overtake the fixed version and power the technology's future growth in spite of hurdles presented by regulatory uncertainty and spectrum availability [71,73]. According to In-Stat, the market-share leader is Alvarion, which markets its gear globally. Most WiMAX end users are located in Asia, which is likely to continue to lead in the rollout of the new 802.16e technology [72].

A recent study by In-Stat found the following:

- With Sprint being the exception, In-Stat does not believe most 3G carriers will deploy WiMAX in the near term [74].
- Alvarion had the largest share of WiMAX equipment revenue during the first half of 2006.
- In-Stat expects sales in 802.16e equipment to quickly overtake those in 802.16d.
- Regulatory uncertainty and spectrum availability continue to hamper the growth of WiMAX [74].

Mobile WiMAX: Brazil and China

Mobile WiMAX will be rolled out in China next year, said Samsung Electronics [76]. The first customer would not roll out a national mobile WiMAX network; instead it will be using the technology for special applications in several provinces.

Mobile WiMAX is currently used to provide commercial services in South Korea and is being rolled out elsewhere. Samsung also signed a contract to commercialize the mobile WiMAX platform in the city of Curitiba, Brazil, with provider TVA. TVA plans to commercialize mobile WiMAX services in Curitiba first, Parana State in southern Brazil from 2007, and then extend it to other Brazilian cities over the ensuing years [76].

WiMAX Climax

If WiMAX was not a hot wireless broadband technology already, some serious fuel was added to the fire during the summer of 2006. Intel Corp. and Motorola Inc. unveiled plans to invest more than $1 billion in Clearwire Corp., which is building a network that will offer the longer-range broadband access. Sprint Nextel Corp. meanwhile committed $3 billion in the coming years to build a wireless high-speed network [78]. Unlike Wi-Fi, WiMAX also offers the QoS needed to support VoIP services. Simply put, many users can overburden a Wi-Fi access point, making it difficult to ensure consistent bandwidth and service for each user. With WiMAX, the base station allocates a slot for each subscriber. The slots can expand or contract, based on the bandwidth and QoS required by each user at particular times. Intel plans to begin incorporating WiMAX functionality in laptops. The company has funded a variety of start-ups that develop technology supporting long-range wireless broadband, including Orascom Telecom WiMAX Ltd., Worldmax, Pipex Wireless, Navini Networks Inc., Beceem Communications Inc., and Clearwire. The Clearwire investment marked Intel Capital's largest deal ever and was necessary to help get WiMAX off the ground. But, Sprint Nextel's announcement in August 2006 that it would spend $1 billion next year and up to $2 billion in 2008 to create a high-speed wireless network based on WiMAX technologies will provide a big boost to the emerging technology. The company said it plans to offer wireless broadband services to 100 million people in 2008, with deployment beginning in the last quarter of 2007. With the nearly ubiquitous broadband coverage WiMAX could offer, salespeople could tap into their home office's network and access data needed to respond to customers more quickly than what is possible with current wireless technologies. A police department could provide officers in the field easy access to driver's-license databases. A digital dispatch system could send information into the field accompanied by maps or access cameras within a bank [78]. But for chief information officers (CIOs) weighing their companies' wireless strategies, the possibilities are tempered by concerns that linger from the advent of Wi-Fi in the enterprise. Industry research suggests that CIOs remain concerned about the security of Wi-Fi systems running in their businesses. Many of these worries tend to be unfounded, and most real security problems in wireless local area networks can be solved by a host of available protections. But Forrester Research Inc. recently found that Wi-Fi still receives less in corporate investment than devices that run on traditional phone carrier networks.

Despite improved security features, WiMAX may face equal suspicion. The original 802.11 wireless LAN standard, on which Wi-Fi is based, was developed without inherent security, deterring many companies from deploying it. Safeguards to protect data were later added to Wi-Fi, but the stigma remains. By contrast, WiMAX already has security features that are built in. Experts say that with both wireless technologies, the real problem usually lies within a user's network. The other hurdle companies face is how to administer their greatly expanded computer network once WiMAX is running. A whole new layer of IT management and control must be put in place to grapple with workers connecting to the network wirelessly from all types of locations. For Cisco Systems Inc., a major supplier of Wi-Fi gear to enterprises, that built its offerings through hundreds of millions of dollars worth of acquisitions, the applicability of WiMAX in the enterprise still is not totally clear. For now, the company is biding its time [78]. WiMAX proponents counter that the technology is not intended to replace Wi-Fi but to complement it. Eventually, enterprise users will barely notice what technology they are using for wireless access because their devices will automatically choose the best connection path [78].

WiMAX to Trail Mobile Broadband Market by 2010

New alternative technologies will add just 6 percent of the forecast 500 million mobile broadband global users by 2010, reported Strategy Analytics [79]. Despite all the hype surrounding alternative technologies like WiMAX, iterations of existing technologies will dominate the mobile broadband arena in the short term. According to the research firm's report, "Beyond 3G: Looking for True Mobile Broadband," technologies such as mobile WiMAX and UMTS TDD will lead the alternative technology camp. However, enhancements to existing technologies, including HSPA and EV-DO Revision A+, will constitute the bulk of the market and that is where the money lies in the short term [79].

Cellular versus Wireless Broadband in Asia-Pacific

Against a burgeoning mobile subscriber base in the Asia-Pacific region, which currently stands at 859.4 million with over 130 million being 3G subscribers (including CDMA1X subscribers), a robust growth in data usage BWA technologies has entered the wireless space [80]. Telecom providers introduced BWA technologies to tap into the wireless trend, accelerate wide market diffusion, and to provide consumers with an alternative or complementary value proposition. However, a lack of standardization and interoperability issues have not augured well in adoption rates for most proprietary BWA technologies, although much attention and interest in the recent past has been given to WiMAX, an evolution of BWA. WiMAX is gaining momentum now, considering the new opportunity offered by the 802.16e standard (mobile version of WiMAX). In-Stat's recent reports show that WiMAX subscribers will exceed 14 million by the end of 2011, which shows WiMAX is still largely lagging behind 3G adoption [80]. This report discusses the key initiatives for wireless broadband technologies and gives a comparison of current broadband, cellular, and wireless broadband services for all 13 countries in the Asia-Pacific region.

WiMAX Considered by 75 Percent of Operators

It has emerged that the wireless broadband access technology Wimax would be considered for use by three-quarters of telecom operators across the globe [81]. According to a survey by Pyramid Research [6], 75 out of 100 operators said they were thinking about building a Wimax network. Seen by many as a competitor to 3G mobile technology, Wimax could potentially be cheaper to introduce into the telecom market, yet some experts are warning that it may not offer a difference in cost [81].

3G Rival WiMAX Promises Much: Will It Deliver?

WiMAX supporters say it will be cheaper and faster than rival 3G mobile networks, which explains why many operators are interested, but industry specialists warn that the emerging wireless technology may not deliver all it promises. A survey by market research group Pyramid Research showed that out of 100 cable TV and telecom operators around the world, 75 said they were considering building a WiMAX network [81]. WiMAX allows super-high-speed Internet access and file downloads from laptops, phones, or other mobile devices over greater distances than previous technologies. That two-year lead is not a good enough reason for a cellular operator to rip out their mobile phone network — which cost billions of dollars to build — but it does create an opportunity for anyone else who wants a wireless broadband business to complement fixed-line or mobile voice networks [83]. Sprint Nextel's rollout, helped by Intel, Motorola, and Samsung, will make wireless broadband much cheaper to deliver — up to ten times cheaper than current 3G cellular telephony networks. Even better, the radio spectrum for WiMAX networks is rented out by regulators at more affordable prices, and WiMAX equipment vendors claim that the infrastructure and handheld devices will be cheaper than 3G mobile phone systems. WiMAX supporters hope that low cost will also result because it is a technology developed by more than 1500 companies. With so many companies contributing, the WiMAX Forum is hopeful everyone will just chip in their patents and keep royalties at zero or an absolute minimum, which would give it another edge over 3G cellular technologies, which have royalties of between 5 and 10 percent of wholesale mobile device prices. The WiMAX Forum hopes wireless broadband will become so cheap that it can be part and parcel of any electronic device, enabling consumers, for example, to send pictures to friends straight from their digital camera. Nokia, another major patent holder, is equally skeptical. Even if royalties are modest, low prices will only come if WiMAX chips are being produced in the hundreds of millions, and that may take a long time [83].

WiMAX to Benefit the Broadband Disenfranchised

According to Kagan Research, U.S. households that have lacked broadband availability comprise a last frontier in telecom, but are now being corralled. Terrestrial wireless WiMAX network installations are scheduled to start in 2007 [84]. Sparsely populated towns may be nominally serviced by some broadband service. But usually coverage is patchy, prices high, and capabilities limited. WiMAX standardization is lowering equipment costs, and first-wave deployments overseas prove WiMAX service is viable. Other WiMAX advantages are equipment that consumers can quickly self-install and robust service. However, WiMAX faces challenges as well. The WiMAX Forum consortium set 3.5 GHz as a standard frequency globally — well, everywhere except in the United States, where it will be a nonstandard frequency. That frequency band is not available because it is occupied by U.S. government services. As a wireless medium, WiMAX also would not deliver fast speeds unless large amounts of spectrum are available [84].

Will WiMAX Be the Basis for 4G?

Wi-Fi has been an unqualified success even though it does not come close to the vision of ubiquitous Internet access [85]. Wi-Fi's limitation is that it is essentially a technology for wireless local area networks. What you need to blanket large areas are wireless wide area networks (WANs). That is where 3G comes in. Theoretically, 3G can cover the whole country, but it is going to take a while before that happens, if ever. The problem with 3G is that it is an incredibly expensive wireless technology. The licenses are astronomical, and the infrastructure required is very costly, too. So, most likely, only urban areas will have 3G. So, will we ever have ubiquitous wireless Internet access? WiMAX holds a lot of promise. It is the wireless technology that will bring the Internet to the next billion people. WiMAX is interesting because it offers transmission rates of up to 280 Mbps and has a service range of up to 50 km per base station. It is viewed as a wireless alternative to DSL broadband. As such, most likely, it will be offered by telcos as a cost-effective means of providing last-mile delivery of broadband Internet access in rural areas, where it is not commercially viable to lay telephone lines. Fixed WiMAX is expected to roll out around the world by 2007. But that is not what has got everyone excited about WiMAX. What people are really looking forward to is mobile WiMAX. Major mobile phone makers such as Motorola and Nokia are not even looking at fixed WiMAX and are working toward incorporating WiMAX into their phones [85]. This naturally begs the question, would anybody want to use 3G for Internet access on their mobile phones when they can get faster speeds at lower costs via WiMAX? That's something that is bound to worry mobile carriers around the world, as most of them have already begun deploying their costly 3G networks. But 3G providers need not worry that much. Mobile WiMAX is still at the development stage and is easily still years away. When it becomes ready for prime time, it will probably be time for everyone to move to 4G anyway. In fact, WiMAX could very well serve as the foundation for 4G. Motorola believes it should. It announced last month that it plans to converge WiMAX with 4G to create something it calls Wi4 [85], which includes a light-infrastructure solution for rural areas, which involves very low costs in deployment. In other words, a WiMAX-based 4G service would be relatively inexpensive. Nokia and Intel announced a nonexclusive partnership to collaborate on several areas in support of mobile WiMAX technology, including mobile devices or clients, network infrastructure, and market development. So, WiMAX, far from being a 3G killer, could very well end up becoming the successor to 3G someday [85].

Why WiMAX for Developing Countries?

Backers of WiMAX are touting it as a solution to two problems: as an alternative to wired broadband in North America and Europe, and as a way to provide broadband in developing countries that lack the infrastructure to deliver the service. A recent report from U.K. research and consulting firm Analysys offers some caveats on the second part of the WiMAX value proposition. Although acknowledging the lack of infrastructure in developing countries, Analysys says that WiMAX is not the answer, at least for companies looking to profit from deploying the technology and offering broadband service [86]. The lack of PCs and low disposable income will hold WiMAX back in developing countries, according to the study, and recent Internet usage statistics appear to support that view. Only 3.6 percent of Africans are Internet users, according to Internet World Stats [86]. Looking at hardware, as of 2004, there were only 1.74 PCs per 100 inhabitants in Africa, compared to 28.48 in Europe, 69.82 in Canada, and 76.22 in the United States, according to figures compiled by the UN's International Telecommunication Union. When the lack of hardware and income is combined with the widespread availability of inexpensive cellular phones, the short- and medium-term prospects for WiMAX look bleak. 3G networks may end up thwarting WiMAX in many developing countries. It will likely prove easier to upgrade current wireless network infrastructure to support 3G technologies in many areas than undertake large-scale WiMAX deployments [86]. There is also a word of caution for those hoping WiMAX will become a viable third alternative to DSL and cable in North America and Europe. WiMAX will need to demonstrate a distinct performance advantage in regions where it is in direct competition with wired broadband services, especially with ISPs offering full-featured service bundles like the triple play of voice, data, and television. Analysys believes that the wireless technology will even face difficulties in rural areas once wired alternatives eventually turn up [86]. The report serves up some difficult news for those who see WiMAX as a panacea for the world's broadband ills. But it is not all bleak news. For those in North America and Europe who currently sit outside broadband's reach, WiMAX has a lot of potential. Urban areas in developing countries are also good candidates for WiMAX deployments because there are more PC users there. WiMAX investment, development, and deployment may be starting out slowly, but the demand is there, if you know where to look [86].

WiMAX: The Promise of the Future

The promise of a new technology always brings hope and optimism. WiMAX provides distinct advantages in cost, flexibility, and performance, and because it is standards driven, it ensures long-term competitive choices. It improves the capability of wireless to compete with DSL and cable in the broadband market. It provides serious competition to existing cellular networks [87]. History gives us reasons for caution. Several technologies/implementors promised a lot but fizzled out: local multipoint distribution service (LMDS), Teligent, NextLink, and, more recently, 3G. The free market has not really thrown up lots of choices with decreasing prices. The United States still lags in broadband access, far from leading the world with the latest implementations. In spite of these cautionary words, the vision of WiMAX is bright and shining [87].

Waiting for WiMAX

In the high-speed networking arena, plenty of people and businesses are waiting for WiMAX. That includes today's 3G wireless data service providers, who have the most to lose from a widespread WiMAX deployment [88]. But 3G carriers can breathe easy, because WiMAX probably would not be a major technology, at least in North America and Europe, for many years. In-Stat's forecast is impressive, but most of the projected subscribers are in the Asia-Pacific region. And as far as mobility goes, well, all current subscribers are using a fixed service, with the exception of those in South Korea. So what is holding WiMAX back [88]? The problems have both business and technical roots. Competition from existing 3G services is certainly a major deterrent to any company planning a major WiMAX deployment. Also, as the number of Wi-Fi systems grows, the case for WiMAX service begins to fall apart. In just a few years, most major cities, and more than a few smaller communities, should have municipal Wi-Fi systems covering large swaths of territory. Additionally, most major hotels, airports, schools, stores, office buildings, and other public places will have their own Wi-Fi hot spots. So what is the point of blanketing a region with WiMAX, when the best (i.e., most potentially lucrative) areas will already be covered by both Wi-Fi and 3G services? Then, there is the client hardware problem. Most mobile handsets and smart phones are sold with some type of service agreement. With carriers offering handsets at greatly reduced prices in service bundles, are they going to want to offer models featuring WiMAX capabilities? Not likely. In fact, many existing handsets do not offer Wi-Fi support, simply because the carrier partner does not want the feature included. Although it is true that WiMAX operators could create their own vendor and bundling deals, they would have to work very hard to overcome the momentum generated by today's 3G handsets. If all of this is not bad enough, prospective WiMAX operators also face a bunch of regulatory and spectrum availability issues. So, is WiMAX a dead deal [88]? No, not entirely. WiMAX will certainly find a place in undeveloped regions and locales, where the only practical alternative is expensive satellite service. WiMAX might also have a chance in more densely populated markets if the operator can deliver superior QoS [88,89]. There is also the chance that some of today's 3G carriers could eventually turn to WiMAX as a 4G technology, although that possibility looks like a long shot because of other high-speed technologies already in the pipeline [89].

How Can New Network Operators and Service Providers Maximize the Chance of Success of WiMAX Services?

The growing availability of WiMAX equipment and the early announcement of a number of deployment plans have led to a surge of interest in WiMAX and its potential to complement or disrupt fixed and wireless broadband services [90]. The WiMAX Forum and equipment vendors are strongly promoting the application of WiMAX in a variety of market situations in both developed and developing countries. However, in developed markets, WiMAX will face growing competition from DSL, whereas in developing markets, its progress will be hindered by limited disposable income [91]. A research report from Research and Markets comes to grips with the real opportunities of WiMAX for existing and new network operators [91].

The business case for WiMAX answers your key questions [91]:

■ Under what circumstances might there be a viable business case for WiMAX, e.g., type of market, competitive landscape, operator characteristics, service mix, and technology requirements?
■ What are the critical factors that will define the success of WiMAX in different situations? How do they affect the potential return of a WiMAX business?

■ What is the business case for WiMAX in a number of developed and developing market scenarios, and what financial returns can be expected?

■ How can new network operators and service providers maximize the chance of success in operating WiMAX services?

■ How significant are the opportunities and threats to incumbent fixed and mobile operators, and how should they respond to WiMAX?

WiMAX and Its Future Importance

WiMAX also has every potential to replace a number of existing world communication infrastructures. In the fixed wireless region, it can replace the telephone copper wire networks and cable TV coaxial cable infrastructure, and in the cellular zone WiMAX has the capacity to take the place of existing cellular networks. The most important point about it is that you get all its services cheaper compared to the services from established technologies such as ADSL, cable, and fiber optics, etc. [92]. The working system of WiMAX is very different from that of Wi-Fi, which is described as Internet hot spots. WiMAX is potentially better in terms of coverage, self-installation, power consumption, and bandwidth efficiency when compared to Wi-Fi. WiMAX is capable of full mobility support. It has broken away many of the Wi-Fi limitations by providing increased bandwidth and stronger encryption. It provides connectivity between two network terminals by completely avoiding the use of wires and cables.

The magnitude of WiMAX and its bandwidth make it suitable for wide possible usages [92]:

■ It is a powerful wireless alternative to ADSL and cable broadband access.

■ It can connect existing Wi-Fi hot spots with one another and to the rest of the Internet.

■ It can provide high-quality mobile communication services. WiMAX wireless broadband and WiMAX mobile service probably work within a local loop.

Many cable and telephone companies are considering installation of WiMAX to extend their services in areas where they are not reachable, thus providing users complete broadband services. So, in areas where physical cables or telephone networks were not feasible until now, WiMAX will be a viable alternative for broadband access. WiMAX service packages are available in indoor and outdoor models from their providers. Self-install indoor models are convenient, but the user needs to be significantly closer to the WiMAX base stations. WiMAX working indoors is comparably similar to ADSL or cable broadband. As far as distance is concerned, WiMAX outdoor models allow users to access it from much farther away from the WiMAX base station. Still, WiMAX has some of the characteristics of ADSL. One is that WiMAX shares bandwidth between users in a given ratio. So, if there are many active users in a particular sphere, each user will get a shared bandwidth [92].

It is quite possible to use WiMAX with existing cellular networks. WiMAX aerials can share a cell tower without making any changes in the function of existing cellular arrangements. Companies providing cellular services are evaluating WiMAX with a view to increasing their bandwidth, so that users can be provided with an array of data-intensive services. As a result, this will cut down the costs of the cellular service providers, thus enabling them to provide users with a wide array of services at low cost. WiMAX can very effectively enhance wireless communications in an inexpensive, decentralized, and installation-friendly manner. However, it may be a futuristic aspect of WiMAX. But, just as broadband technologies such as ADSL or cable became functional within just a few years, WiMAX too will be implemented before long. It is going to be a world-shattering replacement of all the existing forms of telecommunications, the beneficiary being the broadband user [92].

WiMAX Cost and Performance

The WiMAX-Forum-Certified device is a few months old, and already the market is awash with a variety of products. The competition is intense. In telecom, cost plays a big role. WiMAX was initially projected as the wireless broadband technology for rural areas. Off late, some operators are into its deployment. But, this has been limited, as the effort was to provide WiMAX as an alternative for those areas not covered by existing broadband technologies. Whether the wide deployment of WiMAX becomes a reality depends on the cost [93]. A customer encountering a new technology expects better performance, and by "better" he means at lower costs also. For the operator, the criterion is operating costs, so a delicate balance between these two is the key for wide deployment. As mentioned earlier, when the competition gets intense, price plays an important role in decision making. At this point in time, it appears that WiMAX has caught the attention of specialist applications. WiMAX is still an emerging technology, and IEEE has ratified 802.16e as the standard for WiMAX, so where does it go from here? When there is a variety of solutions available in the market, each manufacturer will try to provide a unique feature/attraction to differentiate its products from the rest. The major thrust has been on improving the QoS to the end user. For example, people are looking into adaptive techniques and MIMO techniques to support more simultaneous users, and thus increase the coverage area. Some companies such as Samsung are trying to develop their own WiMAX standard. With the telecom industry already looking forward to 4G, WiMAX still has got a long way to go. Cost–performance trade-off is always relevant. The ideal situation would be to achieve a reduction in cost with zero compromise in the performance. Many companies are providing solutions that are flexible and compact, yet cost-effective. They can be used across continents that have different frequency bands. For example, Texas Instruments offers the TRFxxxx series of chipsets, which can be configured to support both CPE and base wireless terminal (BTS) performance levels. This greatly reduces the time to market of many WiMAX solutions. LNAs with very high levels of performance are available, provided WiMAX receivers provide reliable performance over difficult transmission paths. Vendors also want to have high-end and low-end stations for the price-sensitive market. Even though the market has not seen any killer applications that force the consumers to move to 3G from 2/2.5G, the developers are hoping that the requirement for higher-speed wireless communication, faster movie/music downloads, and anywhere connectivity will be pushing 4G. WiMAX is also based on OFDMA technology which is recommended for 4G. Overall, WiMAX has to face stiff competition, both on the performance and price fronts. To become the technological market leader, it has to overcome the threat from upgrades of existing technology also [93].

WiMAX: Worth Banking On

WiMAX technology offers a lot of promise, but it is necessary to separate the hype from the facts to adopt a balanced approach. Any technology, and promises made by a technology, must be workable and viable. A particular technology represents a snapshot in time. For that period, it can be useful and beneficial to the extent that it solves a particular problem set. WiMAX seeks to provide BWA that goes way beyond Wi-Fi capabilities. It does not seek to replace Wi-Fi, but complements it. For instance, although Wi-Fi is standard-based, popular, and works well, the Wi-Fi hot spots still need to connect to the Internet backbone, and that is where WiMAX can provide a cheaper and better alternative to the ones available right now [94]. It can work at both the back end and in solving the last-mile connectivity problem. Apart from cable/DSL, it adds to the customer choices, hopefully driving down the costs through competition for better services. As of this moment, WiMAX shows tremendous promise but is still regarded as unproven. This is the perception, in spite of all the current deployments across the globe. Most of these deployments are based on the fixed version, IEEE 802.16-2004, and they are still trying it out. The real deal is IEEE 802.16-2005, which will provide full mobility. Products certified on this standard are expected early next year. Many vendors and companies have skipped the fixed version in favor of the mobile version, because it can provide all possible configurations and cater to all possible needs for now. Given the kind of hype that media tends to generate, there are many who question or argue if WiMAX has a real business case at all. WiMAX can work in licensed and unlicensed spectrums. Radio spectrum is always a precious commodity. Realizing the potential of WiMAX, most countries have acted upon this, and so far, more than 500 licenses have already been granted. All kinds of players are taking an active part in the adoption — from chip vendors, system integrators, network providers, and mobile handset makers to service providers; everybody is cooperating on an unprecedented level to make this happen. The WiMAX Forum is not just a voice for this technology. With its more than 400 members, it actively seeks to provide certification for products from various vendors and remove barriers to interoperability and adoption. Both enterprises and the individual consumer will benefit from the success of WiMAX technology [94].

Mobile WiMAX Technology Set to Make Huge Gains in the Years to Come

The mobile version of WiMAX broadband technology is in for rapid growth over the next few years, according to a recent report by market research firm In-Stat. At this point in time, there are an estimated 222,000 WiMAX subscribers worldwide, most of whom use the 801.16d fixed wireless version of the technology [95]. The more recently standardized 802.16e mobile WiMAX specification will make up the bulk of future growth, however, In-Stat predicts, with the global penetration of both technologies reaching 19.7 million by the end of 2010. WiMAX, which is often described as a longer-range version of Wi-Fi, has already begun to pick up steam in rural and remote markets, where wired and cellular Internet access is limited or nonexistent. To gain market share in more densely populated regions, however, the technology is in for some tough competition from a number of existing cellular broadband solutions [95].

Can WiMAX Challenge 3G?

Seventy-eight percent of operators surveyed said that they had considered an investment in WiMAX, according to Pyramid Research's new report titled "Can WiMAX Challenge 3G? Performance, Economics, and Opportunities" [96]. Sixty-two percent of those operators plan to invest in WiMAX as early as next year, with nearly 10 percent suggesting an investment level of more than $100 million. The report examines real-world examples of pre-WiMAX deployments and reviews practical issues, such as time to market, business models and pricing, device availability, economics of scale, and spectrum availability. All of these factors are evaluated and summarized to answer the burning question: can WiMAX challenge 3G? The answer will eventually be determined by the operator community. As part of its due diligence, Pyramid surveyed about 100 operators to tune into their views, investments plans, expectations, and concerns with respect to WiMAX [82].

WiMAX in Asia

Asian companies — like consumers — love new technology. The continent has been at the forefront of everything from multitasking mobile phones to Internet TV. Now, Korea's Samsung Electronics is plowing $300 million a year into mobile WiMAX, betting on burgeoning demand for wireless broadband access in 2008. WiMAX has already won over some big names. Sprint Nextel of the United States plans to install a nationwide network in 2008, and Samsung itself is in talks with carriers in some 20 countries to export the technology. It would appear to supersede old-style hot spots — which give wireless access in coffee shops and airports, for example — by enabling subscribers to access broadband over distances of 70 mi. In reality, however, that coverage shrinks, along with bandwidth, as more subscribers tap in [97]. At first sight, Asian operators have as good a chance as any of turning a profit out of new technology. Consumers are more tech-savvy and more given to running up big phone bills — an estimated 7 percent of Korean household expenditure is spent on telecom services. Unlike, say, the United States, Asia boasts of many densely populated areas, allowing cheaper network build-outs, and governments, keen to promote themselves as cutting-edge, are often happy to subsidize infrastructure. That can be done directly, as in the case of Singapore, or by allowing operators to cross-subsidize. Partly reflecting these factors, research consultant In-Stat estimates Asia-Pacific will account for 45 percent of the WiMAX market by 2009. However, even in these technology friendly territories, WiMAX faces challenges, and competition is predictably fierce. Two Korean mobile operators are pushing High Speed Downlink Packet Access (HSDPA), which in some ways is an inferior technology, but one that has industry support. That should help terminals become cheaper. As is often the case with new technologies, consumers may have more to gain than investors [97].

WiMAX May Challenge Asia 3G in Five Years

Despite the hype and heavy investment, the WiMAX WAN standard is still a long way from challenging existing mobile phone technology as the Asia-Pacific region's primary means of mobile Internet access [98]. It will be at least another five years before WiMAX can pose a serious threat to 3G in the region [99]. South Korea has already launched a mobile version of WiMAX in a few urban areas, although anecdotal evidence suggests uptake has been slow so far. Korean consumer electronics giant Samsung is attempting to take advantage of its early lead by opening a WiMAX factory and research center in China, where 3G service introduction has been delayed for more than a year, according to recent press reports. Samsung is promoting WiBro, a Korean variant of mobile WiMAX. However, 3G has already entered a period of very rapid growth in Asia. The number of 3G subscribers will grow by more than 50 percent annually, from 2005 to 20011, to reach 178 million in the region by the end of 2011, predicts Frost & Sullivan Research Analyst Lenny Koay. Globally, 3G mobile users will account for one-third of a three billion user wireless market by 2010, research firm Strategy Analytics recently forecast [98].

Research Report Presents the Best Business Case for WiMAX

The growing availability of WiMAX equipment and the early announcement of a number of deployment plans have led to a surge of interest in WiMAX and its potential to complement or disrupt fixed and wireless broadband services. The WiMAX Forum and equipment vendors are strongly promoting the application of WiMAX in a variety of market situations, in both developed and developing countries. However, in developed markets, WiMAX will face growing competition from DSL, whereas in developing markets, its progress will be hindered by limited disposable income. Research and Markets has released a report, "The Best Business Case for WiMAX," and the questions answered are the following [100]:

1. Under what circumstances might there be a viable business case for WiMAX, e.g., type of market, competitive landscape, operator characteristics, service mix, and technology requirements?
2. What are the critical factors that will define the success of WiMAX in different situations? How do they affect the potential return of a WiMAX business?
3. What is the business case for WiMAX in a number of developed and developing market scenarios, and what financial returns can be expected?
4. How can new network operators and service providers maximize the chances of success of WiMAX services?
5. How significant are the opportunities and threats to incumbent fixed and mobile operators, and how should they respond to WiMAX?

Cellular Base Station Silicon Makers Face WiMAX and Other Challenges

Just as 3G is deployed after years of delays, there is now a new potential fly in the ointment, WiMAX, reports In-Stat. However, WiMAX is not the only threat to cellular base station semiconductor manufacturers. Not only has cellular subscriber growth started to slow, but also cheaper semiconductors from Asia are starting to enter the base station market. As a result, total semiconductor revenue from base stations is forecast to drop over the next few years [101].

A recent report by the high-tech market research firm found the following [101]:

■ Total cellular base station semiconductor revenue is forecast to reach over $4.5 billion in 2006.

- The rate of major cellular technology updates is slowing.
- Providers are upgrading to the fastest cellular technology as quickly as they can, and doing it while maintaining the price pressure on infrastructure equipment makers.

"Cellular Base Station/PA Semiconductor 5-Year Forecast" explores some of the factors influencing the base station semiconductor, the cellular power amp, and power amp semiconductor markets. Five-year forecasts are included for new base stations, base station semiconductor revenue, cellular power amps, power amp and power amp semiconductor revenue, categorized by CDMA, GSM, PDC, and WCDMA [101].

The Future as Samsung Sees It: 4G Is WiMAX

4G is WiMAX. We are very clear about that, said Samsung [102]. Although the company sees mobile WiMAX as the future, currently mobility and connectivity will come through a variety of wireless interfaces, including EVDO Rev A, HSDPA, and HSUPA, mobile TV, satellite broadcasts, and dual-mode Wi-Fi/cellular phones. "MediaFLO will be big next year," said Garrison. What adds to the authenticity of Samsung's prediction is that it has few axes to grind as it is a developer of wireless technologies across the board, including GSM/GPRS/EDGE as well as the 3G IMT2000 CDMA-based variants. In addition, its commitment to mobile WiMAX was demonstrated on August 6, 2006 when it signed a deal with Sprint-Nextel to supply the operator with the equipment needed for its planned U.S. rollout of mobile WiMAX starting, potentially, by the end of 2007. Intel and Motorola were cosignatories on that deal. According to Samsung, the benefits of mobile WiMAX include time to market, greater throughput, low latency, multimedia centricity, greater broadcast capacity at 2 Mbps per user, vehicular mobility at up to 75 mph, and broad global support with over 380 companies in the WiMAX Forum [102].

WiMAX Applications

IBM and Alvarion to Deliver Wireless and WiMAX for Public Safety

Alvarion and IBM offer and deliver wireless systems to municipalities and their public safety agencies [103]. The alliance will enable a new approach for delivery of scalable, multilayer IP-based wireless networks that support data, voice, and video for both fixed and mobile applications. Based on a unique pilot wireless network implementation in Fresno, the sixth largest city in California, the IBM and Alvarion information communication technology (ICT) system comprises IBM's suite of productivity-enhancing mobile applications built on Alvarion's broadband and mobile wireless systems. Customizable to deliver broad functionality and support a myriad of applications while enabling citywide broadband coverage at a fraction of the cost of competing systems, this cooperation now brings affordable broadband within reach of most U.S. communities. The Fresno public safety network is intended to enable police officers to send and receive text messages, still images, and even full-motion video using their car-based mobile data terminals and their handheld personal digital assistants (PDAs), greatly enhancing productivity and their ability to deter crime and capture criminals. Built by IBM using Alvarion broadband wireless systems and IBM's WebSphere Everyplace Connection Manager, the network features government-grade wireless encryption, roaming, and compression to the city's 250-police-vehicle fleet. Using 900-MHz-based mobile technology requiring less than one-tenth the number of nodes generally required by competing Wi-Fi-based solutions while providing superior net service speeds, the network employs Wi-Fi to extend the network to low-cost, end-user devices. To protect the city's existing network investments while ensuring seamless connectivity over a wider area, the broadband network features seamless switching at vehicular speeds, as it maintains session persistence with the police department's legacy 800-MHz narrowband network. The network provides the optimum balance of minimum infrastructure and maximum access [103].

WiMAX Promises to Help Narrow "Digital Divide"

WiMAX is not a perfect technology. Still, it promises in some applications to help narrow the digital divide in rural markets. WiMAX is touted as the tool that will bridge the digital divide and lack of affordable telecommunication infrastructure that is critical to future economic and social development of a community, region, or nation. The UN is pushing for access to broadband across borders. Its challenge, "Information Society for All," resulted from the World Summit on the Information Society in 2003. A major driver for the development of WiMAX is its potential to reduce the cost and time of deployment and sustain high bandwidth access to phone, video, and data networks to areas too remote for traditional wired telecommunication. This is not just an issue relevant to developing countries; we have communities in our own region that are grossly underserved. We may have dial-up access or even a form of DSL or cable. But without the ability to achieve speeds higher than 2 Mbps download and 256 kbps upload, we will never be able to use the new tools available [104].

The advantages of WiMAX are well known [104]:

- A single station can serve hundreds of users.
- Endpoints can be installed far faster than with wired connections.
- Data rates as high as 280+ Mbps and distances of up to 30 mi are possible.
- Users can operate mobiles within 3 to 5 mi of a base station at up to 75 Mbps.

- No Federal Communications Commission (FCC) licensing is required for its use.
- It is a worldwide standard and equipment using the same frequency should work together.

The possible disadvantages of WiMAX [104]:

- Line-of-sight is required for connections 5 mi or further.
- Rain and weather can disrupt the service.
- Other wireless equipment in the vicinity can interfere with WiMAX.
- Multiple frequencies will be used to deploy WiMAX.
- WiMAX is a power-intensive technology and requires strong electrical support.
- Realities of WiMAX data rates are more like 72 Mbps and reduce as you add distance.

Prespecification WiMAX supported the telecommunications facilities destroyed in the 2004 tsunami in Indonesia and by hurricanes Katrina and Rita along the Gulf Coast. Many wireless solutions providers, manufacturers, telecom and public and private companies fought through the federal roadblocks to establish a make-shift network that supported hospitals, municipal agencies, volunteer organizations, and even the much-maligned federal natural disaster response agency, FEMA. A report by European communications consultant IDATE titled "WiMAX: Ready for Deployment?" forecasts that the worldwide WiMAX market will hit $3.5 billion by 2010. That is a 4 percent share of all broadband use. This growth will be driven by new equipment from an expanding list of hardware suppliers and an increasing number of WiMAX trials and deployments. Among its key findings [104] are the following:

- WiMAX has attracted many leading equipment manufacturers and compo-nent suppliers, and, many are forming strategic partnerships.
- WiMAX systems and services are being evaluated and deployed in subur-ban business districts that lack high-quality DSL access; in urban markets to compete against DSL and broadband cable; and by wire-based carriers and ISPs to compete with mobile carriers. Worldwide, WiMAX systems can be deployed in a large number of licensed and unlicensed frequency bands.
- Delays in allocations and licensing by regulatory agencies, coupled with the lack of a common worldwide frequency band for WiMAX use, may slow market development.
- Companies should realize the benefit of creating a WiMAX network to extend services too expensive to deploy with wire line in underserved areas. If WiMAX can bring broadband communications to remote areas of Africa, it should also serve us well in northwest Wisconsin and northeastern Minnesota.

The world's second-fastest-growing mobile phone market offers challenges for telecom and has serious implications for Indian society. For long a telecom backwater, India is rapidly embracing mobile telephony and is one of the fastest-growing markets on the planet right now. Widespread access to the Internet would have huge implications for the quality of Indian education, health care, and the economic development of the world's biggest democracy. The number of fixed and wireless telephone connections has doubled in the past two years, to about 150 million, and subscriptions for mobile-phone service rose at the extraordinary rate of 5 million new wireless connections a month. The Ministry of Telecom has set a target for 2007 to have 250 million connections and mobile coverage for 85 percent of the country, from about 30 percent today [18].

WiMAX Connects Rural India to the Global Village

WiMAX is the new connector of rural India [106]. This technology is making its presence felt in the country, thanks to its features and possibilities. The future prospects of the technology are lucrative [105]. WiMAX ensures continuous connectivity, high-speed data, voice, and multimedia services, and mobility and affordability. Rural connectivity can be delivered as long as power supply is available, PCs are given, local languages are used in developing content, and people are provided with training to use PCs [18]. According to the RNCOS' recent report "WiMAX — A Market Update (2006–2007)," as the Indian telecom industry is booming and the middle class is growing, a substantial demand for broadband wireless services and WiMAX is expected. It is predicted that Indian WIMAX subscribers will number around 12 million by 2012. Various aspects of WiMAX technology are discussed in the report.

How IT Is Changing Rural India

Farmers in a remote village in Honavar, 600 km away from Bangalore, are using ATM machines to open a bank account. Believe us — it is true. An ATM machine loaded on a van winds its way through the dusty roads of over five villages offering 22,000-odd farmers, perhaps, their first experience with a bank — they can open an account, request a loan, and be able to deposit as well as withdraw cash at will in the near future. The ATM machine is linked wirelessly through Reliance Infocomm's network to the back-end server of the participating bank, which includes Syndicate Bank and State Bank of India. The software on the ATM is simple, in the regional languages, and very easy to understand [107]. For the last few years, state governments, NGOs, and some pioneering companies have tried to crack the technology barrier by developing pilot projects to showcase the marvels of IT in a rural setting. The movement is better known as *Bridging the Digital Divide*. The success of ITC's 6,000 odd *e-choupals* covering over 35,000 villages has made many believe that this model can be made viable. The big boys are jumping onto the bandwagon, including top IT companies, NGOs, technology providers, and the government. There is a need to scale up. The name of the game is clear: how to scale up and still be viable. Microsoft, for instance, has set an ambitious target. It hopes to set up over 50,000 broadband-connected kiosks across villages, covering over 50 percent of the rural population in the next three years under the Saksham scheme. The company is funding NGOs, as well as local companies, with an undisclosed budget to make the project a reality. Not to be left behind, Intel recently joined the club, announcing a new program Jagruti, whereby it will offer PC makers an innovative platform developed exclusively for the rural market. Intel has developed a rugged chassis to withstand dusty and extreme temperatures. It has also integrated a UPS, as well as an AC\DC converter in the machine, so that it can work on a car battery for 6 to 8 hr, to tackle the lack of electricity in many villages. Moreover, it has also tied up with Microsoft in an "affordability alliance" that will look at partnerships to provide solutions for rural India. Yes, the ministry of information technology has set up an ambitious target to set up one lakh "common services centers" across villages where e-governance services will be available by August 2007. It has tied up with ILFS to manage the roll out with support from NGOs, ISPs, and others. The government has also earmarked Rs 100 crore (Rs 1 billion) to fund this Mission 2007. Local Indian companies who have pioneered the rural move but have had problems of scaling up are now embarking on an expansion spree. Jai Kisan, an NGO set up to introduce rural IT technology in Uttaranchal, India, is hoping to put up over 3,000 Kisan Soochna Kendras (a digital hub) across the state. But tobacco giant ITC is concentrating on creating a physical infrastructure to support the 6,000 e-choupals, which are run by entrepreneurship-driven sanchalaks (organizers). It is now creating a second tier of entrepreneurs by appointing *up-sanchalaks* (deputy organizers) in over 14,000 villages — it has already appointed 15,000 — who would directly interact with the e-choupal owners. Also, it is planning to set up over 50 *choupal sagars*, which will have hypermarkets, fuel stations, restaurants, and even an educational service center. Chennai-based n-Logue Communications — part of the Telnet group, which was floated by professors in IIT Chennai — wants to replicate the PCO model to increase per capita incomes in rural India. It has already rolled out over 2,500 kiosks across the country using corDECT (wireless and local loop) technology to provide broadband connectivity to the villages [107]. Ensuring a connected kiosk model as a viable unit is not an easy task. That is why, despite all the noise, there are not more than 13,000 connected kiosks across the country (a large chunk of which is run by ITC's e-choupal). Microsoft, for instance, undertook a study of over 350 kiosks, involving 4,000 users in six states to understand user habits, which could throw up a viable model. The study threw up some interesting insights: kiosks that only offered e-governance services (like registration of life and death, land records, etc.), were unable to sustain themselves very long. The reason was simple: although 70 percent of the revenues, when the kiosk was launched, came from e-governance, in six months time, it dropped to 20 percent. So there was need for offering more comprehensive services in the kiosk for farmers to come in. That is what Microsoft is doing. The company has developed educational content online for children in local languages, which is available for a subscription of Rs 50 to 100 a month. A printer and software for desktop publishing ensures that you can publish marriage or invitation cards, or even a CV for a nominal Rs 10 to 12 a piece. And as PCs are loaded with Windows Media Player, many local kiosk owners have converted themselves into mini movie halls, offering movie shows at a nominal Rs 2 to 3 a show. How does Microsoft ensure that the model is viable? Take, for instance, its tie up with Dhristee, an NGO that has, perhaps, the cheapest-priced kiosk model. Kiosks are not cheap; one connected with a VSAT (Very Small Aperture Terminal), battery pack, and printer requires an investment of over Rs 70,000. The method is straightforward: the entrepreneurs have to pay Rs 20,000 up front. The rest comes from bank loans. Kiosk owners need to pay about Rs 1,666 per month to pay off the loan, but Drishtee offers them a minimum income guarantee of Rs 3,000 a month. Experience has shown that the entrepreneur is cash positive within the first two to three months." On average, in a village of 5,000 homes, at least 20 people go to the kiosk every day, and that is enough to break even and make money. Microsoft, of course, funds Dhristi lump sum or with software support, which can be used to subsidize the overall investment, reduce upfront cost, or the loan burden, depending on individual needs. There are other models, too. Many are using innovative ways to generate revenues. Jai Kisan has, in fact, gone up market by creating a Kisan Soochna Kendra in far-flung villages of Uttaranchal, where road communication is not at its best. The kendra has swanky styling, it is built with glazed tile floorings and equipped with the latest gizmos — laser printers and scanners, and even a movie video camera and PCs connected by VSAT to the outer world. But it also costs money — an investment of a steep Rs 510,000. However, Sanjiv Sharma, CEO of Jai Kisan.org, says that despite the high cost, the model works. The owner of the kendra, who is generally the Gram Pradhan, puts Rs 25,000 up front. Jai Kisan (which gets funds from various agencies, including companies such as Microsoft) forks out Rs 40,000, and banks fund the remaining portion. Then grants are also available from the Khadi Vikas Industry Board, which uses the kiosks for selling and promoting khadi products. To add to the viability, Jai Kisan guarantees the owner Rs 11,000 a month, which ensures that even after paying back the loan installment (Rs 7,500) he or she is making money. The question, though, is how can Jai Kisan afford to give this guarantee? Well, simply put, it has innovative ways of bringing in revenue. The NGO, for instance, has roped in companies ranging from Pepsi to Coke to advertise by using the walls of the kendra to sell their products. Last year, it generated revenue at an average of Rs 5,000 a month from selling advertising space. This year, it expects to hit Rs 11,000, which will take care of the minimum guarantee it offers the entrepreneur. Second, the NGO has helped in floating Jai Kisan Foods (made out of farmer enraptures in the village), which sell farm products ranging from mangoes, herbs, and medicinal plants through the Jai Kisan portal to potential buyers, thus dispensing with the middlemen. Already, companies such as Dabur are using the structure to buy medicinal plants directly from farmers. No doubt, communication costs, through VSATs, are a key impediment in proliferation of the kiosk model. But as Jai Kisan executives tell you, telephone connectivity of BSNL is unreliable (exchanges do not have power for days), and private sector wireless connectivity is conspicuous by its absence, so there is no choice but to go for a VSAT even if it is not cheap. Singh says that if wireless connectivity were available, investment costs would fall by more than half and kiosk owners would have to pay only the monthly running cost of broadband connectivity. That, of course, remains the biggest challenge.

Some are trying to solve the problem. Intel is pushing for WiMAX as a cheaper solution, but with its standards still not fixed, this might be a while away. n-Louge has deployed corDECT (wireless and local loop) technology to bring in connectivity to the villages. It charges between Rs 500 and 1,000 monthly to ensure uninterrupted connectivity. This would require a cluster of kiosks in a 25 to 50 km area to justify the initial investment, which could be around Rs 40 lakh (after all, you need to put in a couple of base stations). So, Jhunjunwala says, you need at least 200 to 300 kiosks to make it viable. At the moment, with most companies spreading the kiosks over a larger geographical distance, it might not be the best option. But that is not deterring many companies and researchers from working out niche applications that can be converted into a viable business model. One such area is banking. Mobile wireless ATMs developed by IIIT Bangalore is one such solution. The solution, which is being implemented in Karnataka, aims to encourage entrepreneurs to invest in a PDA and then go to each home to collect information on topics such as assets, livestock, crop patterns, and income (they are paid for this collection, of course, by the bank or by the data center that wants to collect this information). This information is then sent wirelessly to data centers, which are owned by telcos. Companies can tie up or pay for this information available with telcos. Surely even telcos can make money by selling this valuable information to potential clients. Bridging the digital divide might not be as easy as it sounds; however, companies are taking the first steps to work out viable and scaleable models to make it a reality [107].

India: A Major Market for WiMAX Technology

India has emerged as a major market for WiMAX technology, mainly because of the growing demand for broadband connectivity from urban homes and small and medium businesses that cannot be met by the existing wireline technology [113]. WiMAX, based on 4G technology, promises to bring bandwidth to the masses and is expected to ride on the huge demand for such connectivity in the country.

Beceem Communications, a leading provider of chipsets for Mobile WiMAX technology with significant R&D operations in India, has committed to accelerate WiMAX deployment in India. Several India service providers such as Reliance, Bharti, Sify, etc., have already acquired suitable spectrum licenses to deploy wireless broadband services and are planning early rollouts.

WiMAX: India's Answer to Spectrum Problems and Rural Connectivity

India is on the threshold of a new mobile technology revolution with WiMAX being considered as the new age reality by many mobile manufacturers [112]. With demand for spectrum soaring, WiMAX technology is becoming the way to avert the impending crisis. WiMAX promises seamless connectivity, high-speed data, voice, and multimedia services, mobility, and affordability [109]. Rural connectivity is guaranteed as long as availability of power supply and personal computers is ensured, content is developed in local language, and people are given proper training in handling PCs. Alcatel Research Centre is developing a product that would act as a receiver for WiMAX services. The product will be available by 2007 and cost less than $100 [108].

Latin America: First Great Battleground for WiMAX

China, India, and Russia are most commonly held up as the great battlegrounds for wireless technologies in the second half of this decade. But in broadband wireless, in particular, we should not underestimate the significance of Latin America, which is at the forefront of WiMAX deployment and will have a strong impact on its future success.

Although start-ups and competitive telcos such as Ertach in Argentina are in the vanguard of WiMAX, incumbents, like Telmex in Mexico and Argentina or Telefonica, are also looking to deploy the technology. The most significant move so far has come from Brazil, where Samsung has won the first contract outside Korea for its WiBro technology, which will form the basis of the upcoming 802.16e mobile WiMAX standard. This is a victory for Samsung's claim that WiBro is a general purpose pre-WiMAX technology with international relevance, rather than a variant specific to the needs of Korea; especially as the Brazilian project is in the 3.5-GHz spectrum, not the 2.3-GHz and 2.5-GHz spectrums for which WiBro was created. For Samsung and its compatriot LG, WiMAX is a strong opportunity to start to penetrate telco markets in the West at the equipment end, rather than just with handsets [109]. Brazil is interesting, as one of the most likely countries where operators could look to leapfrog 3G by moving directly to a post-3G technology such as WiMAX. The country's regulator, Anatel, has yet to auction

3G licenses. However, interest from carriers has been lukewarm, whereas there is a growing list of trial lists for WiMAX, including the major fixed-line operators Telefonica, Telemar, and Brasil Telecom.

Growth in Brazilian cellular communications is rapid, with the total number of subscribers reaching up to 42 percent between 2003 and 2004, and reaching almost 70 million in 2005 — the fourth largest base in the world. Brazil has already been the most active Latin American nation, along with Mexico, in promoting broadband fixed wireless services and testing portable or mobile extensions. The Brazilian administration has a program called Service of Digital Communications (SCD), which aims to bring Internet access to remote areas. Intel is working with government agencies and will have a WiMAX pilot, probably in partnership with Siemens. The network will not only serve rural communities but will generate most of its revenue from business users and providing services to ISPs and hosting companies. Also in Brazil, Neotec, a consortium of mobile operators, has tested a NextNet-based system in urban areas in the Multi-channel Multi-point Distribution System (MMDS) spectrum that many Brazilian operators own for television services [109].

Nigeria: WiMAX — Technology for Cheaper Internet Access

Different technology initiatives for Internet access have all been confronted with challenges requiring an improved and affordable alternative. Efem Nkanga writes that with the introduction of the WiMAX technology and its potential to reduce the cost of acquiring Internet access, the country's telecommunications landscape would be the better for it. It is a fact that in the world of communications and technology, change occurs quite fast. As one technology is being celebrated, a new one is introduced into the market, thus rendering the others immediately obsolete. However, a new technology that looks as though it will be around for a while has been introduced — WiMAX technology [110,111]. A unique feature of this technology is that it focuses on economies of scale, thereby leading to a reduction in the cost per unit resulting from increased production realized through operational efficiencies. This in turn causes the cost of acquiring Internet services to drop. It provides bandwidth and range improvements that enable the adoption of advanced radio features in a uniform fashion, which reduces the cost of the radios. It can deploy voice, data, and video. It has fast speeds and runs at zero downtime. The main attraction of mobile WiMAX will be that it will ensure personal broadband wireless access on the move. It is fast, easy to operate, easy to connect, and works seamlessly with the IP multimedia subsystem that is the basis for the common core network of the future, providing lower overheads and easier service deployment. The system will help in extending broadband access to rural areas, as well. However, the primary advantage of the WiMAX standard is that it enables the adoption of advanced radio features in a uniform fashion aimed at reducing costs of all the radios made by companies that are members of the WiMAX Forum. The WiMAX Forum works to remove the barriers to broadband wireless adoption by promoting the adoption of broadband wireless gear beyond the technical standard. The forum maintains working groups formed to address specific elements such as regulatory, technical, certification, marketing, service provider, applications, and networks. The WiMAX Forum was formed to coordinate testing and ensure the interoperability of WiMAX equipment. This forum is made up of industry leaders and technology giants like Intel, Motorola, Nokia, Samsung, Ericsson, Alcatel, etc., who have joined together to invest in the development of chipsets, devices, and other components, which ensures that the WiMAX technology is future proof. These providers are so focused on making WiMAX a success that they have created an ecosystem. Soon, every laptop will contain a WiMAX chip, and in three years, mobile phones and PDAs will have WiMAX chips, according to Anudu. A powerful advantage of the WiMAX technology is that it benefits from widespread industry cooperation and support. This collaboration among the major telecommunications companies will ensure that products are developed and launched at the same time, thereby creating an ecosystem with all elements in place. This will therefore remove the need by service providers to provide their own solutions and accelerate the deployment of WiMAX services by users. A fundamental goal of the communications industry is to provide wireless broadband access across a wide geographical area at an affordable rate. That the Internet has changed the way people communicate cannot be overemphasized, and ever since Nigeria embraced GSM technology five years ago, the communications landscape, which was constrained by a dearth of reliable communications technology, has changed forever. Mobile phone technology and the Internet have become part and parcel of our lives. Very soon, almost everything people do will be done through the World Wide Web. In Nigeria, most activities are now done online — banks, airlines, embassies, large corporations, among others, are all hooking up to the online method of transacting businesses.The online phenomenon cuts across different segments of the society. From applications for jobs, which are sent online to embassy appointments for visas and bank transactions being done online, it is certain that the Web culture is here to stay. It is a fact that those who deploy the Internet in their business and leisure interactions have a great advantage over those who do not. Most Nigerians now deploy the Internet to interact and build relationships, browse, and transact business online. A new technology that will ensure that most Nigerians have affordable access to the World Wide Web is WiMAX. The technology is set to change the face of the communications sector and help bring down the cost of Internet access to the barest minimum. Over the years, various technologies have been deployed in a bid to ensure effective communication to subscribers. Different technology initiatives for Internet access like dial-up, DSL/ADSL, VSAT, among others, were brought in to ensure that the goal of creating and ensuring access to the world was accomplished. But they have all been confronted with various challenges, necessitating a better technology that will meet the needs of the sector at an affordable cost. VSAT technology, for example, is known

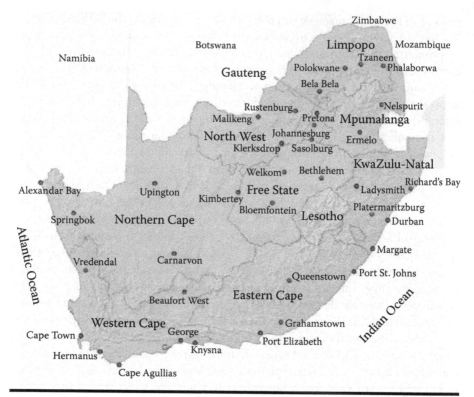

Figure 6.6   Map of South Africa

to be interference prone, especially in bad weather. The dial-up technology connection can be frustrating, as the connection gets cut off intermittently, making the subscriber reconnect again and again. Besides, most of the other technologies have high start-up costs and natural availability limits that cannot be mitigated [110].

A Feasibility Study of WiMAX Implementation at Dwesa-Cwebe Rural Areas of Eastern Cape of South Africa

South Africa (22 to 34° S, 16 to 32° E) is a country (Figure 6.6) located at the southern-most tip of the African continent, having its borders with countries like Namibia, Botswana, Zimbabwe, and Mozambique. South Africa's vast mineral wealth has always been the backbone of its market economy. The country contributes about 30 percent of the world's total gold output. It is also the world's largest producer of manganese, chromite, vermiculite, and vanadium. But years of international trade sanctions and political instability have taken an enormous toll on South Africa's economy [127].

South Africa ranks 23rd in telecommunications development in the world. Telkom, South Africa, provides the basic telecommunication services in the rural areas.

a

Figure 6.7(a)   Map of Dwesa.

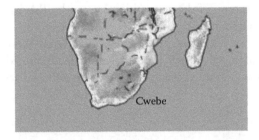

b

Figure 6.7(b)   Map of Cwebe.

But, the rural areas of South Africa have peculiar features such as low population density (typically, 10.50 persons per square kilometer). Out of the nine provinces of South Africa, five have over 50 percent of the population living in rural areas. The analysis of the global survey on the communication for rural and remote areas has revealed the disparity in information and communication services between urban and rural areas in the developing countries. Telecommunications service provision in rural areas is a very demanding enterprise because of inadequate infrastructure and scattered settlements. The provision of rural telecommunications to disadvantaged rural areas remains the only way to usher these rural areas into the information age, thus enabling the narrowing of the digital divide between the rural areas and the urban areas.

Dwesa (32° 17' 60" S, 28° 49' 60" E)-Cwebe (32° 13' 0" S, 28° 55' 0" E) is a rural community area located in the Mbashe Municipality of the Eastern Cape (Figure 6.7a and b). It is situated in the central Wild Coast bordered on one side by the Indian Ocean and on the other by rugged grasslands of the former Transkei.

The region is a very good starting point for rural information communication technologies development research, because it has a well-documented history and an established dialogue with Rhodes University. The region has little or no preexisting infrastructure (electrical, communication, etc.). There is an original research effort currently underway at University of Fort Hare, Eastern Cape, South Africa.

Rural areas encompass a range of geographical terrain, including forest, grasslands, mountainous regions, and isolated islands. This constitutes a primary challenge for many rural areas, as difficult terrain compounded with poor levels of transport infrastructure increases the cost of establishing, operating, and maintaining a telecommunications infrastructure. Delivering affordable and accessible services to populations with very low disposable income and general lack of capital to acquire telecommunication equipment is another challenge. Furthermore, for many rural areas, ancillary services such as electricity supply are nonexistent or insufficient. Solar energy is another alternative; however, it has its own problems. The major problem is theft of the solar panels. The impact created by such thefts has affected some sections of the network permanently. This has impacted the network heavily, leading to its distraction.

The South African Government has set up a Universal Service Agency that has established nationwide approximately 68 telecenters in disadvantaged rural communities. The purpose of setting up these centers is to provide universal access to information

Figure 6.8   Connectivity work in progress.

and communication technologies (ICTs) to communities in unserved and underserviced areas. Work is currently on (Figure 6.8) to connect the community utilizing proven technology. The VSAT was found to provide connectivity to this area, thereby utilizing WiMAX technology to extend the wireless cloud over the whole area.

A second-generation multipurpose telecenter would be established to provide the community with access to telecommunication and information center using VSAT. The WiMAX system would be deployed in this area, and the hope is to be able to offer the communication services that have been sought by the community. The further objectives are to test and evaluate the effectiveness of the access technologies in Dwesa-Cwebe rural and remote areas, to develop and field-test the prototype of a simple, cost-effective, and robust integrated E-business/telecommunication platform, and to deploy it in marginalized and semimarginalized communities in South Africa, where the majority of the South African population live. These communities, by their sheer size and current political dynamics, represent a strategic emergent market for the industry partners in this project.

Furthermore, it is necessary that some kind of economical activity be present, or be stimulated, to sustain the telecenter and gain from it. Based on extensive field research, we envisage that WiMAX connectivity in the rural areas such as Dwesa and Cwebe, where natural resources are abundant, could make a significant contribution to promote rural development [127–132].

References

1. www.marketwire.com.
2. http://www.researchandmarkets.com/reports/c21014.
3. http://www.expresscomputeronline.com/20061030/market07.shtml.
4. http://www.thewirelessreport.com/2006/10/31/wimax-is-the-future/ [dated October 31, 2006].
5. http://www.techworld.com/mobility/features/index.cfm?featureID=2876&pagtype=all [dated October 17, 2006].
6. http://www.pyramidresearch.com/.
7. http://www.dailywireless.org/2006/11/15/wimax-market-projections/.
8. http://www.wimax.com/commentary/spotlight/spotlight11132006mw1/ [dated November 14, 2006].
9. http://www.telegeography.com/cu/article.php?article_id=14034&email=html [dated August 29, 2006].
10. http://www.wimax.com/commentary/spotlight/spotlight11072006mw1/ [dated November 7, 2006].
11. www.heavyreading.com.
12. http://wirelessfederation.com/news/wimax-adoption-to-rise-dsl-to-gain-ground/ [datedOctober 28, 2006].
13. http://www.earthtimes.org/articles/show/news_press_release,12469.shtml [dated October 30, 2006].

14. http://www.redorbit.com/news/technology/712248/mass_adoption_of_wimax_is_possible_in_developing_countries_with/?source=r_technology.
15. http://www.newswire.ca/en/releases/archive/Octoberober2006/10/c6303.html.
16. http://neasia.nikkeibp.com/topstory/004580 [dated June 30, 2006].
17. http://www.techweb.com/wire/mobile/191801662.
18. http://www.rbcnews.com/free/20060828191924.shtml [dated August 28, 2006].
19. http://www.digitalmediaasia.com/default.asp?ArticleID=17836 [dated August 29, 2006].
20. http://www.sda-india.com/sda_india/psecom,id,102,site_layout,sdaindia,news,12038,p,0.html [dated September 27, 2006].
21. http://www.digitimes.com/telecom/a20060807PB202.html [dated August 7, 2006].
22. http://www.techdirt.com/articles/20060809/1149258.shtml [dated August 7, 2006].
23. http://www.wirelessweek.com/article/CA6360929.html [dated August 9, 2006].
24. http://www.suntimes.com/output/business/cst-fin-sprint09.html [dated August 9, 2006].
25. http://www.eetasia.com/ART_8800432097_499488_ca67284b200609.HTM [dated September 1, 2006].
26. http://australianit.news.com.au/articles/0,7204,19921619%5E15306%5E%5Enbv%5E,00.html [dated July 27, 2006].
27. http://www.sci-tech-today.com/story.xhtml?story_id=12200DMDPXPI [dated July 26, 2006].
28. http://www.wi-fiplanet.com/columns/article.php/3634386 [dated September 26, 2006].
29. http://www.theregister.co.uk/2006/09/29/oz_wimax_roaming_alliance/ [dated September 29, 2006].
30. http://www.rethinkresearch.biz/.
31. http://www.stuff.co.nz/stuff/0,2106,3815128a28,00.html.
32. http://www.technologynewsdaily.com/node/4126 [dated August 18, 2006].
33. http://www.abiresearch.com/home.jsp [dated September 1, 2006].
34. http://www.rncos.com/ [dated September 15, 2006].
35. http://www.zdnetasia.com/news/communications/0,39044192,61957298,00.htm [dated October 5, 2006].
36. http://www.prminds.com/pressrelease.php?id=3497 [dated September 11, 2006].
37. http://www.maroc-it.com/blogs/amine/?p=148.
38. http://www.rfglobalnet.com/content/news/article.asp?DocID=%7B317EEF2A-11C0-4CDF-AA48-823AA8545F94%7D&Bucket=Current+Headlines.
39. http://www.digitalopportunity.org/article/view/136442/1/1138.
40. http://www.telegeography.com/products/wimax/.
41. http://www.eetasia.com/ART_8800417528_499488_0b7c2b75200604_no.HTM [dated May 12, 2006].
42. http://www.researchandmarkets.com/reportinfo.asp?report_id=342995&t=o&cat_id=.
43. http://www.latinbusinesschronicle.com/app/article.aspx?id=419 [dated October 2, 2006].
44. http://www.mobiletechnews.com/info/2006/05/16/111931.html [dated May 16, 2006].
45. http://australianit.news.com.au/articles/0,7204,20568832%5E15321%5E%5Enbv%5E,00.html [dated October 12, 2006].
46. http://www.boston.com/business/technology/articles/2006/10/09/wimax_may_give_broadband_a_lead_over_cellular_service/?page=2 [dated October 9, 2006].

47. http://www.wirelessweek.com/article/CA6380796.html [dated October 13, 2006].

48. http://www.informationweek.com/news/showArticle.jhtml?articleID=193300202&subSection=Breaking+News [dated October 12, 2006].

49. http://www.macnn.com/articles/06/10/03/idf.special.report.2.wimax/ [dated October 3, 2006].

50. http://www.itwire.com.au/content/view/6231/127/1/1/ [dated October 11, 2006].

51. http://www.wirelessnetworksonline.com/content/news/article.asp?DocID=%7BCA1ED781-C778-4A90-A0D3-239142661248%7D&Bucket=Current+Headlines [dated October 16, 2006].

52. http://www.tmcnet.com/voip/ip-communications/articles/3180-yankee-group-standards-vital-mobile-wimax-adoption-will.htm [dated October 19, 2006].

53. http://www.cellular-news.com/story/19871.php.

54. http://www.in-stat.com.

55. http://www.digitalmediaasia.com/default.asp?ArticleID=19969 [dated November 22, 2006].

56. http://www.enterprisenetworkingplanet.com/netsp/article.php/3642721 [dated November 8, 2006].

57. http://www.toptechnews.com/news/WiMAX-Wireless-Gains-Head-of-Steam/story.xhtml?story_id=003000AMBC5C [dated November 3, 2006].

58. http://sourcewire.com/releases/rel_display.php?relid=28016&hilite=.

59. http://research.analysys.com.

60. http://business.maktoob.com/itnew.asp?id=20061106024729 [dated November 6, 2006].

61. http://www.business-standard.com/common/storypage.php?autono=263919&leftnm=8&subLeft=0&chkFlg= [dated November 7, 2006].

62. http://www.unstrung.com/document.asp?doc_id=109851&WT.svl=tease3 [dated November 6, 2006].

63. http://www.marketwire.com/mw/release_html_b1?release_id=181008 [dated November 7, 2006].

64. www.nsr.com.

65. http://www.researchandmarkets.com/reports/c44490.

66. http://www.techworld.com/mobility/features/index.cfm?featureID=2877&pagtype=samecatsamechan [dated October 16, 2006].

67. http://www.computerworld.com/action/article.do?command=viewArticleBasic&articleId=9004678 [dated November 1, 2006].

68. http://www.cbronline.com/article_news.asp?guid=D069E848-438C-4B6F-8FDF-05E284581D16 [dated November 9, 2006].

69. http://www.digitimes.com/systems/a20061110A9051.html [dated November 10, 2006].

70. http://www.digitimes.com/systems/a20061116PR201.html [dated November 16, 2006].

71. http://news.yahoo.com/s/cmp/20061116/tc_cmp/194400318.

72. http://www.informationweek.com/news/showArticle.jhtml?articleID=194400318&subSection=All+Stories.

73. http://www.eetimes.com/news/latest/showArticle.jhtml?articleID=194400169 [dated November 15, 2006].

74. http://www.mobiletechnews.com/info/2006/11/15/174040.html [dated November 15, 2006].

75. http://www.wirelessdesignonline.com/content/news/article.asp?docid=2c6e2848-c0e9-4469-8b2a-a24b255a5cb1&atc~c=771+s=773+r=001+l=a&VNETCOOKIE= NO [dated November 15, 2006].
76. http://www.dailywireless.org/2006/11/13/mobile-wimax-brazil-china-germany/ [dated November 13, 2006].
77. http://abcnews.go.com/Technology/ZDM/story?id=2652428 [dated November 14, 2006].
78. http://www.law.com/jsp/legaltechnology/pubArticleLT.jsp?id=1163757925766 [dated November 20, 2006].
79. http://www.eetasia.com/ART_8800442997_499488_e5a44ce1200611.HTM [dated November 23, 2006].
80. http://www.wirelessdesignasia.com/article.asp?id=3909.
81. http://www.tuvps.co.uk/news/articles/wimax-considered-by-75-of-operators-18004252.asp [dated December 7, 2006].
82. http://www.pyr.com/downloads.htm?id=1?sc=pr1.
83. http://today.reuters.co.uk/news/articlenews.aspx?type=reutersEdge&storyID=2006-12-07T110246Z_01_NOA739546_RTRUKOC_0_ITU-WIMAX.xml&pageNumber=0&imageid=&cap=&sz=13&WTModLoc=NewsArt-C1-ArticlePage4 [dated December 7, 2006].
84. http://dhdeans.blogspot.com/2006/12/wimax-to-benefit-broadband.html [dated December 8, 2006].
85. http://rosleemj.blogspot.com/2006/12/will-wimax-be-basis-for-4g.html [dated December 6, 2006].
86. http://arstechnica.com/news.ars/post/20061207-8377.html [dated December 7, 2006].
87. http://hotfromsiliconvalley.typepad.com/hotfromsiliconvalley/2006/11/the_promise_of_.html.
88. http://www.telecomdirectnews.com/do.php/150/21630?199 [dated December 13, 2006].
89. http://www.pwc.com/.
90. http://home.businesswire.com/portal/site/google/index.jsp?ndmViewId=news_view &newsId=20061201005277&newsLang=en [dated December 1, 2006].
91. http://www.researchandmarkets.com.
92. http://www.articlesbase.com/communication-articles/wimax-and-its-future-importance-77194.html [dated December 2, 2006].
93. http://port-70.blogspot.com/2006/11/on-wimax-cost-and-performance.html [dated November 23, 2006].
94. http://hotfromsiliconvalley.typepad.com/hotfromsiliconvalley/2006/11/wimax_worth_ban.html.
95. http://class.cas.msu.edu/tc375/?p=198 [dated November 27, 2006].
96. http://home.businesswire.com/portal/site/google/index.jsp?ndmViewId=news_view &newsId=20061129005706&newsLang=en [dated November 29, 2006].
97. http://www.euro2day.gr/articlesfna/24718013/ [dated November 29, 2006].
98. http://www.computing.co.uk/vnunet/news/2169816/asia-3g-wimax-forecasts.
99. http://www.itweek.co.uk/vnunet/news/2169816/asia-3g-wimax-forecasts.
100. http://www.bbwexchange.com/pubs/2006/12/05/page1423-370048.asp.
101. http://www.rfglobalnet.com/content/news/article.asp?DocID=%7B4C60F4B7-9ED3-4036-B103-D3B95BCEF1C4%7D&Bucket=Current+Headlines&VNETCOOKIE=NO [dated December 13, 2006].

102. http://www.eetimes.com/news/latest/showArticle.jhtml?articleID=196604360 [dated December 14, 2006].
103. http://www.wirelessweek.com/article/CA6333878.html?text=wimax.
104. http://www.wimaxxed.com/wimax_reports/20060224/wimax_holds_pro.html.
105. http://india-movingforward.blogspot.com/2006/10/how-it-is-changing-rural-india.html [dated October 26, 2006].
106. http://www.newswiretoday.com/news/9606/ [dated October 17, 2006].
107. www.rediff.com.
108. http://www.hindu.com/thehindu/holnus/008200609160311.htm [dated September 16, 2006].
109. http://www.cybermedianews.co.in/.
110. http://allafrica.com/stories/200610260545.html.
111. http://news.zdnet.co.uk/communications/0,1000000085,39150906,00.htm.
112. http://www.netstumbler.com/2006/11/28/intel-touts-wimax-as-fix-for-indias-digital-divide/.
113. http://www.pcworld.in/news/index.jsp/artId=4653067 [dated October 31, 2006].
114. http://www.technewsworld.com/story/54854.html.
115. http://www.toptechnews.com/news/Get-Ready-for-the-Big-WiMAX-IPOs-/story.xhtml?story_id=11100AWXQWN6.
116. The Implications of WiMAX for Competition and Regulation, OECD document [dated March 2, 2006].
117. http://gigaom.com/2006/12/19/wimax-scale/ [dated December 19, 2006].
118. http://www.wimax.com/commentary/blog/blog-2006/wimax-iptv-hdtv.
119. http://www.wimax.com/commentary/spotlight/analystscorner2005_04_20.
120. http://www.knowfirst.info/forums/showthread.php?t=22177 [dated December 20, 2006].
121. http://www.convergedigest.com/Wireless/broadbandwirelessarticle.asp?ID=20248.
122. http://dewantoro.org/2006/12/23/wimax-the-future-of-wireless-network/.
123. http://www.mobiletechnews.com/info/2006/12/21/131855.html.
124. http://www.cellular-news.com/story/21090.php.
125. http://www.cxotoday.com/India/News/WiMAX_Competing_with_3G_Services_FS/551-77988-912.html.
126. http://www.efytimes.com/efytimes/fullnews.asp?edid=16254 [dated December 19, 2006].
127. Krishna Rao, G.S.V.R., Terzoli, A., Muyingi, H., and Mandioma, M.T., A Study on Addressing Digital Divide through ICT initiatives in South Africa, *Proceedings of IEEE-ICTE Africa*, Kenya, 2006.
128. Chipangura, B., Terzoli, A., Muyingi, H., and Krishna Rao, G.S.V.R., Design, Development and Deployment of a Mobile E-Commerce Application for Rural South Africa? A Case Study, *Proceedings of IEEE-ICACT 2006 International Conference* [ISBN 89-5519-129-4], Vol. III, pp. 1479–1484.
129. Mpofu, N., Terzoli, A., Muyingi, H., and Krishna Rao, G.S.V.R., Design and Development of a User Agent for Streaming Lectures? A South African Case Study, *Proceedings of IEEE-ICACT 2006 International Conference* [ISBN 89-5519-129-4], Vol. I, pp. 553–555.

130. Gary Ndlovu, G.O, Terzoli, A., Petersen, A., Muyingi, H., and Krishna Rao, G.S.V.R., Development of A Localised E-Commerce Platform for Music Using Indigenous Knowledge — A South African Experience, *Proceedings of IEEE-ICACT 2006 International Conference* [ISBN 89-5519-129-4], Vol. III, pp. 2219–2222.
131. Nkomo, P.T., Terzoli, A., Muyingi, H., Krishna Rao, G.S.V.R., Smart Card Initiative for South African E-Governance — A Study, *Proceedings of IEEE-ICACT 2006 International Conference* [ISBN 89-5519-129-4], Vol. III, pp. 2231–2232.
132. Mpofu, N., Terzoli, A., Muyingi, H., and Krishna Rao, G.S.V.R., MR.MPOFU-A SIP User Agent for Streaming Lectures, *Proceedings of IEEE-ICTE Africa*, Kenya, 2006.

Index

Milton Keynes UK
Ingram Content Group UK Ltd.
UKHW021823071024
449327UK00021B/1404